D1564047

ONE NATION DIVISIBLE

ONE NATION DIVISIBLE

What America Was and What It Is Becoming

Michael B. Katz and Mark J. Stern

Russell Sage Foundation • New York

The Russell Sage Foundation

The Russell Sage Foundation, one of the oldest of America's general purpose foundations, was established in 1907 by Mrs. Margaret Olivia Sage for "the improvement of social and living conditions in the United States." The Foundation seeks to fulfill this mandate by fostering the development and dissemination of knowledge about the country's political, social, and economic problems. While the Foundation endeavors to assure the accuracy and objectivity of each book it publishes, the conclusions and interpretations in Russell Sage Foundation publications are those of the authors and not of the Foundation, its Trustees, or its staff. Publication by Russell Sage, therefore, does not imply Foundation endorsement.

Library of Congress Cataloging-in-Publication Data
Katz, Michael B., 1939–
    One nation divisible : what America was and what it is becoming / Michael
  B. Katz, Mark J. Stern.
        p.   cm.
    Includes bibliographical references and index.
    ISBN 0-87154-445-8
        1. United States—Social conditions—20th century.   2. Social problems—
    United States—History—20th century.   3. Social change—United States—
    History—20th century.   4. Equality—United States—History—20th century.
    5. Pluralism (Social sciences)—United States—History—20th century.
    I. Stern, Mark J.   II. Title.

    HN57.K355 2006
    973.91—dc22   2005054319

The paper used in this publication meets the minimum requirements of American National Standard for Information Sciences—Permanence of Paper for Printed Library Materials. ANSI Z39.48-1992.

RUSSELL SAGE FOUNDATION
112 East 64th Street, New York, New York 10021
10 9 8 7 6 5 4 3 2 1

For Reynolds Farley, who set the standard

Contents

Acknowledgments

IN RESEARCHING and writing this book, we have received extraordinary help from a large number of individuals and organizations. Because the original manuscript was too long and detailed, we faced the difficult task of cutting it—by the end, in half. For this reason, a number of research assistants will not find their work explicitly represented in the final version. We want to assure them that it was all of value—invaluable, in fact—and shaped our thinking. We also want to apologize to anyone inadvertently omitted from this list of those to whom we owe thanks.

This book began when the Russell Sage Foundation conducted a competition for support to write a book accessible to general readers that put the 2000 census in the context of social and economic trends in the twentieth century. We are grateful for the generous support the foundation gave us for this project and in particular to Reynolds Farley, who worked with us on the proposal. We were inspired throughout the project by the example of Ren's outstanding books on the 1990 census. A Senior Scholar Award to Michael Katz from the Spencer Foundation also helped fund the project. An award from the University of Pennsylvania's Boettner Center funded research on the history of old age.

Matthew Sobek, one of the principals in the creation of the magnificent IPUMS database at the University of Minnesota, without which this book would have been, quite literally, impossible, consulted with us on technical matters and prepared files that proved essential to the analysis. Steven Fraser read the entire manuscript, offering his usual keen insight and outstanding editorial judgment. With their usual brilliance, Joel Katz and Will Bardel transformed our workmanlike tables and charts into stunning graphics. Chris Brest produced outstanding maps. Several figures contain demographic data from GeoLytics, East Brunswick, New Jersey. Michael Kahan, Lorrin Thomas, Eric Schneider, Sarah Igo, Alice O'Connor, and Michael Zuckerman read portions of the manuscript and offered excellent comments. Viviana Zelizer not only read sections and offered helpful comments but pointed us to essential sociological literature that we would otherwise have missed. Mehreen Zaman proved an energetic and imaginative photo researcher; she found terrific photos, sometimes in obscure places. Sarah Katz finished procuring the photos. Randall Couch advised on a website for the book.

Undergraduates also helped us with the research. Evan Thomas and Edward Swigert searched early-twentieth-century publications for reactions to the new century. I-Heng Hsu charted economic and demographic characteristics of mid- and late-twentieth-century communities whose early features we already had studied. Sydette Harry worked on tracing narratives of family history.

A large number of the outstanding graduate students at the University of Pennsylvania helped and sustained us in various ways. Jamie Fader began with bibliographic work on women and African Americans, moved on to the preparation of tables and figures, and then joined us in coauthoring three articles. Audra Wolfe and Jeremy Vetter educated Katz in the importance of agricultural history and read early drafts of chapters. Audra prepared an outstanding bibliography on the subject. Leah Gordon and Daniel Amsterdam prepared masterful annotated bibliographies that underlie chapter 4 and the epilogue. Leah also corrected and edited endnotes and references. Dominic Vitiello wrote a stunning comparison of Philadelphia and Los Angeles, which in the end could not be included for reasons of space but should find independent publication. Jordan Stanger-Ross and Christina Collins worked on the history of the transition to adulthood and, along with Mark Stern, coauthored an article on the topic. Julia Rabig, Kara Sabalauskas, and Julie Kaplan produced outstanding case studies of early-twentieth-century communities. Hwa-ok Bae and Sara Bressi assisted us with the analyses of migration and old age, respectively.

Six graduate students—Leah Gordon, Dominic Vitiello, Jordan Stanger-Ross, Peter Siskind, Julia Rabig, and Christina Collins—composed an informal reading group that dissected what were then the first two chapters with insight, skill, and tact.

We presented aspects of the research in a number of settings and are grateful for the constructive responses. These were: the twentieth-century seminar at Columbia University; the Miller Center seminar at the University of Virginia; the Political Science and Sociology colloquium at the University of Michigan, Ann Arbor; the Population Studies Center and Sociology Department and School of Social Work Ph.D. colloquia at the University of Pennsylvania, as well as the Penn Institute for Urban Research faculty forum on Immigration, Race, and Urban Inequality. We thank Thomas Sugrue and Camille Charles for comments at the latter.

We also are grateful to the anonymous reviewers—many in number—who reviewed articles for journals and the whole manuscript for the Russell Sage Foundation. We did not accept or act on all their suggestions, but we considered all of them with care. They made this a much tighter book. With all the help we have received, we would like to think that the resulting book is air-tight. But, alas, that is never the case. For whatever errors or misinterpretations remain, we take full responsibility.

The staff of the University of Pennsylvania's Van Pelt Library, as always, provided skilled, generous support. The Rangeley Public Library in Maine provided Katz with books on interlibrary loan and, to distract him, fiction from its excellent collection.

We also want to thank the excellent editorial and production staff at the Russell Sage Foundation, notably Suzanne Nichols and Genna Patacsil, and, for outstanding copyediting, Helen Glenn Court. For his general support of the project, we are grateful to the foundation's president, Eric Wanner.

We want to acknowledge with thanks permission to reprint portions of articles that appeared in the *Journal of American History* (June 2005), "The New African American Inequality," and the *Journal of Social History* (September 2005), "Women and the Paradox of Inequality in Twentieth-Century America."

As we were finishing the first draft of this book, we wanted a title that reflected its theme of persistent and durable inequality as a feature of American history. The title *One Nation Divisible: What America Was and What It Is Becoming* struck us as exactly right. We had forgotten the publication, twenty-five years earlier, of a book with a similar title: *One Nation Divisible: Class, Race, and Ethnicity in the United States Since 1938,* by Richard Polenberg. We want to acknowledge the importance of Polenberg's pioneering efforts at placing inequalities at the core of twentieth-century American history and hope that our work proves a worthy successor.

Finally, but not least, our personal thanks to our families who endured the long and often tortuous project with its demands on our time and dispositions that resulted in this book.

Prologue

Introducing the
Twentieth Century

A T THE dawn of the twentieth century, two articles flanked the front page of the *New York Times*. One focused on South Africa and the Boer War, the other on China, the Open Door policy, the prospects for trade, and the competition among nations. The *Times* anticipated the new century with barely tempered optimism. The year 1899 was "a veritable annus mirabilis, in business and production." Nothing remained untouched. "It would be easy to speak of the twelve months just past as the banner year were we not already confident that the distinction of highest records must presently pass to the year 1900." American progress seemed all the more miraculous because the country was emerging from the lean years of the mid-1890s, when it had suffered its greatest yet depression. Renewed health showed in three areas, reported the *Times*: the remarkable growth of infrastructure, especially railroads; the great increase in foreign trade, notably in the products of industry that resulted from innovation and industrial reorganization; and in the stabilization of financial markets on account of the "practical disappearance of the issue of silver inflation" and the solidification of the gold standard. The prospect of inflation—the "rapid advance in prices"—remained the one small cloud on the *Times'* otherwise cloudless horizon.[1]

The *Times* marveled at the changes in America in the previous century. A hundred years earlier, President Thomas Jefferson led an agricultural nation with "slight foreign commerce" that occupied only a portion of its continent. By the century's end, the products of industry had surpassed those of agriculture as an America that spanned the continent invaded the markets of Europe and the Far East. Worried about competition where they competed with America for manufacturing outlets, European countries looked for ways to counter the new American threat. France's leading economist proposed "a commercial union of all the countries of Europe to establish free trade within their borders and to protect their industries by import duties on American products."

1

American manufacturing required a massive increase in workers. Immigrants from southern and eastern Europe poured into America in unprecedented numbers to fill the demand for unskilled and semi-skilled labor in factories and on railroads, although legislation driven by fears of competition from cheap labor and xenophobia had virtually stopped immigration from the Far East. As America became a more diverse nation, nativist fears and calls for immigration restriction, which culminated two decades later in quotas, surfaced and helped fuel the anxieties of labor unions. Old stock Americans, worried about the nation's capacity to absorb and assimilate newcomers with different cultures, designed programs of Americanization for the nation's schools and settlement houses.

Optimistic accounts of America at the opening of the twentieth century, like the *Times'*, elided poverty and race. As the *Times* celebrated American material abundance terrible poverty—soon to be documented by Robert Hunter—haunted the streets of New York City, where perhaps half the population was poor and where poverty, in the absence of a public safety net, meant hunger, malnutrition, cold, and rags. America had become more than ever a land of extremes—of wealth and poverty and of racial privilege and discrimination. The twentieth century began at the nadir of American race relations. Segregation excluded African Americans from jobs, housing, and public space. Recent legislation in many places disenfranchised them. Violent racial hatred erupted in beatings and lynchings. Respectable social science proclaimed their inherent inferiority. Social scientists and public spokespersons also worried about the future of families. Despite warnings by cultural authorities and public officials, married couples turned increasingly to birth control and concentrated resources on their smaller number of children, notably by keeping them longer in school as preparation for entering the changing world of work. They also divorced more often. Women, still largely disenfranchised, remained excluded from most paid employment and from public office, although in the century's early years affluent women pioneered in new careers and the daughters of the poor found work in the new sweatshops and factories of the industrial world. Very few women—whatever their race or class—worked for wages after they had married, unless they found themselves widowed.

At the end of the twentieth century, many of the issues on the national agenda were remarkably unchanged. Among the most important were foreign trade, relations with Europe and China, the dislocation and inequality that accompany changes in the mode of production, the management of massive immigration and heightened cultural diversity, the legacy of racial discrimination, and the redefinition of family and gender roles. These echoes across the century do not mean that America in 2000 was closer to America in 1900 than America in 1900 had been to the nation a century earlier. In fact, everything had changed. The experience of a century past gives us a benchmark against which to measure and observe the distance traveled and to assess the forces driving change. It shows, as well, how social and economic transformation reordered work, family, space, politics, and even culture.

It is the contention of this book that America is undergoing a transformation as profound as the one driven by the industrial revolution of past centuries. This great transformation began in the years following World War II; it underlay the many changes observed in the post war decades, although it was not understood very well at the time; it burst through the old structures with great force following the oil shock of 1973; and it gained a name—globalization—mainly in the 1990s. In *The New American Reality*, Reynolds Farley describes two revolutions: the 1960s transformation in family and sexuality and the economic polarization after 1973.[2] Both, in retrospect, highlight the discontinuity that distinguishes the end of the millennium from earlier eras in American, indeed in world, history.

As we view America across a century, four major themes link the analysis of a vast body of data. First is inequality. Throughout its modern history, durable, overlapping inequalities have marked America's social structure. It was—and is—one nation, divisible. Despite repeated contractions and expansions in the degree of economic inequality, the income and wealth pyramid has remained durable and steep, with continuities in the distribution of rewards by work, ethnicity, and gender. At the same time, immense individual and group mobility has accompanied this structural durability. We call this coexistence of structural rigidity with individual and group fluidity the paradox of inequality. Inequality, however, has not always worked in the same way; we pay special attention to its changing expression and to its complex and intricate interactions with the history of diversity, which constitutes so large a part of the American experience.

Diversity is the second theme, and it takes three forms: demography, geography, and personal experience. Twentieth-century American history began at a moment when massive immigration from southern and eastern Europe was transforming the nation's demography and culture. Twenty-first century American history began at a similar moment, only the newcomers came largely from Latin America and Asia, and, as a century earlier, their impact on the United States remained uncertain and contentious. The story of the twentieth century is, in part, the working out of the relation between the nation and its new arrivals. The history of demographic diversity is also about race and gender. With race, the story this book tells focuses on the tortuous and paradoxical emergence of a new African-American inequality. It also traces the supersession of the black-white model of race relations by an emerging multiracial and multiethnic pattern that will characterize the nation's future. With gender, the point is not only that the experience of women underwent revolutionary change—the most, in fact, of any group. Rather, the history of gender intersects with the history of immigration and race because the work experience of women and men went at such different angles, with black and immigrant women often pioneering the route to the middle class and reaching near parity with native-born whites more quickly than men. Diversity has always had a geographic side as well. Here, too, there are paradoxes in the story: the reduction of regional diversity through the economic incorporation of the South into the rest of the nation and the hegemony of a national economy, on the one hand, and the segmentation and diversification of urban form with increased racial segregation and suburbanization, on the other. Finally, the history of personal experience exhibits the diversity theme, too. Both the stages in human lives (adolescence, old age) and the characteristics of families traveled a complicated road from diversity toward standardization and then, after about 1960, back toward diversity. All these forms of diversity—demography, geography, personal experience—have intersected with the history of inequality, this book's first theme, in myriad intimate and detailed ways.

The third theme is the role of government. Americans tend to undervalue the contributions of government to economic and social history. Especially in an age that celebrates the market, the role of government in forming the institutions that shape the experience of individuals, families, and communities is not well understood. In our analysis of social and demographic trends in the twentieth century, we found the hand of one or another level of government everywhere, played with increasing visibility and power throughout the century. The institutions of the state and labor market, we show, reduced inequalities after World War II and proved central to the economic and social progress of blacks and women. The erosion of these institutions in recent decades is a prime source of the increasing inequality that defined the history of social structure in the late twentieth and early twenty-first centuries—a story tragically embodied in the aftermath of Hurricane Katrina in the summer of 2005. At the same time, government policies reshaped personal experience, redefining what it meant to "grow up" and "grow old," expanding the chances of ordinary families to educate their children or purchase a home, and forcing Americans to alter their everyday assumptions about women and ethnic minorities. None of the important economic and social trends of the twentieth century can be understood apart from the role of government.

The great transformations at both ends of the twentieth century exploded existing ideas. This impact of events on the ideas that underpin public life is the book's fourth theme. At both millennia, violent, disruptive change upset patterns of work, family, and social experience. What must be grasped is that change was discontinuous. It did not simply intensify existing practices and trends. It was as much qualitative as quantitative, and at both ends of the century eventually reconfigured the nation's economy and society. Whatever the pace of revolutionary change, however, the break with the past is never clean, immediate, or total. Americans therefore lived with a tension between what their nation was and what it was becoming. Social, economic, and demographic transformation, as is often the case, proved swifter than intellectual regrouping. Americans confronted a transforming world with old ideas whose underpinnings had been exploded.

These four themes—the nature of inequality, multiple forms of diversity, the role of the state, and the intellectual impact of discontinuous change—run through the chapters that follow. It is a story with several subplots about individual and group experience, changing opportunity structures, new geographies, and the role of government. What weaves these stories into a larger narrative is their influence on one another. All are prisms refracting two great waves of economic globalization—bookends to the century. At both the start and close of the twentieth century, the reconfiguration of work registered in new patterns of inequality among women and minorities. Immigration resulted in novel social geographies. Fresh channels of mobility forced families to reconsider old strategies. Public policy rearranged the life course and rebuilt structures of opportunity. Events on the ground shattered the categories used to interpret public and private life. In both 1900 and 2000, the impact of massive economic and social change left America one nation divisible, its great fault lines redrawn but potent as ever. The story starts at the turn of the twentieth century with Americans negotiating the excruciating tensions between the local world they knew and the new age of manufacture with its great factories, industrial cities, millions of newcomers, and intimate links to a world economy.

Chapter 1

What America Was: The Early Twentieth Century

A T THE start of the twentieth century most Americans lived on farms or in small communities where, on an ordinary day, they would not encounter unfamiliar faces. Few things underscore the differences between America then and now as dramatically as the size of the places in which most people lived and the thin dispersal of the population across the continent.

Most historical accounts of the late nineteenth and early twentieth century—at least outside the South—focus on a different view. The major themes are industrialization, urbanization, immigration, and imperialism. Drawn by plentiful jobs and relatively high wages, immigrants from eastern, central, and southern Europe poured into America, fueling the spectacular rise of its industry and the catalytic growth of its cities. During the same years, the products of American industry drove the search for new markets and the creation of the nation's first empire.[1] The unprecedented problems generated by massive demographic and economic transformation made "the response to industrialism" the leitmotif of politics and public policy.[2] This narrative, of course, does not apply to the South, where separate labor markets and racial politics created a nation apart.[3] Nor does it capture a fundamental fact about America: in the first decade of the twentieth century it remained a vast and lightly populated nation, most of whose people lived on farms or in villages and small towns. The America of conventional narrative—industrial and urban—clustered along a stretch of the northeastern and middle Atlantic coasts, extended partly across the Great Lakes, and appeared in places along the Pacific shore. A picture of small-scale settlements—not the smokestacks of Pittsburgh or the sidewalks of New York—captures the image of where most Americans lived.

It was, however, a moving picture composed of millions of immigrants entering America from other countries, rural people leaving farms

7

and villages for towns and cities, and men and women crossing the continent from east to west, displacing American Indians, gradually filling up the vast empty spaces of the nation. It was also a complex picture in which the ethnic character of communities varied by their regional location and size and where even small towns as well as cities were home to many immigrants and harbored men and women who followed diverse occupations.

The two Americas of the early twentieth century—one looking toward the past, one to the future—existed in tension, not isolation. Linked by transportation, trade, and communication, the older and newer versions of the nation joined in elaborate, mutually supportive networks that, in turn, attached them to the wider world during the first modern era of economic globalization. This first wave lasted from the late nineteenth century through World War I. This chapter is about its impact on social structure, demography, family, and life course. Refracted through technology, trade, finance, and migration, economic globalization widened patterns of inequality, pushed and pulled people across continents, and forced them to reconstruct their family strategies, redesign their governments, and redefine many of their ideas. The same might be said about the next significant wave, whose impact we are experiencing and debating today. In this sense, profound parallels join America at the start and end of the twentieth century. But parallels should not be extended too far—for we fail to understand the earlier America unless we realize that it was, also, a world utterly unlike our own.

What is astonishing about this complicated and contradictory world— so different from our own—is how recently it flourished. It was the world entered by the grandparents of working Americans in 2000, the world still visible when their parents were born. Surely, reflecting on what America was, rather than on what it was becoming, is a way to comprehend the rapidity and immensity of the changes that marked the century just ended.

What America Was

In 1900, more than half—54 percent—of the U.S. population lived in villages with fewer than one thousand people. Another 10 percent lived in towns of one to five thousand and only 36 percent in regional centers or cities of five thousand or more. Even in the first era of industrial capitalism, nearly two of every three Americans spent most of their days on farms or in villages and towns with fewer than five thousand residents (see photograph 1.1).

It is easy to forget that America's early twentieth-century epoch of immigration, urbanization, and industrialization was also the golden age of American agriculture. In 1900, 44 percent of the nation's land mass

Photograph 1.1   Steam Plowing in Colorado Between 1900 and 1920

In the early twentieth century, more Americans worked in agriculture than in any other industry. *Source*: Denver Public Library, Western History Collection.

was covered with farms, and most of the rest was prairie, mountain, or forest.[4] Sandwiched between the farm depressions of the 1890s and 1920s, the agricultural prosperity of the century's first two decades was reflected in the growth in the number of farms and farmers and in increasing land values. More than four of ten men in the United States worked as farmers or farm laborers.[5] In the next decade the number of farms and the rural population both rose about 11 percent: by 1910, there were 6.4 million farms in the United States. What marked rural America was its diversity. Any attempt to capture it in a single snapshot founders on variety: crops varied by region; the ethnic mix of rural populations differed from place to place; tenancy and hired labor were far more prominent in some regions than in others; and local social structures and economies proved surprisingly complex.

Like the rural counties of which they were a part, America's towns were remarkably diverse in their economies, demographics, and social structures. The places in which most Americans lived may have been small, but they were at the same time complex, impossible to reduce to simple images or glib generalizations, though most of them, it is safe to say, played a critical role in trade. In *Village Communities,* a book sponsored by the Institute of Social and Religious Research, Edmund deS. Brunner explained the commercial functions of villages.

> In the first place, the village is the shipping point for the community. . . . In the second place, the village is the storage point for such products as are not taken immediately to market. . . . In the third place, the village frequently adds to the value of the farmers' product by manufacture. . . . Finally, the village assembles and sells to the farmer and his family most of the goods that they need, such as clothes, hardware, dry goods and groceries; and it even furnishes such things as credit, secondary education, and the professional services of the lawyer, the doctor, and the minister.[6]

By 1900, towns and farms composed a great Corn Belt that stretched from the middle of Ohio to the middle of Nebraska, reaching into the southern parts of South Dakota and Minnesota and the northern borders of Missouri and Kansas.[7] A Winter Wheat Belt, located primarily in Kansas, reached south into the tip of Oklahoma and New Mexico and north into a corner of Nebraska. A Spring Wheat Belt ran north and west of the Corn Belt, through Minnesota, the Dakotas, and across the border into Manitoba. North and east of the Corn Belt stretched a huge Dairy Belt from New England and New York through Michigan, Wisconsin, and Minnesota. A Cotton Belt reached across the South from North Carolina into central Texas, touching only northwestern Florida and the northern section of Louisiana.[8] And California, once a major source of wheat, was developing its specialty in fruits and vegetables. Still, everywhere, farms kept a variety of livestock and produced more than one crop—thus furnishing their own need for food as well as local markets. In 1910, 88 percent of farms raised chickens, 81 percent dairy cows, 74 percent horses, 68 percent swine, and 76 percent corn; 48 percent had fruit orchards. In the course of the century, this local diversity and potential self-sufficiency nearly disappeared, marking a great transition in the organization of agricultural life and weaving new webs of dependency between producer and consumer, town and country, agriculture and commerce.[9]

Everywhere, crops increased in value. Per capita, between 1899 and 1909 crop value rose 66.4 percent overall. (By far the most profitable crop per acre in these years was tobacco.) Expenses for farm machinery and hired labor grew as well, though at different rates across the nation.[10] The impressive growth in crop value and in the number of farms in the first decade of the twentieth century pales beside the astonishing doubling in the value of farm property. The total value of farm land increased 118 percent as the average value of an acre of farm land leaped from $15.57

to $32.40 in just ten years—a decade of only modest inflation. Increases, reflecting population growth and urbanization, varied by region from $61.32 in the East North Central census division to $16.06 in the West South Central.[11] This rising land value inflated a bubble of prosperity that burst with devastating effect in the 1920s, initiating a fierce agricultural depression.

Although the demand for food—fueled by burgeoning cities—escalated rapidly, agricultural productivity rose only modestly. Indeed, as late as 1930, agricultural productivity, which grew by about two-thirds during the nineteenth century, was about the same as in 1880; it soared only after 1940. Between 1840 and 1910, mechanization accounted for between one-half and two-thirds of increased labor productivity. An early twentieth-century farmer tilled the land with sharper and more refined tools than his counterparts a century earlier, and the horse-drawn mechanical harvester, introduced in the 1830s, followed by the steam-powered thresher and seed drills, expanded his productive capacity. To take one example, the time needed to produce a bushel of wheat declined from 2.96 man hours between 1840 and 1860 to 0.71 in the 1900 to 1910 decade.[12] Nonetheless, the great innovations that would transform farming—the internal combustion engine, electricity, telephones, and hybridization—lay in the future. America's farms could barely keep up with the demands of its cities. In this situation, prices soared, giving American farmers their brief window of prosperity.

Along with increased demand, railroads—the source of cheaper and faster transportation—drew farmers into markets throughout the nineteenth century. During that period, farmers usually concentrated on production for commerce as rapidly as consumer demand and transportation permitted. Although huge farming operations developed in the Midwest and California, most farms remained relatively small family operations, and hired labor contributed only a minor share to farm production. Even though northern farms were often small and family run, by historical and world standards, most American farmers were highly commercialized and depended on national and international markets for their prosperity.[13]

Not all farmers owned their land, however, and rising tenancy disturbed observers worried about loss of the nation's Jeffersonian yeoman tradition. In North Carolina, the number of tenant farmers—augmented by the movement of former slaves into sharecropping—increased by one-third between 1880 and 1900. Around major trading centers, the rise was even more dramatic: more than half the farmers in Charlotte's hinterland were tenants in 1900. Tenancy varied by ethnicity and region: 33 percent of native white farmers, 18 percent of foreign-born, and 74 percent of blacks were tenants. High rates of black tenancy occurred mainly in the South; in the middle Atlantic states, 79 percent of black farmers owned their land, a situation roughly paralleled in the North and Midwest (see figures 1.1 and 1.2).[14]

Observers at the time considered tenants poorly educated transients who overworked staple crops and exploited the soil. Tenancy, they feared, undermined the independence and character that resulted from land ownership. In fact, worried critics exaggerated the problem. Not only were many tenants good farmers, in the northern states they operated only a little more than a quarter of farms, and tenancy there appeared more a phase in the life cycle—a step on the ladder from hired hand to owner—than a permanent condition.[15]

Rural America was home to an array of other industries besides agriculture, which, along with forestry, and husbandry, employed only six of ten adult men in even the smallest communities.[16] Rural mining and gendered forms of rural manufacturing attracted industries employing women and children. Cigar and tobacco factories, silk mills, and factories making men's and women's clothes, to take three examples, ap-

Figure 1.1   Percentage of Farmers Who Are Tenants, by Region and Age of Household Head, 1910

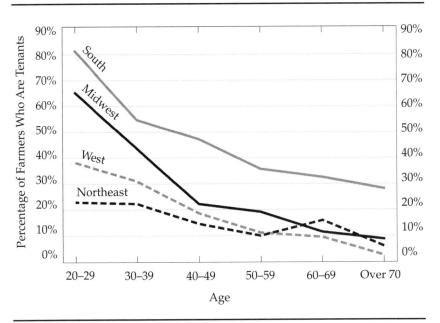

Note: In most parts of the country, younger farmers were much more likely to be tenants rather than to own land. In the South, however, even among farmers in their forties and fifies, a large proportion remained tenants. Source: Data from Ruggles et al. (2004).

Figure 1.2   Tenants as Percentage of All Farmers, 1900

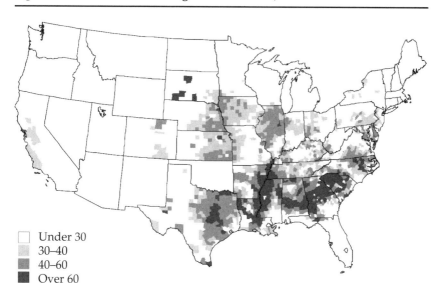

Under 30
30–40
40–60
Over 60

Note: Although farm tenancy was not unknown in the Midwest, the highest rates were in the South. In many counties, more than 60 percent of farmers were tenants, usually because of the proliferation of sharecropping. *Source*: Inter-University Consortium for Political and Social Research, 197-(date uncertain).

peared in areas known for mining coal and iron. The silk industry, for instance, was found in the anthracite coal-producing portion of Pennsylvania.[17] Jobs for women and children undoubtedly compensated for the seasonal layoffs of men who worked in rural manufacturing and mining and in slack times, unlike factory workers, in cities, could not find alternative work nearby.

A major industry in early twentieth-century America, mining employed more than a million workers; 47 percent of the value of its products came from coal with the next most important item, petroleum and natural gas, accounting for only 15 percent. It was, moreover, highly concentrated by geography: for instance, iron mining dominated the Lake Superior District encompassing Michigan, Minnesota, and Wisconsin and anthracite coal mining Pennsylvania's northeastern region. Mining's products were worth more than $1.2 billion, an amount that had increased an astonishing 52 percent in the previous seven years. In large part, mining's heightened productivity reflected increased use of machinery. But the use of machinery varied greatly by region, from 42 percent in Pennsylvania to 17 percent in Arkansas. The rise in horsepower generated by steam—218 percent between 1902 and 1909—illustrates the mechanization of mining, as does the increased use of electricity—1,319 percent—in the same years.[18] Mining's growth depended on new sources of labor as well as on machines. This labor was supplied by recent immigrants, who, despite their concentration in cities, also found their way into rural America's mines and onto its farms.

What America Was Becoming

The forces that changed this older America rode into towns and villages along railroad tracks, slipped in through electric wires, and sailed in on steamships. By 1902, there were 3,620 electric power stations across the nation, 75 percent of which were in towns with populations under five thousand. Between 1890 and 1902, the length of electric street railway tracks had increased 1,636 percent, from twelve hundred to twenty-two thousand miles. The transcontinental railroad had been completed in 1869, and by 1900 a dense network of railroads crisscrossed the nation, reaching into virtually every town and village. Transportation and power were two midwives of the new America; a third was communication—the telegraph that had revolutionized communications in the decades before the Civil War and, since the mid-1860s, linked continents under the Atlantic Ocean. In the early years of the twentieth century even newer, more exciting technologies, the telephone and radio, were coming into prominence as national systems of communication.[19] They reached out to a growing and newly diverse population as immigrants from southern and eastern Europe changed the ethnic composition of the nation.

A Diverse, Mobile Nation

In the first decade of the twentieth century America's population grew from 76 to 92 million—a large increase but, in percentage terms, the smallest since 1800, when fewer than 5 million people lived in what was then the United States. Numbers alone, however, do not tell the story of population growth in the early twentieth century, because the years from 1900 though 1910 saw what would prove to be the largest immigration in the nation's history until the late twentieth century. By 1910, 14.5 percent of the population, and 20 percent of the workforce, was foreign born, and the number of immigrants was increasing much faster than the native-born population. (In 2000, by contrast, the foreign-born were 10.4 percent of the population.) Many others, of course, were not far removed from immigrant origins: about 20 percent had at least one parent born outside the United States. Not only did the immigrants surge upward in their numbers, but they also arrived from new places. In 1900, more than two-thirds were from northwestern Europe; a decade later the proportion was less than half as immigrants from southern and eastern Europe increased by more than 3 million (over 175 percent). As a result, the share of the population born in Italy and Russia doubled and large numbers also arrived from Poland, Austria, Hungary, Romania, and Greece. In 1910, two-thirds of the adults from southern and eastern Europe had been in the United States ten years or less, compared to a little more than a quarter of those born in northern and western Europe.[20] The massive wave of newcomers from southern and eastern Europe aroused apprehension, and in 1907 the U.S. Senate appointed a commission (the Dillingham Commission) to research the new immigration and make legislative recommendations. The commission issued its forty-two-volume report in 1911.

The old immigration had consisted of permanent settlers; the new of birds of passage, "individuals a considerable proportion of whom apparently have no intention of permanently changing their residence," coming instead, in search of higher wages, the commission pointed out. The new immigration, moreover, had arrived "during a period of great industrial expansion and . . . furnished a practically unlimited supply of labor to that expansion." A great many came to America intending to earn money and then return to their native lands. Among immigrants from a number of regions, notably Italy, other parts of southern Europe, and central Europe, rates of return were astonishingly high. Among others—the mid-nineteenth-century Irish escaping famine, and decades later Jews fleeing persecution—very few went back. During the five years from 1908 to 1912, which is the first period for which relatively reliable figures are available, 4.75 million immigrants arrived in the United States and 2.36 million non-citizens departed. The rate of return migration, then, was about 50 percent. More than 43 percent of Italians who left for the United States in the 1880s returned to Italy; this rate increased to 53 percent in the first decade of the twentieth century and 63 percent in the second. Equivalent numbers of non-Jewish emigrants from Greece, Hungary, Russia, and the Balkans went back to their native lands.[21]

The reasons for return varied. In some cases, migrants were in fact seasonal laborers moving back and forth across the Atlantic; some return migrants were target earners who stayed in the United States long enough to save for a small business and comfortable life in their homeland; still others were dissatisfied with what they found or missed friends and family."[22]

Most were unskilled laborers who came with little money. Many were illiterate. Recent immigration regulations, fortunately, had assured that "although drawn from classes low in the economic scale, the new immigrants as a rule are the strongest, the most enterprising, and the best in their class." Still, the commission worried, the new immigrants might lower wages, increase crime, overburden institutions, and fail to assimilate into American society as smoothly as—in the terms of the day—the less racially different older immigrants had done. Legislation, the commission agreed unanimously, should begin with this principle: "While the American people, as in the past, welcome the oppressed of other lands, care should be taken that immigration be such in both quality and quantity as not to make too difficult the process of assimilation."[23] The commission's recommendations touched off a debate that resulted in the now infamous legislation that in the 1920s introduced immigration quotas based on the nation's population in 1890—thereby virtually shutting off all but a trickle of immigration from southern and eastern Europe, just as other legislation, beginning with the Chinese Exclusion Act of 1882, had reduced immigration from Asia.[24]

International migration was just one type of population movement ubiquitous in late nineteenth- and early twentieth-century America. Everywhere, both native-born Americans and immigrants were in flux, reshuffled between towns and cities, states, and regions, as well as between nations. Writing in the late nineteenth century, the astute British observer James Bryce observed,

> Nowhere is population in such constant movement as in America. In some of the newer States only one-fourth or one-fifth of the inhabitants are natives of the United States. Many of the townsfolk, not a few even of the farmers, have been till lately citizens of some other State, and will, perhaps, soon move on farther west. These Western States are like a chain of lakes through which there flows a stream which mingles the waters of the higher with those of the lower.[25]

Indeed, Americans often did not stay in one place very long. Wherever historians have looked, the population of individual towns and cities turned over rapidly, less in rural than in urban areas, but still at remarkable rates.[26]

The settlement patterns that resulted from population mobility, of course, did not spread evenly across the nation, and America emerged a spatial patchwork of ethnicities, one nation politically indivisible but demographically balkanized. Everywhere across America, even in rural New England where young people were leaving farms, the population of some counties grew while that of others shrank. Population density, which averaged only 25.6 per square mile for the nation, was highest in the mid-Atlantic states and parts of New England—250 in New Jersey and 349 in Massachusetts, for example, and lowest in the West—1.6 in New Mexico and 4.4 in Oregon. The frontier may have officially closed, as the Census Bureau announced in the 1890s, but settlers had barely be-

Figure 1.3   Persons per Square Mile, U.S. Counties, 1900

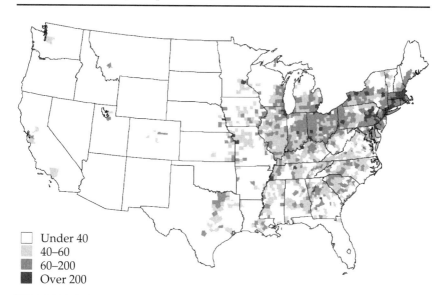

☐ Under 40
40–60
60–200
Over 200

Note: In 1900, population concentrated in the Northeast and around the Great Lakes. Most of the nation remained lightly populated, with fewer than forty residents per square mile. *Source*: Inter-University Consortium for Political and Social Research, 197-(date uncertain).

gun to join the American Indians in the vast stretches from the Canadian to the Mexican borders west of the Mississippi (see figure 1.3).[27]

Nonetheless, population was shifting out of villages and towns— places with fewer than 1,000 residents declined from 63 percent of households in 1880 to 42 percent in 1920; in the same years, cities grew, and the share of households in medium-sized towns held steady at around 10 percent.[28] In 1906, one observer lamented:

> Many towns are injured . . . by the proximity of stronger industrial and social centers. Their citizens go abroad for trade, for acquaintance, for social fraternization, and even for school and church. They look to the adjacent thriving village or city as their true centre with consequent alienation from their own political and social circle. The trolley widens the sphere of this influence; the rural delivery of mails diminishes contact with the village; and the telephone, though it unites the people, keeps them also apart.[29]

Still, despite the loss of population and competition from large towns and cities, it is a remarkable and important fact to remember that even after World War I and decades of high immigration and rapid industrial-

Figure 1.4   Population Change, U.S. Counties, 1900 to 1910

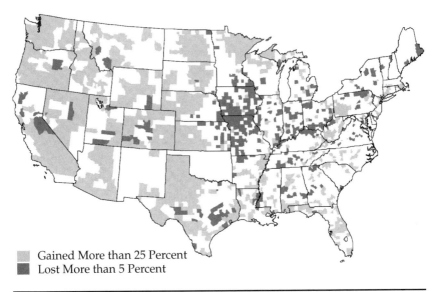

Gained More than 25 Percent
Lost More than 5 Percent

Note: Between 1900 and 1910, most of the fastest-growing counties were in the mountain and Pacific states; counties in the eastern half of the country by and large grew more slowly. Significant parts of Iowa, Missouri, and other midwestern states lost more than five percent of their population during the decade. *Source*: Inter-University Consortium for Political and Social Research, 197-(date uncertain).

ization more than half of American households were still in villages and small or medium-sized towns.

Hundreds of thousands of native whites left the northeastern, southern, and midwestern states in the century's first decade—only the West gained native-born residents. More than 1.1 million native whites, for instance, left the states in the north central census division and more than 1.3 million moved west—often following the same latitude—in just these ten years. (Farmers stayed in the same latitude to capitalize on their human and physical capital because their knowledge of soil conditions, crops, and other factors and the seeds and livestock were adapted to a specific climate.)[30] The outcome was regional population diversity, with significant variation from state to state in the origins of their populations.[31]

Clearly, in the early twentieth century, Americans were a restless, ambitious people, leaving their native states by the thousands in search of new opportunities. Except for the far West, 30 to 60 percent of adults had left the states of their birth (see figure 1.4). The lure of opportunity farther west drew many from the Midwest, sometimes to fertile land in a nearby state, at other times to the shores of the Pacific, a destination and birthplace that relatively few abandoned. The Northeast, by contrast, held on to its residents in this period because industrial opportunity kept Massachusetts and adjoining states attractive. The South, as in so many other ways, remained a nation apart. Six of ten adults born in Mississippi, for example, remained there. What interstate movement occurred in the early twentieth-century South flowed mainly—though not entirely—to other parts of the region. In 1910, neither the Great Migration of African Americans nor the move of native whites into northern industry had begun. Thus, migration was common and immense—a great stream of Americans flowing through the nation. But it was a complicated stream, interweaving opportunity, location, and demography.

Massive population movements resulted in ethnic and racial differences among regions. Whites, including the children of immigrants, spread themselves relatively evenly across the nation, as did immigrants from northern and western Europe, though not in the South. The two groups most unevenly distributed were blacks and immigrants from southern and eastern Europe, whose residential patterns were mirror images: 73 percent of blacks lived in the southeast, and 75 percent of immigrants from southern and eastern Europe lived in the Northeast and elsewhere in the nation's industrial heartland. The location of other newcomers also reflected particular migrant streams: Canadians in New England; Hispanics and Asians along the Pacific Coast; Hispanics near the southwestern border.[32]

In 1910, most immigrants—for instance, eight of ten from southern and eastern Europe—lived in cities. Immigrants, in fact, clustered in a small number of locations. In 1910, six states with 34 percent of the population were home to 57 percent of immigrants; five metropolitan areas—New York, Chicago, Boston, Philadelphia, and Pittsburgh—with 16 percent of the population housed 36 percent of the foreign born. (In 2000, immigrants were even more concentrated.) By contrast, three of five men, women, and children in rural and small-town America had been born in the United States to American-born parents. In fact, people of native stock were primarily rural: about three of every five adults lived in a place with a population under 1,000. In this they were almost the exact opposite of U.S.-born adults with immigrant parents. Nonetheless, a great many immigrants, more than one-third of those not in cities farmed in the Great Plains or Pacific regions.[33] The most rural, however, were African Americans: 70 percent of blacks lived in communities of less than 1,000.

In early twentieth-century America, outside cities, the spatial separation of immigrants, blacks, and native-born whites resulted in "balkanized" settlement patterns, to use the demographer William Frey's description of the late twentieth century. Blacks remained clustered in the

South; the new immigrants from eastern and southern Europe concentrated in industrial cities. Additionally, 55 percent of counties had no African American population, nearly 90 percent had no American Indian or Asian, and 38 percent had no foreign-born. Although immigrants from southern, central, and eastern Europe clustered in cities far more than in small towns or on farms, they did not find their way equally to all of urban America. In 1910, the largest two immigrant groups in New York City were from Russia and Italy, in Philadelphia from Russia and Ireland, in Buffalo from Germany and Canada, and in Chicago from Germany and Austria. Consider the proportion of foreign-born in four industrial cities reasonably close in size: Baltimore, 14 percent; St. Louis, 18 percent; Pittsburgh, 26 percent; Cleveland, 35 percent.[34] In its social geography, America was becoming more a patchwork quilt than a melting pot.

A Manufacturing Nation

In early twentieth-century America, the spectacular development of manufacturing accompanied the new immigration, the redistribution of population, and the growth of cities. In fact, as the historical geographer D. W. Meinig describes them, all the prerequisites for a great manufacturing future had been in place by the Civil War: "the coal-iron-steam complex, the machine-driven factory, the new 'American system' of mass production, the space-conquering railroad, established areas and centers of specialized production and distribution, and all the vigorous workings and potentials of an essentially 'unfettered market economy' fueled by vast resources and growing population." In every region of the country since the decades after the Civil War, manufacturing—driven mainly by steam engines (77 percent of industrial horsepower in 1900)— had taken off with stunning velocity. By 1900, America produced a third of the world's industrial output—more than England, France, and Germany combined.[35] The leading quality of American manufacturing— which was located in towns and cities across the nation—was diversity. In large and small work settings, in factories and the shops of craftsmen, Americans made everything (see photograph 1.2).

In the twenty years between 1870 and 1890, the size of workplaces— represented by the number of employees per establishment—doubled and then continued to grow early in the twentieth century. In the first decade, aside from small hand and neighborhood industries, the number of manufacturing establishments grew 23 percent, the number of wage workers in them 29 percent, and the value of their product 45 percent— a mark of the increased productivity that resulted from technological and organizational change. The nation's manufacturing plants employed more than six and a half million wage workers and produced nearly $21 billion in products. Manufacturing reshaped the nation's for-

Photograph 1.2   Ford Factory, First Moving Assembly Line, Detroit, 1913

By the second decade of the twentieth century, technology made it possible for industrialists to reorganize manufacturing using assembly lines. Automobile production led the way. *Source*: Courtesy of the Francis Loeb Library, Harvard Design School.

eign trade as well as its domestic economy and surpassed agriculture as the dominant export. Indeed, as a share of total exports, manufacturing increased from 28 percent in 1860 to 60 percent in 1910. Despite these exports, consumer demand within the United States, fueled by high fertility and massive immigration, was so great that most production targeted domestic markets.[36]

As manufacturing activities spread across the nation, their old location in the Northeast gave way to a new concentration in the Midwest, with the South still home to very little industry.[37] The result was a new industrial heartland, which Meinig defined as approximating a parallelogram whose corners were Milwaukee, St. Louis, Boston, and Baltimore (see figure 1.5). Its western boundary stretched to include Dubuque and the Davenport area, and its northeastern corner extended to the rivers of southern New Hampshire and Maine.

In 1900, despite the catalytic growth of manufacturing in the Midwest, New York and the New Jersey cities sharing its harbor ranked first on all measures of industrialism. New York's $1.5 billion industrial product was about double Philadelphia's and much higher than the next leading industrial city's, Chicago's $889 million. With economies composed of all

Figure 1.5   Total Manufacturing Production, U.S. Counties, 1900

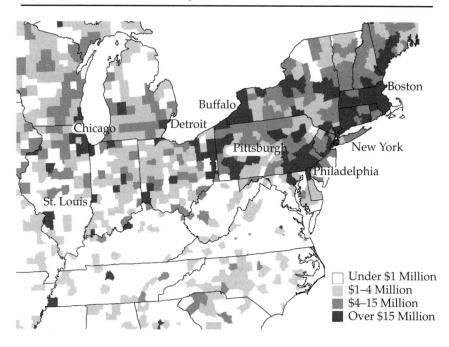

Note: In 1900, manufacturing production was concentrated in a region bounded by Boston and Philadelphia in the east and Chicago and St. Louis in the west. *Source*: Inter-University Consortium for Political and Social Research, 197-(date uncertain).

major trades, these cities shared a dazzling industrial diversity. Although textiles remained the largest industrial employer, iron and steel along with engineering and machinery led in investment and industrial output. These massive industries notwithstanding, the historian Walter Licht stresses, "it is the *completeness* of the manufacturing system that deserves emphasis." Americans produced everything—and in settings that ranged from great iron and steel mills in Pittsburgh and huge meatpacking plants in Chicago to small manufactories turning out limited amounts of fine goods in cities and towns throughout the nation. To be sure, manufacturing was located disproportionately in large cities—home to 19 percent of the population in 1900, cities of over 100,000 produced 40 percent of the total value of manufacturing products. But small cities and towns remained significant industrial locations, too: those with a population under 10,000 produced 31 percent of the total value. Manufacturing was ubiquitous, diverse, and specialized.[38]

Within this diversity, three patterns of industrial development marked American industry: modern, traditional, and sweated. Modern firms were often found in large industries like iron and steel or railway car production. They were distinguished by above average wages, the use of technology, and modern management—they employed a high proportion of salaried workers. Within them, productivity and value-added per worker, not surprisingly, were also high. Traditional industries also paid above-average wages. But they used less advanced technology, and their management relied on fewer salaried employees. Their productivity and value-added were generally low. Neither modern nor traditional industries, it is important to remember, were distinguished by their size or rate of growth: they could be small or large, slow or fast growing. Sweated industries, by contrast, often had grown rapidly, paid low wages, and did not rely very much on advanced technology or modern management. Within them the value of product per worker remained low, but the value added by each worker was high—the result of sweated labor. Modern firms took the high road to the extraction of value from their workers, sweated firms the low. They were also the industries most likely to employ large numbers of women. Women who entered manufacturing, especially immigrants from southern and eastern Europe, were in fact found in the worst-paying industries more often than men.[39]

Within large industries, a range of wages separated workers by income—with the newest immigrants at the bottom. In the iron and steel industry, for instance, about 9 percent of male jobs were white collar, 36 percent crafts, 28 percent operatives, and 26 percent laborers. But they were distributed disproportionately by ethnicity: 13 percent of whites, no blacks, and 2 percent of immigrants from southern and eastern Europe held white-collar positions; 14 percent of native whites, 71 percent of blacks, and 59 percent of southern and eastern European immigrants were laborers. A similar pattern characterized the railway industry, in which 93 percent of the "new" immigrants, 42 percent of the "old," and 68 percent of blacks were laborers—compared to 37 percent of the white male workforce.[40]

A wave of mergers concentrated the organization of manufacturing into huge companies whose power and operations stretched across the continent. International Harvester, U.S. Steel, and Standard Oil Trust represented enormous "horizontal consolidations of formerly competitive firms that took place in most sectors of American industry"—a form of organization soon reworked into vertical integration that controlled manufacturing from processing raw materials through marketing finished products. Vertical integration was pioneered by Swift and Armour in the meatpacking industry, which—in an astonishing burst of growth driven by consolidation and consumer demand—overtook iron and steel between 1900 and 1910 as the nation's leader in the value of goods produced.[41]

Neither industrial consolidation nor growth, however, could have happened without increases in two other factors: capital and labor. In the late nineteenth century, capital came from a surge in investments. After the Civil War, banking laws became more favorable to industrial expansion and, in the 1890s, the introduction of industrial securities to stock markets made new sources of external finance available, which provided the capital for the expansion of manufacturing. In most places immigrants provided the labor. Newcomers from central, southern, and eastern Europe flooded into factories producing both durable and nondurable goods. Native whites, on the other hand, did not respond with anything like the same enthusiasm to the new opportunities opened up in manufacturing. Blacks, still largely in the South, were excluded. Among working men aged ten to sixty-four in 1910, 53 percent of Polish, 25 percent of Italian, 29 percent of German, and 31 percent of British immigrants worked in manufacturing compared to 16 percent of white and 11 percent of black Americans.[42]

Cities Ascendant

Most manufacturing growth took place in cities, and the result transformed the residential profile of Americans. Between 1910 and 1990, the share of the national population living on farms plummeted from 35 percent to 1.8 percent as the nation reorganized into a new urban hierarchy linking a transcontinental network of cities.[43]

The growth of industrial cities, of course, did not start in the twentieth century. In some parts of the nation, it can be traced to the 1840s and 1850s. The years 1900 and 1910, then, are less baselines for measuring change than arbitrary starting points for cutting into a process that had accelerated in much of the nation in the years after the Civil War. Writing in 1913, William Bennett Munro, professor of municipal government at Harvard, summarized the "the great urbanizing forces" transforming America: "It is the combination of cheap fuel for motive power, cheap labor, and cheap transportation which now determines the location and governs the growth of great cities."[44]

Across the nation, the average size of large cities (population more than one hundred thousand) rose 33 percent in the century's first decade, medium size cities (twenty-five to one hundred thousand) 38 percent, and small cities (twenty-five hundred to twenty-five thousand) 36 percent. Although still increasing, the rural population grew much more slowly, only 11 percent. The degree and pattern of urbanization across regions, however, varied sharply. Most urbanized were the middle Atlantic states of Pennsylvania, New Jersey, and New York; New England was also heavily urbanized; the South remained the most rural. Although lightly populated, the Pacific Coast states were also surprisingly urban. Settlement there clustered along the coast: more than a third of the region's people lived in one of the six cities with a population of more than one hundred thousand—making Pacific Coast urban growth spectacular. In California, the combination of commerce, service industries, foreign trade, and tourism meant that urban growth depended less on manufacturing; this pattern prefigured an alternate economic route that other cities would find later in the century.[45]

Even in the early twentieth century, the links between metropolitan areas and agricultural hinterlands gradually gave way to central cities surrounded by suburbs. In 1910, central cities still dominated suburbs with a population of 17 million compared to 5 million, but suburbs were growing faster—a harbinger of things to come. (Because many central cities in this era grew by annexing their suburbs, the real difference in growth rates was probably even larger than statistics suggest.)[46] Patterns of metropolitan size and growth, however, varied, highlighting the complexities subsumed under the general process of urbanization. Local influences—rail lines that made suburban commuting feasible or decisions about industrial location based on proximity to transportation, for instance—clustered manufacturing and population into a myriad of new urban patterns.

Nonetheless, by 1915 the nation functioned economically as a "vast network of cities" organized into an urban hierarchy. In the nineteenth century, the economic historian Carol E. Heim points out, agriculture and manufacturing in new regions drove spatial change, "expanding the boundaries of the economy." In the twentieth century, by contrast, "extension of the system of cities" took "center stage."[47] This urban hierarchy—a shifting but powerful urban system—had been knit together inadvertently by national banking legislation. At its apex, "New York provided an array of financial and commercial services for the entire nation; Chicago was the principal financial and marketing center for a huge portion of the midsection of the country"—branching to Minneapolis, Milwaukee, Denver, Portland, Kansas City, San Francisco, Seattle, and Indianapolis, and beyond them to still another tier of widely separated cities: Quincy, Omaha, St. Joseph, and Spokane. St. Louis's dominance extended southward to Houston, Dallas, and Fort Worth. There is, in this historical creation of an urban hierarchy, a paradox. Within America's federal system, cities were officially powerless; they were, and remain, creatures of state governments, their capacity to act autonomously circumscribed by state law. However, as Meinig points out, even in the early twentieth century, "insofar as one might choose to view the United States as a vast market and unified world of business and commerce it already functioned as a great system of cities."[48]

Rural-Urban Tensions

The spectacular growth of cities resulted in tensions between the older, rural America and the new urbanism. These tensions lay at the heart of late nineteenth-century politics. At the Democratic national convention of 1896, William Jennings Bryan warned advocates of the gold standard:

> You come to us and tell us that the great cities are in favor of the gold standard; we reply that the great cities rest upon our broad and fertile prairies. Burn down your cities and leave our farms, and your cities will spring up again as if by magic; but destroy our farms and the grass will grow in the streets of every city in the country.[49]

Even as it acknowledged the ties that joined city and country, Bryan's fiery rhetoric highlighted the tension between them. Underlying the bravado were resentment and insecurity that grew out of asymmetries in power. True, without farms the cities would starve. But city businessmen controlled the cost of transportation, access to credit, the supply of currency, and the conditions of international trade—factors that could bring success or failure to farmers. With agriculture depressed in the 1870s and 1880s, farmers had turned to new political movements—the Grange and Farmers Alliance—that spoke for rural interests. When farm prices collapsed in the depression of 1893, intense rural and western anger underwrote populism and, in 1896, with Bryan's nomination and Free Silver as its banner, captured the Democratic Party. To a degree unimaginable in twenty-first century America, the currency issue aroused the passions animating the fierce partisan politics of the late nineteenth century— unimaginable to Americans but not to Europeans caught up in the debate over the euro in this second age of economic globalization.[50]

With Bryan's defeat by William McKinley, rural-based populism lost a major political battle. On the national political stage, the election of 1896 was a major defeat for a local and rural America in its confrontation with a national system of capital and commerce.[51] The struggle, of course, was waged on other fronts as well. There, too, asymmetries of power resulted in the spread of urban hegemony, though not without significant resistance. Young women and men flocked from farms to cities, aging farmers moved to town, and farm families consumed the artifacts of urban culture in mail order catalogues. In politics, rural interests took second place to urban; in social life and culture, the lure of city lights and the comforts of towns threatened to depopulate farms and erode distinctive rural values. But agriculture, as we have seen, nonetheless prospered. Indeed, the first two decades of the twentieth century were a more prosperous time than farmers had ever known. Not surprisingly, rising prices for agricultural products and land muted farm-based protests. Instead, a movement for rural social and economic change originated in the cities. Its audacious aim was the fusion of rural and urban life in a new American culture that resolved the tensions between what America had been and what it was becoming. The project began by attempting to recast the relations among families, communities, and public institutions—most notably, schools.

Urban-based critics of the countryside idealized rural life as the fount of national strength and virtue, but they worried about its future. President Theodore Roosevelt warned Americans "that the great recent progress made in city life is not a full measure of our civilization; for our civilization rests at bottom on the wholesomeness, the attractiveness, and the completeness, as well as the prosperity, of life in the country."[52]

As Roosevelt and other critics said, prosperity by itself neither measured the vitality of rural life nor guaranteed its future. Cityward migration threatened the agricultural labor supply and robbed the countryside of its most intelligent, energetic, and ambitious population. Depletion of the soil through exploitative farming methods threatened productivity while intemperance, stolidity, and excessive individualism blocked the organization, efficiency, and cooperation essential to successful modern agriculture. Underlying specific criticisms was the worry that rural Americans would fail to produce the agricultural products needed by an urban population whose expansion showed no signs of slowing.

When Roosevelt appointed a Country Life Commission in 1907, concern about rural life had been growing for a number of years. The commission was chaired by Liberty Hyde Bailey, a leading agricultural scientist who taught at Cornell, and composed almost entirely of non-farmers—a clear sign of the national and urban concerns that prompted its formation. After holding many hearings around the country and soliciting responses through questionnaires, the commission reported in 1909.[53]

The commission wanted to haul rural society into the mainstream of modernity. Judged by historical standards, the American farmer never had been "as well off as he is today" in terms of both "earning power" and "the comforts and advantages he may secure," but his progress had not kept pace with the "complete and fundamental change in our whole economic system within the past century. . . . In all the great series of farm occupations the readjustment has been the most tardy, because the whole structure of a traditional and fundamental system has been involved." The results—"arrested" development, "marked inequalities," "positive injustice"—were to be expected. Instead of a forward-looking spirit of cooperation, a commitment to the public good, and a healthy ambition, a narrow materialism undercut the future of rural America. "So completely does the money purpose often control the motive that other purposes in farming often remain dormant. The complacent con-

tentment in many rural neighborhoods is itself the very evidence of social incapacity or decay."[54]

But the commission did not want to lay the blame for rural backwardness solely on country people. "The social structure," it pointed out, "has
been unequally developed. The townsman is likely to assume superior-
ity and to develop the town in disregard of the real interests of the open
country or even in opposition to them. The city exploits the country; the
country does not exploit the city." The goal was to fuse the best of country and city in a new American culture that transcended geography. "The
good institutions of cities may often be applied or extended to the open
country," it wrote. Thus, "country ideals, while derived largely from the
country itself, should not be exclusive; and the same applies to city and
village ideals. There should be more frequent social intercourse on equal
terms between the people of the country and those of the city."[55]

The commission did isolate a number of specific problems—for instance, inadequate rural mail delivery, the lack of parcel post, and poor
highways. It criticized the working conditions of rural labor and the
harsh isolation of women. It chided farmers for their poor methods and
lamented the absence of effective social organizations, the excessive
competition among rural churches, and the absence of cooperative economic practices. Most of all, it worried about the quality and relevance of
rural education. "The subject of paramount importance in our correspondence and in the hearings is education. In every part of the United
States there seems to be one mind, on the part of those capable of judg-
ing, on the necessity of redirecting the rural schools. There is no such
unanimity on any other subject."[56]

To both Country Life reformers and professional educators, nothing
seemed to hamper rural education as much as its organization into a
myriad of tiny, ungraded, one-room schools controlled by small, local
school districts.[57] In the conflicts over rural school consolidation, the tension between what America was and what it was becoming emerged
with unmatched clarity. By pitting "those who were oriented toward the
city and the larger society and deferred to outside expertise and authority against those who continued to stress the privacy of the local community, the sanctity of home rule, and the virtues of self-reliance," school
issues, the historian Hal Barron points out, "highlighted the conflict between two competing visions of society."[58]

Consolidation was the essential first step toward reducing the educational differentiation between country and city, but the challenge was
immense: in the early twentieth century, to take one example, Iowa had
about fourteen thousand country school districts and subdistricts, most
with their own locally controlled one-room schools; about 65 percent of
the state's children were educated in country schools. Thus, the base for
grass-roots opposition to reform, though widespread and potent, was

Photograph 1.3   Rural School in Cavalier County, North Dakota, 1896

In the early twentieth century, schooling for many children took place in one-room, wooden schoolhouses. To reformers, these schools symbolized rural backwardness. *Source*: Fred Hultstrand History in Pictures Collection, NDIRS-NDSU, Fargo.

uncoordinated, lacking the consolidators' resources and networks. Often overlooked by historians, district school consolidation was the major rural arm of administrative progressivism—the attempt to reform education through efficiency, professionalism, and systematic reorganization—and one of the most significant social movements in Progressive-era America. It was also a key platform of the Country Life Movement (see photographs 1.3 and 1.4).[59]

Reactions of rural parents to school consolidation paralleled rural responses to other modernizing, city-based technologies such as the telephone, electricity, and the automobile. Progressives who viewed them as backward, stubborn people, fearful and resentful of whatever was new, missed the point. They were, rather, cautious, anxious not to destroy their way of life or to give up local control, ready to ingeniously adapt new technologies to their own uses. Farm men and women, argues the historian Ronald R. Kline, "contested efforts to urbanize the farm by resisting each

Photograph 1.4   Osnabrock, North Dakota, Public School, 1918

By the second decade of the twentieth century, reformers had successfully consolidated many one-room schools. School consolidation proved to be one of the most contentious issues in early-twentieth-century America. *Source*: Fred Hultstrand History in Pictures Collection, NDIRS-NDSU, Fargo.

new technology and then weaving it into existing cultural patterns in their own way." One important difference, however, distinguished between resistance to school consolidation and other technologies. After an initial, fairly brief period of resistance, farm people adapted and then adopted the telephone and the automobile. Indeed, in the 1920s, they purchased automobiles and radios at extraordinary rates. But they did not give in on school consolidation for decades. More than any other force of urbanization, school consolidation struck close to the bone, blending issues of family, economy, and community into a powerful nexus of resistance and highlighting the tension between what America was and what is was becoming.[60]

Domestic Links

The unity of apparent opposites defined early twentieth-century America. The opulence of Fifth Avenue and the poverty of the Lower East Side, the economic prosperity of the North and the backwardness of the South, the opportunities open to white immigrants and closed to black Americans: these, and many others that could be enumerated, point to multiple, simultaneous, and overlapping dualities and striking inequalities as the essence of the nation. But first appearances can deceive. For in none of the binaries did the two sides exist in isolation. In every instance, bonds of interdependence bound them in intimate, although frequently not harmonious, relations. In these tensions between seeming opposites the multiple meanings of the era were found. None of those dualities was more misleading than the contrasts between domestic and foreign, the fictive line that separated America from the rest of the world in the first modern era of economic globalization, or that which divided rural and urban, town and country.

Nature's Metropolis, William Cronon's magnificent history of nineteenth-century Chicago's relations with its hinterland, explodes the binaries between town and country and city and nature. Chicago's growth depended on the products of the countryside: grain, lumber, and livestock. In turn, the demands of the city's market reshaped the countryside into what Cronon calls a "second nature" as hogs and cattle replaced buffalo, and prairie grasses gave way to grain. Less immediately visible, but no less powerful, links joined country merchants and farmers to Chicago through the extended reach of the city's banks and suppliers.[61]

Chicago's experience underscores the superficiality of one of the great, enduring binaries in ideas about history: the separation of town and country, farm and city, rural and urban. It directs attention away from the separate features of the "America that was" and the "America that was becoming" and toward the tensions that linked them. These were, of course, perfectly obvious to observers at the time. In *The Country Town*, first published in 1906, Wilbert L. Anderson, a New England clergyman and student of rural life, contrasted the "age of homespun" with the "age of machinery" or the "age of cities" and described the "partnership" of the rural with the "urban population in one economic enterprise." The age of homespun may have predated the age of machinery, but it did not disappear with the emergence of industrial cities. In the early twentieth century, the distinction between the two reflected space as much as time, and it was the contemporary links between them, not the succession of one by the other, which marked the era. Anderson tried to deflect attention away from the depletion of some rural villages and toward the larger picture: the "magnitude of the rural population and the rapidity of its increase." Cities, he was clear, "may multiply and grow to an amazing extent without diminishing the rural population as a whole."

> Country and city are united in an indissoluble partnership, which is equitable and for their mutual profit. The farms feed and clothe the urban mil-

lions, forests and mines furnish dwellings and indispensable mechanism; the city repays the service in honest work, which its mills and factories make efficient in the highest degree. So great is the advantage of costly machinery, that the city can take the toll of its maintenance and even of its wealth out of the traffic, and then return to the rural partner what he needs of his product wrought into the form for consumption that the highest civilization approves.[62]

The growth of cities thus assured "corresponding rural development and prosperity." Anderson was optimistic: within ten years agricultural overproduction had given way to "a condition in which the city and country are in delicate equipoise, with many intimations of the demands in the near future that will tax the resources of the farmer to the utmost."[63] Anderson may have been overly sanguine about the future of agriculture—in particular the size of the labor force that it would take to feed urban Americans and the continued tilting of the balance between supply and demand in favor of the farmer—but he was right about the urban-induced growth of agricultural prosperity in the early twentieth century and the intimate links between his "age of homespun" and "age of manufacture."

The Circulation of Products

The links between town and country took many forms. Most apparent in some ways was the circulation of products: raw materials brought from farms to towns and cities for processing and, in many instances, returned in the form of finished goods—clothing, furniture, and canned foods. The urban "talent for exchange," Anderson observed, worked so well that

> in addition to his own grains, and meats, and fibres, passed through the processes of manufacture, the farmer receives for his labor furnishings and adornments for his home, books and papers for his instruction, and a liberal contribution to his bank account. The farm has a double significance for commerce, for from it are derived the materials of manufacture and trade, and to it return the rich products of the toil and skill of the city.

Manufacturers did more than meet rural demands; they induced them. In need of an outlet for the new products of mass production, manufacturers enlisted advertisers and merchants to enlarge rural markets. Faced with problems of distribution in some industries such as meatpacking and sewing machines, they constructed a national marketing system.[64]

In 1872 a salesman named Aaron Montgomery Ward with connections to the Grange, the leading farmers' movement, opened a mail order house that within ten years offered rural families a catalogue with more than ten thousand items. By 1890 he faced competition from an aggressive new mail order firm founded in 1886, Sears, Roebuck and Company, which also directed its wares to rural customers. Rising standards of rural consumption pointed to a circuit of culture as well as merchandise, in this case an asymmetrical exchange as "goods designed, manufactured, advertised, and sold by urban businesspeople," permeated the countryside.[65]

The United States, Delos Wilcox pointed out, was rapidly becoming "a nation of cities, and even while the majority of the American people" remained "rural, so far as residence is concerned, the influence of the cities upon the national life" had grown "quite out of proportion to their population." The city served as the "distributing centre of intelligence as well as goods." It stood at the "centre of the complex web of national life." A number of developments—"rural free [mail] delivery . . . systems of trolley lines focusing in the cities, the expansion of the mail order business, the concentration of the publishing interests"—all these placed cities in "direct and dominating relations with country people, making the country essentially suburban." The trend of the age, said Wilcox, was "urban imperialism."[66]

Although the products of farms and forests sustained urban populations, cities controlled both the processes that turned them into the mass produced goods and the sources of credit and capital that nourished agricultural expansion and trade. In these exchanges, cities held the greatest power, sending back to the countryside a new culture of consumption along with the products of mass production, setting the costs of transportation, and controlling credit. Relations between town and country may have been reciprocal, but they were uneasy, filled with tension, exacerbated by the cityward migration of rural people. Towns and cities were great magnets, drawing people, especially youths, away from farms. Between 1860 and 1920, the size of the urban population grew about nine times; the rural population scarcely doubled.[67] Thus, people as well as products linked town and city.

Finance, Communications, and Labor Markets

Finance also linked town and country. The financial links that joined an older, rural America to the new nation growing up in the cities had their ultimate source in New York City. By allowing country banks to count deposits in New York as legal reserves, the National Banking Act of 1865 intensified their reliance on the metropolis's banks, which had long served as correspondents for interregional or international transactions. The New York banks usually invested the money from country banks in short-term loans in the city. A shortfall anywhere in the nation could thus put pressure on New York to scramble for funds and raise interest rates. This pattern fluctuated with the seasons as money flowed from New

York to the interior in the fall to pay for crops and then back again during the rest of the year, notably in the spring when farmers spent what they had earned.[68] Without a bank of last resort, the system remained unstable, subject to crises that, as in 1873, 1893, and 1907, swept across the nation. In 1913, Congress responded with the Federal Reserve System that, for the first time since the demise of the National Bank of the United States in the antebellum era, linked banks into a national financial system and completed the domination of the nation's financial system by large, urban institutions.

A national financial system required a uniform currency. In nineteenth century United States, the multiplicity of local currencies acted as a brake on financial integration. Before the Civil War, more than five thousand different kinds of state bank notes circulated along with a bewildering variety of coins issued in Europe and Mexico. Starting in the 1860s with the National Banking Act, the federal government tried to force the substitution of a single national currency for the many state and local varieties. Although the late nineteenth and early twentieth centuries witnessed considerable financial integration, including the spread of a national currency, a variety of notes remained in circulation until 1913 and the Federal Reserve system. Paper money did not, in fact, become entirely uniform until the 1920s.[69]

The circulation of goods, the diffusion of a new culture of consumption, the migration of rural people to cities, and the integration of financial markets: all were links joining an older to a newer America. They were facilitated by innovations in communication, notably the telegraph in the nineteenth and the telephone and radio in the early twentieth century, which for the first time permitted the virtually instantaneous flow of information about prices, credit, markets, and products across vast distances at minimal cost. But none of these links would have been possible without dramatic innovations in transportation—methods of moving large quantities of goods quickly, efficiently, and at reasonable cost. Early in the nineteenth century the major transportation innovation had been canals. The Erie Canal spurred the economic ascendancy of New York City and Chicago, which, in effect, was its western terminus. For a time, it made Buffalo, the point where goods were transshipped from the Great Lakes to the Canal, one of the nation's great cities. But by late in the century, canals had been eclipsed by railroads.

On May 10, 1869, the Union Pacific and Central Pacific Railroads met in Utah, joining East and West in the first transcontinental railroad. The great era of railroad building, however, still lay in the immediate future. Between 1870 and 1910, railroad mileage increased from 53 to 243 thousand miles. In the decades between 1870 and 1890, the nation added one hundred and ten thousand miles of track; in the next twenty years it completed nearly another eighty thousand. The introduction of Bessemer steel after the Civil War combined with organizational innovation made this spectacular growth possible. Before then, the small amount of steel the nation produced was twice as expensive as the iron used for tracks. In the decade after 1866, improved steel rails, which dropped in price and proved stronger and better than iron, facilitated the introduction of larger and heavier locomotives and increased the capacity of railroads to carry freight. At the same time, a host of organizational innovations by railroad managers not only facilitated the expansion of railroads but created the template for modern corporations.[70]

Today, as railroads struggle to survive, it is hard to recall that once they drove the economy. In the late nineteenth century, railroads absorbed about 70 percent of the steel output, from 12 percent to 15 percent of coal, around 10 percent of lumber, and a very large share of foreign investment. Three large railroad lines—Central Pacific, Union Pacific, and Illinois Central—each employed more than ten thousand workers; in the 1880s, railroad construction reached its maximum employment, about 200,000 a year. In the same years, in both Britain and North America, financiers focused on mobilizing capital to invest in railroads. In the process, they forced financial institutions to modify their practices to service the new global economy. Until World War I, railroads were the nation's second-largest consumer of capital, exceeded only by the construction industry.

Railroads, as historians have stressed, reduced the cost of freight and diffused goods across the nation. But they had three other key economic effects as well—all of which forged stronger links between the America of farms and villages and the new nation of manufacturing and cities. The railroad, first, freed economic growth from its dependence on proximity to the coast or inland waterways. Second, as the railroad penetrated the trans-Mississippi West it connected previously inaccessible resources to transportation. And, third, it fueled demand for natural resources—iron ore, fuel, lumber—and heavy manufactured products—for instance, steel, engines, and railway cars.[71]

The intensified links between farm and city, forest and factory, East and West reinforced one another. Together, by the first decade of the twentieth century, they built a national economy and labor market unique in the world.[72] Unlike its European counterparts, "the American market was essentially a mass market. It demanded and obtained large quantities of cheap low-to-medium quality goods with comparatively little variation from one part of the country to another." It was, moreover, a market whose resources were found within the same nation state. British and German manufacturing required that large volumes of materials be imported; American manufacturing for the most part did not. It did, however, require mobile labor. With resources irregularly distributed across the continent, manufacturing depended on the willingness of workers to remain on the move.[73]

With the help of self-replicating institutional networks, a relatively integrated labor market had emerged across the nation, with the exception of the South. Two features mark integrated labor markets. First, information moves quickly and easily between workers looking for jobs and potential employers located elsewhere. Second, both parties to the market—workers and labor—share the ability to respond quickly to labor shortages in different locations. In the late nineteenth and early twentieth centuries, helped by the telegraph, telephone, and post office, information about jobs and opportunities flowed along networks defined by kinship, ethnicity, friendship, and location. With railroads crisscrossing the nation and ticket prices falling, potential emigrants faced minimal difficulties in moving in search of better jobs and higher wages—special "emigrant trains" even offered reduced fares to the nation's interior where demand for labor was high.[74]

Because it is difficult, if not impossible, to directly measure information flows and the speed with which workers and employers respond to labor shortages, empirical studies rely on indirect measures of which the most promising, for domestic as well as international markets, is wage convergence across different locations. "As the labor supply increases in the high-wage location and decreases in the low-wage location, the differences in wages will fall," the theory contends. Of course, in the real world many factors intervene to make the process less than perfect. Workers do not have full information; they may have preferences unrelated to work that hold them to where they live; there are costs associated with moving. Nonetheless, over time, converging wages do signify an integrating national as well as international labor market. This national labor market linked all parts of the nation, with the exception of the far West and the South. Huge labor demands sustained higher wages in the West, but remained lower in the South than in the rest of the country. Although the flow of population from the low wage south Atlantic to the higher wage south central regions helped integrate labor markets within the South, until at least 1914 real wages there continued to decline relative to those elsewhere.[75]

In the decades after the Civil War, the South remained separated from national and international labor markets. Southern planters, politicians, and business people managed to exploit black labor through a host of techniques, such as laws that held them in virtual peonage or restricted travel, and the threat of violent reprisal reinforced by lynching. A captive labor force left little incentive to modernize and diversify a largely rural economy. But the reasons for the South's distinctive labor market also go beyond race, because poor white southerners also proved slow to move northward, despite a huge need for labor in an expanding manufacturing economy, which European immigrants eagerly filled. Instead, tradition joined with the absence of networks and labor market institutions to keep white and black southerners within the South. The Civil War had reinforced the historic separation of North and South and the reliance of northern industry on immigrant labor. Furthermore, southerners who might have welcomed unskilled or semi-skilled jobs in the North lacked the networks of friends and relatives that initiated and sustained the chain migration that brought waves of immigrant workers to the nation's factories, mines, and railroads. Nor did employers, who might have wanted to turn to the South for low-wage workers, have any clearly defined means for finding and recruiting them. The South may have lost political nationhood in the Civil War, but on the eve of World War I it remained in many ways economically and socially a nation apart.[76]

Global Links

The links that joined the older and newer Americas were global as well as homegrown. In fact, the years between the Gilded Age and World War I formed America's first important age of economic globalization. The global economy's reach extended from factory to farm and from the Atlantic to the Pacific Coast. Consider, for example, Frank Norris's description of the office of a large wheat rancher in California at the turn of the century:

> The office was the nerve-center of the entire ten thousand acres of Los Mertos, but its appearance and furnishings were not in the least suggestive of a farm. . . . no doubt, the most significant object in the office was the ticker. This was an innovation in the San Joaquin. . . . The offices of the ranches were thus connected by wire with San Francisco, and through that city with Minneapolis, Duluth, Chicago, New York, and at last, and most important of all, with Liverpool. Fluctuations in the price of the world's crop during and after the harvest thrilled straight through to the office. . . . The ranch became merely the part of an enormous whole, a unit in the vast agglomeration of wheat land the whole world round, feeling the effects of causes thousands of miles distant—a drought on the prairies of Dakota, a rain on the plains of India, a frost on the Russian steppes, a hot wind on the llanos of the Argentine.[77]

The first truly international economy reached not only from the grain markets of Liverpool to the wheat ranches of California, but also to every corner of the globe, economic historians Kevin H. O'Rourke and Jeffrey G. Williamson emphasize:

By 1914, there was hardly a village or town anywhere on the globe whose prices were not influenced by distant foreign markets, whose infrastructure was not financed by foreign capital, whose engineering, manufacturing, and even business skills were not imported from abroad, or whose labor markets were not influenced by the absence of those who had emigrated or by the presence of strangers who had immigrated. . . . poor regions had enjoyed significant convergence gains by erasing part of the gap between themselves and rich regions, and flourishing export sectors enjoyed the benefits associated with the global trade boom.[78]

In America, the modern history of economic globalization moved through three phases: a period of intense globalization between the later nineteenth century and World War I; years of de-globalization—a turning inward in both public policy and economic activity—from, roughly, the 1920s through the 1950s; and the current era of re-globalization that started after World War II and accelerated in the 1960s. Although the overuse of "globalization" often robs the term of its precision and analytic power, we understand it to have a specific meaning. Economic globalization refers to increasing internationalization in four areas: trade in goods and services, financial markets, labor markets, and population flows. Together, the force of these connections reshaped the distribution of people and economic activity in space, the content and demography of work, the level of personal well-being, and the experience of individuals and families.[79]

Trade and Finance

Between the late nineteenth and early twentieth centuries, with the share of exports and imports in gross domestic product (GDP) as the measure, the United States showed little increase in international economic activity. As a share of GDP, imports between 1870 and 1913 hovered between 6 and 7 percent and exports between 5 and 6 percent. But volume and share of GDP can reflect influences on supply and demand other than the integration of global markets, for instance, "population growth, colonization of empty lands, capital accumulation, technological change, and a variety of other factors." These influences on GDP masked the growing internationalization of the U.S. economy, signified, according to O'Rourke and Williamson, by the convergence in the price of commodities—*the only irrefutable evidence that globalization is taking place.*"[80] In other words, the market for goods becomes increasingly worldwide with prices subject to the same influences wherever they originate.

For prices to converge at least one of two things must happen: transport costs or barriers to trade, such as tariffs, must fall. In the late nineteenth and early twentieth century, tariffs did not decline. (In Asia, however, with the opening of Japan, trade barriers disappeared with lightning speed.) But transport costs plummeted spectacularly around the world—at an annual rate of about 1.5 percent over many years. The convergence of commodity prices followed. In 1870, the cost of wheat in Liverpool exceeded the cost in Chicago by 57.6 percent, in 1895 by 17.8 percent, and in 1912 by 15.6 percent—and these numbers almost certainly understate the decline. The pattern was repeated for other foodstuffs. For meat, the gap went down from 92.3 percent in 1895 to 17.9 percent in 1913. For cotton textiles, the price difference between Boston and Manchester was 13.7 percent in 1870 and 0 in 1913. The same trends marked prices in iron rails, pig iron, copper, hides, wood, coal, tin, and coffee. Price convergence took place, too, between Britain and Buenos Aires, Montevideo, and Rio de Janeiro and was facilitated between London and Asia by the opening of the Suez Canal and the substitution of steam for sail on long distance routes, which reduced the time and cost of transport.[81]

International financial markets—highly integrated in the early twentieth century—supported the globalization of trade. Sustained by the gold standard and the complex of financial institutions in London, early twentieth-century capital flowed around the world searching for the highest returns. Three measures highlight this financial integration: capital accounts, the correlation between savings and investment, and the duration of capital flows. Capital accounts, which combine imports and exports, measure capital mobility. Aggregating them for twelve major nations yields a higher average for the pre–World War I period than from 1989 to 1996. The relation between savings and investments points in the same direction. Where international markets are integrated, the correlation between them should be low because capital should flow where returns are highest. This, in fact, was the case in the early twentieth century. In 1907, for instance, 40 percent of British savings was invested abroad, and, in sharp contrast to today, as primarily long-term investments. Investors bought government bonds and shares of railroads and other public utilities. Increasingly, therefore, returns to investors depended on developments around the world.[82]

Wages and Labor Markets

Global links, in fact, defined the "age of machinery." International financial exchanges, wages, and labor markets provided the capital, incentives, and manpower that underlay America's industrial ascendance. As the flows of international capital locked nations into a global financial system and the prices of commodities traded in increasingly integrated markets became more similar, the wages paid to ordinary workers also converged. In the early nineteenth century, the simultaneous impact of industrialization in labor-abundant Europe and the exploitation of rich natural resources in labor-scarce America drove a huge gap between wages. The U.S. advantage over Great Britain in real wages soared from 40 percent in 1830 to 86 percent in 1846. In 1870, real wages were 136 percent higher in the New World than in the Old.[83] By 1913, this gap had fallen 36 percent. Between 1870 and 1910, the wage gap between Britain and the United States dropped 17.2 percent.[84] This wage convergence signaled the emergence of an international labor market.

More than any other factor, migration accomplished this internationalization of labor. The flow of people—even more than of commodities or capital—is both the source and the sign of economic globalization. Population flows across oceans and the American continent constituted two sides of the processes that integrated international and domestic economies in the years from the latter nineteenth century through World War I. Between 1850 and 1914, fifty-five million Europeans moved to North and South America and to Australasia. Emigration rates of fifty per thousand per decade and immigration rates of one hundred per thousand per decade were common in the years just before World War I; they have rarely been matched since then. In the four decades before World War I, this migration increased the labor force in the New World by a third and decreased it in the Old World by an eighth. Even California and Mexico in the last four decades of the twentieth century did not exceed these proportions. Constraints that had prevented poor European workers from seeking high wages in the Americas dissipated after 1870: the cost of transportation fell; remittances from the first generation of emigrants financed the migration of relatives; and, with the spread of industrialization across Europe, income rose in previously depressed regions, increasing family resources available for a move. As the impediments to emigration eased, workers found themselves pushed out of low-wage and drawn into high-wage countries, and redistributed around the world from areas of labor surplus to labor scarcity.[85]

New "entrepreneurs of the international labor market" channeled many of the migration streams that linked country and city across both the Atlantic and the North American continent. These were "padrones" who recruited workers in southern Europe to supply areas of labor shortage in America and Canada and to railroad construction in the West. Once in the New World, laborers recruited by padrones remained subject to their control, commodities shuffled between work sites to meet shifting demands. "By linking diverse and isolated sites of labor demand such as Kootenay Landing, British Columbia, Bingham Canyon, Utah, and Minnesotan sugar beet fields with equally isolated sites of labor supply in the countryside of Italy, Greece, and Mexico," the historian Gunther Peck writes, padrones "helped build truly international labor markets."[86]

In the United States, the redistribution of the global labor force registered in the spatial mobility of American workers, described earlier. Mobility was one facet of the interaction between native and immigrant workers. The others were wages and structures of opportunity. In the late nineteenth and early twentieth centuries, immigrants took the least desirable jobs in the slowest-growing parts of the economy, freeing native workers to pursue higher wages in faster growing industries. As they entered the slowest-growing occupations, immigrants crowded out unskilled native workers, often motivating them to move west. For every additional one hundred immigrants entering northeastern states, Timothy Hatton and Jeffrey Williamson estimate, forty native workers left. The availability of immigrants for unskilled factory work also probably blocked black migration north to better jobs until World War I and the immigration quotas of the 1920s. Immigrants, who appear to have received the same wages as natives for similar work, flooded labor markets. Thus, despite the absence of wage discrimination, they lowered wages—either absolutely or by lowering the rate of increase that otherwise would have occurred. In the absence of immigrants, according to Hatton and Williamson, real wages would have been 4.7 to 5.9 percent higher after 1890, or 10.9 to 13.7 percent higher after 1879.[87] Even in the older cities, however, immigration did not reduce opportunity structures for the native-born workers who remained. Their occupational rank, as measured by a socioeconomic index, rose as the numbers of immigrants increased. Immigrants entered at the bottom of the labor market queue, bumping the native-born workers who stayed up the ladder into better jobs.[88] Immigrants may have reduced wages, but they also opened opportunities.

The displacement of native by immigrant workers worried the U.S. Immigration Commission, which studied the problem with care. Displacement, the committee concluded, was a complex phenomenon. Native-born Americans and immigrants from Britain and northern Europe were abandoning a number of industries, especially coal mining and iron and steel making; those who remained, however, moved up into more skilled jobs and, even, executive and technical positions, as immigrants from southern and eastern Europe flooded in; but their children refused to enter the same industries. This reluctance resulted from three influences: advanced education that enabled the move to better occupations, degraded working conditions accepted by recently hired unskilled workers, and the social stigma attached to occupations of the new immigrants.[89]

The transnational integration of trade, finance, labor markets, and people marked the first era of economic globalization. They were, of course, the same factors that knit the northern United States into an integrated economy. Globalization and national economic integration were two sides of the same coin. Thus, international migration and population movement within the United States, usually written about separately by historians and social scientists, were part of the same process—a redistribution of labor representing a massive adjustment of supply and demand linking an older, rural America to the age of machinery.

The consequences of this massive population movement across oceans and continents were huge. It forever changed the nation's demography, and its political and cultural impact registered on every aspect of American life, with reverberations that have not yet ceased. Together with the other sources of discontinuous social and economic change, it exacerbated inequalities and built into early twentieth-century experience a tension between old and new that forced Americans to redesign everything—from their governments to their families.

The Limits of Government

Governments—federal, state, and local—that fit an older, rural America proved unsuitable for the age of manufacture. Their limits forced Americans to rethink the characteristics of the state and what it should do.

Early twentieth-century Americans remained a lightly governed people. Federal, state, and local governments all began the century better suited to an agricultural-commercial nation than to one dominated by manufacturing and great cities. Compared to the end of the century, the federal government was small. Excluding defense and the post office, there were only 58,760 federal employees in 1901, or one for every 1,293 Americans. In 1999 the number was 1,685,000, or 1 for every 161. (The post office, the great source of federal patronage, accounted for 70 percent of federal civilian employees in 1901; reformed by Civil Service regulations, its share of federal civilian employment in 1999 had dropped to 32 percent.) Although it was small, the size of the federal government was increasing faster than the population: the number of federal employees went up 132 percent between 1880 and 1900, and would grow another 133 percent by 1910. In the same decade, population increased 21 percent. (Much of this growth in the federal workforce resulted from the expansion of the armed services during the Spanish-American War and the occupation of new territories and war in the Philippines.) [90]

The cost of government grew less than the number of its employees— 98 percent in the last two decades of the nineteenth century and 25 percent in the twentieth century's first. Cost lagged behind employment partly because of declining interest payments on the national debt, which, swollen as a result of the Civil War, dropped from $95 million in 1881 to $40 million in 1900 and $21 million in 1910. The federal government paid this interest and other expenses from sources of revenue quite different from current-day ones. In 1900, it received 41 percent of its income from customs and 52 percent from internal revenue, which, in turn, received 82 percent of its revenue from excise taxes on alcohol and tobacco. The first federal income tax was coterminous with the Civil War; the modern version was introduced in 1913. With the importance of customs to federal income, it is not surprising that the tariff question dominated early twentieth-century politics. In an era of economic globalization tariffs and free trade inevitably proved powerful and divisive issues. To its partisans, free trade promised unlimited benefits through the expansion of exports and consequent growth in jobs and income. To its opponents, by opening the nation to competition from lower wage economies, it threatened working-class incomes and jobs. This clash, so powerful in America's first era of economic globalization, repeated itself nearly a century a later in the debates over the North American Free Trade Agreement and other trade issues. Only the sides had changed. Whereas labor remained suspicious of unregulated international commerce, manufacturing interests, supporters of high tariffs a century earlier, were now, with a few exceptions, ardent champions of free trade.[91]

The largest single expense in the federal budget in the early twentieth century was veterans' services and benefits (swollen by the late-nineteenth century expansion of Civil War pensions), which, in turn, was followed closely by the cost of the army and, at a distance, the navy, and interest on the public debt. Even with generous veterans' pensions, the federal government, helped by high tariffs, still ran a surplus equivalent to almost 9 percent of its expenses. For a few fortunate decades its problem was how to spend its revenues, not how to increase them. Within the government, the Interior Department, a catch-all agency whose most important responsibilities included lands and railroads, Indian affairs and territory, patents, printing, and public documents had the most employees—7,699 in 1900—followed by the Treasury Department with 5,587. Other departments remained very small: State 101, Labor 103, Justice 143—tiny compared to now, even accounting for population increase.[92]

In the late nineteenth century the presidency remained a less powerful and far more informal agency than it became in the twentieth. Presidents concerned themselves mainly with dispensing patronage. James Bryce remarked, "The business of nominating is in ordinary times so engrossing as to leave the chief magistrate of the nation little time for his other functions."[93] The historian Morton Keller describes the office as "small in scale and limited in power, caught up more in the vicissitudes of party politics and patronage than in the formulation and conduct of public policy. Late nineteenth-century presidents had little say over the estimates, appropriations, expenditures, and policies of government bureaus and departments." "He has less influence on legislation," wrote Bryce, "than the Speaker of the House of Representatives."[94] At the start of the twentieth century, the president's staff consisted only of "a secretary, two assistant secretaries, two executive clerks, four lesser clerks or telegraphers, and a few doorkeepers and messengers." This weakness and informality gave way in the early twentieth century. Already, late in the nineteenth century, McKinley's administration had improved the efficiency of the presidential office. Indeed, heightened executive power during the Spanish-American War and the fierce politics of the late 1890s initiated the transformation of the presidency led by Theodore Roosevelt and Woodrow Wilson.[95] Nonetheless, the presidency began the century a faint shadow of what it would become by its end.

In 1885 Woodrow Wilson called Congress the "predominant and controlling force, the centre and source of all motive and regulative power." With the presidency weak and in the absence of a capable, independent civil service, Congress, dominated by state party leaders, controlled fiscal and budgetary power and initiated legislation. It was also an institution undergoing change as the congressional leadership exerted increasingly tight control. The vehicle for congressional government was the committee system, through which Congress exerted administrative influence on the federal government.[96]

Growth in the number of civil service positions following the Pendleton Act of 1883 and the presence of more skilled civil servants in the government's technical branches—such as Carroll Wright at the Bureau of the Census, Walter Moseley at Agriculture, and Henry C. Carter at the Interstate Commerce Commission—improved its administrative capacity. Still, American national government remained far less professional and far weaker than its counterparts in England and continental Europe. Americans, by and large, Keller observes, lacked "any broad conception as to what the central government might *do*, save collect taxes, provide patronage, guard the coasts, fight Indians, and preserve order."[97] Expansion of the federal government's activities to include the protection of children, provision for the elderly, the relief of unemployment, and the construction of housing would require a conceptual as well as an administrative revolution. This revolution is a central theme in the history of American government in the twentieth century, with vast consequences for every topic discussed in this book, as later chapters make clear. In the years before World War I, new beliefs about the uses of government remained just a glimmer on the federal horizon, but they had moved much closer to the center of state and local government.

Because of the way American federalism worked, crucial power over education, welfare, law enforcement, infrastructure, corporate charters, and other activities that affected the intimate experience of Americans on a daily basis remained with the states, which, in turn, often delegated them to cities, towns, and counties. In the late nineteenth century, many states, hostile to "active government," wrote new constitutions or revised old ones that crimped state legislatures' lawmaking powers. But strict constitutional language could not hold back the pressures of industrial growth and urbanization, which forced legislatures to intervene,

if reluctantly, in economic and social affairs. Thus, state governments extended their authority in education, social welfare, corrections, public
health, and other important matters. "There is," Bryce noted, "visible in
recent constitutions a strong tendency to extend the scope of public administrative activity."[98] Indeed, the early twentieth century witnessed the
emergence of modern, activist state government. "Whereas the nineteenth-century state was spare, with little administrative muscle," historian Jon C. Teaford observes, "during the course of the twentieth century,
the state expanded beyond recognition, becoming a governmental gar-
gantuan in comparison with its earlier self." In these years, with their
role redefined, "states emerged as dynamic molders of domestic policy
and vital providers of government services."[99]

The growth of spending and employment illustrates the dynamic
transformation of state government in the early twentieth century. State
expenses increased much faster than population. Consider the growth in
state spending in three periods: from 1880 to 1900, from 1900 to 1910, and
from 1910 to 1920. In Illinois the percentage increase was 71 percent, 49
percent, and 116 percent compared to population increases of 57 percent,
17 percent and 36 percent. In Pennsylvania, a state that grew more
slowly, spending also rose much faster than population. Even in the
South, the pattern was the same. Considered on a per capita basis, the
rise in spending becomes even more striking: in Illinois, which was not
exceptional, from $2.75 in 1880 to $3.00 in 1900, $3.83 in 1910, and $6.09
in 1920. The second decade of the century was, in fact, the period of catalytic growth in state government and of major reorganization. Per
capita state employment increased in Illinois from four per thousand to
seven per thousand during the decade, numbers almost identical to
Pennsylvania's, whereas in Alabama it rose from two per thousand to
three per thousand.[100] (To pay for this growth, state governments began
to experiment with financial reforms, notably by decreasing reliance on
the property tax which, in 1902, was the source of 53 percent of all state
tax receipts.)[101]

As a result, the early twentieth century witnessed new specialized
state administrative agencies, staffed increasingly by experts, and designed both to modernize and extend old responsibilities, such as education, and to administer new ones, such as mothers' pensions or workers'
compensation. In the same years, the automobile posed entirely new
problems for state governments, which carried most of the burden for financing highways, which they met through borrowing and levying new
taxes. State highway department allocations leaped from $24 million in
1914 to $107 million in 1919, and $910 million in 1929.[102]

"During the second decade of the twentieth century," writes Teaford,
"demands for administrative reorganization swept the nation." Reformers emphasized the need to reorganize the executive branch and to re-

duce the "multitude of irresponsible state commissions and boards" that state legislatures had created in the last decades of the nineteenth and the first of the twentieth century. In their place, reformers advocated "a limited number of departments headed by gubernatorial appointees subject to the governor's removal power."[103] The administrative history of Illinois' state government illustrates these patterns. Between 1903 and 1914, the number of state boards and commissions proliferated, from approximately eighteen to sixty-one. Within a decade, by 1924, the government had been radically reorganized into ten departments under the executive branch and a small number of permanent boards and commissions. A new Department of Labor and Department of Public Welfare spoke not only to administrative reorganization but to new functions and a self-conscious professionalization widely shared throughout the nation.

Local government remains the hardest branch to describe. With more than ten thousand incorporated units, it took a variety of forms. In the South, the most important unit was the county, in New England the town. Elsewhere, Bryce described a third pattern that combined "some features of the first with some of the second, and may be called the mixed system. It is found, under a considerable variety of forms, in the middle and north-western States." Everywhere, though, local autonomy remained strong. Municipal expert Delos Wilcox described American city government as a "chaos of forms."[104]

The problems identified by early twentieth-century urban reformers ring with an eerie familiarity. As they groped toward the definition of a novel urban form—the industrial city, as new in its time as the "edge city" is today, they wrestled with the consequences of recent immigration, the lack of affordable housing, the growth of poverty and homelessness, crises in public health and sanitation, and the impact of growing concentrations of wealth on society and politics. At the same time, they grappled with private corporations' operations of municipal services and facilities, the heavy hand of state government, the weakness of mayoral executive authority, the corruption of machine politics, the inefficiencies and inequities of the courts, and the regressive and inadequate foundation of city finances on property taxes.[105] By 1910, American urban government had acquired the underlying structures, critiques, and dilemmas that would endure for at least the next century.

Cities governed by political machines posed a special problem: reformers called them corrupt, inefficient, and impotent. "There is no denying," Bryce claimed in an often-quoted observation, "that the government of cities is the one conspicuous failure of the United States."[106] Because they were (and are) creatures of state legislatures, cities retained limited capacity to control their own institutions and economies or to replace political machines. Home rule—defined as greater municipal autonomy from the state—thus composed a key component of municipal reform.

Nonetheless, cities tried to meet the immense challenges they faced. With the growth of population and manufacturing, they found themselves confronted with wretched slums, unsanitary streets, inadequate infrastructure, and overcrowded schools. Municipal government suitable for an older America could not cope with the age of machinery. As Wilcox observed, "the world can never again be the same as it was before steam and electricity were engaged in the service of man, and one of the hardest problems for democracy to face is the necessary readjustment of political habits to fit the new conditions."[107]

As they exhorted Americans to grapple with new problems, Progressive-era writers on urban reform tried to steer a course between Bryce's condemnation of American government—which they cited—and their own optimism about the possibilities of urban democracy. Within the chaos of early industrial cities they saw the potential for both civic revival and the development of innovative urban policies that harnessed the energy and vitality of cities and the fruits of technology to clean, effective, responsive governments. They were not naïve. They realized the obstacles. They thought, however, that the struggle was winnable and crucial. Cities, agents of a new "imperialism," now dominated the country, and their power would only increase. In their character, therefore, lay the fate of the nation.[108]

Like states, city governments in the early twentieth century responded to the age of machinery by expanding and modernizing and by redefining their roles. Among them, as among state governments, the second decade proved the crucial turning point, although some reforms had started in the 1890s. In 1913, Harvard municipal expert William Bennett Munro pointed to civil service reform, changes in election procedures, reductions in the size of municipal legislatures, the substitution of at-large for ward-based elections, and the increased authority of mayors. But, he asserted, "the real renaissance in American city government has come in the last ten or twelve years."[109]

Municipal spending also revealed the growth in city government. In Philadelphia, for example, expenditures grew 164 percent between 1913 and 1920 as population increased only 12 percent. From 1890 to 1913, municipal per capita expenses hovered around $25; in the next seven years they leaped to $58.87. In 1920, the City of Philadelphia employed 15,372 people excluding teachers, 12,817 under civil service. Most of these, 6,754, were employed in the Department of Public Safety and many of the rest, 3,239, in the Department of Public Works. The story in Chicago was similar. There, municipal expenses grew 201 percent between 1913 and 1920 as population increased only 15 percent.[110]

These were, after all, years of tremendous accomplishments in cities, despite their often inefficient and corrupt governments. Cities built water works, bridges, and schools. They dug sewer systems and tunnels for subways. They created parks, public health systems, and departments of public welfare, introduced zoning, and professionalized their courts. They employed experts and founded municipal reference bureaus.[111] Between 1900 and 1920, for example, Philadelphia's Bureau of Health, housed in the Department of Public Safety, became the Department of Public Health with its own network of specialized bureaus. The Bureau of Charities and Correction also became a department overseeing four specialized agencies, including Social Service (a term not used in 1900). Looking back from 1913, Munro pointed to progress on a number of fronts, with the result that in municipal services and infrastructure cities had "made more progress in efficiency during the last twenty years than they [had] in the preceding fifty."[112]

Thus, America's early twentieth-century government, like its economy and population, looked back to what America was and forward to what it was becoming. Its weak authority, impermanent and unspecialized civil service, pervasive patronage, and diffuse structure worked reasonably well in a nation of widely scattered farms, villages, and towns, loosely connected to a few large cities. But it could not cope with the responsibilities and problems of the world's leading industrial nation, with the flood of immigrants from new sources, the burst of urban growth, or the acquisition of an empire. In the strengthening of the presidency, the professionalization of the federal civil service, the expansion of state administrative authority and competence, and the initial modernization of municipal government lay a new idea of government and the basis of a government capable of confronting a transformed America. But government was modified and adapted, not wholly rebuilt. The old remained visible in the new, revamped rather than rejected. The same can be said of American families.

Family Strategies

Government was the public and families the private face of the process through which Americans negotiated the transition to the age of manufacture. In 1900 and 1910, the hand of government rested more lightly on the shoulders of families than it would later in the century. Still, like the divide between rural and urban or local and global, the division between public and private existed as much in the imagination as on the ground. In the real world, the links that joined them blurred the distinction between separate and autonomous spheres. One of those links, as we have seen, was education. Schools intervened between parents and children; with schools, governments tried to structure the daily patterning of family life. In the countryside, the tension between state and family around schooling played itself out vividly in the contest over rural school consolidation. In cities, it appeared in myriad ways: rigid age grading, Americanization programs that introduced conflicts to the relations between immigrant parents and their children, and, most of all, in compulsory education, which moved decisions about how children should spend their time from parents to the state. Public authorities infringed more on the private space of poor than of well-off families. Child protection societies, nominally private but vested with state authority, could remove children from families in cases of suspected neglect or abuse, and their efforts focused almost exclusively on the poor. Even well-off families, however, felt the influence of the state on the most intimate aspects of their lives when they wanted to practice birth control and found access to contraception criminalized by state law.

In early twentieth-century America, families confronted difficult and delicate tasks. They looked for methods to at once protect and advance their interests in a context of momentous and discontinuous change. They met this challenge in countless different ways, but amid the numbing variety two clusters of practices—or strategies—emerged: one anchored in the past, one pointing toward the future. What is interesting and distinctive about a great many families of this time is that they deployed both at once, registering the tension between the old and the new in their day-to-day lives.

Whether they think about them consciously or not, all families have strategies. All of them need resources and must make similar decisions: how to divide economic and domestic responsibilities; whether to bring relatives, friends, or boarders into the household; how many children to have (or at least to try to have); and how long children should remain in school. Family decisions about these matters reflect many influences—custom, culture, education—and are often inconsistent. But patterns as well run through the ways families respond to their life circumstances. Economic, demographic, and spatial changes register in the everyday lives of ordinary people who reorder their families and life plans to meet them.

In the late nineteenth and early twentieth centuries, industrial working-class families faced enormous challenges. With few resources, immigrants needed to recreate households in a new country whose language they very often did not speak. The spectacular industrialization of the time structured the lives of a great many wage earners and their families around the daily rhythm of mills and factories and disfigured them with low wages, periodic layoffs, and industrial accidents. In the same years, urbanization drew young people from farms, disrupting family economies. Professional, technical, and business careers ratcheted up demands for human capital, the importance of education, and the cost of children. Yet, even middle-class families lacked a safety net.[113] Without public or private old-age pensions or unemployment insurance, with public assistance limited to miserly outdoor relief and wretched poorhouses, with private charity uncertain and scarce, aged, disabled, sick, or out-of-work individuals had only their families to whom to turn.

Although individual families responded to the tugs of obligation and modernity in many ways, two basic strategies emerged. What can be called the protective approach responded to change with conventional practices that looked inward, mobilizing families' resources as bulwarks against a threatening, often bewildering new world dominated by unemployment, sickness, and untimely death. It emphasized large, complex households with multiple wage-earners, including children, and large families to manage short term crises, accumulate collective assets, and shelter parents in old age. What can be called the anticipatory approach looked to the future, mobilizing discipline and human capital to equip families for competition in a tough, new economic environment. It stressed limiting family size, excluding non-members of the nuclear family, and educating children. To some extent, these strategies reflected differences in class, ethnicity, and gender, and one or the other often dominated the choices made by individual families. But they were not mutually exclusive. Rather, as they negotiated the tensions inherent in an era of immense change, families combined strategies creatively, devising their own ways of mediating between disaster and mobility.

American families at the beginning of the twentieth century were usually much larger than their counterparts at its end. But size was only one axis along which fundamental family change occurred. Not only were there more children, but assorted extensions—relatives, boarders, employees—swelled the size of many households.

All these generalizations are also valid for families in the mid-nineteenth century. It is not that there had been no change: every feature of families and the life-course was in motion. As a result, early twentieth-century families were in transition. In a great many instances, however, the past was still more visible than the future, and many families, uncertain about their prospects and worried about emergencies, hedged their bets, keeping a foot in each world.

Coming of age in early twentieth-century America also echoed familiar practices. As in the nineteenth century, many young people, who took a long time to negotiate the transition to independent adulthood, still spent several years between work and marriage living as boarders or servants in households other than their parents'—a practice described in detail in chapter 3. In this slow transition, young people in early twentieth-century America reflected the experience of earlier generations more than they forecast the compressed passage to adulthood of the future.[114]

Of course, all families did not change at the same rate, even if almost all were moving in the same direction. The pace varied by class, ethnicity, race, gender, and location. For example, in older, stagnant communities, such as Chelsea, Vermont, it was retired parents who most often lived with kin. In Indianola, Mississippi, among poor, sometimes fragmented African American families, relatives were more often grandchildren, nephews and nieces, or siblings.[115] Families based in professional and white-collar work were the first to adopt new family strategies. Working-class families followed more slowly, not because middle-class norms somehow trickled down or were diffused, but because it took longer for their life circumstances to change enough for new strategies to make sense. Within immigrant groups, the second generation usually pioneered new family forms when they surmounted the tenuous foothold in the American economy that had attached the first generation to the security of older family strategies. Widows were, in important ways, a case apart. Dependent throughout most of the twentieth century, as they had been in earlier times, on the wages of working children supplemented by income from boarders, their family strategies changed the least.

Most families, it is true, were nuclear: fewer than one in three housed a relative, as is clear in figure 1.6. But this is a misleading statistic because families were too large and death came too early for all but a small minority to include a member of the older generation at any one time. In fact, in the early twentieth century, most of the elderly lived with one of

Figure 1.6   Presence of Relatives and Nonrelatives in Households, by Age of Householder, 1910

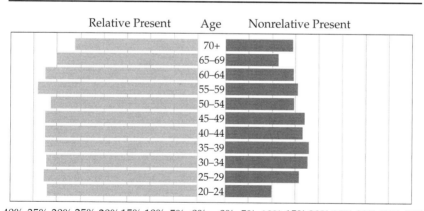

Note: The composition of households varied across the life cycle. For example, relatives more often lived in households with older heads while nonrelatives (mainly boarders and servants) more often lived with younger families. *Source:* Data from Ruggles et al. (2004).

their children whenever they could. At the same time, families and households were fluid. Boarders, servants, and relatives moved in and out, constantly varying the composition of individual households. Watched over time, at some point almost all households included members other than the nuclear family.[116] (It is significant, as we point out in chapter 4, that the concept "nuclear family" first appeared in social science journals only in 1941.)

Between the late nineteenth and early twentieth centuries, families changed only modestly, though for the most part in directions that would accelerate later in the century. The average number of children, for instance, declined by 16 percent and the number of servants and employees living with families by 59 percent. Some trends, however, pointed in the opposite direction: the number of relatives held fairly steady, and the number of families with an employed child living at home increased by a quarter, and the number with boarders and lodgers by more than half. Families thus faced both forward toward the smaller, more stripped down competitive form most would assume in succeeding decades and backward toward a time when kinship obligations were stronger, children were integral to family economies, and education mattered less.

The decline in the number of children born to married couples pointed to the future. "Advancing civilizations," warned Charles Franklin Thwing, president emeritus of Western Reserve University and Adelbert College, in a jeremiad reflective of the eugenic ideas prevalent at the time, "are in peril of becoming declining social stages by reason of a diminished birth-rate. The diminished birth-rate obtaining in France and in the early native stock of the United States is the cause of public lamentation." It was, he noted, "more conspicuous in families of the Protestant than of the Roman Catholic faith," and it was "most evident" among "what are known as the educated classes."[117] Thwing's observations, if not his lamentation, were accurate. What demographers call the standardized fertility ratio fell 20 percent between 1880 and 1910. Clearly, couples were deciding to limit the size of their families. Ethnic and racial differences in fertility for the most part were not large, as is clear in figure 1.7. Black fertility, in fact, fell more precipitously as a percentage of previous fertility than native white. Among the new immigrants, fertility fell sharply between the first and second generations, although Italians continued to have more children than Russians (mostly Jews). Fertility rates did differ sharply, however, among occupations. Professionals, managers and proprietors, and business employees had the lowest fertility. Fertility was highest by far for agricultural families, and a little lower for manual workers, among whom laborers had the most children.[118]

To some extent, the number of children born to a couple depended on where they lived. On the boom and bust plains of Kansas, where land

Figure 1.7 Change in Standardized Marital Fertility Ratio, by Ethnicity and Occupation, 1880 to 1910

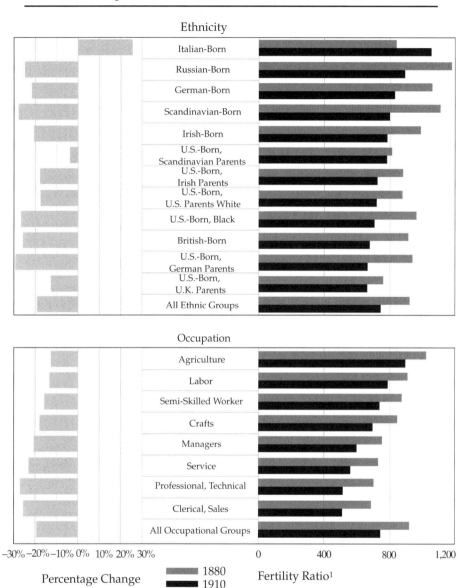

Note: Between 1880 and 1910, married couples began to have fewer children. This trend held among all ethnic and occupational groups except Italian-born. For example, marital fertility declined 27 percent among U.S. blacks and 13 percent among laborers. *Source*: Data from Ruggles et al. (2004).
[1]Number of children zero to four per 1,000 married women, fifteen to forty-nine years of age. Figures are age-standardized using the aggregate distribution of the married female population for the three census years.

was available and extra hands useful, families in Haskell County had many children. On the stagnant farms of rural Vermont, couples in Chelsea, worried about expenses, uncertain of the future, sharply limited the size of their families. In El Centro, California, and Indianola, Mississippi, places less touched by either the fever of land and crop speculation or the backlash of early globalization, couples practiced older forms of family limitation, increasing the spacing between births rather than adopting the more modern practice of choosing a target number of children.

For farm families, children usually remained an important economic asset, their labor central, not incidental, to family economies. The same incentives also often held true for manual workers. With one income inadequate to sustain a family, children's labor sometimes prevented destitution and made buying a house possible. In Homestead, Pennsylvania, social investigator Margaret Byington found that among the families she studied with a total income of at least $20 a week, sons in English-speaking European families contributed 29 percent and in native white families 11 percent. "Some of these boys of nineteen or twenty earned as much as their fathers. The period before they leave home is, therefore, the high-water mark of financial prosperity for the family. During this time a home can sometimes be bought."[119] Thus, among both farming and working-class families, children insured against homelessness and pauperization in old age. For white-collar groups, this calculus had begun to change by the early twentieth century. With education increasingly important to occupational success, the cost of children rose. With children in school rather than at work, many white-collar families needed to get by on one income, and large families became a burden rather than a source of support.[120] It was "both natural and right," reasoned Delos Wilcox, "that the number of children in city homes should be reasonably limited; for under existing conditions, while a child in the country may become practically self-supporting at ten years of age or younger, a city child must ordinarily be an increasing burden upon the family until he is about grown to manhood."[121] Nonetheless, among all groups, income and living standards rose in the early twentieth century. With economic pressure reduced, families were able to think about a future that did not necessitate as many children. All faced rising expectations for schooling. In these circumstances, fertility went down among all families, although the size of the drop roughly paralleled class structure.

Overall, women remained a fairly small fraction, 12 percent, of household heads in these years. Because many of them were widows, the frequency with which they headed households increased with age: for instance, from about 20 percent of all households headed by a person aged fifty-five to seventy to 28 percent of those over seventy. Their economic stress was apparent. Compared to households headed by men, they contained nearly twice as many boarders and lodgers, more parents and siblings, many fewer servants, and twice as many working children. To some extent, the ethnic distribution of women heading households tracked economic vulnerability: they were most common among poorer groups, the Irish, African Americans, second-generation Italians, and Russian Jews. But their vulnerability—not their race, ethnicity, or geographic location—dictated the household structures and strategies of widows.

Like their urban counterparts, families rooted in agriculture were changing fast. Farm families were larger; contained fewer boarders and more employees; and housed more parents, siblings, and grandchildren. But between 1880 and 1910, the number of employees fell by more than a third, and the size of farm households declined more steeply than others. As they balanced often precariously between past and future, farm families refracted the transitional status of American agriculture with its uneven prosperity, new urban and global markets, and declining family farms.

With one instructive exception—the role of boarders and lodgers—changes in both working- and middle-class families flowed in the same direction. Professional and white-collar workers, with the smallest families, sent their children to work least often. Along with managers and proprietors, however, they were the most likely to house their parents and siblings—they were, after all, the families with the most space and resources. In the early twentieth century, however, the social structure of boarding reversed (see figure 1.8). In 1880, boarders lived least often with farmers, laborers, and operatives. By 1910, the share of laborers' households with boarders had doubled and operatives' had increased as well. In fact, laborers and operatives now housed boarders and lodgers more often than any other occupational group.

As with other aspects of family life, the social structure of boarding was in transition in 1910. Professionals and others in white-collar occupations did not take in boarders less often. Rather, the swift rate at which boarding increased among the families of laborers and operatives reversed the rank order. Here was a signal of change. In 1880, boarding still reflected nineteenth-century practice. Young people lived in a condition of semi-autonomy, neither children nor independent adults. Through boarding, well-off families performed a public function, supervising young people in the years between the time they left home and married. In the twentieth century, this pattern reversed. Families began to take in boarders primarily as a way to supplement their income, not to watch over unattached youth. In this, they responded not only to their own changing preferences but as well to shifts in the social structure of demand as massive numbers of new immigrants desperately sought housing, very often, understandably, with families of similar ethnicity.[122] Black families resembled those of immigrants. Like immigrants, they took in

Figure 1.8   **Percentage of Households with a Boarder Present, by Occupation of Household Head, 1880 to 1910**

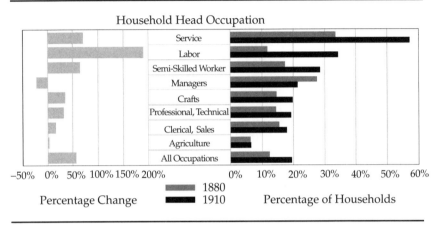

Note: Boarders became more common between 1880 and 1910. The increase was especially high in the households of service workers (57 percent) and laborers (34 percent). *Source*: Data from Ruggles et al. (2004).

boarders to augment their inadequate household incomes, and they also helped kin. Compared to whites, blacks more often housed boarders and relatives—only the relatives, more than among other groups, were grandchildren, cousins, aunts, and uncles. For hardship left many black families in fragments, with young children or unattached relatives in need of home and care.[123]

Working children played an increasingly important part in older families. Overall, in 1910 families were 1.5 times more likely to include an employed child than in 1880 (see figure 1.9). In 1910, 52 percent of forty-five- to fifty-year-old parents, well over 60 percent of those in their fifties, and over 70 percent of those sixty or older lived with at least one working child. Within families of practically every rank, the prevalence of working children increased, though least often in families of professionals. They also were more prevalent among black than white families, but differences in race and ethnicity were not large.

It seems odd that more families included a working teenager in 1910 than in the late nineteenth century. With teenage school attendance rising, the trend should have gone in the opposite direction. "Education," Thwing claimed, "has come to be the dominant force in modern American life." Education also promoted individualism at the expense of families. "In education the family and the school exist for the individual. . . . The presence, therefore, of education, as the most potent of all social

Figure 1.9   Percentage of Households with a Working Child Present, by Ethnicity and Occupation of Household Head, United States, 1880 to 1910

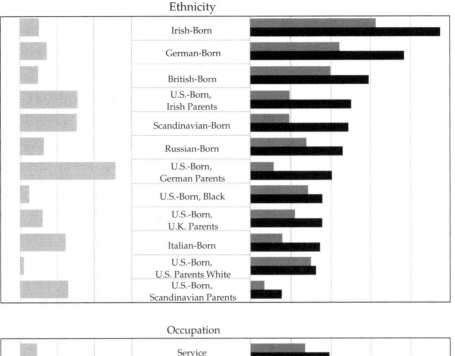

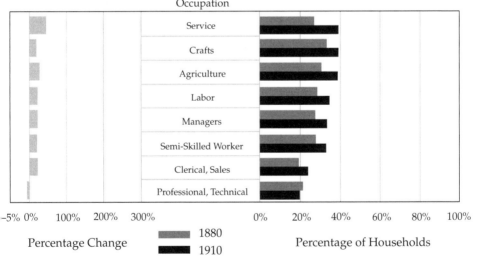

Percentage Change   1880
                           1910

Percentage of Households

Note: Children's wages were a critical element of the family economy during the early 20th century. Between 1880 and 1910, the proportion of households with an employed child of any age increased among all occupational groups, except professionals, and among all ethnic groups as well. For example, among managers, the proportion with an employed child living at home rose 21 percent and among the German-born, 74 percent. *Source*: Data from Ruggles et al. (2004).

forces, has resulted in the appreciation of individualism and in the depreciation of the family."[124] Yet the number of working children within families went up. For immigrant working-class families the logic is easiest to understand: more than other families, they needed the income from teenage children just to get by. The growth of large industries helped because it brought more jobs within reach; young people less often needed to leave home to find work. The burgeoning world of white-collar work also opened large numbers of new clerical and sales jobs to young people while they still lived with their parents. Nor was school a clear alternative to work. Many youngsters combined them. Although they appear two very different family strategies, work and school coexisted, often complementary rather than competitive. Teenagers and their families frequently balanced individualism and family solidarity in ways that defied Thwing's overstated predictions.

By 1910, most children aged seven to fourteen attended school at least part of the year; very few attended after the age of nineteen, when, indeed, attendance had dropped to 15 percent. Between 1880 and 1900, teenage school attendance (defined here as age fifteen through nineteen) remained at 30 percent. It then increased to 39 percent in 1910 and remained there through 1920. By 1940, it had passed the halfway mark: at 56 percent, school attendance had become the norm for the majority of teenagers. Thereafter, it rose each decade, reaching 80 percent in 1990. Increased teenage school attendance resulted from the spread of high schools—the cutting edge of educational transformation in early twentieth-century America. Indeed, high school graduation leaped from 9 percent in 1910 to 40 percent in 1935.

School attendance, presented in figure 1.10, reflected the influence of both family and community. Teenagers, not surprisingly, were more likely to attend school if their parents spoke English and owned property. Girls—reflecting the growth of clerical work described in chapter 2—also stayed longer in school. Most influential, however, was the occupation of parents: children of professionals led the way in school attendance, followed not far behind by children of white-collar workers and self-employed parents. The chances that the teenage children of manual workers would attend were much lower. Where youngsters had been born mattered, too. Among youngsters with foreign-born parents, those who had been born in the United States remained in school longer. More than 20 percent of Polish teenage boys born in the United States, for example, went to school, compared to 9 percent of those born in Poland. Among the new immigrants, Russians, whether born in Europe or in the United States, were more likely to attend than Italians, Poles, or Germans and Central Europeans. Among all the U.S.-born children of immigrants, second-generation British and Irish youngsters went to school most often.

Investment in school constituted one component in the bundle of

Figure 1.10   School Attendance, Persons Fifteen to Nineteen Years of Age, by Gender, Ethnicity, and Occupation of Household Head, 1910

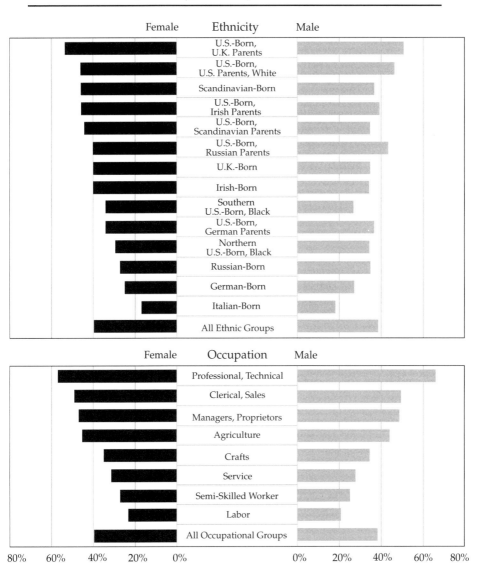

Note: School attendance among older teenagers remained strongly dependent upon family background in 1910. The son of a professional was three times more likely to attend school than that of a laborer. The children of second-generation ethnics were generally more likely to attend than those of immigrants. *Source*: Data from Ruggles et al. (2004).

characteristics that distinguished Russian Jews from Italians and Poles. Jews moved more quickly into business and white-collar work and more rapidly reshaped their families along modern lines, reducing the number and prolonging the education of their children. Among blacks, major differences separated the northern and southern born. Northern-born black teenagers attended school almost as often as native whites, more often, even, than second-generation Russians. Although southern-born black teenagers attended less frequently, they went about as often as many second-generation ethnics. In Philadelphia in 1900, to take a concrete example, northern-born blacks sent more of their teenage sons to school than any other racial or ethnic group. Rates were high for their daughters, too, and even for those born in the South.[125] Despite poverty, poor facilities, and segregation, black youngsters attended school in remarkable numbers—dramatic proof of commitment to education among a people whose faith, unfortunately, was not met with corresponding rewards.

The dynamics of school attendance also depended partly on the characteristics of communities. Attendance was high in socially and economically diversified small towns and rural areas—ones with a substantial middle class; it was low in large, ethnically diverse cities and manufacturing districts. In fact, the center of the high school movement economic historians Claudia Goldin and Lawrence Katz show (see figure 1.11), moved away from the large cities and manufacturing districts of the Northeast and Mid-Atlantic and toward an "education belt," extending "from the Pacific States through Utah, Colorado, Nebraska, Kansas, Iowa, Indiana, and then jumping to New England."[126]

The situation in large cities is not hard to understand: clearly, the explosive growth of semiskilled jobs in manufacturing opened many opportunities for teenagers to trade the enforced dependence of school for the allure of wage-earning and to help working-class parents buffeted by the pressure of whirlwind change. In Philadelphia between 1850 and 1900, school attendance among all working-class boys aged fifteen to sixteen went down during the city's massive industrialization. Attendance, in fact, fell most for the children of skilled workers—parents hit hardest by technological change and the eroding value of old skills—as distinctions between unskilled and semi-skilled workers began to collapse with the deskilling of much manufacturing work.[127]

Many families held on to older ways of coping with economic insecurity and low incomes even as they embraced new ones. Young people contributed to family economies as they prepared themselves for a world in which advanced education promised heightened rewards. For families, prolonged school attendance—along with the decision to limit births and shed the expense of servants and household employees—was a response to the heightened cost of children and increased importance of human capital in an era of qualitative economic change.

Figure 1.11   Percentage of Fifteen- to Twenty-Year-Olds Attending School, U.S. Counties, 1910

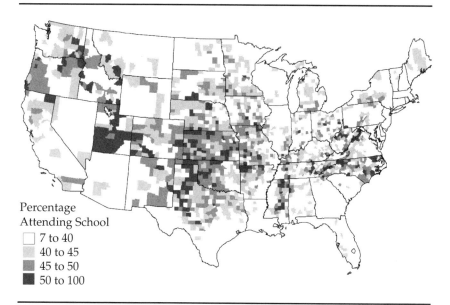

Percentage
Attending School
- [ ] 7 to 40
- 40 to 45
- 45 to 50
- 50 to 100

Note: In 1910, great regional variations persisted in the opportunity for a high-school education. Fifteen- to twenty-year-olds were most likely to attend school if they lived in the "education belt" that extended from the northwest through the mountain states and Midwest and then jumped to parts of New England. *Source*: Inter-University Consortium for Political and Social Research, 197-(date uncertain).

The intricate family patterns etched onto America's social landscape in the early twentieth century led, then, to two dominant strategies: protective and anticipatory. The first responded to the pressures of poverty and crisis with long-standing practices for increasing income and security based on the family's resources. Practiced by farmers, laborers, operatives, and many craftsmen, protective strategies combined sending children to work with taking in boarders and lodgers and, at the same time, keeping the number of their children high enough to guarantee security in old age. Women who headed households also practiced protective strategies, notably relying on the work of their children and income from boarders as well as help from co-resident relatives. Still, all families were changing in some of the same directions. Even the groups that practiced protective strategies were reducing their fertility and the size of their households. The protective strategy was a variation within a larger story.

Professionals and white-collar workers took another tack by responding to new structures of work and opportunity with anticipatory strategies that tried to adapt to what America was becoming. As they reshaped their families and households, they began to strip away household extensions and send fewer of their children into the workforce. Concerned with the increasing cost of raising children, professional and white-collar workers also curtailed their fertility sharply and kept their children in school longer.

Many immigrants arrived in America accustomed to protective strategies, which they deployed in their often difficult struggles to survive in a new land. But their children, raised in America, by and large modified their parents' family practices, thereby reducing distinctions among ethnic groups. Reduced marital fertility and prolonged school attendance point to anticipatory strategies among black families as well.

A great many families bridged the older American and the age of manufacturing by practicing both protective and anticipatory strategies at the same time, with the balance among different groups tipped one way or the other. In their personal lives, as they redefined ideas about family, they lived the tension that pulled the nation in opposing directions. And, in the late nineteenth and early twentieth century, they worked out for themselves ways of mediating between the tugs of familiarity and the pressures for change.

Chapter 2

The Paradox of Inequality in the History of Gender, Race, and Immigration

I N THE last half of the twentieth century the Civil Rights movement and the Women's movement swept across the United States. Although neither reached all its goals, each gained many of its objectives and, in the process, transformed the nation. Yet, in the decades of these movements' greatest successes, Americans became massively more unequal.

How did this happen? This chapter answers the question by tracing multiple inequalities across the century and finding a common pattern among them. In the late nineteenth and early twentieth centuries, inequality—deep, durable, pervasive—emerged from the clash of the old and new Americas. Whether named or not, it haunted public life and drove the politics of both reform and reaction. The same could be said for the turn of the next century. In both eras, economic globalization registered in deeply divided social structures, making America one nation divisible. This chapter, then, is about the outcome of the processes set in motion early in the century and described in chapter one. It is a story of both continuity—the persistence of deep enduring divisions based on wealth, work, gender, race, and ethnicity—and of astonishing change and mobility along each of the same axes of social experience.

Understanding inequality requires burrowing deeply into the history of America's social structure and political economy. It calls for historical analysis because inequality is always changing and in motion, a set of usually self-replicating relationships captured only incompletely and imperfectly by the coefficients with which it is measured by social scientists. Measures that gauge the distribution of resources remain, of course, essential. By themselves, however, they tell little about how unequal distributions of resources took shape or what sustains or challenges them over time. Because inequality always rests on comparisons between at least two individuals or groups, it is by definition a relational idea—and relations are always in motion. That is why measures taken at single moments are at best snapshots, partial glimpses into a moving process, starting points for analysis, not its end. In this chapter, we take some snapshots that portray inequalities at points in time, but we focus on the process as well. Ultimately, our concern is with how and why the character of inequality has changed in twentieth-century America.

What is Inequality?

In modern American history, inequality has been a process with six primary features. It is paradoxical, historically and geographically contingent, multidimensional, state-sponsored, gendered. and self-replicating. We first define each of these terms and then illustrate them with examples drawn primarily from the history of African Americans, women, and immigrants. The approach to inequality sketched here does not intend to ignore or minimize the force of racism, sexist beliefs, or ethnocentrism. Its intent, rather, is to shift the focus away from individualist interpretations and toward structures and processes erected partly on beliefs in group difference or inferiority but, which once set in motion, operate with their own logic. These structures and processes give inequality its durability, and its history.

Inequality is both durable and fluid. This is why it is paradoxical. What sociologist Charles Tilly terms durable inequality runs through American history. By durable inequality, Tilly means persistent inequalities among paired categories (for instance, black and white, male and female) over time. To these may be added the rough shape of the inequality pyramid and the relative rewards flowing to different occupations. Tilly identifies a set of mechanisms that reproduce durable inequalities. We will return to these after describing inequality's twentieth century history.[1] For now, the point is continuity: the remarkable resilience of major configurations of inequality. But there is more to the story. Inequality is also fluid. The amount of movement always has been vast with individuals and groups losing as well as gaining economic and social rank. In recent decades, poverty among blacks has declined dramatically even though the ratio of black to white poverty remains about the same or is worse. Women have demolished one gender barrier to work after another, but still earn much less than men. This is the paradox of inequality.

Inequality has a history and geography; it varies with time and place. This is why it is contingent. Changes in income distribution—for example, the share of income flowing to percentiles of the working population—do not by themselves capture inequality's history. For the way in which inequality manifests itself alters over time. In twentieth-century America, inequality shifted from an overlapping system of oppression to a cumulative process, a series of screens progressively dividing populations into more or less favored statuses. At the same time, inequality depends on regional and local factors determined in America's federal system by political institutions (for instance, slavery and segregation), social welfare policies, and local labor markets. In American history, the gulf between North and South composed the most striking example of geographic contingency in inequality, but today inequality varies more with the structure of local labor markets, as the work of sociologist Leslie McCall reveals.[2]

Inequality is a less straightforward concept than it at first appears. It is, in fact, multidimensional. Of what, exactly, does it consist? One way is to divide it into realms: economic, social, and political. Individuals and groups differ in wealth, social position, and power. Although pronounced, the overlap among them remains far from perfect, and the causal relations are maddeningly complex. Does wealth result in political power? Would the devolution of political power downward to the poor decrease economic inequality by redistributing resources? Even within realms, the metric of inequality varies. With economic inequality, our primary concern in this chapter, income and wealth are not synonymous. With wealth rather than income the measure, for instance, inequality appears a good deal more severe. To parse inequality's dimensions it helps to employ five lenses. They are: participation—the share of groups who work; distribution—the kind of jobs they hold; rewards—the relative income they receive; differentiation—the distance among them on scales of occupation and earnings; and geography—where they live. Each lens shows something different; together they produce a rich, multidimensional history of inequality.

It is easy to think of economic inequality as the consequence of free market processes at work over time. Although markets have played a crucial role, inequality has always been state sponsored as well. Sometimes this sponsorship has worked indirectly through policies that structure market outcomes, such as tariffs, the regulation of monopolies, or subsidies to industries. But government has also structured inequality directly. Most blatant was state-sanctioned slavery and racial segregation. Other examples, however, are legion—tax policy, labor laws, civil rights legislation, and affirmative action. At every point in its history, distinctive patterns of inequality have resulted from actions of the state as much as from the market.

Everywhere, inequality has been, and remains, deeply gendered. An abundant literature traces the historic economic, social, and political inequalities between women and men. A recent literature exposes how the structure of America's welfare state has disadvantaged women. Less has been written, however, about gender inequalities over time within racial and ethnic groups. In fact, everywhere inequality has been, and remains, deeply gendered. Evidence of these in-group differences between women and men emerges from the gender gap that has opened among African Americans and Mexican Americans.

Inequality is reproduced by actions of market and state and by individuals and groups protecting their interests. But, once in place, structures of inequality prove powerful mechanisms for channeling the distribution of economic, social, and political rewards along existing lines. They are, in short, self-replicating. Upwardly mobile individuals and groups divide internally, moving into and reinforcing rather than challenging social and economic structures. This process of differentiation resolves the paradox of inequality—the coexistence of durable inequality with individual and group mobility. It is the outcome of the stories told in this chapter.

Contexts of Group Inequality

The inequality story among women, African Americans, and immigrants took place within three contexts, each with its own distinct history. They are wealth, work, and government. Their stories are too long to tell in any detail in a single chapter. Here we highlight some of the major trends underlying the experience of specific groups.

First is wealth and income. Think of the distribution of income or wealth as a pyramid built of blocks of a material that expands and contracts. From time to time, in response to any one of a number of forces, the width of the blocks at the top or base widens and narrows. Both individuals and groups clamber up from one block to another or slip downward. The pyramid itself, however, remains solid, its shape unmistakable.

Income and wealth inequality both increased during the nineteenth and early twentieth centuries, rising sharply in the decades after 1900. World War I exerted a brief equalizing effect that ended around 1920 when inequality began to rise again, climbing to its pre–World War II peak in 1929, or, some economists would argue, in the Great Depression of the 1930s. Beginning in 1940, inequality plummeted, drifting downward until 1967. After that the trend reversed, accelerating after 1979. By the end of the twentieth century, income inequality had risen to approximately the same level as the late 1940s. A simple statistic based on personal earnings—the coefficient of variation—dramatically highlights the trends. Between 1940 and 1950, it went down, indicating declining inequality, and did not vary a great deal until after 1980. However, in the century's last two decades it gained 48 percent.[3]

Ordinary workers did not just lose ground relative to the affluent; they also watched their economic positions deteriorate in absolute terms. Starting in 1973, the real wages of average workers began to go down. From 1973, in 1982 dollars, the average weekly wage of production and nonsupervisory workers on nonfarm payrolls dropped from $315.38 to a low of $254.87 in 1993 before recovering a bit to $273.64 in 2001.[4] Faced with declining wages, families relied on two practices to maintain their standard of living. One was to add a second income, accomplished by the massive increase of married women in the workforce. Wives' contributions to family income jumped from about 14 percent of family income in 1967 to 36.1 percent in 2001.[5] This resulted in a modest rise in household income. The other practice that sustained family standards of living was the explosion of credit card debt and its concomitant—bankruptcy. Between 1970 and 1995, the number of personal bankruptcy filings per million of the population skyrocketed from a bit more than 1,100 in 1960 to about 4,500 in 1999.[6]

Conventional explanations for the declining wages of American workers and the rise in earnings inequality stress supply and demand. Research in the 1970s and 1980s stressed supply-side influences, notably the impact of government benefits on incentives and the size of the baby-boom cohort. Neither of these, it turned out, had very much influence on inequality. By the mid-1980s, therefore, attention shifted to demand, notably technology and the globalization of markets. Explanations based on globalization stressed the role of international competition in encouraging corporations to move operations overseas and lower wages. Interpretations based on technology stressed the "skills mismatch" between the demands of a new economy and the skills of the workforce. Other researchers stressed demographic factors, such as birth cohorts, the employment of women, and the impact of immigration. All these explanations had merit, but each ran into problems of evidence. As a consequence, the rise in inequality remained a puzzle. The missing piece, neglected by most explanations, was institutions, notably the decline in union density (the share of the workforce belonging to trade unions), the effectiveness of collective bargaining, and the reduced government role in the labor market—for instance, the steep decline in the real value of the minimum wage, in constant dollars, a drop of 21 percent from 1970 to 1997.[7]

The critical role of institutions highlights the second contextual factor in the inequality story: the role of government. Government has influenced the trajectory of inequality as powerfully as have private corporations. Early twentieth-century governments lacked programs designed to redistribute income and wealth more widely. In fact, the federal government's promotion of high tariffs, its support of capital in its struggles with labor, and its imperial foreign policy worked in precisely the opposite direction. Beginning in the 1930s, however, the state combined with labor market institutions to reduce economic inequality. Together, through social insurance, taxation, education, labor law, and labor unions, they proved very effective. Especially important were the Wagner Act (1935), which legitimated labor unions and set the stage for their meteoric growth, and the Fair Labor and Standards Act (1938) which introduced a national minimum wage and limited hours of work. Other examples from later years include the G.I. bill, which helped millions of veterans attend college and buy homes, and Great Society legislation, such as Medicare and Medicaid, which transformed the availability of health care. Most potent of all was progressive taxation. During the World War II years, the base of the income tax broadened and its rate structure became more progressive, the highest bracket reaching a peak of 94 percent before starting to fall in the 1960s. Other tax measures, notably tax credits and deductible expenses for health insurance and pensions, also promoted equality.[8]

But other government policies moved in precisely the opposite direction, widening inequality. The federal government's support for racial segregation retarded homeownership and the accumulation of wealth among African Americans. In recent decades, policies widened inequality by supporting anti-union practices and opposing affirmative action and by lowering the value of public assistance and the minimum wage, implementing restrictive social insurance regulations, and massively reducing taxes on corporations and wealthy individuals. Tax cuts, which started in the 1980s, and the erosion of public benefits and the assault on wages, increased inequality and produced an income pyramid at the start of the new century that resembled 1945 more than 1975 or 1980. Between 2001 and 2010, according to Citizens for Tax Justice, President George W. Bush's 2001 tax cuts would reduce the taxes of the poorest fifth of Americans by 1.2 percent, or $947, and of the wealthiest one percent by 51.8 percent, or $662,569.[9] Tax cuts resulted in the erosion of public services and infrastructure. The outcome—whether in health care, education, housing, or flood control—widened the gulf between those people capable of compensating for public inadequacy by purchasing services and protection for themselves and those whose poverty left them vulnerable to the ferocious consequences of a collapsing public sector.

Work has been the third contextual factor underpinning twentieth-century inequality. Three major eras mark the occupational and industrial history of the twentieth century. The first, from the late nineteenth century through about 1940, included the shift out of agriculture, the growth of manufacturing and big business, and early professionalization in social work, teaching, nursing, and related occupations (see figure 2.1). Call it the transition to mature industrialism. The second, the mature industrial era, lasted from roughly 1940 to 1960 (see photograph 2.1). The third is harder to capture in a phrase. Post-industrial, one common way of referring to these years, characterizes it more by what it was not than what it became, and deflects attention away from the continued importance of industry. The idea of an information and service society—an occupational structure dominated by both highly skilled and lower level service jobs—better captures the essence of the post-1960 decades.

The major story, of course, is the decline of agricultural work. In 1910,

Figure 2.1   Changes in the Industrial Distribution of the Labor Force, Selected Industrial Categories, 1900 to 2000

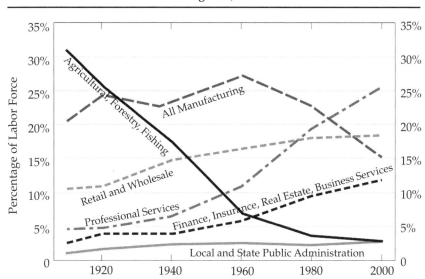

Note: America's labor force went through two revolutions during the twentieth century. Between 1920 and 1940, manufacturing replaced agriculture as the nation's largest industry. Later in the century, professional services overtook manufacturing. At the end of the century, agriculture employed only two percent of the labor force. *Source*: Data from Ruggles et al. (2004).

nearly one of every three employed Americans worked in agriculture. In 2000, the ratio was only one in forty-seven. Manufacturing employment, however, was not the major beneficiary of the emptying out of agriculture. It grew from 20 percent in 1910 to a peak of 27 percent in 1960 before falling to 15 percent in 2000. Growth occurred proportionally more in the professions, business, and the public sector. By 1990, professional services employed more people than manufacturing, for instance. Outside of agriculture, even early in the twentieth century, most people worked for someone else. The self-employed made up 15 percent of the nonagricultural workforce in 1910 and 10 percent of the entire labor force in 2000. In its towns and cities, the idea that America once was a nation of independent craftsmen, professionals, and small businessmen is a myth.

As the balance among industries shifted during the twentieth century, the demography and content of occupations changed as well. Several examples illustrate their varied histories. Some occupations simply did not

Photograph 2.1   Dodge Truck Plant, Detroit, 1942

The mass production of standardized products dominated America's economy in the middle decades of the twentieth century. *Source*: Reproduced from the Collections of the Library of Congress.

change very much. Construction laborers remained almost entirely men. The regularity of their work was shaped by the seasons, and, despite technological change and new materials, the basic tasks they performed—shoveling, carrying, mixing—changed very little over the century.[10] Indeed, the proportion of the total labor force in construction remained remarkably stable at around 6 percent. Carpenters also remained primarily native white males (except for 1910, when many more were immigrants) who worked partly to the rhythm of the seasons.[11]

Two other manual occupations changed more. Textile work illustrated, first, geographic change—from the North to the South and, increasingly, from rural to urban locations. Always a poorly paid occupation that suffered from deskilling, regional shifts, and decreased wages under the impact of technological change after World War II, its demography has reflected America's various recent immigrant streams, from the Irish and Germans in the nineteenth century to Italians and Jews in the early and Asians in the late twentieth century. To some extent, textile work's racial makeup reflected its location. In the Northeast and Midwest it remained predominantly white (over 90 percent) until the 1970s; in the South many more workers were African American. Textile work feminized early: the proportion of women workers rose from 43 percent in 1880 to 60 percent by 1910 and 81 percent in 1990. Almost all the early women textile workers were unmarried, a situation that began to change markedly after 1970.[12] Teamsters had an opposite experience. They exchanged their low status as unskilled workers early in the century for a position of more respect and better pay by its latter decades. The key was technology—the internal combustion engine—combined with the crucial role of transportation in the economy and, after the 1930s, a strong union. It remained, like construction work, a male preserve: 99.5 percent male in 1910 and 94.1 percent in 1990. At about 10 percent to 13 percent of teamsters, blacks were represented roughly in proportion to their share of the population. Teamsters earned relatively high wages, and in 1990, more than 80 percent of teamsters aged fifty to fifty-five owned their homes.[13]

Other occupations feminized massively during the twentieth century. In 1880, bookkeepers were 96 percent male; by 1990, the proportion had dropped to 10 percent. In 1880, however, 96 percent of the women bookkeepers had been unmarried, a figure that dropped by two-thirds in the course of the next hundred years. Bookkeeper was notable, too, as an occupation that underwent internal differentiation. Influenced by professional accounting standards, reflected in the CPA exam, accounting separated from bookkeeping and became a more managerial and male occupation. Both bookkeepers and accountants, however, remained mainly white.[14] Stenographers also feminized between 1890 and 1910 when the proportion of women in the occupation increased from 10 percent to 85 percent. In those years, as businesses expanded, the number of clerical jobs escalated but, at the same time, lost the role as an avenue into management. Primarily white, stenographers' demography reflected immigration and ethnic change, and, as with bookkeepers, the share of married women among them increased from about 6 percent to two-thirds during the century.[15] Women physicians, by contrast, remained unmarried or widowed more often than men. The share of women among physicians increased from 1880 to 1910 and, then, remained stable until 1970. Still, women's proportion of physicians increased from only about 2 percent to 12 percent between 1910 and 1990—a rise of 600 percent that left them very much a minority. Furthermore, 25 percent of them, compared to 11 percent of male physicians, had not married. These changes took place in an occupation whose outward stability belied immense internal redefinition with the introduction of professional standards and associations, licensing laws, and improved medical education, on the one hand, and re-orientation around the dominant role of hospitals, the growth of specialization, and the introduction of new technologies after World War II.[16]

Taking the workforce as a whole—men and women together—the most dramatic change was the decline in farmers from one in five workers in 1900 to 0.6 percent in 2000 and of farm laborers from 13 percent to 1 percent in the same years. The enormous rise in all kinds of nonmanual work constituted the second major change in occupational structure. This growth in white-collar and service work registered the emergence of technical and professional specialties, the heightened importance of retailing and service, and massive bureaucratization. An army of lower-level workers staffed the offices that had become the factories of the late twentieth century. Huge declines in general unskilled labor and domestic service composed two other important occupational trends. Craft and semi-skilled work, on the other hand, remained at about the same proportion of the workforce across the century despite many changes in the content of the jobs.

Occupational change did not happen at a uniform or even pace throughout the century. Instead, it varied across different kinds of work. The share of the workforce employed in manufacturing peaked in 1960; it is with this year as a baseline that its drop appears so steep. By 2000 it had declined one-third from its high point. The timing of other major occupational shifts followed somewhat different rhythms. Farming and farm labor declined slowly from 1880 to 1920—farmers' share of the workforce, in fact, remained quite stable from 1910 to 1920, the golden age of agriculture. The decline resumed in the 1920s and 1930s, accelerating after World War II and, finally, plummeting after 1960—a reflection of the impact of technological and organizational change on farming. The increase in professionals as a share of the workforce, in contrast, did not start until after World War II; in 1940, it had reached only 3 percent. Its subsequent tripling registered the explosive growth of higher education and profound changes in the organization of professional life, as in, to take two examples, medicine and science. The semi-professions (for example, social work, teaching, nursing) began to expand in the 1920s, a result of both demand and the availability of specialized training in universities. The increase in managers, officials and clerical workers followed a steadier course from decade to decade, a result of the continuous expansion of jobs in both the private and public sectors.

A differentiation of occupational structure resulted from these massive changes in work. In 1900, only nine major job titles accounted for the occupational designations of 70 percent of men aged eighteen to sixty-five. In 2000, it took twenty-five occupational titles to account for the same fraction of the labor force. Despite these enormous changes, the relative rewards attached to the major jobs—as measured by the typical income they provided—remained surprisingly consistent across the century. Historian Matthew Sobek showed that men's income variation by occupation in 1950 accounted for 85 percent of variation in 1890 and 86 percent in 1990.[17]

Nonetheless, in the half century after 1950, the gaps between the pay associated with the rungs on the occupational ladder widened—an ominous trend because of changes in workforce demography. Between 1980 and 2002, employment rose faster than population, and American policy makers celebrated the increase in jobs. But it was the entrance of women and teenagers—many of whom worked part time—that boosted employment. (In these years, teenage employment grew 63.2 percent.) And a large fraction of the new jobs opened in occupations that paid relatively low wages as jobs that had paid high wages disappeared. The "new jobs created by" Wal-Mart and McDonald's, writes political scientist Andrew Hacker, "alone made up for the combined job losses of the dozen downsized firms" whose employment history he charted. "Yet it hardly needs saying that the typical new job at Wal-Mart's or McDonald's, even if pursued full-time, pays about a third of the wage for a lot of the jobs that no longer exist."[18] And because Wal-Mart and McDonald's have remained free of unions, their expansion has helped fuel the decline in union density (see photograph 2.2).

The result of this history is a twentieth-century world of work characterized by both immense change and remarkable continuity and by a massive growth in inequality. The rewards earned by workers, which had grown much closer by mid-century, had widened at its end. One reason was the dramatic change in the content of jobs—the kind of work men and women did. If we think about the modal occupation of Americans, a nation of farmers became a nation of service workers with an intervening period in which a large share found employment in manufacturing. The post–World War II manufacturing era marked the high point for American workers. The service sector jobs that replaced manufacturing not only paid less; they also often lacked the security and protection provided by seniority, collective bargaining, health insurance, and pensions. The great transformation in occupational structure itself, therefore, contributed to inequality. How this story intersected with—and provided the context for—the history of inequality among women, African Americans, and immigrants follows.

In one area, however, inequality was not so durable, and the reason is instructive. That is inequality among regions. After the Civil War, the South remained virtually an economic colony of the North, though one with a peculiarly large political influence on its metropole. Despite the emergence of manufacturing and mining in the late nineteenth and early twentieth centuries, the region's economy rested mostly on the export of staple crops, primarily cotton, and depended on credit from other re-

Photograph 2.2   Wal-Mart Employees in Cafeteria, Late Twentieth Century

While many women became professionals and managers, many others remained in low-wage retail jobs. Wal-Mart had become the largest private employer in the nation. *Source*: Capitol Broadcasting Company.

gions and abroad. Until after World War II, the South, almost a nation apart, remained poorer and less developed than the rest of the United States. This colonial relation broke down after World War II. As the South depended less on agriculture, its manufacturing and service-producing sectors grew, resulting in a more differentiated occupational structure and personal earnings more like those found in other parts of the nation. The reasons for the crumbling of this durable regional inequality lay in the collapse of the North's ability to exploit the region and its resources. With the growth of the defense industry in the Sunbelt, the shift of manufacturing southward in search of non-unionized labor, the invention of air conditioning, and improvements in transportation and communication, the ability of the North to extract surplus from the South ended, reordering the spatial dynamics of population, economic growth, and inequality.[19]

As regional occupational structures melded, differences in personal earnings (available only from 1940) also converged (see figure 2.2). In 1940, median personal earnings in the South were only 65 percent of those in the Northeast and Midwest and 60 percent of those in the West.

Figure 2.2   State Poverty Rates, 1949 and 1999

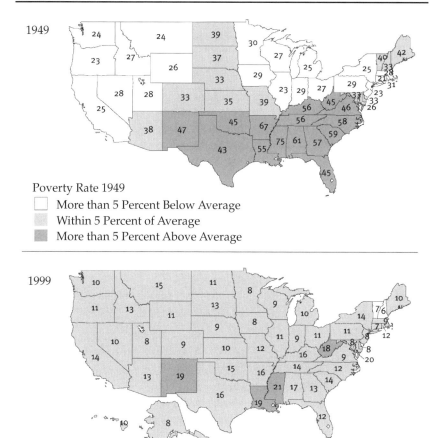

Poverty Rate 1949
- More than 5 Percent Below Average
- Within 5 Percent of Average
- More than 5 Percent Above Average

Poverty Rate 1999
- More than 5 Percent Below Average
- Within 5 Percent of Average
- More than 5 Percent Above Average

Note: In 1949, fifteen states had poverty rates more than 5 percent above the national average. All but New Mexico were located in the South. By 1999, almost all states were within 5 percent of the national average. *Source*: Data from Ruggles et al. (2004).

By 2000, the South's ratio had increased to 83 percent of the Northeast's, 92 percent of the Midwest's, and 90 percent of the West's. No longer, moreover, did more people in the South live in poverty than in other regions. Instead, between 1940 and 2000, the social structure of poverty became national. The South's pre–World War II colonial economy, like those everywhere, had resulted in sharp inequalities of wealth. In 1940, this was greater in the South than in other regions. The transformation of the southern economy at first reduced the inequality until the 1980s when it began to rise (as it did across the country), reaching its 1940 level in 1990 and exceeding it in 2000. The shattering impact of economic globalization on existing structures of work, income, and security registered in a sharp rise—as it did everywhere in America—in inequality in the South.

Inequality Narratives

The histories of wealth, work, and government shaped the changing contexts of inequality in twentieth-century America. They defined the avenues along which women, African Americans, and immigrants strode with mixed success to enter the American mainstream. Together, they exerted a powerful influence on the combination of durability and mobility that defined the paradox of inequality.

Women

Until the last decades of the twentieth century, gender segregation relegated women to a small fraction of available jobs and many employers refused for some time to hire married women. Women eventually broke through these exclusionary practices and dismantled most of the barriers to employment. Indeed, in the last decades of the century powerful exogenous forces joined to interrupt the processes that had reproduced the most blatant gender inequalities. Together, they mounted a powerful assault on the enduring inequalities that separated the experience of women and men. However, despite many successes, a major theme in women's economic history remains inequality: women forced by necessity into low-wage, dead-end jobs, excluded from work altogether, relegated to occupational ghettos, or paid less than men.

Married women's movement into the work force constitutes the most important strand in women's twentieth-century employment history. In 1900 about 6 percent of married women were in the paid labor force; by 1990, the figure had multiplied to 50 percent, where it remained in 2000 (see figure 2.3).[20] The first great burst of women into market work occurred in the two decades after 1940, led primarily by older women who no longer had young children at home. A great barrier to married women—the prohibition against employing women in many white-collar

Figure 2.3   Women Aged Eighteen to Sixty-Four in Labor Force, by Marital
Status

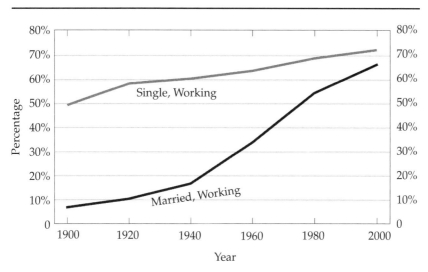

Note: After 1940, the percentage of married women who worked outside their homes went up dramatically. In 1900, less than 10 percent of married women held a job; in 2000, almost 70 percent of them did. *Source*: Data from Ruggles et al. (2004).

industries and in teaching—thus began to crumble in the face of labor shortages and the demands of educated women. Nonetheless, in 1960 paid work remained a minority experience for married women; by 1990 it had become the norm. Single women, of course, always worked more often than those who had married, but the difference between single and married women narrowed over the century. As a result, the sex composition of the American labor force looked very different at the century's beginning, middle, and end. In 1940, only about one-quarter of the labor force consisted of women; by 2000, the proportion had reached nearly half.[21]

Of course, married black women always had worked more than white women, but the difference narrowed sharply as married white women entered the labor force (see figure 2.4).[22] The trend among one category of white and black women, however, went in an opposite direction. This was women-on-their-own (women with an absent spouse, formerly married women, or those who had never married). In 1950 and 1960, young white women-on-their-own began to work more than black women. In fact, the labor force participation of black women-on-their-own began to fall until 1970 when it turned upward. In 2000, though, it still remained below the rate for white women. Why did this happen? It did not result

Figure 2.4   Female Labor Force Participation, by Marital Status and Race

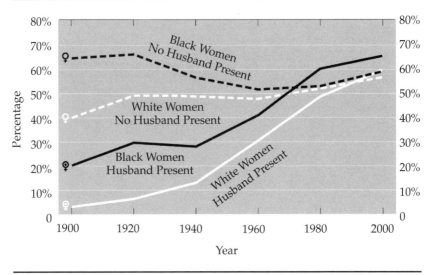

Note: Early in the twentieth century, married black women held jobs much more often than married white women. In 2000, the proportion of both black and white married women with jobs had increased steeply, and the difference between them had nearly disappeared. *Source*: Data from Ruggles et al. (2004).

from the shift of black women out of agriculture—it took place regardless of where they lived. Nor did it happen because welfare allowed some unmarried black mothers to withdraw from the labor force.[23] Rather, job opportunities for black women declined when domestic labor—their principal form of work—nearly disappeared.

Domestic service was women's major non-agricultural occupation at the start of the century; by century's end, it had dwindled to insignificance. The alternative occupations into which women first moved, however, still represented an extension of their traditional work—taking care of children, tending the sick, or minding the home.[24] Clerical work was the exception, and its rise was spectacular—from 9 percent of employed women in 1910 to 35 percent in 1970. Increasingly feminized, clerical work lost its place as the first step on the ladder to management, becoming, instead, a largely permanent status identified not by decision making but instead by the exercise of routinized skills such as typewriting.[25] In part, but only in part, the shift of women into clerical work responded to changes in occupational structure—the growing prominence of office work in the economy. But women's clerical employment grew at nearly twice the rate of clerical work itself and outstripped overall job growth

**Figure 2.5   Percentage of Women Workers in Selected Occupational
Categories, 1900 to 2000**

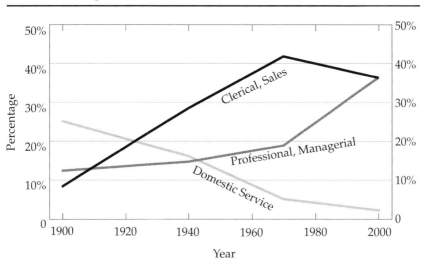

Note: During the twentieth century, clerical and sales work replaced domestic
service as the typical "women's" job. The proportion of women employed as domestic servants went down dramatically, from 25 percent to less than 5 percent,
and the proportion with clerical jobs increased sharply, from 9 percent to 30 percent. *Source*: Data from Ruggles et al. (2004).

among women.[26] The feminization of the office, then, represented a real
shift in women's work (see figure 2.5), not simply a response to compo-
sitional changes in workforce demography or occupational structure.

In the 1880s, technological change—specifically, the widespread adoption of the typewriter, which had been patented in 1868—transformed
clerical work. Other new technologies soon followed: cash registers and
machines for dictating, mimeographing, calculating, and tabulating the
1890 census. A second surge of office machine invention followed in the
1910s. A list of the machines commonly found in American offices in
1919 included thirty items, none of which had been available before the
1880s. Machines facilitated the standardization of tasks. In 1871, one authority described clerical work as requiring "knowledge of languages,
skills in accounts, familiarity with even minute details of business, energy, promptitude, tact, delicacy of perception"; by the early twentieth
century, for most office workers, it had become "routine and mechanical"[27] (see photograph 2.3).

However, even before machines were introduced a great deal of clerical work was nonetheless dull and routine, and most male clerks spent

Photograph 2.3   Clerical Staff at Work, U.S. Bureau of Chemistry, About 1900

In the early twentieth century, women increasingly dominated clerical occupations, where they were supervised by men. *Source*: Reproduced from the Collections of the Library of Congress.

the bulk of their time copying correspondence and other documents. The main skill they needed was good penmanship. In the long run, office machines may have routinized clerical work, but in their early years, the skills demanded by the typewriter and adding machines were new and challenging. Thus, women did not take over clerical work because it became less skilled. More to the point was the conjunction of rising demand—the sheer increase in the number of office jobs to be filled in the late nineteenth and early twentieth century—with the availability of young women who wanted work. Young women, now more often high school graduates than earlier, wanted work commensurate with their educations. Compared to other available jobs, clerical wages were good: unemployment was low, working conditions were usually clean and safe, and status was relatively high. At the same time, young men educationally qualified for clerical jobs increasingly went on to college or sought jobs in management. Employers, who could absorb only a fraction of male clerks into managerial positions, worried about what to do with them in the long run and looked for workers whose job tenure would be temporary. Young women, therefore, were ideal: they were cheap, available, and educated, and they understood that they would leave when they married.[28]

Throughout the century, relatively few women worked in skilled manual crafts or as unskilled laborers. Self-employment also remained a minor theme in their work experience. Semi-skilled factory work as operatives, however, became increasingly important through mid-century, and in the 1980s, large numbers of women finally entered the ranks of management. Between the 1960s and the 1990s, the proportion of women working as managers tripled from 3 percent to 9 percent and the fraction of managers who were men went down from 86 percent in 1950 to 61 percent in 2000. The same trend held among professionals, excluding teachers. As a result, the share of women employed as either managers or professionals more than doubled from 12 percent in 1970 to 28 percent in 2000.[29] Government directly facilitated this movement of women into managerial and professional work: important measures were the Equal Pay Act of 1963, Title VII of the 1964 Civil Rights Act, the formation of the Equal Employment Opportunity Commission, and other regulations mandating affirmative action.

Married women's new ability to find jobs did not erase gender inequality. Among managers and professionals men still dominated the best work. Women remained clustered at the bottom of managerial hierarchies where they often supervised other women, and they less often held decision-making authority. They also dominated the less-prestigious human services professions (nurses, librarians, social workers) yet remained, despite rising numbers, a minority among scientific and technical professionals. They did make real inroads in some other categories, such as technicians, but again usually those with less prestige, pay, and authority. Broken down by actual jobs, as contrasted to broad occupational categories, women's occupational segregation emerges even more clearly. One large study found the average woman in an occupation 65 percent female but an actual job that remained 88 percent female. In this study, the allocation of women to segregated jobs and the devaluation of jobs dominated by women accounted for 75 percent of the gender gap in earnings.[30] There is, however, a more optimistic way to look at women's occupational history. One researcher found that 75 percent of the growing similarity in the work of women and men resulted from occupational desegregation and only 25 percent from shifts in occupational structure. In 2000, women still faced a long road to occupational parity with men, but they already had traveled a great distance.[31]

Even when they broke into industries, women purchased their advance at the expense of differentiation, which at once preserved the overall advantage of men and stratified women in ways that reinforced rather than challenged existing inequalities. Although women made large in-roads into commerce (banking and credit, insurance, security and broker-age services, real estate, advertising, accounting, auditing, bookkeeping), only a minority were managers. More entered the ranks of foot soldiers—the secretaries and clerks who performed the routinized work in the new white-collar factories. In 2000, for instance, 63 percent of women in the banking and credit industries held clerical jobs.[32]

What explains the inroads made by women into so many occupations after 1970? The answer, according to one persuasive interpretation, lies in the intersection of changes in labor queues—the attractiveness of women as workers to employers—and job queues—the attractiveness of jobs to women. In some occupations, men became increasingly unavail-able because the service sector had expanded so rapidly that demand had exceeded the supply of men with the appropriate qualifications. At the same time, automation combined with reduced pay to make many jobs unattractive to them.[33] In this situation, employers turned to women for a variety of reasons. Antidiscrimination legislation and lawsuits filed by women against employers coupled with government affirmative ac-tion regulation made discrimination costly. In some occupations, too, newly automated tasks seemed extensions of "women's work"—as in the introduction of keyboards that resembled typewriters or the empha-sis on communications skills in dealing with clients. Women were sought, too, in occupations where the clients were, increasingly, other women. With the pressure of competition from de-regulation at home and glob-alized industry abroad, many employers also looked for ways to cut costs. In large part because they would work for less pay, women sud-denly became much more attractive. They also responded readily to in-creased employer demand. Anticipating opportunities, confident of the impact of affirmative action and public opposition to discrimination, many enrolled in MBA programs and other varieties of professional training traditionally dominated by men. As women entered new kinds of work, their presence created a virtuous circle that led to the employ-ment of still more women. Employers less often preferred men, the gen-der-typing of many forms of work eroded, women used their informal networks to get jobs for other women, and some men fled from jobs in-creasingly dominated by women.[34]

Despite their occupational progress, between 1940 and 1980 the main story in women's earnings was its stability as a share of men's. Among full-time workers, women earned 58 percent as much as men in 1940 and 56 percent in 1980. Then, in the 1980s, women's earnings moved upward, rising, by 1990, to 69 percent and more or less remaining there during the century's last decade.[35] However, black women's wages, which had in-creased in the 1960s and 1970s, began to reverse direction in the 1980s, partly as a result of the cutback in publicly funded jobs, which, as the next section of this chapter shows, employed a great many of them.[36] The gap between the earnings of men and women did not result from occupational segregation. In fact, in all major categories of nonagricultural work women consistently earned less than men, even though in most occupations women improved their economic position. Although women managers earned a good deal more than women operatives, they still earned less than men, for instance. Job titles inflated to show progress toward ending sex discrimination often masked the real content of work, the relegation of women to less remunerative positions, and the glass ceilings against which they bumped. Women's lower earnings did not result from less education. At every educational level, in 2000 as well as in 1940, women's earnings were lower than men's. The gap had shrunk but the distance still remained wide. In 2000, for instance, among individuals with four or more years of college, women earned only 68 percent as much as men. In the same years, the fraction of women in poverty dropped sharply. But women composed a larger fraction of the poverty population, and the ratio of their poverty to men's widened.[37]

Relative earnings of younger women, however, have improved. By 2000, the ratio of women's earnings to men's had risen from 67 for women born between 1946 and 1955 to 77 and 93 for the next two cohorts. If young women continue on this trajectory—if the gain toward income parity with men persists over time—the result will herald an important shift in one of the nation's most durable inequalities. There is another side to the story, however. Young men and women started with similar earnings, but men advanced further and faster. For example, among women born between 1956 and 1965, the ratio of women's to men's earnings declined from 82 in 1980 to 75 in 1990, and 68 in 2000. Over time, men capitalized a relatively small initial advantage into a commanding lead. Thus, women's economic history illustrates the paradox of inequality: evidence of both solid progress and durable inequality.

The contradictory trends in women's occupational and economic history—evidence of both progress and continued inequality—emerge clearly by looking at banking and credit, an industry that feminized during the twentieth century. In 1910, 95 percent of its employees were men; in 2000, 69 percent were women. The share of women increased steadily after 1910, reaching a majority during the 1960s. Until 1990, most of the women in banking—80 percent to 90 percent—worked in clerical jobs. And, as banking feminized, most of the industry's clerical jobs went to women, jumping from 14 percent in 1910 to 43 percent in 1920—a reflection of the second wave of feminization in clerical work. By 1950, the industry was nearly 65 percent women and, in 1980, 85 percent. As women moved into clerical work, taking over teller positions, men moved into management and professional positions. Men composed 93 percent of managerial workers in 1920, 80 percent in 1970, and 61 percent in 1980.

Banking had been a traditional man's domain for two reasons: gender stereotypes about women's interests and mental capacities and the physical demands of the job:

> Men handled financial matters because it was assumed that women were not interested in such activities and furthermore women's minds were incapable of and unaccustomed to what was referred to as, "doing figuring" and making financial transactions. [Because the] early medium of exchanges included heavy gold and silver commodities as well as currency, women were presumably unable to handle such heavy items. Moreover, large posting and accounting books used in banking were presumed difficult for women to lift.[38]

Bank jobs opened to women in the twentieth century after the increased volume of work required many more clerks to file paperwork and record transactions. Their numbers swelled briefly during World War I and then fell back again until World War II caused another labor shortage, which brought many more women into banks as tellers, bookkeepers, and minor officers—positions previously held by men. As bankers developed new services, expanded their customer base, and introduced new technologies, they needed to increase both the overall size of their staffs and the number with advanced training. For the latter, they turned increasingly to college-educated men who began their banking careers in managerial-training positions, rather than, as in earlier times, as clerks and tellers. Thus, "the teller's position diminished in prestige, responsibility, skill, and advancement opportunities. And in keeping with tradition, the teller's salary remained low." Few men applied for jobs as tellers, and, "by default rather than by design," women were hired in their place. "Teller" was now "redefined as a typical 'woman's job.'"

Nonetheless, after 1970, women made striking inroads into both management and professional and technical positions in banking and credit. Until the late 1960s, in fact, women generally were not allowed in banks' managerial training programs. In the 1970s, however, de-regulation put more competitive pressure on the industry, and banks consolidated and opened many more branches. Branch managers, often, were women. During the 1970s, bank employment grew 50 percent and the number of bank managers 86 percent. At the same time, the earnings and prestige of bank managers deteriorated, and young men began to look elsewhere for white-collar careers. Banks also hired more women because of the pressure of federal regulations and antidiscrimination laws and because women launched successful and highly publicized suits against them for employment discrimination. Although many women were hired or promoted into managerial positions, they were shunted primarily into the less prestigious, powerful, and remunerative managerial specialties, which included retail banking. Men still filled most of the managerial jobs in commercial banking, the most attractive branch of the industry.[39]

In 1970, women composed 21 percent of bank managers. In a decade, this fraction had almost doubled to 39 percent; in 2000, it was 55 percent. In the same three decades, the share of women among professional and technical employees also increased dramatically, from 34 percent to 52 percent. By 2000, 33 percent of women in banking, compared to 63 percent of men, held managerial or professional positions. Women remained underrepresented in the best work, but had made genuine inroads into the better jobs. In this, their experience in banking and credit encapsulated the wider economic history of women, the paradox of inequality: an increase in participation, a shift upward in occupational distribution, and a differentiation that brought their social structure closer to the overall structure of inequality.

But occupational improvement did not erase disparities in earning. Within the major occupational categories in banking and credit, women continually earned less than men. Women in managerial and professional positions earned a lot more than clerical workers: in 2000, the median annual earnings (in 1990 dollars) for women managers were $25,869 compared to $13,536 for women in clerical jobs. Movement up the occupational ladder, therefore, brought substantial increases in pay for women and boosted the number of women in banking and credit earning higher salaries. But in 2000, male managers' median annual earnings were $39,856—much higher than women's in the same category of work, and as late as 1970, the median earnings of male clerical workers were only slightly less than those of women managers. In fact, between 1940 and 2000, there was little change in the ratio of women's to men's earnings: for managerial employees it hovered between 50 and 65 percent, for professionals and technicians from 56 percent to 75 percent, and for clerical workers, from 39 percent to 87 percent (a sharp increase from 73 percent in 1980). Nonetheless, younger women in banking were closing the economic distance between themselves and men. In 2000, among managers, fifty- to fifty-nine-year-old women earned 57 percent as much as men; forty- to forty-nine-year-olds earned 53 percent; thirty- to thirty-nine-year-olds 63 percent; and twenty- to twenty-nine-year-olds, 76 percent. Among clerical workers, the ratio jumped from 56 for fifty- to fifty-nine-year-olds to 89 among twenty- to twenty-nine-year-olds. But, over time, as elsewhere in the economy, men outpaced women in economic gains. Consider, for example, the managers born between 1956 and 1965. In 1980, the ratio of women's income to men's was 88. By 1990, it had fallen to 71 and by 2000 to 54. For managers born between 1966 and 1975, the decline was similar. The pattern even held with clerical workers. Young men and women started out at similar salaries, but, over time, men moved up the economic ladder faster, leaving women increasingly behind.

Throughout the economy, young women could count some major gains. But the structures they attacked were so powerful that victories remained only partial. At the beginning of the twenty-first century, whether women would continue to modify this ancient form of categorical inequality, whether young women had finally begun to dismantle the durable walls that have limited women's economic achievements, or whether they had reached the limit of their power, remained to be seen. Similar questions emerge from the twentieth-century history of African American inequality.

African Americans

At the start of the century pervasive and overt racial discrimination barred blacks from most jobs, denied them equal education, and disenfranchised them politically. After mid-century, slowly and sometimes with violent opposition, the situation changed dramatically. Courts and Congress—prodded by a massive social movement, national embarrassment on the world stage during the Cold War, and the electoral concerns of urban politicians—extended political and civil rights. Affirmative action and new "welfare rights" contributed to the extension of social citizenship—guarantees of food, shelter, medical care, and education. By the end of the century, legal and formal barriers that had excluded blacks from most institutions and from the most favorable labor market positions largely had disappeared. Black poverty had plummeted, and black political and economic achievements were undeniable.[40]

Yet, for many people—both white and black—the sense remained that racism still pervaded American society, operative in both old and new ways, removing some barriers but erecting others. Observers found discrimination in racial profiling by police; verbal slips by members of Congress; disproportionate poverty, incarceration, and capital punishment; and in the workings of institutions and public policies that disadvantaged blacks. Racism, they maintained, kept blacks residentially segregated and clustered disproportionately in the least desirable jobs, if not out of the workforce altogether, and circumscribed their opportunities for education, high incomes, and the accumulation of wealth. Far more often than whites, blacks lived in poverty. Most black children were born out-of-wedlock, and a very large fraction of them grew up poor. And in the 1980s and 1990s, some indices of black economic progress began to reverse direction. In the summer of 2005, television images of New Orleans's African Americans, segregated in low lying sections of the city, a great many without automobiles, trapped as flood waters rose, brought home in a horrible way the persistence and consequences of black inequality and poverty.

Was the glass half empty or half full? Could past black achievement be projected into the future, or had it stalled, leaving this enduring categorical inequality etched deeply into the soil of American life?[41] The question should not be framed in either-or terms or answered using a single scale of progress. For the historic pattern of black inequality based on social, economic, and political exclusion largely shattered in the course of the century—replaced with its features rearranged in a new configuration of inequality. In the early twentieth century, the sources and results of America's black-white divide overlapped with and reinforced one another. What stands out about the new pattern of inequality is the cumulative process from which it results and the internal differentiation which is its product. Inequality among African Americans no longer grows out of a massive and mutually reinforcing, legal and extra-legal, public and private system of racial oppression.[42] Rather, it is a subtler matter, proceeding through a series of screens that filter blacks into more or less promising statuses, progressively dividing them along lines full of implications for their economic futures and, in the face of natural disaster, their very lives. The history of African American experience, like the economic history of women, reflects the paradox of inequality in twentieth-century America.

The history of black economic inequality is very much a story about gender. African American women, who at mid-century fared much worse than black men or white women, have vaulted ahead of men in educational and occupational achievement. They have closed the gaps between themselves and white women more successfully than black men have reduced their distance from white men. This story of inequality, thus, is not only about the relation between blacks and whites. It also traces the emergence of the gender gap between black men and women.[43]

The story begins with geography. Throughout American history blacks have clustered disproportionately in the nation's most unpromising places. Because the sources and features of inequality have always been tied so closely to where they have lived, changes in the spatial distribution of blacks have mapped the reconfiguration of inequality among them. A southern, rural people at the start of the twentieth century, by its end—with 55 percent still living in the South—they had become the most urbanized Americans, and many more blacks than whites lived in central cities.[44] They were also the most segregated Americans. In the twentieth century, racial segregation reached unprecedented levels from which it retreated only very modestly after 1980 as many blacks moved to suburbs. But even in suburbs they often remained in relatively segregated neighborhoods. By the century's end, the typical black still lived in a neighborhood where two-thirds of the other residents were black.[45] This segregation resulted partly from racism, concern with property values, and the venality of realtors who exploited white fears through blockbusting and similar tactics designed to encourage white flight. It emerged as well from local, state, and federal policies—mortgage under-writing practices, interstate highway construction, and the segregation of public housing, to identify three of the most important.[46] As a result, the overwhelming number of blacks started the twentieth century clustered in America's poorest spaces—southern farms; they ended it also concentrated disproportionately in the nation's most disadvantaged locations—central cities, where only one of five whites remained.[47]

Black disadvantage registered in work as well as residence. Official unemployment rates among black men went down but remained about twice the rate for white men.[48] Labor force participation rates show an even worse situation for black men—but not for black women, among whom a large fraction always had worked. As slaves, they were forced to labor; after slavery, and in the North, they worked to supplement meager men's wages or because they were more often widowed.[49] In post–World War II cities, disincentives built into public assistance kept many of them from employment until after 1996, when new welfare legislation forced them into the labor force—for some a welcome opportunity, for others a chance to join the ranks of the working poor.[50] At the same time, better education, the impact of the civil rights movement, and the expansion of government and health care employment opened more attractive jobs to black women.[51] As married white women entered the labor force, the proportions of black and white married women who worked converged until little difference remained between them.

In 1940, more black men than white men already were out of the labor force. In the following decades, the gap grew as a stunning disparity in labor force participation separated black from white men (see figure 2.6). Among black men aged twenty-one to twenty-five, the proportion not in the labor force rose from 9 percent in 1940 to 27 percent in 1990 and 34 percent in 2000. Between 1990 and 2000, nonparticipation increased for older black men as well. In 2000, for instance, more than one of four black men aged forty-one to fifty remained out of the labor force. This means that by 2000, more than twice as many black as white men in their prime earning years were not in the labor force.

Increased incarceration helped fuel this labor force detachment. On June 30, 2002, 1,355,748 inmates filled federal and state correctional facilities. This number represented an 82-percent increase since 1990. Another 665,475 inmates were in local jails, a 64-percent increase since 1990. The federal prison system, which grew 153 percent between 1990 and 2002, had become the largest in the nation. Most of the increase reflected mandatory sentences for drug offenders—57 percent of federal prisoners. America's incarceration rate had become the highest in the world, exceeding those in Western Europe and Canada by 508 times. Black men bore the brunt of America's rise in incarceration. Between 1900 and 2000, as labor force detachment spiked, the fraction of twenty-six to thirty-

Figure 2.6   Labor Force Nonparticipation, Persons Eighteen to Sixty-Four
Years of Age, by Race and Gender, 1900 to 2000

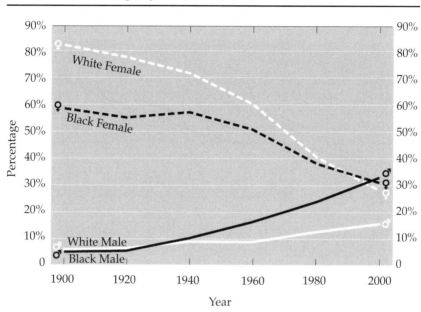

Note: At the beginning of the century, men—both black and white—were rarely
out of the labor force. With the decline of the Southern agricultural economy,
however, black men's rate of joblessness increased sharply and then stayed high
for the rest of the century. In contrast, in 1900 black women were much more
likely than white women to be working outside the home, but by the end of the
century their labor force participation rates had converged. *Source*: Data from
Ruggles et al. (2004).

year-old African American men living in institutions—mainly prisons—
increased by a third, from 9 percent to 12 percent. In the late twentieth
century, 49 percent of prisoners were black compared to 13 percent of the
overall population. On any given day, one of three black males aged
twenty to twenty-nine "is under some form of criminal justice supervision . . . either in prison or jail, or on probation or parole" (see figure 2.7).
The growth of African American men's incarceration fuels inequality.
Since 1994, Congress has prohibited inmates from receiving Pell Grants
with which to continue their education, and many states have cut back
on education for inmates who leave prison lacking the skills needed to
find employment. With employers reluctant to hire ex-convicts, and
without job skills, former inmates have great difficulty finding work.
One consequence is the high rate of black men who remain outside the
regular labor force.[52]

Figure 2.7   Percentage of Black Men Living in Institutions, by Age, 1980 to 2000

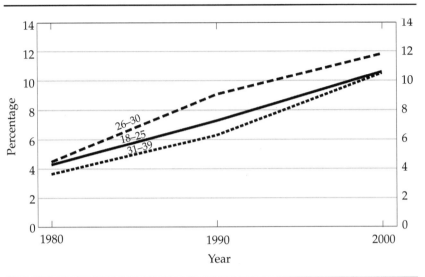

Note: One reason that black men were so often out of the regular labor force is that a very large and growing share of them were in prison and other institutions. *Source*: Data from Ruggles et al. (2004).

At the start of the twentieth century, the structure of black inequality reflected the powerful convergence of geography and work. Clustered in the rural South, African Americans worked mainly in agriculture and household service. As they left agriculture, black women in the workforce passed through two phases: movement into household service—the first major employer of black women who moved North—and, after 1940, out of personal service into an array of other industries. Helped by education and the growth of government and service sector jobs, they began to find white-collar work.

Black men took longer to leave agriculture. In the manual working class into which they moved, they held skilled craft jobs less often than white men and more often worked as laborers. As they left agriculture, black men faced a declining job market for industrial work and often exclusion from the best industrial jobs that remained. With industrial opportunities pretty much gone, they found themselves less able than black women to enter white-collar jobs or find any work at all.[53] There never was a golden age when most African American men worked at well-paying industrial jobs. The difficulties black men faced finding work in the regular labor market did not arise from the deindustrialization of the 1960s and 1970s, and were not solely the consequence of incarceration.

The origins lie, rather, in the shift of black men out of agriculture and their relative inability to move into other forms of work. Black men displaced from agriculture landed often on the margins of the economy, chronically detached from the labor market, with a lack of education and skills compounding the racist discrimination they faced when looking for work.[54]

Many black men found employment in public and state-related jobs (that is, jobs that were nominally private but depended on public funding).[55] In 2000, these state-related industries employed 19 percent of black men. Public and state-related employment proved even more important for black women: at century's end nearly half (43) percent of black women worked in state-related industries (see figure 2.8).[56] Another 39 percent (compared to 35 percent of men) worked in retail and service jobs. The movement of black women into white-collar work had been stunning. In percentage terms, blacks, led by women, outpaced white movement into white-collar work by a wide margin. These were real changes,

Figure 2.8   Percentage of Women Over Eighteen in State-Related Industries by Ethnicity

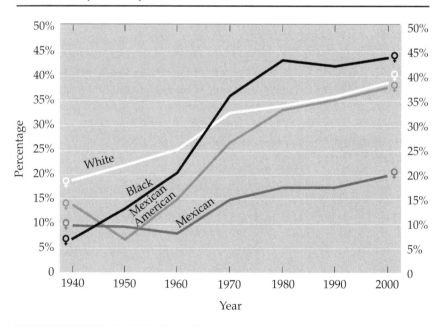

Note: In 1950 less than 15 percent of black and Mexican American women held state-related jobs. By 1980, more than a third of Mexican American women and two-fifths of black women were employed in this sector. Source: Data from Ruggles et al. (2004).

not simply products of shifts in the occupational composition of the workforce. Among black women, the share in white-collar work increased from 2 percent in 1900 to 7 percent in 1940 and about 63 percent in 2000.[57] Clearly, the expansion of government, education, and health care in late twentieth-century America, as well as private sector white-collar jobs, opened a plethora of new opportunities that black women were quick to seize. For them, America's economic transition from manufacturing to service was a source of opportunities gained, not lost. Nonetheless, even when they moved into better types of occupations, blacks clustered in the less prestigious and well-paid positions. Among professional and technical workers, for instance, black women's employment as technicians, the lowest rung on the ladder, multiplied five times between 1940 and 2000. At the same time, since 1940, professional black men have been about twice as likely as white to work in human services.[58]

Public employment became African Americans' distinctive occupational niche.[59] The Brown v. Board of Education Supreme Court decision (1954), which declared school segregation unconstitutional, the Civil Rights Act (1964), the Voting Rights Act (1965), and affirmative action policies in the 1960s and 1970s, all built pressure to desegregate work and expand opportunities for blacks. Racial barriers to employment crumbled most quickly and widely in state-related jobs when the numbers of such jobs exploded in the 1960s and 1970s as the War on Poverty and Great Society escalated spending on social programs. These were good jobs. They paid, on the whole, more than private sector employment.[60] In 2000, the median income for blacks who worked full time in the public sector exceeded the income of black private sector employees by 15 percent for men and 19 percent for women. Public and state-related employment have thus proved the most powerful vehicles for African American economic mobility and the most effective anti-poverty legacy of the Great Society. This dependence on publicly funded work also left blacks vulnerable. Reductions in public employment and spending strike them with special ferocity and undermine their often fragile achievements.[61]

Public employment, more than blue-collar factory jobs, played a key role in lifting blacks out of poverty. High black poverty rates, that is, did not result from deindustrialization. In major cities, aside from Detroit and Chicago, blacks did not find extensive work in manufacturing and were denied the best industrial jobs. Even where black industrial work was common, service jobs remained the core of black urban employment. Black industrial workers, moreover, did not earn higher wages or work more steadily than blacks employed in other sorts of work. In a sample of fifteen representative cities in 1949, Buffalo, New York, had the largest fraction of black industrial workers, except for Detroit, but its black poverty rate was among the highest. In cities with the lowest black

Figure 2.9   Percentage of Employed Persons over Eighteen Years of Age in White-Collar Occupations

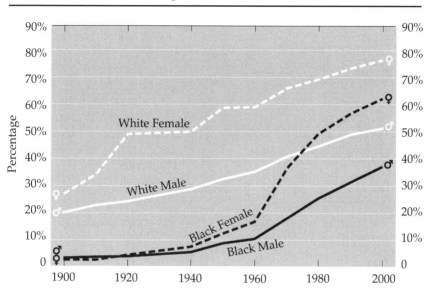

Note: White-collar work increased sharply during the twentieth century among all groups, but it rose most for women, and, after the 1960s, especially for black women. In 1900, almost no black women worked in white-collar occupations but more than 60 percent did in 2000. *Source*: Data from Ruggles et al. (2004).

poverty rates, relatively few African Americans worked in industrial jobs. Instead, government employment, which accounted for 60 percent of the variance in black poverty rates across the fifteen cities, reduced poverty and proved the best predictor of those rates (for the increase in white-collar work across the board, see figure 2.9). Not only did public employment reduce poverty by providing steady, well-paid jobs. African American access to public employment also signaled increasing black political influence, which, in turn, encouraged local welfare bureaucracies to respond more generously to black need. Thus, in cities with the highest levels of public employment more blacks escaped poverty through public transfer programs—the size of black public employment explained 33 percent of the effectiveness of cities' public assistance programs. Overall, the correlation between the black poverty rate and black employment in government was a striking -.7.[62]

This work history increasingly differentiated African Americans by industry and occupation, sorting them into the familiar ranks of America's

Photograph 2.4   Black Women with Brooms, Belton, South Carolina, 1899

During the first half of the twentieth century, African Americans remained excluded from most steady, well-paid employment. Most black women worked in
agriculture or as domestic servants. *Source*: Photographer unknown. United
States Department of Agriculture.

class structure. Among black women, for example, in 1910 just two industries—agriculture and private household service—employed nearly 90 of
100 black working women (see photograph 2.4). At the end of the century
it took 17 industries to encompass the same fraction. Black women's work
experience had bifurcated, with about a third in 2000 still employed in
manual and lower level service work. Men's occupational history splin-
tered in the same way: in 2000 about 39 percent held white-collar jobs.

   In the last half of the twentieth century, African Americans' stunning
educational progress had made possible this mass movement of blacks,
especially women, into white-collar work. However, even though blacks
stayed in school much longer than earlier in the century, inequality in the
kind of education that mattered most did not disappear, and education
continued to stratify, as well as help, black Americans.[63] During the last
half of the century, among both black women and men, educational attainment began to catch up with white levels, although women, for a variety of reasons, progressed more quickly. At the end of the twentieth

century, about 90 percent of both twenty-six- to thirty-year-old blacks and whites had finished at least twelve years of schooling.[64] (This percentage overstates black progress, however, because it equates the GED, a high school equivalency diploma, earned more often by blacks, with high school graduation, which leads more frequently to higher education and income.)[65] College graduation is another matter. There the story is persistent white advantage. In the 1950s, black women began to graduate from college more often than black men, and their lead gradually widened until the 1970s when it accelerated. Nonetheless, the distance separating black and white college graduation rates increased between 1940 and 2000, qualifying black progress. Here, too, black experience bifurcated as the share of the black population with and without some college experience became about equal. Thus, despite great progress, blacks still remained well behind whites where it counted most. This, in fact, always had been the case.[66] Earlier in the century, only when elementary and then high school education no longer were of much use in landing a good job did blacks reach parity with whites. In the late twentieth century, when a college degree had replaced a high school diploma as the key to the best work, blacks lagged well behind. This educational gap was very important (see figure 2.10). In 1940, race mattered more than education in determining earnings. In 2000, education overrode the influence of race.[67] As a result, earnings of the most well-educated blacks and whites grew closer to each other over time, even though white men retained, and even lengthened, their advantage over all other groups.

This persistence of durable racial inequality registered in incomes and wealth as well as in work and education. Improved occupations for blacks meant higher incomes. In 2000, the median incomes of black women professionals and managers were more than one and a half times higher than the incomes of clerical and twice as high as those of service workers. The story was similar among black men. Indeed, some black women made stunning economic progress. In most occupations, they earned as much, or nearly as much, as white women. Black men fared much less well. Although they reduced the earnings gap with whites, sharp differences in earnings separated black and white men within the same occupational categories—regardless of level of education. By 2000, black men were only 51 percent and black women 74 percent as likely to be in the top economic quintile as white men and women. Nonetheless, in the sixty years since 1940 the likelihood that black men and women would be in the top quintile had risen six times and the probability that they would be found among the poorest had dropped by more than half (see figure 2.11).

Trends in median earnings and in poverty point in the same direction. Poverty is mapped in figure 2.12. For men age forty to forty-nine, the black-white earnings ratio increased from about 41 percent in 1940 to 69

Figure 2.10   Difference Between Earnings of College Graduates and of White, Male High School Graduates

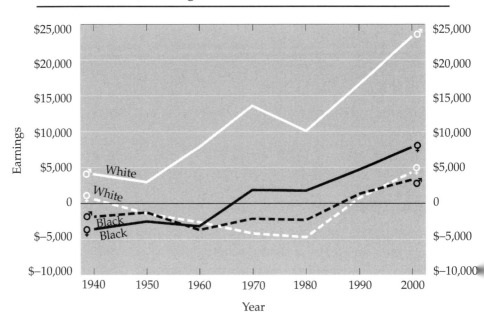

Note: Until 1970, white women and black college graduates earned less, on average, than white male high school graduates. After 1990 all groups gained relative to high school graduates although a college degree benefited white men more than any other group. Figures are real 1990 dollars. *Source:* Data from Ruggles et al. (2004).

percent in 2000; for women it grew from 40 percent to 96 percent, near parity. Women's earnings gains, however, proved precarious. They began to erode in the 1980s and 1990s, not because the absolute earnings of black women dropped but because the earnings of white women rose faster. Still, black women's relative earnings remained far higher than in 1940. Although poverty rates plummeted for all groups, including African Americans, the differences among groups remained surprisingly durable. Black poverty dropped from 75 percent in 1939 to 24 percent in 1999. Nonetheless, it was about twice the white rate in the first and quadruple in the second year.

Measures of economic well-being need to distinguish between individual and family earnings. With family earnings the measure, black women's earnings, relative to white women's, went down late in the century.[68] The reason was that many more black than white women were single mothers, surviving on one income (chapters 3 and 4 discuss black family structure). At work, a black woman earned as much as the white

Figure 2.11   Ethnic and Gender Groups in the Top and Bottom 20 Percent of Income Distribution

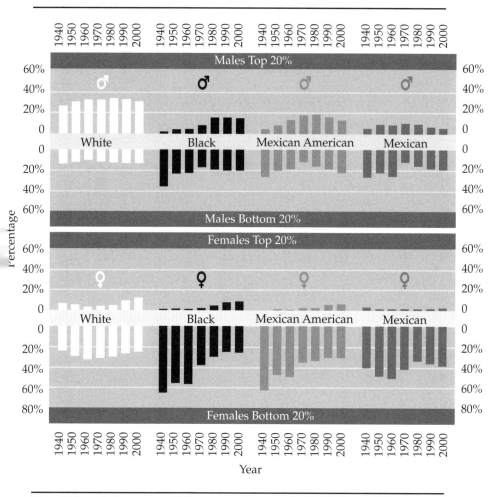

Note: Although intergroup differences in income declined during the twentieth century, white men were more likely to be in the top income quintile in 2000 than they were in 1940. Mexican American and black women's chances of being in the bottom income quintile declined rapidly after World War II, but they still were unlikely to be in the top 20 percent of the income distribution. *Source*: Data from Ruggles et al. (2004).

woman with a similar education who sat next to her. But she more often went home to a husband who earned less than the white woman, or to no husband at all. She also lived in a household with few assets other than earnings.[69]

Whether black men experienced mobility during their prime working

Figure 2.12   Percentage of Total Population Living in Poverty, by Ethnicity, 1940 to 2000

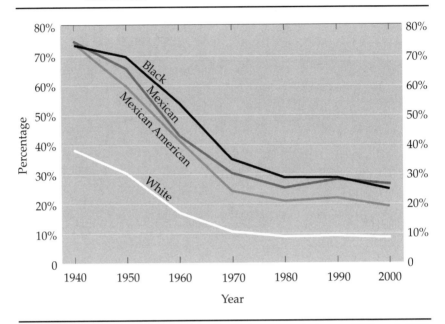

Note: Poverty declined rapidly for all ethnic groups between 1940 and 1980. However, the poverty rate of blacks and Mexicans remained more than twice that of whites. *Source*: Data from Ruggles et al. (2004).

years depended in part on when they were born. Those born earlier in the century made the most dramatic gains as the post–World War II economic boom combined with migration from southern farms to boost their earnings throughout their working lives. Men who entered their prime working years during the difficult period from the mid-1970s to the mid-1980s did not experience the same economic mobility. Their adult earnings hardly budged over time (for a breakdown of earnings over time by age, see figure 2.13). Indeed, among men the black-white earnings ratio reversed direction and declined during the economic hard times of the 1980s, when most workers' incomes—regardless of race or ethnicity—went down (see photograph 2.5).[70]

Earnings are only one component of family wealth. Others include real property, savings, and securities—assets held much less often by blacks than whites, as the research of Melvin Oliver and Thomas Shapiro and of Dalton Conley has shown.[71] Throughout the twentieth century, a smaller fraction of blacks than whites owned homes, which is one reason

Figure 2.13   Median Earnings for Black Male Workers, by Age and Year of Birth

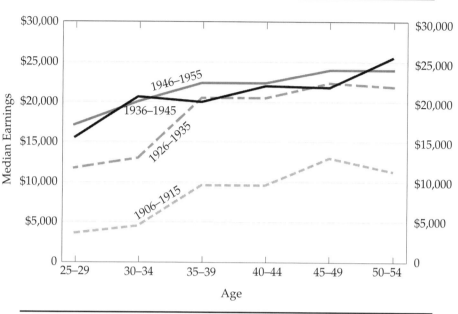

Note: Black men who were born early in the century experienced very rapid earnings increases as they aged, thanks to their move to the urban North and the decline in overt discrimination. Those born after 1936 began their careers with higher average wages, but did not enjoy as rapid an increase over their working life. Figures are real 1990 dollars. *Source*: Data from Ruggles et al. (2004).

why blacks have much less wealth than whites, whatever their incomes. Among both groups, homeownership rose after 1940. Figure 2.14 tracks homeownership by ethnicity in the United States from 1940 to 2000. In 1940, the black-white ratio was 49; it reached a high of 67 in 1980 and stood at 66 in 2000 when 72 percent of whites and 47 percent of blacks owned their own homes. The homes that blacks did own were worth less than those owned by whites, although their relative value increased greatly over time—from 20 percent in 1940 to 67 percent in 2000.

A view that combines earnings, education, and property qualifies the record of black economic progress. Blacks less often acquired a four-year college education; men (but not women) who did enter remunerative jobs earned less than whites; whatever their jobs or educations, they could not bundle individual into family earnings as large as those of whites; more of them were poor; more men were in prison; they owned

Photograph 2.5   Mother Working at Home, Late Twentieth Century

By the end of the twentieth century, many more African Americans and Latin Americans held jobs in business and the professions than earlier in the century. Opportunities had improved more quickly, however, for women than men. Nonetheless, a great many women faced a difficult challenge balancing single-motherhood with careers. *Source*: © Jose Luis Pelaez/CORBIS.

homes less frequently; and the homes they did own were not worth as much. As a consequence, they lived in segregated neighborhoods, owned automobiles less often, died younger, and, when disaster hit, proved the most vulnerable. Economic inequality, thus, was a cumulative process. It did not result from a single form of inequity or discrimination but from a series of screens that filtered blacks into less favored compartments whose cumulative result was a new configuration of inequality.[72]

Patterns of economic inequality separating blacks and whites shattered and then recomposed between the end of World War II and the turn of the century. Although blacks did not reach economic equality with whites, the configurations of inequality among them had been transformed irrevocably. A differentiation within African American social structure—a differentiation by labor force participation, industrial employment, occupation, education, income, and wealth—was one result.[73]

Figure 2.14 Percentage of Households Living in Owner-Occupied Housing, by Ethnicity, 1940 to 2000

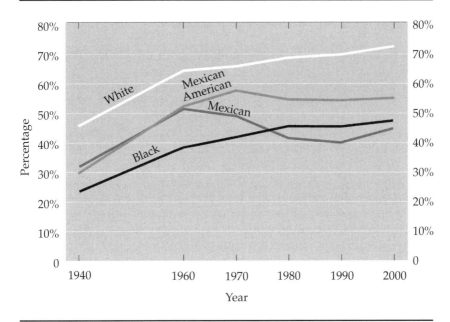

Note: The general rise in homeownership after World War II affected all ethnic groups. However, residential segregation and limited access to mortgages caused blacks to fall behind other groups between 1940 and 1960. Efforts to expand opportunities for homeownership later in the century did not overcome this setback. *Source*: Data from Ruggles et al. (2004).

It was through this process of differentiation—the accumulation of many small and not-so-small distinctions—that black social structure increasingly came to resemble that found among whites and that black inequality endured despite individual and group mobility.

Immigrant Generations

There is a heart-warming story usually told about immigrants who arrived from southern and eastern Europe early in the twentieth century. Poor, uneducated, but hard-working, they found jobs in America's factories. Over time, their pay increased. With ruthless underconsumption, they managed to save enough to buy homes and move from poverty to modest security and comfort. Their children, educated in American schools, found even better work and joined the great American middle class. The question for many of today's analysts of immigration is whether history will repeat itself, or whether the massive wave of current immigrants will follow a different path, one that leaves them economically marginal, imperfectly assimilated, and heavily dependent on public aid. The question seems especially urgent when asked about Mexicans because more immigrants now arrive in the United States from Mexico than from anywhere else. Will the Mexican story replicate the black experience rather than the Italian, Polish, and Jewish? Will the Mexican second generation join the white American middle class or add to the "underclass" in the nation's central cities?[74]

The answer requires probing both the conventional story of immigration and the experiences of today's Mexican immigrants and their children. Set against data on immigration today, the historical evidence qualifies some of the worries about the future of Mexican immigrants and their children and calls into question the argument that their incorporation into America is following an unprecedented path in immigrant history.[75] An interpretation that uses the paradox of inequality—the coexistence of durable inequalities with individual and group mobility—to frame immigrant history highlights both the continuities and differences between newcomers from southern and eastern Europe in the early 1900s and Mexicans today and allays the pessimists' worst fears.

Historic Roads to Immigrant Incorporation

The question of comparative immigrant history is important because it stands at the center of the debate over the prospects of today's immigrants, especially Mexicans. The most appropriate comparison for the Mexicans consists of early twentieth-century immigrants who arrived from countries where educational achievement was lower than in the United States and who did not share the predominant cultural origins of the white American population. Like today's Mexican immigrants, displaced by the spread of capitalist agriculture and industrial development, southern and eastern Europeans came in huge numbers to the United States as target earners, remitted massive amounts of money to family members left behind, and often returned themselves. Two of these immigrant groups—Italians and Poles—show suggestive parallels to Mexicans today. A third, Russian Jews, offers a telling contrast.

Immigrant is a broad category that conceals as much as it reveals. It encompasses enormous diversity in origins, culture, and experience. One rough way to think about this diversity in economic experience is to distinguish among the paths followed by immigrant groups as they sought survival, security, and prosperity in their new land. Three major routes defined the paths to immigrant economic incorporation in nineteenth and twentieth century America. Two are still active, one is vestigial. The active routes we call working-class and entrepreneurial-professional. The vestigial is agricultural. In no group did all members follow the same route—even among the earliest entrepreneurial/professional travelers, Russian Jews, for instance, many remained in the working class and a fraction were farmers. Rather, these routes should be understood as main tendencies, dominant patterns among immigrant groups.

The largest number of immigrants followed the working-class route whose outcome was differentiation—ethnic groups divided into working and middle classes. Differentiation occurred primarily between rather than within generations, with the first generation remaining for the most part in the blue-collar world. It was the route followed by the Irish, Italians, Poles, and Mexicans. The entrepreneurial/professional route traced a different pattern—a project of group upward mobility that reduced internal differences. It was the route taken early in the twentieth century by the Jews and, at its end, by Koreans. The agricultural route, of course, has died out as the farming population has dwindled but it was enormously important earlier in the nation's history. Germans bifurcated between working class and agricultural routes and the agricultural path dominated among Scandinavians, and, before World War II, the Japanese.

This division by class tells only one part of the story. Gender composes a distinct strand as well. Most historians and social scientists who trace the economic routes followed by immigrant groups do not differentiate by gender. This is a mistake. As with African Americans, immigrant men and women followed distinctive paths, incorporating into economic life in quite different ways.[76] Immigrant women and their daughters generally moved more quickly than men into the world of white-collar and semi-professional work.

An image of periodic waves, not a steady stream, best captures the rhythm of immigration throughout American history. (Immigration can be measured roughly with official statistics starting in 1821.) The first great immigrant surge resulted from the arrival of massive numbers of Irish and Germans in the 1840s and 1850s. (Large numbers of Scandinavians began their emigration in the 1860s.) A second wave, as chapter 1 has described, gathered force in the 1880s, peaked in 1907, and lasted until World War I. (In 1907, 1.3 million immigrants, a number equivalent to 3 percent of the U.S. population, arrived.) Unlike the older immigrants, who originated primarily in Europe's north and west, most of the newcomers arrived from the continent's south and east.[77]

Between 1850 and 1930, the number of foreign-born in the United States increased from 2.2 million to 14.2 million. Immigration, cut-off by world events and restrictive American legislation, entered a trough during World War I, the Great Depression, and World War II. Its resurgence, following legislation ending the quota system enacted in the 1920s, began after 1965, fueled, this time, not by Europeans but by newcomers from

Asia and Latin America, especially Mexico, with many from the Caribbean, South Asia, and Africa as well. By 2000, the number of foreign-born in the United States had reached 28.4 million.[78] (The inclusion of undocumented, or illegal, immigrants would boost this number considerably. Estimates put the number at 11 million in March 2005.)[79] In 2000, the foreign-born were 10.4 percent of the population, but they accounted for a third of population growth in the 1990s.[80]

Although a nation built of immigrants, America has not responded graciously to cultural difference or to strangers in its midst. In the mid-nineteenth century, nativist fears of Irish immigrants resulted in an anti-immigrant political party, employment discrimination, and violence. In the third quarter of the nineteenth century, Chinese immigrant workers—feared as labor competition by American laborers—bore the brunt of similar racism and stereotyping, resulting in the Chinese Exclusion Act of 1882, with later legislation excluding other Asians. Just as they stigmatized the Irish and Chinese as racially inferior, social commentators racialized the Italians, Poles, Slovaks, and Jews who arrived between 1880 and World War I. Equating them with paupers, criminals, and the insane, nativists worried they would debase American culture, lower wages, and drain the public fisc. This hostility culminated in the nationality-based immigration quotas of the 1920s, finally abandoned only in 1965 with legislation that opened the nation's borders to the current immigrant wave originating in Central and Latin America and in Asia.[81] Today's anti-immigrant sentiments, directed with special virulence at Mexicans—embodied, for instance, in California's Proposition 187, which denies essential services to immigrants—have a long history.

Economic Incorporation: Italians and Poles Versus Russian Jews

From the 1880s to World War I, Poles, Italians, and Russian Jews arrived in massive numbers. In each instance, emigration responded to the dislocations accompanying the spread of wage-labor and intensification of industrialization. Between 1870 and 1914, Polish immigrants numbered more than two million; between 1897 and World War I, about three million nine hundred thousand Italians arrived in the United States, and from the 1880s to 1914, Russian Jewish immigrants numbered roughly 1.6 million. These are figures for gross, not net, migration, which was considerably lower because about half the Italian immigrants and 40 percent of the Poles (but only 5 to 6 percent of the Russian Jews) returned to Europe.[82] When the U.S.-born children of immigrants are added to their numbers, the size of the "foreign-stock" population multiplies, highlighting the ethnic diversity of the nation. In 1910, the foreign-born numbered 13,345,545 and the white "foreign stock" 32,243,382 or nearly one in three of the entire population.

Before 1900, most Italian emigrants were peasants and day laborers from the north. As conditions in the north improved in the early twentieth century, most emigrants came from Italy's south. Many arrived as temporary workers, returning in large numbers to Italy, sometimes moving frequently back and forth between nations. In southern Italy little formal education had been available to emigrants during the nineteenth century. By one estimate, in 1871, 87 percent of Sicily was illiterate.[83] Illiteracy among immigrants reflected both the economic distinctions between Italy's north and south and the lack of schooling in the latter. In 1910, 54.5 percent of the immigrants arriving in the United States from the south and 11.5 percent from the north were illiterate.[84]

In Poland, no industry was available to absorb peasants newly made landless by land subdivision, and emigration proved the only solution to their search for subsistence.[85] Education expanded more rapidly in nineteenth-century Poland than in southern Italy, though it remained far below American standards. Thus, illiteracy among Polish immigrants in 1910, 35 percent, though still very high, was much less than among the southern Italians.[86] Emigration usually took place in stages, first within Poland or Europe and then to the United States.[87] Like Italians, most Poles who emigrated to the United States and elsewhere did not intend to remain. They planned to earn enough money to return to their native homes and buy land, which a large proportion of them did—paradoxically making the situation in Poland worse by contributing to the excessive subdivision of the land into small, unproductive parcels. While in the United States, emigrants sent considerable sums of money back to Poland. Indeed, given the emigrants' concentration in poorly paid work, the amounts, as with Italians and other immigrants, are staggeringly large, testimony to ruthless underconsumption and family commitment.[88]

Restricted by law in occupation and residence, Russian Jews in the years following 1880 faced increased oppression and persecution, including the notorious pogroms. Because they were leaving persecution and discrimination as well as poverty, relatively few Jewish immigrants returned to Russia.[89] Jews were a distinctive population—attracted first into Russia to perform economic functions not carried out by the Christian majority, that is, finance, trade, and services rather than agriculture and the simpler crafts. In time, they moved into consumer goods—especially clothing—that did not compete directly with Christian craft guilds. A people apart within the larger population, Jews were distinctive for their high rate of literacy and low rate of mortality as well as for their occupations, religion, and culture. This low death rate compensated for a below average birth rate and facilitated population growth. Jewish literacy resulted from both urban location—which made schools accessible—and from the pervasive system of religious schools, cheders, attended by men. Literacy, as a consequence, was much higher among Jews than among non-Jews in Russia or than among Italian and Polish immigrants in the United States; and, among Jews, it was higher among men than women.[90] (Illiteracy among immigrants dropped dramatically after the passage of the 1917 legislation mandating literacy as a condition of admission to the United States.)[91] Most Jewish immigrant workers to the United States—64 percent between 1899 and 1914—were skilled craftsmen, primarily in the apparel trades, and many brought their wives with them. Indeed, women and children—families—composed a higher share of Jewish than of most other immigrant groups.

How did these Italian, Polish, and Russian Jewish immigrants and their children fare in the United States? One way to answer the question is to focus on the experience of two cohorts: immigrants born between 1885 and 1894 who, as young adults, entered the United States at the peak of immigration, and the second generation born between 1905 and 1914, roughly the American-born children of the immigrant cohort.[92] Three themes stand out from this history: the continued anchor of the first-generation Poles and Italians in the working class; the mobility of the second generation; and the distinctiveness of the Russian Jews.

In the twentieth century, except during times of depression, most immigrant men found work in the regular labor market. The exclusion of African Americans, so common today, has been the exception. What disadvantaged earlier immigrants was their difficulty finding steady work and low pay—not labor market detachment or long term unemployment.[93] Their sons much more often not only earned more but worked steadily throughout the year.

Polish and Italian immigrants remained primarily blue collar.[94] Despite some movement over time into white-collar work, mobility remained modest, and by 1950, 70 percent of Polish and 63 percent Italian immigrants remained in blue-collar work. Within the working class, immigrant men improved their situations. The declining fraction of Polish and Italian men employed as ordinary laborers offers the best evidence of this limited mobility. When they moved into white-collar work, it was often as proprietors of small businesses. Few worked as professionals, clerical, or sales workers. Although Russian Jews also started out primarily in blue-collar work, few of them, about 2 percent, were ordinary laborers, and by 1970 only 43 percent remained in the manual working class. More Russian Jews than Italians and Poles worked in clerical and sales jobs, a small but increasing share were professionals, and a large, growing fraction—41 percent of forty- to forty-nine-year-olds at its peak—were self-employed.

In the second generation, the proportion of Polish and Italian men who reached white-collar work doubled the fraction among their fathers, but still remained a minority—35 percent of Polish and 30 percent of Italian men—and more of them avoided working as common laborers. By contrast, the share of white-collar workers among second-generation Jewish men had soared to 75 percent. Only a negligible number were laborers, and the share working either in crafts or as operatives was much lower than among their parents. By 1970, an extraordinary 22 percent worked in professional or technical jobs. Over a fifth found employment in clerical and sales work, and self-employment remained very high, peaking at 45 percent of fifty- to fifty-nine-year-olds. Russian Jews worked for themselves and in white-collar jobs more often, even, than native whites.

First-generation Poles, Italians, and Russian Jews developed distinctive industrial profiles. A very large fraction of Poles worked in heavy manufacturing. Italians more often were found in mining, construction, transport, and personal services. Russian Jews dominated trade and worked more often in the garment industries. Second-generation Russian Jewish men, however, worked less often in manufacturing than the immigrant generation had, and the fraction in business, the professions, and government increased. Unlike Italians and Poles, many of whom remained in manufacturing, second-generation Russian Jewish men moved decisively into commerce and government.

Polish and Italian women remained primarily in the manual working class, concentrated in manufacturing and, early in the century, service. The ability of immigrant women to leave household service signaled modest mobility comparable to the exit of first-generation men from work as ordinary laborers. By the second generation, a substantial minority had entered clerical work or found jobs in retail trade. Although most employed second generation Polish and Italian women remained operatives, their occupational structure bifurcated as about a quarter moved into clerical and sales work.[95] Change between first- and second-generation Russian Jewish women was more dramatic. In the first generation, like their Italian and Polish counterparts, they worked very often as operatives, sometimes in small family businesses, but rarely in private household service. Among the second generation, however, the share employed as operatives plummeted to only 4 percent in 1970. Instead, a majority turned to white-collar work, breaking more decisively with their parents' generation than either the Poles or Italians had.

Even more than occupation, earnings point to the economic advantage of the second generation.[96] Among the first generation, Russian Jews earned the most and Italians the least. For each group, second generation earnings grew remarkably. At age fifty to fifty-nine, second-generation Italian, Polish, and Russian Jewish men earned twice as much as had their fathers at the same age. Between generations, the share of each group in the lowest earnings quintile dropped and the fraction in the top quintile jumped—reaching an extraordinary 65 percent for Russian Jews. The earnings of second-generation men increased as they aged with the largest gain registered among men in their thirties and forties, that is, in the years immediately following World War II.

The second generation owed its economic success more to trade unions and labor legislation than to manufacturing employment. Before World War II, manufacturing jobs, after all, had not brought prosperity to their fathers. Self-employment, which included professionals, proprietors of relatively large businesses, petty entrepreneurs, and push cart vendors, proved an uncertain route to economic mobility. Membership in labor unions rocketed from about only 7 percent of the workforce in 1929 to about 25 percent by the end of World War II. In mining, manufacturing, and transportation, which accounted for most of this increase, unions had become the rule rather than the exception. Industries at the forefront of unionization employed a large fraction of immigrants and their children. In 1940, 30 percent of all foreign-born, compared to 25 percent of all blue-collar, workers were employed in the twelve industries leading the unionization wave. Among immigrants, in 1939, 37 percent of Russian, 37 percent of Polish, and 43 percent of Italians worked in these industries, which also employed 29 percent of second-generation Polish and 33 percent of second-generation Italian workers. Immigrants and their children had worked in these industries for a long time. It took unionization, however, to prod employers into offering decent wages and improved stability. Unionization, in turn, rested on New Deal legislation that strengthened the bargaining power of workers.[97]

In the 1930s, the Wagner Act legitimated collective bargaining. The Fair Labor Standards Act set a minimum wage and regulated hours of work. The Federal Housing Authority guaranteed mortgages and facilitated the explosive growth of affordable housing in the suburbs. Social Security opened a path to an old age lived outside of poverty, and the rapid increase in unemployment compensation after World War II and the enactment of disability insurance in 1956 shielded this generation of workers from the two greatest risks to their financial well-being. After the war, unions, helped by an expanding economy, won large pay increases and health and retirement benefits. The GI Bill and expansion of higher education vastly increased opportunities for advanced education. Coupled with extraordinary economic growth, these developments brought unprecedented prosperity to the entire white working class, including the children and grandchildren of immigrants.

Important as they were, higher earnings and steady work were not the only metrics by which immigrants and their children measured economic success. A home of one's own—property ownership—was also a significant goal—a buffer against the inevitable earnings decline in old age and the only realistic means of accumulating capital. Judged from this vantage point, their American experience proved encouraging. After age thirty, homeownership, which was closely linked to age, more than doubled among the immigrant generation, eventually reaching 68 percent for Poles and 75 percent for Italians against only 35 percent for Russian Jews. Despite their anchor in the manual working class, an extraordinary number of first-generation Polish and Italian immigrants managed to buy homes. Russian Jews deployed a different family strategy, investing more in small business than real estate.[98] The homes they did buy, however, usually were worth more than the ones bought by Italians and Poles. Homeownership rates did not change very much in the second generation, although fewer men in their thirties acquired property, a result, probably, of a delay imposed by depression and war, but the homes of second-generation immigrants were worth quite a lot more than those of their parents, again underlining economic mobility between generations. With homeownership rather than earnings as the metric, immigrants emerge more successful.

However, another measure of economic standing—poverty—qualifies the image of modest first-generation success.[99] Despite the economic progress of the immigrant generation, poverty among its households remained high. In 1950, 25 percent of first generation Polish, 24 percent of Italians, and 25 percent of Russian Jewish households had family earnings below the poverty line. Among the second generation, poverty rates dropped, though they were still high for younger families.[100] By 1970, however, these poverty rates had plummeted to 10 percent for Poles and 9 percent for Italians and Russians.[101] The mid-century coexistence of extensive poverty with increased income and widespread homeownership underscores the emergence of economic differentiation as a hallmark of immigrant history.

Economic Incorporation After 1965: Koreans and Mexicans

When Congress finally dismantled national-origin quotas in 1965, massive immigration resumed. Most of the new immigrants arrived from places deeply underrepresented among earlier newcomers. Prominent especially were Asia and Latin America, notably Mexico. Asian immigrants originated in a variety of nations; in their social origins they ranged from well-to-do business people and professionals to impoverished refugees fleeing war and persecution. Among them, Koreans stand out as particularly educated and entrepreneurial, modern day exemplars of the entrepreneurial-professional path to economic incorporation. Mexicans, with much less formal education and access to capital, followed the working-class route, now partially blocked by the erosion of the institutions of the labor market and the state that had facilitated mobility among immigrants and their children a half-century earlier.

Koreans.   Fewer than fifty Koreans lived in the United States before the twentieth century. The first major immigrant wave arrived in Hawaii between 1903 and 1905 as contract laborers for sugar plantations. Between 1950 to 1953 and 1965 a second wave consisted of war orphans, wives, and relatives of American servicemen stationed in Korea. The third and largest wave began when the 1965 Immigration Act abolished discriminatory quotas based on national origins. An annual average of thirty thousand to thirty-five thousand Koreans arrived between 1976 and 1990. In these years, after Mexicans and Filipinos, Koreans were the third largest immigrant group. By 1994, with improved living standards in Korea, the number had dropped to just under ten thousand eight hundred.[102] In 1999, approximately six hundred forty-five thousand first- and two hundred sixty-eight thousand second-generation Koreans lived in the United States.[103]

It was not the poorest Koreans who left for the United States. That group lacked the money to emigrate, and U.S. immigration law effectively prevented entry to the poverty-stricken unable to slip in unauthorized across a land border. Instead, Korean emigration consisted overwhelmingly of the urban middle class—men with white-collar and professional occupations and their families. Despite their education and skills, most of them could not find white-collar work commensurate with their professional qualifications. They turned instead in large numbers to small business for a foothold in the U.S. economy. They drew on various sources of capital, including their own savings, rotating credit associations, and U.S. branches of Korean banks, and kept expenses low by employing family members.[104]

The distinctions between Korean and Mexican immigrants resembled the differences between Russian Jews and Italians and Poles early in the twentieth century. Post-1965 Koreans had received more education than Mexicans, and they often arrived with some financial capital and business skills. Almost immediately they entered business, where by and large they prospered. Like the Jews, the first-generation Korean route to success led through proprietorship, but, unlike the Jews, Koreans were quick to buy property. Because the first generation Koreans were so well-educated and successful, differences between immigrant and second-generation men appeared less dramatic than the advances between generations among Jews or Mexicans.[105] Instead, second-generation Korean men advanced modestly on the achievements of their parents, which still left them more prosperous than the children of Mexican immigrants. Second-generation women, however, broke much more decisively with the occupations of their parents and, as did Mexican American and African American women, moved overwhelmingly into professional and white-collar work. Like other immigrant groups, Koreans remained clustered in a relatively small number of metropolitan areas. The largest was greater Los Angeles followed by New York.

Both immigrant Korean men and women were self-employed more often than the second generation. Lacking English fluency but able to draw on help from a network of compatriots and their own financial capital, these immigrants found in small business the surest route to economic security. The alternative route initially followed by the second generation more often led through public employment. Fluent in English and well educated, the second generation could find opportunities closed to their immigrant parents. Many immigrant Korean women worked in food stores, laundering, and apparel manufacturing—industries rarely entered by their daughters who were found more often in business and professional service and health-related industries. Second-generation women also often found work in the public sector.

Their high level of education helped Korean immigrants to find white-collar work and start businesses. In 1980, for example, 51 percent of immigrant men had attended college for four or more years. For Korean-born women, educational attainment was lower, but still high in comparison to both other immigrant groups and native whites. Second-generation Korean Americans continued to attend college in high numbers, and the educational gender gap of the immigrant generation disappeared. By 2000, slightly more than half of second-generation women and slightly less than half of second-generation men were college graduates.

In earnings even more than occupation, second-generation men advanced beyond their immigrant fathers. Second-generation men not only earned more than their fathers; they were able to translate their early advantages into gains that continued throughout their careers. Immigrant women also lost ground in earnings after age fifty, and they earned considerably less than their daughters, who, in turn, had lower earnings than men but higher than their mothers.[106] For men in the immigrant generation, private and public sector employment resulted in higher earnings than self-employment. For their sons, however, self-employment proved most rewarding. Immigrants often started small, marginal businesses whose profits did not increase greatly over time. In fact, the immigrant men who in time found work in the public sector managed the largest increase in their earnings as they aged. Second-generation men, by contrast, ran larger and more successful businesses, the rewards of which put them among the top ranks of the American earnings distribution. Self-employment less often proved a route to economic success for women than for men. Private and public employment offered the surest rewards.

Not surprisingly, poverty rates were low among adults with Korean origins, well below the national average, and most Korean families managed over time to buy property. By 1980, nearly 50 percent of immigrant men and 32 percent of immigrant women household heads owned property. The high values of their property distinguish Korean owners. The median value of property for Korean male and female household heads was $169,000 and $122,000, respectively.

Like Russian Jews earlier in the century, Koreans traveled the entrepreneurial-professional road to economic incorporation in the United States. Arriving with education, business skills, and some capital, they mounted an escalator that led to relative prosperity. In the immigrant generation, the mechanism was small-scale entrepreneurship; in the second, employment in the professions and public sector and ownership of larger businesses brought even greater prosperity. Along both working-class and entrepreneurial-professional roads the story was partly about gender. Women not only shifted into new kinds of work faster than men, they also began to catch up with and surpass them in education, if not in earnings. Access to the middle-class road wiped out the economic inequality of the first generation, and sometimes left it ahead of native whites. Certainly its children were disproportionately well off. Unlike Mexicans, who followed the working-class route, Koreans undertook a project of group upward mobility.

Mexican Immigrants and Mexican Americans.   Mexicans, of course, are not a new immigrant group. Until the mid-nineteenth century and the 1848 Treaty of Guadalupe Hidalgo, which ended the Mexican-American War, much of what is now the American Southwest was part of Mexico. Mexicans have moved easily and frequently back and forth across the border throughout the nation's history.[107] Federally legislated immigration quotas in the 1920s did not restrict legal immigration from Mexico, though the legislation did create the border patrol. But in the Great Depression of the 1930s, worried about jobs for Americans and the burden of welfare dependency, Washington repatriated more than 400,000 Mexicans.[108] In 1943, responding to the labor needs of American agriculture, the federal government initiated the bracero program, which allowed Mexicans to enter the United States as guest workers. The program ended in 1964 after Congress refused to reauthorize it. Mexican immigration accelerated once more in the 1960s as Mexico's "economic miracle" began to unravel. Rapid population growth and declining economic fortunes in Mexico coincided with the imposition of new U.S. limits on Mexican migration. The result promoted an explosion of undocumented immigration. Especially in California, it met the needs of growers for large quantities of cheap labor, and American border authorities did little to impede the flow. The substitution of undocumented workers for the older bracero system served both sides reasonably well. "As in the earlier era, movement during the undocumented era was highly circular, and crossing the border was not difficult. While working in the United States, Mexican migrants maintained strong contact with their home communities and regularly sent back monthly remittances, and most returned with savings." In fact, most undocumented men returned to Mexico within two years.[109] Two-thirds of Mexican migrants in these years were young married men, with an average age of between twenty-one and twenty-three. Arriving from mid-sized towns and cities, they had spent only five years in school but had worked for many years. Only 25 percent had been employed in agricultural occupations in Mexico; another 25 percent were unskilled workers; roughly 15 percent worked in service jobs; and 10 percent were skilled. They had strong links to the United States: 40 percent had a parent and 18 percent a sibling with U.S. experience; in the towns and cities from which they emigrated, 33 percent (one in three) of the townspeople had spent time in the United States.[110]

After 1986, the stable and circular migratory system between Mexico and the United States broke down. The Immigration Reform and Control Act of 1986 (IRCA), which tried to limit immigration, instead shifted the balance toward undocumented workers and discouraged immigrants from returning to Mexico. On the Mexican side, economic collapse intensified the pressure to emigrate and to remain in the United States.[111] In 1982, as oil prices imploded, the Mexican government floated the currency, which promptly lost half its value. Inflation soared, the GDP fell, real wages plummeted 21 percent, unemployment increased, and a chasm opened between rich and poor.[112] At the same time, in the U.S. mounting hysteria over "illegal" immigration—reinforced by domestic economic problems—helped pass the IRCA, the most visible symbol of the government's attempt to crack down on undocumented workers.

The IRCA provided amnesty for undocumented immigrants, implemented sanctions for employers of unauthorized workers, and strengthened border controls.[113] The war on undocumented Mexicans, however, did not reflect the realities of American labor market demand, which remained strong. The difference was that much of the need for cheap unskilled labor shifted from the farms of California and Texas to new immigrant destinations where population growth, economic restructuring, and demand for low-wage, low-skilled workers (as in the meatpacking and poultry industries) drew Mexican immigrants. Between 1990 and 2000, the share of Mexican immigrants going to non-gateway states (such as Iowa and Nebraska) jumped from 13 percent to 35 percent. Most of these new destinations consisted of "smaller towns and cities" where, for the most part, Mexican immigration has become a "family affair"—as immigrants used the amnesty provision of the IRCA to sponsor the immigration of family members.[114] Aside from sponsored family members, most Mexican immigrants now—about 80 to 85 percent of migrants totaling six million—are undocumented; more of them are dependents (that is, children who do not work); they tend to stay longer, and many more become citizens.[115] American immigration policy, perversely, has helped transform a "permanent flow" back and forth across the border "into a permanent settlement" and *encouraged* additional migration from Mexico to the United States."[116]

An obvious question is whether the large number of undocumented immigrants distorts a census-based analysis. Many of the undocumented were included in the census, and there is no reason to believe that the census presents an unrepresentative portrait of the Mexican population. Undocumented immigrants, however, add a complication to the comparison between early twentieth-century newcomers and current Mexicans because their status poses a barrier to mobility not confronted by Italians, Poles, and others who arrived earlier. In fact, this barrier makes the achievements of Mexicans even more impressive.

The geographic concentration of Mexican immigrants fans the concerns of those who worry about Mexicans' impact on America's economy and culture. It means, first, that the fiscal burden of immigration falls most heavily on a few states. The federal government benefits most from taxes paid by immigrants—income and Social Security and Medicare taxes—but states and local governments pick up most of the burden through Medicaid and other health programs, public assistance, and, especially, education. Concentration also means that the labor market impact of Mexican immigrants and their children is localized. Most American workers compete with immigrants directly, but in the major destination areas, the potential for job competition and pressure on wages is intense.[117]

Concentration also fuels residential segregation and cultural isolation, which reinforce the maintenance of Mexican culture, decrease pressure to master English, and retard economic and social incorporation. For these reasons, the residential concentration of Mexican immigrants worries observers who fear the fragmentation of America and the breakup of its allegedly national culture. Historic parallels, however, sketch a more optimistic view. In the nineteenth and early twentieth century, Scandinavian and German immigrants settled America's midwestern heartland, building ethnically homogeneous settlements where they preserved languages and customs for at least a generation (see photograph 2.6). These settlements were not a minor part of the landscape. Indeed, immigrants composed a very large share of the population of midwestern states. As early as 1880, over half the farmers in Wisconsin, Minnesota, and Dakota, one-third in Michigan, Iowa, and Nebraska, and one-quarter in Illinois were immigrants.[118] Critics at the time, very much like their counterparts today, worried about the influence of foreign cultures, the preservation

Photograph 2.6   **Bohemian National Cemetery, Silver Lake Quadrangle, Rich Valley Township, McLeod County, Minnesota, May 1912**

Throughout the twentieth century, immigrant communities have sought to hold on to their traditions and language, efforts that have often been interpreted as "un-American." Yet, the interest in cultural heritage has rarely impeded processes of economic incorporation. *Source*: Minnesota Historical Society.

of European languages, and reluctance to assimilate. They focused much of their anxiety on religion—the Lutheran and especially Catholic faiths of the immigrants. Over time, their hostility abated as immigrant children joined the American workforce and abandoned the distinctive ways of their parents. The point is this: America's institutions and its social fabric have proved robust, accommodating ethnic settlements and distinctions without disruption. There is no reason to suppose that they are any less capable now. Indeed, the incorporation of earlier immigrants into America took place in the face of hostility as virulent as any faced by Mexicans today.

Comparisons of Mexican immigrants with the Italians and Poles who arrived in the United States early in the twentieth century are even more instructive. All three groups embodied the internationalization of labor markets that accompanied the first and second great waves of economic globalization in the modern industrial period. (The first wave of economic globalization, as chapter 1 explained, extended from the third quarter of the nineteenth century through the start of World War I.) They often came as target earners; clustered in ethnically homogeneous settlements; remitted a great deal of money to family members; and frequently traveled back and forth themselves. In the United States, they often took the worst jobs, hard, dangerous, poorly paid irregular work.

Their educations were modest. Mexican immigrants have graduated from high school or attended college much less often than native whites. In 2000, 59 percent of Mexican immigrants born between 1945 and 1954 had eight or less years of schooling, a fraction that dropped to about a third among immigrants born two decades later. But, early in the century, Poles and Italians only infrequently had the equivalent of a common school education, and, as the figures earlier make clear, many more of them were illiterate than native whites—an educational gap at least as consequential as the differences between Mexican immigrants and native whites today. Educational attainment, however, rose sharply among subsequent generations: in 2000, 42 percent of Mexican American men born between 1955 and 1964 and 47 percent of women had completed at least one year of college.[119] Among younger Mexican Americans, however, the educational trajectories of men and women moved in opposite directions: the proportion of men with at least one year of college dropped while among women it rose to half—highlighting stagnant circumstances for men but not women.[120] As with African Americans, the history of education revealed the emergent gender gap that had opened among Mexicans.[121]

Mexicans arrived speaking English more often than earlier immigrants.[122] This discovery contradicts critics who inject Mexicans' allegedly reluctant and slow acquisition of English language skills into the politics of immigration.[123] Among immigrant men in the United States five years or less, 23 percent of Italians, 15 percent of Polish, and 48 percent of Russian Jews compared to 54 percent of Mexicans spoke English. All groups made rapid progress. Among Mexicans who had lived in the United States more than twenty years, only 7 percent of men and 10 percent of women remained monolingual. Virtually all Mexican Americans spoke English, and many were bilingual. The pessimists' fear of huge numbers of Spanish-speaking children and grandchildren of Mexican immigrants balkanizing America linguistically and displacing the English language clearly represents an imagined disaster, not a realistic future.[124]

With low wages, Mexican immigrants survived economically by combining the earnings of family members. Most of them, 80 percent in 2000, remained in blue-collar jobs—a fraction not very different from among Italian and Polish immigrant men at mid-century. Like African Americans, Mexican Americans found the road to economic mobility in public and publicly funded employment rather than in owning small businesses, a common route among Italian and Polish immigrants earlier in the century.[125] In 2000, 37 percent of Mexican American women and 17 percent of men born between 1945 and 1954 worked in public or publicly funded employment, which paid relatively well and offered the most certain route to modest prosperity.

Mexican immigrant men enjoyed modest economic mobility, evident in earnings that increased over time and in the ability to buy a house. Some 66 percent of Mexican men born between 1945 and 1954 owned their own homes at ages fifty to fifty-nine, a fraction similar to the one for Italian and Polish immigrant men of the same age. Another way to compare groups is through average occupational income score—a measure that approximates general group economic rank. In a regression analysis, for men resident in the United States for five years or less, the occupational income score was 21 for both early twentieth-century Italian and Polish immigrants and 20 for late twentieth-century Mexicans. All groups progressed with length of stay in the United States. For each of the three groups of immigrant men the annual increase in score was an identical .18. Economic mobility, though not dramatic, was solid and unmistakable (see figure 2.15).

Most encouraging of all, they witnessed the mobility of their children. The children and grandchildren of Mexican immigrants reached much higher levels of education and enjoyed modest but unmistakable movement up the occupational and economic ladder. In 2000, about 40 percent of Mexican American workers were in white-collar work—a fraction not far different from the 48 percent of second-generation Italian men and 42 percent of Polish of the same age in 1970.

In earnings as well as occupation, Mexican American women, but not men, began to converge with native whites. In fact, with educational achievement statistically controlled, Mexican American women earned virtually the same amount as native white women. A substantial gap remained between Mexican American and native white men. Both Mexican American men and women, however, earned substantially more than their immigrant parents and grandparents. Members of subsequent generations became, in fact, a more differentiated population than their parents—differentiated by income, occupation, and the mobility trajectories of men and women. As among earlier working-class immigrants, the paradox of inequality played itself out between, more than within, generations (see figure 2.16).

Late in the century, the relative economic position of Mexican immigrants and Mexican Americans began to slip. In this, they paralleled the experience of African American men and the rest of the working class.[126] As the prospects of young native white men began to deteriorate sharply

Figure 2.15   Average Occupational Score by Length of Residence in the United States, Selected Immigrant Groups

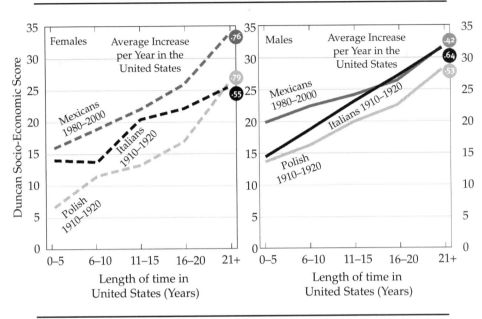

Note: Male Mexican immigrants improved their occupational standing slowly as their length of time in the United States increased. Their occupational standing and rate of improvement were quite similar to those of Italians and Poles earlier in the century. Like Italian and Polish women, Mexican women's occupational progress outpaced that of their male counterparts.

The dependent variable is the Duncan socio-economic score, see O. D. Duncan (1961). These are results of a general-linear model controlling for age differences between groups. Mexican data include 1980 through 2000 censuses. Polish and Italian data include 1910 and 1920 censuses. *Source*: Data from Ruggles et al. (2004).

in the late 1970s and 1980s, it would have been odd, indeed, if Mexican Americans had proved an exception. Between 1970 and 2000, the share of Mexican and Mexican American men in the poorest income quintile increased as their share among the top two quintiles declined. Women—both immigrants and Mexican American—were overrepresented in the two poorest quintiles and badly underrepresented in the top two. Thus, it is not surprising that a large fraction—smaller among Mexican Americans than earlier twentieth-century immigrants—lived in poverty. In general, Mexican poverty rates hovered between that of native whites and blacks.

Especially among men, the upward trajectory of income, occupation, and educational attainment seemed to halt or, even, stagnate and drop back a little. In this it might be thought that Mexican Americans diverged from descendants of eastern and southern European immigrants. But

Figure 2.16   Mean Wage and Salary Income, by Gender, Nativity, and Age, 2000 Controlling for Educational Attainment

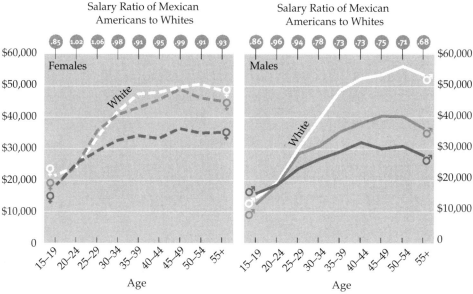

Note: The apparent earnings gap between Mexican American women and white women virtually disappeared when educational differences are taken into consideration. In contrast, Mexican American men with a similar educational background earned, on average, much less than white men.

General linear model results, estimated marginal means, controlling for educational attainment. *Source*: Data from Ruggles et al. (2004).

there is another way to look at the matter. At both ends of the century, the histories of immigrants' children and grandchildren reflected broad economic trends shaping working-class experience. With census statistics, we pick up the incomes of the second generation southern and eastern Europeans only in the aftermath of World War II during a period that combined the fruits of newly won unionization, an expansive welfare state, and tremendous economic growth. Income, education, and opportunity were increasing throughout the nation, benefiting both the children of immigrants and everyone else.

Early twentieth-century immigrants, the usual argument asserts, prospered thanks to the availability of jobs in heavy industry, which now has nearly vanished, leaving the Mexican immigrants without a comparable initial rung on the ladder of economic success. In pay and working conditions, however, the industrial jobs that employed earlier immigrants were no worse than the construction, agricultural, and service work available to today's Mexican immigrants. What differ are labor

Photograph 2.7   Geeta Temple Procession, Jackson Heights, New York

Although the origins of immigrants have changed, the challenges of economic incorporation and cultural adaptation remain. The latest wave of globalization, if anything, has made the clashes more dramatic. *Source*: © Audrey Gottlieb 1989.

market and public sector institutions—unions and an expanding welfare state. These are what brought modest prosperity and security to an earlier immigrant working class and its children, and it is what Mexican immigrants and their children do not enjoy to anything like the same extent today. In this respect, Mexican Americans share the situation of other young Americans. The halt, even slight reversal, among the Mexicans is an instance of a much larger problem—growing inequality and declining mobility among the whole working class. After World War II, a dynamic economy, unions, fair wages, employee benefits, and opportunities in publicly related jobs—supported by an active government—finally began to move the children and grandchildren of early twentieth-century immigrants toward better jobs and incomes. Without a reinvigoration of these influences, current-day Mexican immigrants and their children will not enjoy the same rewards (see photograph 2.7).

Inequality as History

The experiences of women, blacks, and immigrants illustrate the history of inequality in twentieth-century America and highlight its features as outlined at the start of this chapter.

Inequality is Paradoxical

This chapter has illustrated what Charles Tilly calls durable inequality— persistent inequality among paired categories over time. These inequalities retain their power through four mechanisms that Tilly terms exploitation, opportunity hoarding, emulation, and adaptation. By exploitation, he means that the more powerful member of a category uses its resources to appropriate a disproportionate share of what the less powerful member produces and perpetuates its position through any one of a number of means—legislation, work rules, or outright repression. With opportunity hoarding, the less powerful member of the category makes its peace, more or less, by finding ways to promote its own interests; it looks for ways to advance within a category rather than to break down the distinctions between them. The development of ethnic niches—where ethnic groups take hold of an occupation and pass it on to their members—is one historically very important example; another is labor union practices that favor relatives or friends for membership. The third and fourth mechanisms—emulation and adaptation—are general social processes; they can be seen at work outside of as well as within relations of inequality. Emulation is simply the tendency for individuals and groups to reproduce the organizational models with which they are familiar; adaptation refers to the ways in which members of each category build routines and social relationships that facilitate daily interaction and reinforce their interest in maintaining category boundaries.[127]

The historical record provides evidence of how exploitation and opportunity hoarding shaped the twentieth-century inequality narratives discussed in this chapter more than emulation and adaptation. Exploitation took many forms—for example, rules that prohibited the employment of married women and sanctioned paying women less than men; lynching and legalized segregation in housing, transportation, education, and public accommodations; and the neo-slavery of migrant agricultural laborers.

The historical record is also full of examples of opportunity hoarding. Take, for instance, the feminization of occupations. Excluded from most occupations, women seized what openings there were, making them their own, filling vacancies with other women trained in new educational programs—from commercial courses in high schools to social work schools in universities—that channeled women into the expanding slots in a limited number of occupations. Blacks sometimes found themselves bumped from occupational niches as whites invaded trades they had dominated—such as barber in the nineteenth century. In the twentieth century, excluded from the best industrial jobs, a fortunate minority found a private sector niche as Pullman porters on railroads. The most important niche was public and publicly funded employment, though it was one that required educational credentials that many lacked, and proved vulnerable to cuts in public spending. Mexicans, of course, found their niche in farm labor, to which they were often recruited through social networks extending from Mexican villages to the American Southwest. In recent years, they have found another niche in meatpacking and poultry processing.

In Tilly's account, the mechanisms that perpetuate durable inequalities are relentless rather than paradoxical. They do not account for group or individual mobility. Thus, they leave unexplained the massive gains we have just described. Women broke through one occupational barrier after another and pushed past men in educational achievement. As legal segregation crumbled, African Americans entered new forms of work, moved to the suburbs, and went to college much more often. Poverty among them plummeted, and black women earned as much as native white women with similar educations. Among working-class immigrants, mobility took place more often across rather than within generations. The children of immigrants exceeded the accomplishments of their parents on every dimension. Mexican Americans, with women leading the way, broke out of agricultural labor; a large proportion found white-collar work. They stayed in school much longer and earned a lot more than their immigrant parents.

Thus Tilly accounts for only one side of the paradox of inequality. His four mechanisms do not show why groups, such as women, remain unequal despite great individual gains in occupation, education, and income. The answer, a crucial supplement to the theory of durable inequality, lies partly in powerful external forces converging from different directions—the state, economy, culture, higher education, and social movements. All groups could count some major gains. But the structures they attacked were so powerful that victories proved only partial. Thus, the key to the paradox of inequality lies in the process of internal differentiation—in American history, characteristic of women, African Americans, and most immigrant groups. The grooves etched deeply into hegemonic social structures provided the routes along which advancement took place. Women, African Americans, and Mexican Americans assimilated into and reproduced existing economic hierarchies among themselves. For this reason, their mobility did not challenge the structure of inequality; instead it replicated it.

Inequality Is Contingent

How inequality works varies with time and place. Interpretations that squeeze racial, gender, or ethnic group history into a linear "either-or" framework risk turning narratives of qualitative transformation into scorecards that divert attention away from the most important issues.

The question is not only whether groups are more or less unequal but how and why the characteristics of group inequality have changed during the twentieth century and what those changes imply. Until World War II, inequality among women and minorities resulted from an overlapping system of oppression: the combination of legal discrimination, occupational segregation, and social norms resulted in overt, publicly legitimated forms of inequality that stretched from families to workplaces and from housing to politics. Marriage barred women from work; gender discrimination denied them equal pay. Restrictive covenants shut African Americans and Mexican Americans out of entire neighborhoods; racial segregation legally relegated African Americans to poorly funded schools; and employers refused them work with no sanctions—to give just three examples.

By the late twentieth century, this older pattern had shattered, replaced by a new cumulative process of inequality that progressively sifted individuals through a series of screens separating them into more or less favored statuses. Education had replaced race and gender as the factor most closely associated with economic success. Where individuals lived, however, exerted a huge impact on the quality of the education they received, and race remained a powerful influence on residence. With middle-class comforts dependent on two incomes, single-motherhood erected barriers to women's advance and reduced opportunities for their children. Incarceration generally ruined labor market prospects, shunting many minority men away from opportunities for good jobs and, even, marriage. Thus, in myriad ways, the allocation of life experiences among group members progressively hindered or facilitated their opportunities.

Inequality Is Multidimensional

No single measure captures the multidimensional, protean character of inequality. A view through five lenses, however, approaches a comprehensive portrait. The five lenses through which the stories here have been told are geography, participation, distribution, rewards, and differentiation. Geography powerfully shaped the experience of African Americans who always have concentrated disproportionately in the nation's most disadvantaged places: early twentieth-century southern farms and late twentieth-century inner cities. Proximity across a long and until recently mostly unguarded border encouraged the emigration of poor Mexicans. Thus, among Mexicans, geography fostered economic mobility. With other immigrants, spatial concentration sometimes had the same result, such as the opportunities for immigrant entrepreneurs in ethnic neighborhoods. Changes in labor force participation played a dramatic part in the stories of women and blacks with the surge of married women into the labor force and the increased chronic labor force detachment of many African American men. The history of the distribution among types of work also pointed to major change, for example, women's move into clerical and, much later, managerial jobs; African Americans' exit from agriculture and domestic service and into the public sector; and Mexican Americans' generational shift out of farm labor.

Seen through the lens of rewards, images are mixed. In the late twentieth century, women, blacks, and the children of immigrants earned a lot more than they or their parents did earlier in the century. Poverty rates dropped and many more reached the top earning quintile. But earnings ratios, with some important exceptions, did not change very much. In fact, poverty ratios actually widened. The most important exception is the astonishing accomplishment of African American and Mexican American women, who earn as much as similarly educated native white women. Differentiation, the outcome of each of these narratives, emerges as the most powerful lens with which to examine the history of group experience. Bifurcation weaves a central thread through each story: women executives and women on welfare; African American public administrators and African Americans stuck in poverty or unable to find work; Mexican American white-collar workers and Mexican farm laborers all help shape sharply divided social structures.

Inequality Is State Sponsored

Federal, state, and local governments played major roles in each inequality narrative. They reinforced inequality directly through legislation, the courts, administrative regulations, and executive actions, for instance, by legitimating segregation and unequal pay. Governments also added to inequality indirectly, for example, by exacerbating the housing problems of the poor through urban renewal and, as Hurricane Katrina showed, by eroding public services and protection. But government also was the source of the most powerful measures to reduce inequality. Two of the most important of these were progressive taxation, now reversed and driving inequality in the opposite direction, and the expansion of public higher education after World War II. Other measures—civil and voting rights legislation and affirmative action in particular—targeted disadvantaged groups directly. Government also reduced inequality indirectly, by legitimating trade unions and setting a minimum wage, for example, as well as by funding social programs that created massive numbers of jobs for women and minorities.

Inequality Is Gendered

Inequality has worked differently for men and women. Indeed, its gendered character emerges unmistakably from these narratives. Overall, of course, women had to break through barriers erected by men, which has given them distinctive goals. The story of women's inequality reveals both their achievements and frustrations, as men manipulated jobs in ways that helped solidify their advantage—as in finding ways to pay women less for nominally similar work. Within African American and Mexican American history, however, the stories told here highlight the unmistakable emergence of a gender gap—far too often ignored in the scholarly literature—as women pioneered the road to white-collar work, advanced beyond men in education, and closed the distance in income between themselves and comparably educated white women.

Inequality Is Self-Replicating

At this juncture the point that inequality is self-replicating seems almost redundant, but it deserves emphasis, nonetheless. For it adds a dynamic quality to the inequality story and extends the idea of durability beyond Tilly's categorical inequalities—black or white, men or women—to the whole system of stratification, most importantly, the shape of the income pyramid and the hierarchy of occupations whose resilience resulted in remarkable continuities across the century. Membership changed, but structures endured with such force that they channeled successful insurgents, whether women, African Americans, or Mexican Americans, into familiar grooves. Just how this process works requires a great deal of analysis. But its results, sometimes lethal, are plain to see. In the histories of the late twentieth century Women's Movement and Civil Rights Movement, as well as in the aftermath of Hurricane Katrina, the paradoxical consequences of America's inequality narratives emerge clearly in the persistence of inequality amid success.

Chapter 3

Growing Up and Growing Old in a Century of Family Change

Iɴ ᴛʜᴇ early twentieth century, many Americans did not know exactly how old they were, and they did not care. The Census Bureau's report on age statistics from the 1910 census cautioned readers:

> It is impossible to claim entire accuracy for census statistics of age. Some people do not know their true ages; some people seem deliberately to report them incorrectly; and the reports for a good many persons are not made by the persons themselves, but by others who have not exact knowledge as to the age. There is a conspicuous tendency to report ages in round numbers; the number reported as 40 years of age, for example, is far greater than the number reported as either 39 or 41.[1]

Age heaping, as the demographers call it, remained common in the century's first decade. In 1910, there were, on the census, 24 percent more people listed as twenty than as nineteen years old, for example. By 1920, these numbers had started to retreat. In 1940, the number of 20 year olds exceeded the number of nineteen-year-olds by only 7 percent. Age consciousness had permeated American life. "How old are you?" became a question Americans could answer with precision.

The Meaning of Age

The penetration of American society and culture by age consciousness is the story told by historian Howard Chudacoff in his book, *How Old Are You?* In the nineteenth century, Chudacoff claims, "the country's institutions were not structured according to age-defined divisions, and its cultural norms did not strongly prescribe age-related behavior." When this situation began to change, the pace was fast for a transformation of such fundamental importance. "By the beginning of the twentieth century,"

Chudacoff observes, "age consciousness and age grading had become fixed in American institutions and culture."[2]

The looseness surrounding discussions of age before the twentieth century signified inexact ideas of when life's stages—childhood, youth, old age—began and what they included. With the twentieth century's heightened attention to age, this vagueness gave way to precise divisions of the life course fixed by chronological boundaries, a new standardization enforced by institutions and public policy and often justified by science and medicine. Writing in 1933 in the report of the President's Committee on Recent Social Trends, Lawrence K. Frank observed: "One of the most important discoveries of the past thirty years is that the child is not a small sized adult, but is a growing, developing, ever changing individual, whose treatment must differ not merely in degree, but in kind, from that received by the adult."[3]

This momentous shift in thinking about human lives shows that, unlike inequality, personal experience is remarkably malleable, buffeted by American's durable inequalities and subject to reconfiguration as a result of changes in labor markets, state policies, and scientific research.[4] In the twentieth century, many of the same forces drove the histories of both inequality and personal experience. But the inequality pyramid changed less than the shape of families and the life course. In the course of the century, the history of both families and the life course traced a rough arc from diversity to standardization and back again to partial diversity. The first stage occupied roughly the years until World War II; the second, the postwar years through the 1960s and 1970s; the third emerged most clearly in the century's last two decades. Through this sequence, the trajectory of twentieth-century inequality registered in the transformation of personal experience, resulting in a configuration of family forms unprecedented in history.

The standardization of experience by age began in schools with age grading. In the nineteenth century, rough forms of age grading had been in place for a long time. In the United States, for instance, grammar schools were recognized as generally serving children over the age of seven and colleges were for older students. Still, until at least the middle of the nineteenth century, the age range in colleges and academies (before high schools the source of secondary education) remained very wide. Most American children attended one-room schools in which pupils of a variety of ages intermingled. The generation of reformers that created modern public school systems—Horace Mann and Henry Barnard are the most famous—worked to change all this, partly by persuading communities to switch to age graded schools. Starting around the middle of the nineteenth century, they met with success —most readily in cities, where the pressure of numbers necessitated some principle for dividing students into groups, but, over time, in small towns as well.

In the same years, the age spread within academies and colleges narrowed dramatically. Architects built schools divided into rooms for different ages. State governments set minimum ages for entering the hierarchy of schools now characteristic of bureaucratic public educational systems. Publishers aimed textbooks at particular ages. And, by the second decade of the twentieth century, "retardation"—defined as falling behind age-normed achievement levels—surfaced as a major problem in urban schools while the founders of IQ tests exuded confidence in their ability to determine exact mental age.[5] Schools had pioneered the age standardization that took hold in the twentieth century.

Age grading demarcated the line between puberty and the early adult years with unprecedented precision. High school, for example, now implied not only a setting accessed by achievement but a place for young people of a certain age. Anyone younger or older no longer fit. Later in the century, another public policy—Social Security—established an official boundary for old age. Many other policies also reified specific ages: permissible age of marriage, age of sexual consent, draft age, driving age, voting age, drinking age. Age stratification, as some sociologists call it, had become one foundation of public policy.[6]

Life in the twentieth century changed not only because of neat age boundaries enforced by law and public institutions but, as well, because of its increased length. In 1900, at birth, a male could expect to live 47.9 years and a female 50.7. This expected life span increased dramatically during the century. At mid-century, it had reached 65.6 for men and 71.0 for women, and, at the century's end it stood at 74.1 and 79.5. In other words, during the twentieth century men's life expectancy increased 55 percent and women's 57 percent. One result was that in the early twenty-first century a twenty-year-old was more likely (91 percent) to have a living grandmother than a twenty-year-old in 1900 was (83 percent) to have a living mother. Life expectancy in 1900 was so short partly because many people died early—as infants, young children, or in childbirth. Early in the twentieth century, about one hundred of every one thousand infants died. In 2001 the number was 6.8. Those men and women who had reached age sixty-five could expect to live about another twelve years (women a little longer than men); in 2000, men at age sixty-five could expect sixteen years of life and women another nineteen. The difference between the sexes in life expectancy, in fact, had widened during the century.[7] Why did women's advantage increase in these decades when, with advances in medicine, one might have expected it to have shrunk? The answer is smoking, taken up by large numbers of men before it became a widespread habit among women. Smoking cut life expectancy by several years. In the last decade or two a shrinking gender gap in life expectancy at age sixty-five resulted from an increase in smoking by women (see figure 3.1).[8]

Figure 3.1   Age Pyramid, 1900 and 2000

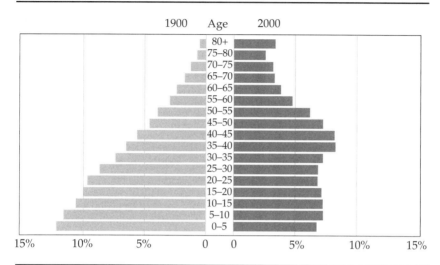

Note: Changes in birth and death rates during the twentieth century transformed the "age pyramid." In place of the broad base and narrow top of 1900, the population in 2000 was distributed much more evenly across age groups. *Source*: Data from Ruggles et al. (2004).

Life expectancy has differed by race as well as by gender. Indeed, race differences have inscribed one of the nation's most durable inequalities into patterns of life and death. Black death rates, like white, went down sharply during the last half of the twentieth century. But the difference between races remained about the same. Blacks improved their absolute chances, but their relative disadvantage hardly changed. In 1950, the death rate for infants (per one thousand live births) was 26.8 for whites and 43.9 for blacks; in 2001, the rates, respectively, were 5.7 and 14.0—a larger gap than at mid-century. These differences persisted into adulthood. At age forty-five to fifty-four, the death rate in 1950 for white men was 984.5 and for black men 1905; in 2001, the two rates were 501.3 and 996. At both times, black men were about twice as likely to die as white men of the same age. The story was similar for women—a decline from 546.4 to 286.8 for white women and from 1576.4 to 579.1 for black women—whose relative disadvantage had worsened.[9]

Longer lives changed the shape of the nation's age structure. In 1900, the median age of the population was only twenty-three; by 2000, it was thirty-five.[10] The average American did not, however, grow older at an even pace. In the 1930s, during the Great Depression, fertility dropped to its lowest point in American history and remained low until after the war. By mid-century, the median age had reached 30.2 before dropping back as a result of the post–World War II baby boom, when the large number of young children offset the increase in life expectancy. Earlier in the century, age structure varied by region. The frontier, for instance, drew large numbers of young men; in the South, agriculture and slavery also tilted age structure toward youth. But, the demographers Irene and Conrad Taeuber write, "the path of the [twentieth] century was toward convergence." No longer regional, "the major differentiations in age structures became those within the metropolitan population itself, particularly between central cities and outer areas."[11]

America's age pyramid looked vastly different at the beginning, middle, and end of the twentieth century. Writing in 1971, the Taeubers observed, "a new demographic vocabulary is required, for the current and prospective age pyramids are neither the broad ones of high fertility, the narrow and eroding ones of declining fertility, nor yet the scarred ones of major wars with the gashes of military dead and the decimated cohorts of the births of the war years. They are, rather, variable from decade to decade, from age to age."[12] The consequences were great. In 1972, the U.S. Commission on Population Growth and the American Future warned: "The postwar baby boom is over, but those born during the boom period are still very much with us. Our society has not had an easy time thus far in its attempts to accommodate the baby-boom generation, and their impact is not likely to diminish in the near future."[13] Early in the century, most of the resources spent on dependent persons went to children, privately for their upkeep, publicly for their schooling. By century's end, the cost of supporting the elderly had risen dramatically. In 1955, there were 8.6 workers to support every person receiving Social Security. By the end of the century, that number had shrunk to 3.3 and continued to fall.[14] It was against this backdrop of immense demographic change—and the pressure it induced—that the history of life's stages took place.[15]

The familiar stages in human lives—childhood, adolescence, adulthood, middle age, old age—are products of culture and history as much as of biology, and they have proved remarkably malleable. This chapter focuses on two that have undergone dramatic transformations in the twentieth century: the transitions to adulthood and to old age. We examine the history of each separately and then set them in the context of the equally profound alterations in family and household structures that occurred in the same years. All these transformations responded to the same forces shaping the history of women, blacks, and immigrants discussed in earlier chapters. They were in large measure set in motion during the first great age of economic globalization, described in chapter 1, and propelled by powerful social and economic changes during the rest of the century. They registered the impact of labor markets and the state as well as of individual women and men struggling to reorder their lives in fluid and uncertain times. Late in the twentieth century, these great domestic transformations crystallized into a new family landscape, a geography of domesticity and inequality that reshaped cities and redefined suburbs.

Growing Up

What defines an adult? Clearly, the answer involves more than biology. By itself, puberty constitutes an important marker—though one whose onset varies with historical circumstances—but is far from sufficient.[16] "The age at which a person becomes an adult," sociologists Elizabeth Fusell and Frank Furstenberg write, "is inherently subjective. It could depend on a person's behavior, their status as a student, worker, spouse, or parent, or their legal status. Adulthood may also be attained through socially recognized rites of passage."[17] Does adulthood begin when young people leave school? When they start to work? Marry? Have their first child? Set up their own households? None of these, by themselves, is a clear index. At least in modern Western societies, the temporal relation of these events to each other, and their cumulative outcome in individual lives, defines adulthood, which is a process of moving from dependence to autonomy, from the status of child to independent householder, rather than an event. It is, moreover, a highly variable and malleable process with its own distinct history.

Most people experience six key events between their late teenage years and early thirties: leaving school, starting work, leaving their parents' home, marrying, setting up an independent household, and having children. These events do not always occur in a neat sequence; they are not universal or unidirectional. Some people move in and out of statuses—back and forth between their parents' homes, for instance, and others follow different routes, never leaving home or marrying, to take another example, or having children and living independently before marriage. Patterns also vary by sex, class, and race, but there is a rough twentieth-century story about these patterns that might be called the historical demography of youth, or the history of the route to personal independence.[18]

The sequencing and relations among life course events define the path away from childhood and toward independence. "By the 1950s and 1960s," Frank Furstenberg and his colleagues write, "most viewed family roles and adult responsibilities as nearly synonymous. For men, having the means to enter marriage and support a family was the gateway to adulthood, while for women, merely entering through the gate—getting married and becoming a parent—conferred adult status."[19] But the late twentieth century witnessed the decoupling of parenthood, independent living, and marriage. Many women and men left home to live on their own or with roommates or a partner. Unmarried women increasingly became mothers, often living alone with their children. The practices varied by race and class, but, to some extent, they could be found among every major group.

This decoupling of marriage from parenthood, Kathryn Edin and Maria Kefalas write, cannot be wholly explained by any of the theories advanced so far by social scientists. "So the reasons remain largely a mystery; perhaps the biggest demographic mystery of the last half of the 20th century." The result shattered the thin boundary between youth and adulthood. For Americans age eighteen and older, a 2002 national survey found, marriage and parenthood no longer defined the border of adulthood. Instead, respondents stressed finishing education, employment, financial independence, and the ability to support a family as the key markers.[20]

In the first half of the twentieth century, young people traveled a long route along the passageway to independence, however its end point was defined. This was true of both blacks and whites.[21] Although they left school as teenagers and started to work, young people either postponed leaving their parents' homes or departed to live with other families before they married. They relied for support on the adult households in which they lived, and these households in turn relied on them for income. After World War II, for two or three decades the length of their journey was compressed. Longer school attendance delayed its onset; relatively quick exits from their parents' homes hastened it; young marriages and independent households brought it to an early close. In this era, young people depended on their parents for longer periods, contributed less to family incomes, and made decisions about the next major stage in their lives—marriage—while they still lived at home, or very shortly thereafter. In neither these years nor in the century's first decades did very many young people, or for that matter anyone else, live alone, separate from parents, without a spouse or partner, nor did any but a very small fraction of women bear children before marriage. By the mid-1970s, this pattern had begun to fray and to differentiate by race and class. Once again, young people delayed their passage to independence. They stayed even longer in school, lived in various kinds of transitional households after they left home, and married later. Most entered the full-time workforce in their twenties, but many remained in school at the same time. These were the first young people who reached relatively autonomous decisions about marriage and the formation of independent households. They nonetheless remained partially dependent on parents for financial and emotional support. A survey found that 34 percent of eighteen- to thirty-four-year-olds received cash help from their parents and 47 percent time help. During these years, the material assistance they received totaled $38,000, or an average of $2,200 per year. Help came from grandparents as well. "For many American families," the *New*

Figure 3.2   Length of Transition to Adulthood

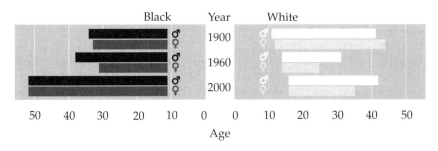

Note: Among white men and women, public policy and labor conditions after World War II encouraged a rapid transition from childhood to adulthood. As these conditions changed later in the century, their transition became more protracted. Blacks neither shared the expansion of opportunities after the war nor the shortening of the transition to adulthood.

These data are based on five conditions: leave school, go to work, leave parent's household, get married, and establish one's own household. A male group's transition begins when ten percent of the group has entered one of these conditions and ends when 90 percent of the group has completed all of these conditions. For women, going to work is not considered in estimating the beginning or end of transition. *Source*: Data from Ruggles et al. (2004).

York Times reported in 2005, "intergenerational help is now moving in a new direction. 'Thirty, 40, years ago, the money went up; you helped your grandparents, you bought them this or that, they might have moved in with you,' said Timothy M. Smeeding, a professor of public policy at the Maxwell School of Syracuse University, 'but now, all the money comes down'" (see figure 3.2).[22]

On the surface, young people appeared to have returned to the long road to independence characteristic of the early twentieth century. The situation was, however, in fact very different. The economic reciprocity between parents and children so common then had given way to a mainly one-way flow of resources, and the years of delayed adult responsibility were much more often passed living alone or with roommates or partners than with parents or other families. A new life stage, Furstenberg and his colleagues argue, had emerged. They call it early adulthood; others, less sympathetic, see it as a phase of indulgent and delayed maturity. A 2002 *Newsweek* story termed it adultolescence. In recent decades "structural and cultural changes," the sociologist Marlis Buchmann writes, have "made youth as a life stage increasingly obsolete, while they have simultaneously extended it indefinitely."[23]

This pattern characterized the experience of whites more than blacks. African American experience became most distinct late in the century when marriage took a radical plunge. By the century's end, most black women gave birth before they married, and most lived on their own. Blacks were pioneering a trend visible in less accentuated form among white women as well—the disconnection of parenthood from marriage.[24]

An initial set of measures highlights the distinct events dominant in each part of the century. The first statistics measure the length of time it took to travel the road from the first to the last event along the way to independence. In 1900, it took thirty years for white men and twenty-five years for white women to travel the road: 10 percent of men had left school, the first event, by age 11; 90 percent did not marry until age forty-one. This span of years, or spread, gradually sunk, reaching its low point for women in 1960 and for men in 1970. For men, the spread had dropped 50 percent and for women 60 percent. What had taken white men thirty years in 1900 took fifteen years in 1970; what had taken women twenty-five years in 1900 took ten years in 1960. The spread then began to increase. By 2000, it was almost as long—twenty-six years for men and seventeen for women, as at the century's start. For most of the century, men took longer to complete the process than women, although the distinction between them fell in the first four decades: in 1940, a year when marriage and family formation still showed the disruptive impact of the Great Depression in the 1930s, women actually took a little longer. But, by the century's end, men's habit of marrying younger women had again stretched out the relative length of their journey.[25]

Another measure shows the overlap among events within the experience of age groups. In mid-century, when white men felt most pressured, as they rushed toward independence, the statuses through which they passed—work and school, for instance—overlapped the most. By the end of the century, with their more leisurely move toward adulthood, the sequencing of these key events once again spread out. In contrast to men, overlap among the events along women's journey increased throughout the century. More than men, women of the same age could be found working, married, or in other circumstances. A third measures reveals that early in the century men and women followed less standardized, more diverse, paths to adulthood than fifty years later, although events in the lives of women were more integrated than in men's. At the century's end, the looser, less standardized journey after the age of sixteen to eighteen—before which rigid age segregation remained nearly universal—started much later than it had in 1900 and proceeded at a slower pace: in 1900, 90 percent of men had left school at the age of nineteen, but 90 percent had not married until age forty-one. At the end of the twentieth century, all the events in the transition started at a later age: 90 percent did not leave school until the age of twenty-nine or thirty, long after they had started to work. Early adulthood was defined for many men and women by the combination of work and school.[26]

These measures describe a sequence that traces a rough arc from diversity to standardization and back again to partial diversity (partial because of the standardization still common before age sixteen or eighteen). This sequence depicts the experience of white, but, only partially, of black Americans. For blacks, it always has taken a relatively long time to experience the events selected here to mark the road to independence. For black men in 1900, it took thirty-three years; in 1950, forty-five years; and in 2000, forty-nine. For black women the span was twenty-seven years in 1900, twenty-two years in 1950, and forty-three years in 2000—vastly longer than for white women. Like white women, black women compressed events most in mid-century, but the change was much less dramatic for blacks than for whites.[27] Spread out over more years, events overlapped less among blacks, and, especially among black women, the integration of events—their sequence within individual lives—became much less distinct. This was because the association between parenthood and marriage began to dissolve.

Throughout the twentieth century, black women had children at younger ages than white women and more of them were born out of wedlock. To take one example, at most points in the century, about twice as many black as white women less than twenty years old had children. Among these young women, many more of the African Americans were not married. Rates of out-of-wedlock birth increased among both white and black women, but the degree of difference among them remained about the same: 6.2 percent of white and 26.7 percent of black women born between 1914 and 1924 gave birth at least once out-of-wedlock compared to 11.1 percent and 46.0 percent born between 1945 and 1954 and 16.2 and 55.8 percent born twenty years later. (Rates of out-of-wedlock birth among Hispanics generally fell between those of whites and blacks.)

Despite higher rates of out-of-wedlock birth, until the late twentieth century, parenthood usually followed marriage for black women. By the century's close, the dissolution of this connection marked a historic change in the African American family and life course. Between 1950 and 2000, for instance, the fraction of black twenty-five-year-old women who had married plunged from 82 percent to 28 percent, but in both years 50 percent had at least one child living at home. Most of these mothers were women living on their own, either household heads or spouses. Marriage had declined sharply among white women as well—from 82 percent to 55 percent of twenty-five-year-olds between 1950 and 2000, but less steeply than among African Americans. And only 35 percent of white women had a child at home—signaling that most of those who remained unmarried also remained childless. Marriage plummeted among black men, too. The proportion of forty-year-old black men ever married dropped from 89 percent to 62 percent between 1950 and 2000.

Figure 3.3   Percentage of Women Aged Twenty-Five to Twenty-Nine Currently Married and with Own Child Present

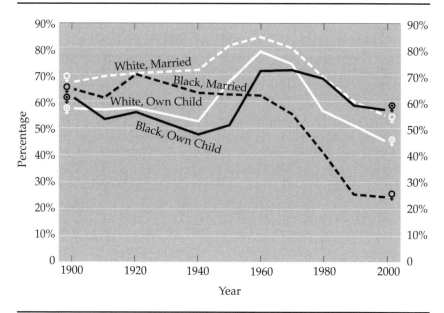

Note: The separation of marriage and childbearing was more complete among black than white women. The proportion of black and white women in their late twenties with a child living at home followed roughly the same path over the century, but the proportion of black women living with a husband declined earlier and more steeply than among white women. As a result, by 2000, nearly 60 percent of African American women in their late twenties lived with at least one child, but only 25 percent lived with a husband. *Source*: Data from Ruggles et al. (2004).

As a result of marrying less and divorcing more often, in 2000, only a minority of black men—34 percent of thirty-five-year-olds—lived with a child (see figure 3.3).

This new family and life course pattern appeared first in the 1960s and accelerated in the 1970s and 1980s.[28] The timing is important because it coincides with trends in inequality and economic stagnation—a point to which we return. The trend did not signify a rejection of marriage. In 2000, by the age of forty, 73 percent of black women had married. Parenthood was preceding marriage, not replacing it. However, young black women may not replicate the relatively high eventual marriage rate of their elders. At age forty, many fewer of them, than of women born earlier in the century, have married.[29] This disconnection of marriage and parenthood does not mean that black women are having more children. Although the fraction married went down, the share with children remained stable. In fact, fertility among blacks is decreasing and is lower than among white women of the same age.

The path to independent adulthood has varied by class as well as race and ethnicity. As a result, among black women, economic differentiation resulted in divided paths to independent adulthood. In 2000, compared to women with only a high school education, more black women with college educations, as shall see, had married and fewer had given birth. Overall, among blacks, whites, and Latinos, late and gradual transitions have remained more common among youth from more affluent families. The disconnection of parenthood and marriage, Kathryn Edin and Maria Kefalas found, appeared more a concomitant of poverty than of race or ethnicity. Furstenberg and his colleagues report, "less educated and less affluent respondents" were "more likely to subscribe to an earlier timetable."[30]

What accounts for differences and changes in the routes women and men have followed on their way to becoming adults? The clue lies in the intersection of the labor market and the state. In the early twentieth century, the wages of children still remained crucial because working-class fathers could not earn enough to support a family adequately. Women (as chapter 2 has shown) left market work when they married. Frequently, they added to family incomes by taking in boarders, growing vegetables, or other kinds of domestic work. But working-age children who remained at home brought in cash, sometimes even made it possible for their parents to accumulate the money to buy a house. In exchange for shelter, food, and the domestic services of their mothers, they turned over most of their wages to their parents. This pattern of reciprocity helped define the era. In any event, youthful wages were too low to marry; independent living was almost unknown; and when they did leave home, young people lived often with other families as boarders, or quasi-family members.

In the first two decades of the twentieth century, as we pointed out in chapter 1, high school entered the lives of most young people. The high school, Robert and Helen Merrill Lynd observed, in their monumental study of a midwestern American city in the 1920s, "has become the hub of the social life of the young of Middletown, and it is not surprising that high school attendance is almost as common today as it was rare a generation ago."[31] As a result, young people stayed at home longer and delayed full-time work. During these years, technological innovation combined with the supply of cheap adult immigrant labor to push young people out of the labor market as a vigorous campaign against child labor undercut the legitimacy of paid work, particularly among young children. For young men, school became an alternative to work and, sometimes, a prerequisite for emerging technical and white-collar occupations. For young women, school became vocational preparation for the exploding number of clerical jobs. This gradual exchange of work for school began to undermine the features defining the early twentieth-century route to independence—a shift reinforced by new psychological theory. Psychologists, most famously G. Stanley Hall in *Adolescence* (1904) redefined youth as adolescence—a sharp, biologically constructed break in the life course rather than a loose passage—and stressed the unique needs of young people in the years following puberty.[32]

By the end of the 1920s, the behavior of young people had changed significantly since the turn of the century. They were staying longer in school, developing a distinctive youth culture, and marrying earlier. Despite the taboo against birth control, they were practicing contraception, and young women were more often in the workforce. The ingredients for a new era in the passage to adulthood were present. Depression and war, however, delayed their combination. In Middletown, marriages declined and the birth rate continued to drop.[33]

After the war, the pace of life course change accelerated, picking up from where it had stalled at the end of the 1920s. Depression and war had postponed marriages and curtailed births. With peace and prosperity and labor in short supply, the wages earned by young men increased. As a percentage of all wages and salaries, they never had been so high. A tight labor market also favored labor unions, supported by the 1935 Wagner Act, which enrolled more workers than at any point in American history and bargained successfully for higher pay and new health and retirement benefits—with, as we showed in chapter 2, enormous consequences for the well-being of working class families. With better pay and prospects and more security, young people married at younger ages than ever before. Not only did birth rates soar, but, with the advent of antibiotics and other medical advances, many more children survived. Fortunately, young couples, assisted by the federal government, could afford to buy houses. Beginning in the Great Depression, federal mortgage guarantees helped extend credit and lower the cost of home ownership. After the war, the GI Bill vastly extended federal home mortgage help to veterans. New suburban housing tracts, reached by federally subsidized roads, increased the supply of inexpensive housing. The trajectory of school attendance, of course, continued to move upward. High school graduation was expected—this era invented the dropout;[34] many more young people went on to college; and transformations in work (chapter 2), which called for increased human capital, tightened the links between schooling and future prosperity. All these influences combined to standardize and compress the sequence of events through which young men and women passed as teenagers and in their early twenties.

The family arrangements and life course that emerged in the years after World War II became American icons. They were the norms against which subsequent change was measured, and found wanting. In fact, the new pattern lasted only for a short span of years—the "leave it to Beaver" family, with working dad and stay at home mom, like the adolescent rushed along a tightly organized route through school to college to work and marriage—defined one of the briefest periods in the history of personal experience. Shaped by a unique confluence of war, prosperity, and a welfare state, it soon began to unravel, partly on account of changed context and partly from its own internal contradictions.

Even at its height, the postwar transition to adulthood contained forces that spelled trouble for some youngsters, proving, incidentally, that many young people deviated from the main path. In 1960, two eminent educators, Robert J. Havighurst and Lindley J. Stiles, observed:

> Forty years ago there were many boys who could not grow up through the school system. But at that time there was a clear alternative road to adulthood—the road to work. A boy could quit school at age 14, 15, or 16 and get work on a farm or in a business. . . . they found work and grew up along that pathway provided by a series of jobs with increasing pay and responsibility. . . . During the past forty years the number of jobs open to juveniles has been decreasing. . . . The employment situation for teen-agers is not likely to improve during the 1960s. . . . Thus there is a strong prospect that the road to adulthood through juvenile work which has been narrowing since 1920 will become even more constricted during the coming decade.[35]

The narrowed path excluded many youngsters, creating a serious problem of youth unemployment that preoccupied observers in the 1950s and 1960s. In 1963, the President's Commission on Youth Employment juxtaposed the vast increase in the number of young people age sixteen to twenty-one with labor market trends. "The kinds of jobs they used to be able to fill are disappearing, and many of the jobs that are available demand much more skill and training than they now can offer." For "hundreds and thousands of boys and girls between 16 and 21," the commission warned, "the problem is immediate and desperate." One of nine out of school and in the labor force was without a job.[36] The "major problem which confronts contemporary youth," the noted psychologist Kenneth Clark advised in 1957, "is not that they will be prematurely exploited by an industrial economy that is insatiable in its demand for manpower, but that they will be excluded from that participation in the economy which is essential for the assumption of independent economic and adult status."[37] For women, the situation proved especially ripe with explosive contradictions. More women went on to college or some other kind of higher education, where they acquired advanced skills. But they still were expected to shelve their skills and leave the workforce when they married. Only when their children were grown was it acceptable, given prevailing ideas, for them to return to work.

After 1973, the high wages and boom economy that had sustained the fragile mid-century era in personal experience with its compressed life-course events, early marriages, single-earner households, and stay-at-home moms collapsed. Declining wages, heightened inequality, poor job prospects, and the increased importance of college education, all these trends (described in chapter 2) encouraged men and women to delay marriage. Rising home prices, and for a time, soaring interest rates, had the same effect while improved contraception—notably the birth control pill—allowed young people to separate sex from marriage as never be-fore. Increasingly embarked on careers, women were in less hurry to marry as were both the men and women flocking in greater numbers to graduate school. The "counter-culture's" emphasis on autonomy added to the influences promoting independence and delaying marriage. Young people followed increasingly diverse paths as they moved more slowly through the events that marked the route away from childhood and adolescence. As never before, they lived on their own, independent of adult influence.

These influences, however, do not account for the steep decline in marriage and the disassociation of marriage and parenthood among blacks. One prominent interpretation stresses the destructive impact of slavery on black families and anchors black family patterns in the pre–Civil War South. The historical record, however, does not support the "legacy of slavery" interpretation of black family experience. Abundant evidence points to an enduring commitment to family; only a miniscule fraction of black mothers living on southern farms never married; and the rate of out-of-wedlock births was not exceptionally high. Even though the number increased from 1910 to 1940, it was still dramatically lower than today. By 1940, black children on southern farms lived much more often with two parents than their counterparts in either southern cities or the North. The prevalence of disrupted families increased 16 percent among southern farm children and 43 percent in the North. Throughout the whole century, the percentage of black children in two-parent families was higher among those with southern than with north-ern origins.[38] The reasons for the decline of marriage and the rise in out-of-wedlock births among blacks lay in northern cities, not the South.

The history of African Americans' passage to adult independence re-flected America's durable racial inequality. Extreme poverty—the prod-uct of farm labor in the South, exclusion from better-paying jobs in the North, and exploitation everywhere—necessitated sharing income and forced children as well as married women into market work. It took black men a long time—longer by and large than it took white men—to earn enough to marry and set up a household. As a result, early in the twentieth century, the age spread between black spouses was greater than between whites. The influences that compressed the events in white youth's experience into a narrower age band did not operate with anything like the same force for blacks. Red-lining, introduced by the federal government in the 1930s, prevented many of them from buying property by denying them mortgages in black neighborhoods. Government-sanctioned segregation denied equal education to blacks throughout the South, even after the Brown v. Board of Education decision declared segregation unconstitutional in 1954. The GI bill discriminated in subtle ways against blacks, who did not benefit nearly as much as whites from its largesse.[39] Labor unions often excluded or marginalized blacks. With incomes low and uncertain, property acquisition blocked, and less education, black income did not rise nearly as much as white, and young men still took a relatively long time to earn enough to begin a family.

Widespread poverty also jostled life's events, preventing the neater sequencing more common among whites. In the century's last decades, as black economic experience bifurcated, many gained the resources to follow the same path as young white men and women. Key events in the lives of black men and women, however, often lacked a clear sequence. The exclusion of black men from the labor force and the high rate of incarceration among them held back the formation of families and households, leaving black women increasingly unmarried, with a passage to adult independence centered around single motherhood. With motherhood the measure, black women reached adulthood early, following a road along which statuses (child, parent, student, worker, householder) overlapped and neat sequencing was impossible. In this way, the history of the life course refracted America's most durable inequality.

Growing Old

Like the route to adult independence, the road followed during life's latter years passed from diversity to standardization and back again to diversity. It, too, was shaped by powerful social and economic changes and by the institutions of the labor market and the state. Early in the twentieth century, men and women lived out their old age very much as they had for at least a hundred years. At work, they used a variety of strategies to hold on to their jobs even as their physical capacities declined. At home, overwhelmingly poor, the elderly, as we described in chapter 1, lived with their children. During the twentieth century, two revolutions interrupted these long-standing patterns. First, the retirement revolution, a product of both actions by employers and government, pushed the vast majority of them out of the workforce within a very few years. Second, in the 1960s and 1970s a rising "retirement wage" reduced poverty among the elderly and allowed them, more than ever before, to live alone (see photographs 3.1 and 3.2).

This history of aging reveals a sharp disjunction in the experience of

Photograph 3.1   Depression Hard on Elderly, 1930s

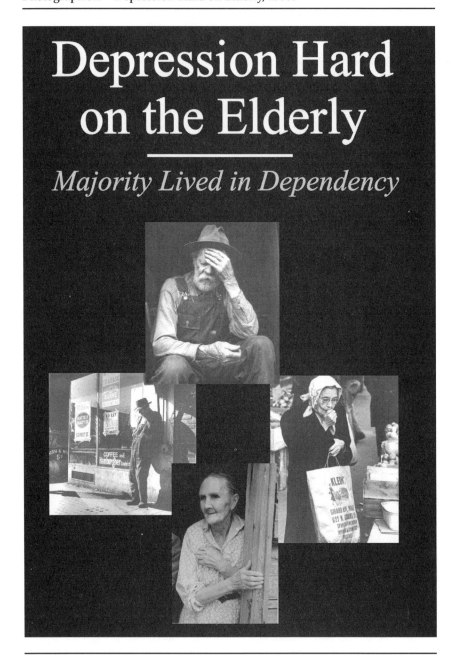

Depression Hard on the Elderly

Majority Lived in Dependency

Before Social Security, the incomes of most elderly Americans remained below the poverty line. *Source:* U.S. Social Security Administration.

Photograph 3.2   Two Senior Citizen Couples Planning Trip, 2002

By late twentieth century, the elderly had a poverty rate lower than the rest of the population. Many enjoyed historically unprecedented prosperity. *Source:* © Jim Craigmyle/CORBIS.

the elderly. In the first third of the century, public policy did not address age-old patterns that left the elderly mostly poor and dependent on their children. The various choices they made—or were forced by circumstances to make—about work and where to live resulted in lives at once diverse and economically impoverished. In the century's middle third, concerns with productivity focused on moving the elderly out of the workforce through the invention of retirement, but the minimal benefits of public and private pensions did not begin to adequately meet their economic needs. In these years, with sixty-five inscribed as the retirement age, old age was defined, increasingly, by the institutions of the labor market and the state. Between the 1960s and the 1990s, unionized workers' concerns with retirement combined with the politically potent force of the elderly to transform old age for many into a new life stage signified by the "empty nest." In these years, the incomes of the elderly became more equal. As government forced the end of mandatory retirement, the elderly faced a variety of options for work and residence. As with women and men moving along the passage to independent adulthood, the experience of the elderly became less standardized, more diverse. Part of that diversity was economic. In the 1990s, the trend toward income inequality also registered among the elderly leading, increasingly, to their economic differentiation. With the retirement of the baby boom looming, the possibility of a new, far less economically equal or adequate, era in the history of the elderly seemed a real possibility.[40]

The history of aging unfolded against the backdrop of a growing elderly population. In 1880, only 12 percent of Americans were over the age of fifty; by 1960 the proportion had nearly doubled to 23 percent. The advent of the baby boom stalled the aging of the population, which resumed in the 1990s as the oldest baby boomers moved into their fifties. By 2000, 28 percent of the population was older than fifty. Both the economic cost of an aging population—and its voting power—introduced a new dynamic, including an undercurrent of generational conflict, into American politics.[41] The elderly became a powerful interest group, active agents in the promotion of public policies that served their well-being.

In the early twentieth century, two patterns dominated the experience of the elderly. First was their slow and uneven transition out of the workforce. In 1910, fewer than 10 percent of men in their late fifties had left the labor force. Among men in their early sixties, the fraction inched up about 3 percent a year until men were in their early eighties. About 70 percent of men in their eighties no longer worked. At no age did men rush out of the workforce in large numbers. The length of time between the exit of 20 percent and 80 percent of the population from the labor force was quite long—eighteen years. Neither class nor ethnicity influenced the timing very much, although blacks tended to remain in the labor force a bit longer—a reflection of their poverty and concentration in the South as tenant farmers. Older workers, however, sometimes did adapt to declining ability by moving to less demanding occupations. Many, for instance, appear to have become watchmen as they aged (see figure 3.4).[42]

Poverty prevented most of the elderly from maintaining their own households in 1940.[43] Typically, they lived with one of their children. High birth rates sustained this practice because couples in their fifties and sixties often had young children and teenagers still at home, and many more women than today were widows who needed the support of adult children. Older women, in fact, lived with children more often than older men. Fewer than half of men in their sixties lived with children, and the figure fell to about a third of men in their seventies, where it stabilized. By contrast, the majority of older women—roughly seven of ten in their late seventies—lived with a child during the later part of their lives. Although by the early twentieth century poorhouses largely had become public old age homes, only a small percentage of the elderly—much more often men—lived in them, or in the private old-age homes that charitable groups set up primarily for widows. In 1919, the *Report of*

Figure 3.4   Percentage of Men over Fifty Not in Labor Force, by Year and Age, 1910 to 2000

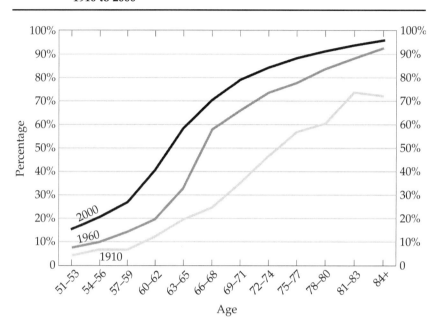

Note: Early in the century, the proportion of men not in the labor force rose steadily among men between the ages of fifty-five and seventy-five, suggesting that there was no clear retirement age. By 1960, Social Security and mandatory retirement led roughly 40 percent of men to retire between the ages of sixty and sixty-six. By 2000, retirement had become more varied with a quarter of men in their late fifties having already left the labor force and more than 10 percent waiting until after the age of seventy-five. *Source*: Data from Ruggles et al. (2004).

the Pennsylvania Commission on Old Age Pensions pointed out that children and relatives would:

> make greater sacrifices . . . to keep an aged mother at home and prevent her going to a poorhouse, than they would for an aged father or other male relative. Aside from the sentimental reasons involved, the presence of an old woman around the house—unless she is absolutely invalided—entails little burden, as she can be made useful in numerous ways. This, however, is not the case with an aged man.[44]

The family living arrangements of the elderly took one of two quite different forms. Either the elderly remained heads of their own households with children living at home, or they moved in with their older children. For the most part, older couples remained household heads and the widowed moved in with a child or other relative. Owning a home—far more common among the elderly—also helped the elderly remain household heads. Indeed, the share of property owners among household heads increased steadily with age, reaching nearly 90 percent of men in their eighties.[45]

In the years between 1900 and the Great Depression, not very much changed in the way the elderly managed their work and family lives. But all around them pressures for change were building. Medical science, for one, was pathologizing old age as a disease. Physicians, the historian Carole Haber writes, "warned the elderly that their normal physiological condition had now become one of disease. Although the individual might appear to be in perfect health, old age alone signified disability." Increasingly, by the early twentieth century, the historian Andrew Achenbaum notes, "observers described [the elderly] as ugly and disease ridden." Sir William Osler, physician-in-chief at Johns Hopkins University Hospital, highlighted the problem of the unproductive older worker, "the uselessness of men above sixty years of age, and the incalculable benefit it would be in commercial, political, and professional life if, as a matter of course, men stopped work at this age." Osler's theme resonated with both employers and progressive-era labor economists seeking to rationalize a labor market characterized by high turnover, decentralized hiring practices, nepotism, and the lack of uniform practices.[46] Older workers, they argued, could not keep up with the pace of modern industry; they retarded production and caused safety hazards.

In the 1920s, the Lynds found that Middletown's employers by and large wanted younger workers. The head of a machine shop commented, "I think there's less opportunity for older men in industry now than there used to be. . . . we find that when a man reaches fifty he is slipping down in production." In another shop, the personnel manager observed, "in production work forty to forty-five is the age limit because of the speed needed in the work. Men over forty are hired as sweepers and for similar jobs." The manager of a large plant with three-quarters of the workers under forty-five explained: "We try to find a place for these older men even when they are as old as fifty-five if there is no danger in their working near machinery." In another major plant the superintendent was blunt: "The age dead line is creeping down on these men—I'd say that by forty-five they are through." Not surprisingly, workers and their families dreaded old age. One forty-year-old laborer said, "Whenever you get old they are done with you." Another, fifty-one years old, often wondered "what he'll do when he gets a little older. He hopes and prays they'll get the State old-age pension through pretty soon." A forty-year-old pattern maker realized that "in about ten years now will be on the shelf. . . . What will we do? Well, that is just what I don't know."[47]

Everywhere, old workers appeared obsolete, a threat to the entire economy. At the same time, social insurance advocates, pointing to the example of Europe, documented the hardships the elderly faced and lobbied for public old age pensions. But in the years before the New Deal the pension plans enacted by most states made little difference in the lives of the elderly. California's plan, for example, one of the more generous, offered a maximum benefit of $23 a month only after a worker had reached age seventy and met a variety of stringent tests. Public pensions met with little support from labor unions, which remained for the most part wedded to privately negotiated retirement plans. Instead of negotiating pensions, however, a number of large employers turned to "welfare capitalism," which, at its height, failed to offer any significant form of retirement support. Workers did have a few private alternatives—fraternal organizations, life insurance, and savings banks.[48] These, however, all called for personal savings, which, given low wages, was often impossible.

The economic crisis occasioned by the Great Depression struck the elderly with special ferocity. Savings banks failed, welfare capitalism collapsed, city and state governments ran out of money, work was unavailable. Labor unions abandoned their commitment to voluntarism; economists' arguments for clearing the elderly from the workforce made increased sense; and the elderly, a potent political force, mobilized. When he took office, President Franklin Delano Roosevelt confronted not only the immiseration of the elderly but radical political movements—the Townsend Movement, which proposed a flat monthly pension for the elderly, and the Lundeen Bill, which advocated greatly increased income supports—that were rapidly gaining adherents. Aside from increasing direct relief, he responded by creating a Committee on Economic Security, whose report influenced the passage of the Social Security Act of 1935. This legislation introduced two new supports for the elderly: an immediate system of federal-state public assistance called Old Age Assistance, which remained the predominant form of federal "welfare" until the mid-1950s, when it was surpassed by Aid to Dependent Children, and Social Security, which did not pay benefits until 1940. Social Security was a cautious, limited response, which institutionalized age sixty-five as the normal age for leaving the workforce. Exit from the labor force, in fact, became a "retirement test," a condition for receiving Social Security. Initially, as the price of southern congressional support, Social Security excluded domestic and agricultural workers—hence, most African Americans and many women; it did not cover surviving spouses; and it paid very modest benefits.[49] Over time, incremental reforms removed these limitations. At its start, Social Security began to influence the age at which men left the workforce but not where they lived.

In 1940, when Social Security paid its first benefits, the way in which men left the workforce had not changed very much since early in the century. During the Great Depression, the share of men leaving the workforce in their fifties—almost certainly not voluntarily—was double the 1910 fraction. Nonetheless, after the first 20 percent had withdrawn, eighteen years passed before the next 60 percent had exited. Under the influence of Social Security, retirement spread dramatically during the next twenty years. By 1960, forty percent of men were leaving the workforce between the ages of sixty and sixty-six. Uniform retirement peaked in the 1960s and 1970s—a pattern of slow exit before age sixty followed by a rapid exit in the next decade and the slow withdrawal of remaining workers after the age of seventy. As women's share of the labor force increased, their exit from the labor force also followed a clear pattern with retirement concentrated in a short span of years. With the spread of mandatory retirement, employers reinforced the institutionalization of the years around sixty-five as the normal age for leaving the workforce. Between 1920 and 1970, as a result, the number of years required for the central 60 percent of men to leave the labor force dropped from sixteen to eleven.

Social Security, however, did not have an immediate impact on where the elderly lived. This is because its low initial benefits did not guarantee an income adequate for independent living. As a result, they continued to live often with children or other relatives. One change in living arrangements did emerge from the small families of the depression and war years, however. Couples entering old age in the 1950s had fewer children than earlier cohorts and found themselves alone at much younger ages. The result was a new phenomenon—the empty nest—that began to appear in the postwar years. But it was still a transitional empty nest most common in the years immediately before and after retirement. As white couples entered their late sixties and early seventies, the number of empty nest households went down while the fraction of the elderly living with their children increased. By the time whites had reached their eighties, 40 percent of women and a third of men were living again with children. Black men and women did not experience this empty nest as often as whites. With higher fertility, they had more children at home. Social Security also influenced them less because, concentrated in farm work and domestic service, more of them remained excluded from benefits.

The expansion of Social Security benefits helped engineer a revolution in the living arrangements of the elderly. The first expansion occurred in 1939 with amendments that added insurance for survivors and shifted Social Security from a system financed for the most part through reserves to one based on current contributions. Social Security now protected families as well as individuals—protection for the two parent family had become the center of policy. Another major benefit expansion took place in 1950. Disability Insurance was added in 1956; and benefits were expanded four times between 1968 and 1972. In 1972, they were indexed to protect against inflation. The formulas used to expand benefits deliberately tilted them toward low income workers. In the 1970s, low income workers could expect to receive benefits equal to 90 percent of their average indexed monthly earnings—the index used to calculate benefits. Higher income workers' benefits rose only about 15 cents for each additional dollar in their indexed earnings. Social Security had become a tool for modest income redistribution as well as a means of assuring adequate income support for the elderly. In 1965, Medicare brought national health insurance to the elderly, a benefit hard to quantify on an individual basis but one that worked a transformation in experience and also reduced inequalities.

The expansion of Social Security benefits dramatically and quickly reduced poverty among the elderly to levels inconceivable earlier in the century. By 1999, poverty among the elderly had plunged to 10 percent.[50] At the same time, their range of residential choices widened, and, by the century's end, among most of the elderly the empty nest had become permanent. The change was revolutionary. In 1900, only a little more than one of four married couples over the age of fifty lived without children; by 2000, that number had leaped to nearly three of four. (The fraction had reached half around mid-century.) In their early sixties, more than 70 percent of men and women lived alone or with a spouse—a fraction that did not change very much among those in their eighties. When widowed, women were more likely than men to live with their children—in 2000, about 15 percent of women over eighty-four—double the share of men—lived with children. Compared to earlier generations, these numbers were very low. A great many more of the elderly lived by themselves. The number of persons over sixty-five living alone more than doubled from 14 percent in 1900 to 33 percent in 2000 (42 percent among women).[51] Even with increases in Social Security, elderly people living alone often remained in or near poverty, isolated and vulnerable in times of crisis, as their death rate in Chicago's great heat wave of the 1990s underlined with appalling detail (see figure 3.5).[52]

Unwilling or unable to live with children, a modest but growing share of the elderly turned to institutions. For most of the century, the share of the elderly in institutions—mainly old age homes of one sort or another—hovered around 2 or 3 percent. In 1950, among women over the age of eighty-four, it had increased to 10 percent and in 2000 to 25 percent. The jump in the fraction of older women living in institutions highlighted an important trend. A substantial, but indeterminate, share of the

Figure 3.5   Household Status, Persons over the Age of Fifty, 1900 to 2000

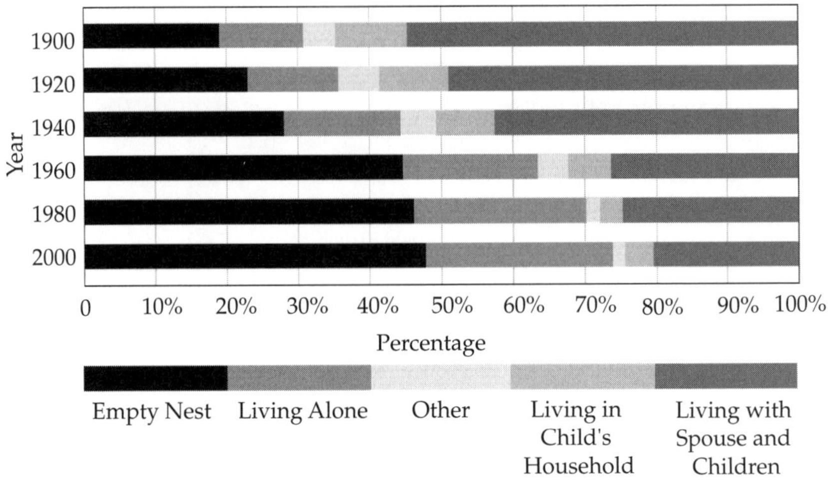

Note: Early in the twentieth century, most older Americans lived with their children. By the end of the century, most older Americans lived in empty-nest households or alone. *Source*: Data from Ruggles et al. (2004).

elderly moved into retirement communities—developments of single-family homes restricted to senior citizens or continuing care or assisted-living facilities—as well as nursing homes. Medicaid—the income-tested public health insurance program—covered most of the 1.5 million seniors living in nursing homes in 2004, but the expansion of other residential options resulted from the elderly's new economic status. Between 1998 and 2001, the number of assisted living facilities increased 48 percent. In 2004, nine hundred and ten thousand seniors lived in thirty-six thousand assisted-living facilities and six hundred thousand lived in twenty-one hundred continuing care communities.[53]

The ability of so many to afford expensive options reflected both the increase in Social Security benefits as well as post–World War II pensions and the great rise in the value of the homes now owned by most elderly Americans. Earlier in the century—with children more likely to take in their mothers than their fathers—most of the elderly in old-age homes were men. By the century's end, with women living much longer than men and widowhood the main spur to institutional living, most of the residents of nursing homes and assisted-living facilities were women. The feminization of old-age homes is one of the major institutional stories of the twentieth century. Together, independent living and, later, increased reliance on institutions among the very old, signified a revolution in the experience of the elderly.

As with young people, the 1950s and 1960s composed the most uniform moment in the social history of aging. As never before or since, strict public and private retirement tests channeled them into a retirement officially bounded by age and supported in part by Social Security and expanded pensions won for the most fortunate workers by labor unions. By the late 1970s, nearly half of workers were covered by private pensions. With advances in longevity and health care, however, mandatory retirement began to appear irrational, and older workers worried about the age discrimination they experienced themselves or saw around them. Old age discrimination became a civil rights issue, unacceptable in light of the rejection of discrimination against minorities and women. Slowing the move of workers out of the workforce, moreover, promised to relieve burdens on public pension systems. Encouraging workers to remain longer in the workforce appeared sound as well as humane policy. Congress acted by progressively banning mandatory retirement and by changing requirements for Social Security benefits. The 1967 Age Discrimination in Employment Act (ADEA) outlawed discrimination against workers between the ages of forty-five and sixty-five. In 1978, Congress raised the retirement age to seventy, and, in 1986, unanimously amended the act to ban compulsory retirement, except in colleges and universities, where the ban was postponed for seven years. Many states already had outlawed compulsory retirement.[54] At the hearings on the amendment before a House Select Committee on Aging, witnesses underscored the dissolution of chronological age as an accepted marker of old age. Their testimony accentuated the diversity increasingly characteristic of the years after sixty-five. Dr. T. Franklin Williams, director of the National Institute on Aging, pointed out the absence of "convincing evidence to support a specific age for mandatory retirement. Rather, each person, each situation should be considered on its own merits."[55]

Changes to Social Security gave workers incentives to stay employed. In 1983, Congress raised the retirement age—the age for full Social Security benefits—to sixty-seven, and in March 2000, unanimously lifted the retirement test on the earnings of Social Security recipients. Women and men now could collect full Social Security benefits while working and, by delaying Social Security to age seventy, could substantially increase their monthly checks. Kenneth S. Apfel, commissioner of Social Security, explained:

> Beneficiaries who are 65 years young should be allowed to contribute their energy, talent, and experience to the workplace without being penalized for doing so. . . . The earnings test is counterproductive in an economy in which employers want and need the skills and talents of older workers. . . .

It is an outdated policy that discourages healthy seniors from continuing to work past age 65 if they choose to do so.[56]

That, of course, was precisely its original purpose. Like the boundary to adulthood, the gate to old age had crumbled.

As the idea of an official retirement age dissolved, the compressed transition of women and men out of the workforce ended. In 2000, the central 60 percent of the workforce took fifteen years to move into retirement. This was a span of years almost as long as the sixteen-year transition in 1910 and 1920 and much longer than the eleven-year span of a few decades earlier. Rigidly institutionalized retirement had given way to a diverse and individualized process of leaving the workforce. Diversity also characterized the economic condition of the elderly. Traditional defined benefit pensions increasingly had been replaced by defined contribution schemes, under which employees made their own investment decisions.[57] With 60 percent of the elderly population reporting some income from pensions or private retirement accounts in 2000, this shift impacted the well-being of millions. Some did much less well than others. The result was a new economic inequality among senior citizens.

The 1990s wiped out thirty years of movement toward income equality among the elderly. Women and men without private pensions did worst of all. About 25 percent of the elderly relied on Social Security and other government programs for their primary support. They concentrated in central cities and were disproportionately black and Latino. They were also the poorest retirees. The majority of the elderly in the bottom forty income percentiles depended solely on Social Security; the richest relied mostly on investment income. In 2000, the top 10 percent accounted for 44 percent of all income, a 13-percent rise in one decade and the most unequal distribution since 1960. (These figures omit the rising cost of prescription drugs and other medical care, which have proved crippling to the less well-off elderly.) Nothing on the horizon of the labor market or state, including the federal prescription drug benefit scheduled for 2006, promised to reverse this new inequality. Trends, in fact, moved in precisely the opposite direction. A slack labor market, stagnant wages, demographic pressure from an aging population, and declining union density all worked against economic equality among the elderly, as well as among everyone else. With pension coverage in retreat, and many people employed in temporary or contingent work lacking benefits, more workers could expect to enter old age without significant private retirement funds. President George W. Bush and his allies threatened to exacerbate the problem and heighten inequality by partially privatizing Social Security through individual retirement accounts, which would intensify risks and, almost certainly, lower benefits for the least well-off workers.⁵⁸ Inequality and diversity promised to characterize the experience of the elderly for the indefinite future.

Defining Family

Huge changes in the way Americans grew up and old transformed the families in which they lived. Like the life course, families traversed a sequence from diversity to standardization and back again to diversity—a sequence also powerfully impacted by the institutions of the labor market and the state and by the nation's durable inequalities.⁵⁹

In the twentieth century, four trends interacted to produce the changing configuration of families. The first and third, as we have seen, already were in motion at the start of the twentieth century; the others began later. They were, first, the drop in the number of children born to married couples; second, the decline in marriage and its partial disconnection from parenthood; third, the lessened co-residence of the elderly with their children and of others—relatives and boarders—with families; and, fourth, the increased number of unmarried adults living together, that is, of nonfamily households.

Nothing is more intimate than decisions about how many children to have and when to have them. They are intensely personal, bound up with love, sexuality, and primordial pulls of parenthood. Yet, most married couples living in the same time and place make them in remarkably similar ways, and the shifting historic patterns that result show they are malleable, subject to widely shared hopes and fears, buffeted by the same forces that have shaped and reshaped growing up and growing old. In the twentieth century, the product of these decisions—what demographers call marital fertility—followed an arc similar to youth and old age, moving from a diverse to a more standardized and back to a more diverse pattern. These decisions about family size were, in fact, both shaped by, and shapers of, the life course, expressing America's durable inequalities in intimate ways, yet not wholly reducible to market and state.

The number of children born to married couples plummeted during the twentieth century. For a social change of such enormous importance it happened with remarkable speed.⁶⁰ The decline, as chapter 1 noted, began in the later nineteenth century. Between 1880 and 1900, the fertility rate went down from 925 to 800. Then, by 1940, it tumbled to 456 before reviving to 644 in 1960—the baby boom years—and falling back to 382 at the century's end. This drop in marital fertility meant that the size of families was going down. In 1900, six of ten households where the mother was forty to forty-nine years old had three or more children at home. In 2000, the number was less than one in five. Families not only limited the number of their children but changed when during their lives they were born. Early in the century, couples tended to spread their children out through the mother's twenties and thirties. By the middle of the century, reflecting young people's compressed, accelerated life course, the number of children born to families peaked when parents were in their twenties and then dropped rapidly when they were in their thirties. After 1970, this pattern reversed: births to married women in their twenties went down—more than in the first seventy years of the century—and to women in their thirties climbed sharply. Indeed, women born in the 1950s, 1960s, and 1970s all had rather low marital fertility in their twenties but historically high rates in their thirties. Very young women, teenagers who married, also had more children in 2000 than in earlier decades. Diversity had become the hallmark of fertility, with some very young women choosing to start families and other women deciding to delay marriage and childbirth while they went to school and worked (see figure 3.6).

Inequality registered on family decisions through both gender and class. Before married women's massive entry into the labor force, class influenced fertility decisions directly through the occupations of husbands. Families with fathers who worked as professionals, managers, clerks, or service workers lowered their fertility more than manual workers or farmers—a pattern observed and discussed in chapter 2. This pattern lasted through the 1940s; the fertility of farmers and laborers remained 20 percent higher than that of white-collar workers and professionals. With the standardization of family experience and the life course in the years after World War II, these sharp divisions diminished; measured by husbands' occupations, fertility decisions became more alike.

As women entered the labor force, however, their aspirations became a new source of differentiation in childbearing, reflected in the varied experiences of women with an eighth-grade education from those with at least some college—a rough proxy for class. Everywhere in the world, in fact, increased education for women appears the surest route to reducing fertility.[61] In 1940, the fertility of the best-educated women was about 75 percent below the average, and that of the least educated 14 percent above it. These differences shrunk with the standardization common to the baby boom era but reappeared again after 1970. In the last three decades of the century, married college-educated women's fertility was 92 to 94 percent of the average and that of women with an eighth-grade education or less was 120 percent. Among unmarried women, differences by education were most striking of all. In 2000, for instance, the fertility of unmarried black women with a high school diploma was 231 compared to 91 for those with a college education; for Hispanic women the same rates were 172 and 58. Similar differences separated white and Asian women with high school and college educations. For the most

**Figure 3.6   Age-Specific Fertility Ratios for Women Aged Fifteen to
Forty-Nine, 1880 to 2000**

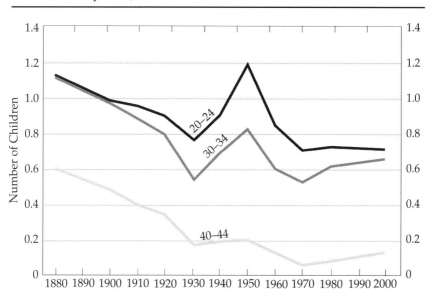

Note: As couples began to control their fertility, the most striking change was
the rapid decline in the fertility of women in their thirties and forties, a decline
interrupted briefly by the baby boom. After 1960, however, the fertility of
women in their twenties declined steeply, while that of women in their early
thirties began to rise after 1980. By the end of the century, women in their
twenties were having fewer children than at any time in American history, but
women in their thirties had fertility ratios comparable to those of the pre–World
War II generation. (Fertility ratio is number of children, 0–4, per 1,000 married
women.) *Source*: Data from Ruggles et al. (2004).

part, with education controlled, the similarities rather than the differences among groups stand out. With fertility, as with earnings, reported
in chapter 2, by the end of the twentieth century, education trumped
race. In family as well as income, a college education had become the
prime agent dividing the experience of women.

America's durable inequalities registered most visibly in the history
of out-of-wedlock births. The stark numbers underline the growing disconnection of parenthood from marriage evident, as well, in measures
that describe routes to adult independence. The first point to emphasize
is that the rise in out-of-wedlock births did not signal an "epidemic of
teenage pregnancy," as alarmists in the 1980s claimed. Teen pregnancy
has not varied a great deal in past decades; recently it has been going

down. What has risen, though, is the proportion of children born outside of marriage. Many fewer of those children, however, are born to teenagers. In 1970, 50.1 percent of out-of-wedlock births were to women less than twenty years old. By 2001, that number had dropped almost by half to 26.6 percent as the share born to women age twenty-five and older had nearly doubled from 18.1 percent to 35.2 percent. Along with improved contraception, this increase in the age of mothers suggests that for many unmarried women parenthood has become a choice, not an accident.[62]

Overall, the fraction of births to unmarried women more than tripled from 10.7 percent in 1970 to 33.5 percent in 2001. This sharp rise varied by race. Out-of-wedlock births spiked most sharply among whites at 404 percent. They rose, too, among blacks by 82 percent and, since 1980, among Hispanics by 80 percent. For blacks, the 1970s was a decade of catalytic growth in the proportion of children born out of wedlock, though the fraction kept rising until it peaked in 1995. Among whites, both the 1970s and the 1980s proved years of great change, with the percentage of births to unmarried white women reaching its highest point, 27.7 percent, in 2001—compared to 68.4 percent for black and 42.5 percent for Hispanic births. Among black women, out-of-wedlock birth had become the norm.

In part, the rise in out-of-wedlock births reflected the hard economic times that made marriage more difficult after the early 1970s, including, for blacks, joblessness and incarceration and for whites, declining real wages. But, clearly, something else also was at work. The Great Depression, a period with much worse unemployment, even less of a safety net, and much less reliable contraception, did not witness anything like the increase in out-of-wedlock births of the late twentieth century, even though women and men delayed marriage. Rather, the increase—and especially the rising share of older women among unmarried mothers—signified an emergent new definition of family and marriage. A 1955 Frank Sinatra song claimed, "love and marriage go together like a horse and carriage. . . . you can't have one without the other." By the end of the twentieth century, the sentiment was as obsolete as the horse and buggy.

For the young women Edin and Kefalas interviewed, parenthood was a necessity—childlessness was unthinkable and selfish—and marriage was a desirable goal that followed the advent of a stable relationship and economic security. Stable relationships, however, remained elusive because of the pervasive domestic violence, infidelity, alcoholism, drug abuse, and incarceration among men. These young women exuded confidence in their capacity to be good mothers and support their children economically. They did not feel that motherhood imposed impossible economic or personal demands, and children gave meaning, satisfaction, and order to their lives.[63]

This disconnection between parenthood and marriage underlines the relative autonomy of intimate personal decisions from public policy. Early in the twentieth century, state laws criminalized contraception; the federal government banned the sending of contraceptive information through the mail; and, as chapter 1 pointed out, cultural authorities—worried about "race suicide" among educated, middle-class whites—inveighed against birth control.[64] Yet births to married couples plummeted as husbands and wives made decisions about the size of their families. In the late twentieth and early twenty-first centuries, public policies attempted to promote marriage. Cultural critics joined by some social scientists decried the allegedly damaging effects of single-parenthood on children. Yet, the separation of marriage from parenthood did not slacken. Instead, it picked up steam, especially among U.S.-born white women.

Early in the century, families had balanced protective and anticipatory strategies, at once looking backward to a world they knew and forward to one emerging. Middle-class families tilted toward anticipatory and working-class toward protective strategies that emphasized large numbers of children as sources of modest capital accumulation and support in old age. By mid-century, declining economic inequality, rising wages, and a new national consumer culture encouraged a melding of class aspirations and behavior—a focus on anticipatory strategies reflected in smaller family sizes and investments in children. Like the life course itself, across the nation, the intimate decisions of wives and husbands grew more similar. In tandem with the history of the life course as well, after the 1970s, they again grew more apart. Women stayed in school longer and began careers; some women and men grew concerned about the high cost of raising children and found it more and more difficult to earn enough to sustain an independent family. As a result, they increasingly delayed marriage and did not begin to have children until in their thirties. Others chose radically different routes: the minority who married in their teen years had more children earlier than ever before. A new version of the protective strategy emerged in the small but increasing number of couples remaining voluntarily childless—protective because childlessness now involved the least risks, rather than as early in the century, the most. In 2000, about 18 percent of women age forty to forty-four had never given birth—an 80-percent increase since 1976.[65] Most couples, however, wanted children and chose the anticipatory strategy, focusing resources on a small number of children in the hope of giving them the education necessary for economic success in an era when human capital made all the difference.

The lineaments of the anticipatory strategy, which emerged ever more clearly over time, included not only smaller families and prolonged schooling but, as well, stripping away the household extensions—relatives and boarders—common in earlier times. Households became much smaller. Average household size for whites went down from 4.6 in 1900 to 3.3 in 1960 and 2.4 in 2000. Black household size, which followed the same trends, was just a little larger. Patterns were similar for Latinos, too, though they had larger households at each point in time (3.1 in 2000). In part, smaller households reflected the decline in the number of children born to married couples. It also reflected the departure of others who augmented households in earlier times. Aging parents, as the discussion of the life course showed, were among the groups whose departure reduced household size. Their exit, which depended on adequate public pensions, occurred primarily after World War II. The fraction of white households with a parent of the householder or spouse present dropped from 6 percent in 1900 to 5 percent in 1960 and 2 percent in 2000. The trend among black households was almost identical. Latinos, by contrast, always housed more of their parents, though the share in 2000, 4 percent, was still quite small. Asian families were the most likely in 2000 to include an aging parent. The share of households with boarders, other relatives, and servants also all went down sharply. In 1900, 33 percent of white, 35 percent of black, and 50 percent of Latino households included someone not related to the family (a boarder or servant, for the most part). By mid-century these numbers had been more than halved and remained more or less the same through the end of the century, except that the difference between whites and blacks had widened.[66] About one of four black households, a larger fraction than among whites or Latinos, included grandchildren—about 9 or 10 percent throughout the century. Nonetheless, all ethnic groups shared the trend toward stripped down families.

The anticipatory strategy called for keeping children in school longer—a decision that reduced the number of family incomes. With one wage insufficient to support a family—increasingly the situation after the 1970s—women, as noted in chapter 1, took up the slack. Family economies switched from depending on children to depending on wives to supplement men's wages. The fraction of white families with a working child at home dropped from 36 percent in 1900 to 12 percent in 1960, where it remained. The trajectory was similar among black and Latino families, though more Latino, nearly one of five, included a working child in 2000. (This was a slight increase from 1990 signaling, perhaps, economic strain.) The share of families with an employed wife, of course, went in just the opposite direction—for whites, from 2 percent in 1900 to 30 percent in 1960 and 52 percent in 2000. With more married black women always employed, the jump in the African American percentage—from 21 percent in 1900 to 61 percent in 2000—was less dramatic, roughly three times compared to fifteen times among whites. The 25 percent of Latino wives who worked in 1960 increased to nearly 65 percent by the century's end. Among all groups, the contribution of wives to family income increased sharply as the importance of children's earnings plummeted. In 1940, the small share of family earnings supplied by wives in young families dwindled to insignificance as contributions from children increased. In 2000, children's contributions at their height were only 2 percent.

The twentieth century began with families living in large households which often included boarders, servants, aged parents, and other relatives. They were supported by the wages of men and of children from their mid-teenage years through their early or mid-twenties; women supplemented family incomes by looking after boarders, tending gardens, or through other kinds of domestic work. The century ended with vastly smaller families—couples with fewer children—who lived for the most part by themselves. Children generally stayed in school through age eighteen if they did not go to college, much longer if they did. When they left school, they made only minor contributions to their family's economy and, often, took money from it instead. Frequently, they left home as well. With men's wages declining, families survived only because of the earnings of women. Two adult earners composed the hallmark of stripped-down families as they faced the new century. With jobs insecure, benefits eroding, and the expense of higher education increasing, whatever prosperity they managed was fragile and their future security remained uncertain.

Most precarious were single-parent families—for the most part, women living alone with their children (see photograph 3.3). In 1939, 59 percent of female-headed households were poor. Contrary to common impressions, the share of households headed by women remained remarkably stable throughout the century. The fraction of women householders not married or living with a husband was 28 percent in 1900, 29 percent in 1950, and 30 percent in 2000. For white women the fraction hovered between 24 percent and 25 percent. For black women it increased from 38 percent to 46 percent during the century, with most of the increase after 1960. What changed most were the reasons women lived alone with their children. Early in the twentieth century, they were mainly—80 percent—widows.[67] In fact, two-thirds of them still were widows at mid-century when only 12 percent were divorced and 2 percent unmarried. By the century's end, all this had changed. Only one of five was a widow, more than three of ten were divorced, and more than one of four had never married. With fewer children and no spouse, their households were smaller than average, but more often included members other than the nuclear family.[68] Early in the century they often depended on income from boarders or relatives and from working children—a practice that dwindled by century's end. In 2000, instead, they frequently relied, as early twentieth-century women could not, on support from government—never generous but, in the century's last

Photograph 3.3   Homeless Family in Shelter, Philadelphia, 1990s

By the late twentieth century, rising inequality and a shrinking welfare state left many families, especially ones headed by women, unable to support themselves. *Source:* Harvey Finkle.

decades, declining and increasingly insecure. Balanced on the edge of survival, women living on their own with children could not fully adopt modern anticipatory strategies. Instead, they retained vestiges of the older protective strategy, looking for support to traditional sources, now supplemented by government, and trying to help their children to a more prosperous future.[69]

By the end of the twentieth century, many of these single mothers had been divorced. Divorce grew steadily in the century following the Civil War. In the period right after the war, about 5 percent of marriages ended in divorce. By 1964, the proportion had grown to 36 percent. The real burst, however, took place between the mid-1960s and late 1990s, when the divorce rate rose from 10.6 in one thousand in 1965 to 22.8 in 1979. In the 1980s and 1990s, though it began to level off, the divorce rate remained high. In 1996, two Census Bureau demographers estimated that more than half of twenty-five-year-olds who married would eventually divorce. Divorce rates have been higher among blacks than among non-Hispanic whites. In the mid-1980s, ten years after marriage, 47 percent of blacks and 28 percent of whites had divorced. The Hispanic rate, which masks variation among Latino groups, was between the other two.[70]

Divorce increased the economic fragility of single mothers, because only a minority received the child-support payments to which they were legally entitled and because government supports were very low. Like divorced men, they were increasingly unlikely to remarry. However, despite the steep decline in the value of public assistance benefits, the newly expanded Earned Income Tax Credit combined in the 1990s with other supports to raise the incomes of working mothers substantially, often over the poverty line, if not by much. In 1999, poverty among female-headed households had dropped to 16 percent, but for most of them, just getting by remained very difficult.[71]

Single mothers pioneered one new family form—parenthood without marriage. Young people in early adulthood pioneered another: the nonfamily household. The late twentieth century's slow route to independent adulthood meant that a great many young women and men enjoyed a span of years when they lived independently of their parents. Decades earlier, they would have spent most of the years between leaving school and marriage at home. Now, they lived by themselves or with other single young people of the same age. Demographers interested in these trends have focused primarily on what they call cohabitation—unmarried "persons of the opposite sex sharing living quarters," a kind of quasi-marriage. "The increase in heterosexual cohabitation that has accompanied the delay in marriage and increase in divorce is one of the most significant changes in family life to take place in the last half of the [twentieth] century," the sociologists Lynne M. Casper and Suzanne A. Bianchi write. Cohabitation is, in fact, hard to pin down. Does it refer to a relatively stable arrangement that lasts over some long period? Does it cover as well shorter term relationships, or ones where less commitment is involved or expected? How, in this definition, should homosexual couples be classified? Rather than a neatly bounded status, cohabitation exists along a continuum of living arrangements that shade into each other.[72] What characterizes them is that they consist of unmarried women and men between roughly the ages of eighteen and thirty-five living alone or together as friends, roommates, or romantic partners. Together, these nonfamily households, like single mothers, are forcing a redefinition of family in America.

Nonfamily households have grown at an astonishing pace. Their percent of all households increased from 5 percent between 1940 and 1960 to 23.1 percent in 2000. There were, in fact, more nonfamily households, 12.9 percent, in 1900, than in 1950. Yet, the reasons were not the same. In 1900 and 1910, men were more than twice as likely as women to live in nonfamily households. Immigrants were the most likely of all. A 1910 investigation of nonfamily households in Chicago linked them to the preponderance of men over women in most immigrant groups. In their introductory note to the study, Sophonisba Breckinridge and Edith Abbott pointed out that many of the men were married. "In many cases . . . they have not yet been able to locate their families on this side, and during their periods of unemployment, they establish themselves with other members of their nationality in fairly permanent domestic relationships." The study's author, Milton B. Hunt, divided these domestic relationships into two types:

> Two arrangements seem to have been worked out; either the men attach themselves to a family group as lodgers or boarders, or they form a nonfamily group of their own. This may be organized either under a houseboss or on a co-operative basis. The predominance of the one kind of organization over the other . . . seems to depend largely on the length of time during which immigration of that particular nationality has been in progress, and the non-family type prevails among the most recently formed colonies.[73]

Most often collections of young men new to the city, nonfamily households grew out of the preponderance of men over women among most immigrant groups and in the West. In 1900, boarders constituted about 85 percent of the members of nonfamily households, which concentrated in the core of major cities. In large measure, the decline of nonfamily households in the early twentieth century registered the virtual disappearance of boarding, one hallmark along the route to adulthood before the middle of the twentieth century.

At the end of the twentieth century, nonfamily households remained more a central city phenomenon—30.3 percent of households in 2000 compared to 19.9 percent in the suburbs and 20.4 percent outside of metropolitan areas. But education, not immigration, now distinguished them most clearly. Women and men who had spent at least four years in college lived in nonfamily households much more often than high school graduates—in 2000, 32.6 percent of college graduates compared to 19.0 percent of high school graduates—remarkable increases for both groups since 1940.[74] These were, of course, also class differences. And the fractions for a given moment greatly understate the numbers who, at some point, shared this status.[75] For the college educated urban middle class, time spent living alone, with roommates, or a partner had become a normal part of early adulthood.[76] (Homosexual couples were also an important component of nonfamily households. But existing data make it impossible to chart their numbers or growth.)

From everywhere on the demographic spectrum new family forms emerged: single mothers who separated parenthood from marriage, young college educated men and women enjoying a period of independence with minimal responsibilities, and the elderly with their empty nests. As a result conventional families—married couples with children—plummeted as a percentage of all families from 55 percent in 1900 to 45

Figure 3.7   Change in Type of Household, 1900–2000

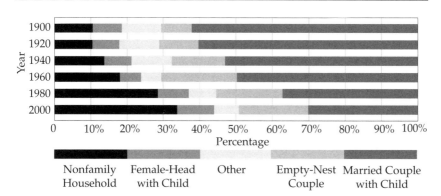

Note: The proportion of traditional family households—married couples with children—in the population declined from 62 to 30 percent during the twentieth century. They were replaced by "empty-nest" families and nonfamily households. Although single-mother households provoked much anxiety, they increased only from 8 to 10 percent of all households between 1900 and 2000. *Source*: Data from Ruggles et al. (2004).

percent in 1960, and 25 percent in 2000. Among these families, the drop in the fraction with a nonworking spouse was even greater: from 52 percent in 1900, to 33 percent in 1960, and to 8 percent in 2000 (see figure 3.7).

In both 1900 and 2000, a combination of four family and household types accounted for almost all the settings in which people lived.[77] Changes in the content of these family and household forms and the balance among them, however, had strained the conventional meaning of family. Nonfamily households were either young adults working for a few years before marriage or cohabiting couples rather than, as earlier in the century, immigrant men in boarding houses or sharing rooms while they earned money to send back to their families. Empty-nest households were couples looking forward to old age alone together or in a retirement facility rather than women and men anticipating a move in with children when they grew feeble or ran out of money. Single mothers were divorced or never married rather than, as earlier, widows. In 1900, these were the approximate shares of different household and family types: traditional families 55 percent, nonfamily households 10 percent, single-mothers 28 percent, and empty-nest households 6 percent, with a small remainder of different forms. By 2000, the balance had shifted dramatically: traditional families 25 percent, nonfamily households 25 percent, single-mother families 30 percent, empty-nest households 16 percent.[78] As never before, the question—what is a family?—required a new answer.

The New Family Landscape

Massive family change rearranged America's domestic landscape. The result was a new, more diverse social geography of family. From the baby-boom families of the 1950s to the adultolescent roommates of 2000, each emergent family form traced fresh patterns in America's cities and suburbs. Three facts about this new family landscape are especially important. First, it appeared with astonishing speed in the last few decades of the twentieth century. Second, it altered the geography of inequality. Third, it redefined the character of the nation's suburbs.

American suburbs began to develop in the nineteenth century with the extension of railroads and street railways outward from central cities. With the burst of automobile ownership in the 1920s, suburbanization accelerated, and suburbs started to grow faster than cities. But at the end of World War II, more Americans still lived in cities. All this changed very quickly in the decades that followed. Large, young baby-boom families found themselves cramped by a severe housing shortage in the nation's cities—housing construction had virtually stopped during the depression and war. At the same time, powerful influences—federally backed mortgages, more readily available for suburban than central city homes; highway construction, which eased commuting; the mass production of inexpensive homes; and the blockbusting tactics of real estate brokers who frightened whites into fleeing central cities—all lured families toward the suburbs. In the 1950s, suburbs grew ten times faster than central cites. By 1970, more Americans lived in suburbs than in any other type of community, reversing the historic pattern.[79] In these early years, the primary function of the suburbs was to provide housing for families with children. In time, they acquired an infrastructure of retail shopping, services, and jobs that serviced and supported their young populations. In both popular image and demographic fact, suburbs were dominated by married couples with children (see photograph 3.4).

During the last three decades of the twentieth century, the demographics and functions of suburbs changed, and in some important ways suburbs and central cities grew more alike. The first of these lines of convergence is the vanishing traditional family—married couples with children. In both suburbs and cities, the fraction of the population living in census tracts where more than half the families consisted of married couples with children plummeted. (In the following paragraphs, unless otherwise noted, all numbers refer to a sample of 14 metropolitan areas.) In suburbs it went down 80 percent—from 59 percent to 12 percent—and in central cities 77 percent—from 12 percent to 3 percent. In cities, the change began after 1920. In Philadelphia and Chicago, for instance, between 1900 and 1920, about six of ten households consisted of married couples with children. The change in the suburbs began later, stabilized by mid-century, and then plummeted after 1960. Already a small minor-

Photograph 3.4   A Family Poses in Front of Their Cape Cod House, Levittown, New York, 1948

After World War II, married couples with children dominated the new, mass-produced suburban landscape. *Source:* Bernard Hoffman/Stringer, Time & Life Pictures.

ity in 1970, traditional families had by 2000 become a minor element in central city populations. The major story, however, is the suburban trans-formation. By 2000, the great majority of the nation's suburbanites lived where married couples with children were a small share of families. Al-though the magnitude of this decline varied by metropolitan area, it hap-pened everywhere. The largest fraction of a suburban population, in the sampled metro areas, living where more than half the families were mar-ried couples with children, was in Houston, and there it was only 25 per-cent, down from 78 percent in 1970. No longer did traditional families dominate America's suburban landscape.

Women living alone with their children—female-headed families—re-placed many of the traditional families in both suburbs and cities. Here the change was greatest in the suburbs. Between 1970 and 2000, the proportion of the suburban population living in census tracts where at least 25 percent of families were headed by women jumped an extraordinary 440 percent, from 5 to 27 percent. In cities it rose 84 percent—from 32 percent to 59 percent. Most people in central cities—in some central cities nearly everyone—lived where female-headed families made up over a quarter of families: in Detroit the fraction was 99 percent, in St. Louis it was 92 percent. In 1970, residents of central cities were about six times more likely than residents of suburbs to live in census tracts where female-headed families composed at least a quarter of the families; by 2000, the central city lead had shrunk to a little over double (see figure 3.8).

What we have called nonfamily households—young, unmarried people age eighteen to thirty-five living alone or without relatives—also replaced traditional families in both cities, where the young adult districts dominated early in the century by boarders had long disappeared, and in suburbs. Again, the pace of change, fastest in the suburbs, accelerated with astonishing speed after 1960. Between 1960 and 1970, the share of the population living in census tracts where nonfamily households were 30 percent or more of the population multiplied four times in the suburbs and fourteen times in central cities.[80] Between 1970 and 2000, it shot up from 8 to 35 percent in suburbs, while in central cities it rose from 28 percent to 57 percent. In these three decades, the central city lead in nonfamily households had dropped by half. Again, the pace of change varied among metropolitan areas, but everywhere the trend was the same. In suburbs a very sizeable minority, and in most central cities a majority, of people lived where at least three of ten households were nonfamilies. Suburban developers responded with new housing styles. "In Chester County [Pennsylvania]," according to the *Philadelphia Inquirer*, "more neotraditional villages are taking shape on drawing boards—a movement driven largely by childless singles and empty nesters who prefer an urban-like environment." The Philadelphia Chamber of Commerce now "holds two of its Young Professional network events *outside* the city. . . . At the Pottery Barn, unattached young singles are registering for housewarmings and significant birthdays rather than waiting for a mate, and single women are hefting power tools in home-improvement clinics at the Lowe's Plymouth Meeting."[81]

Empty-nest households became more common as suburban populations aged and elderly people less often lived with their children. The share of the population aged sixty-five or older increased in suburbs from 11 percent to 16 percent—or 45 percent—while among central city populations it remained virtually the same—18 percent and 17 percent. During the twentieth century, as we have seen, empty nests, as a fraction of all households headed by a person over the age of fifty, went from 26 to 73 percent. Suburban populations reflected this trend. The share of the suburban population living in census tracts where empty-nest households

Figure 3.8   Concentration of Selected Household Types, by Metropolitan Status, Census Tracts for Fourteen Metropolitan Areas, 1970 to 2000

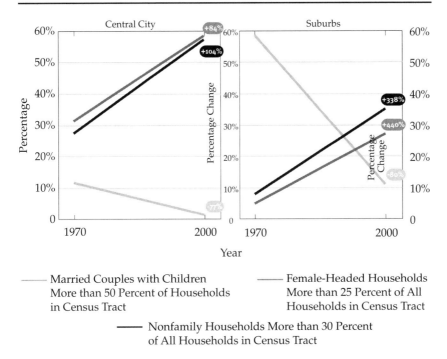

Married Couples with Children More than 50 Percent of Households in Census Tract

Female-Headed Households More than 25 Percent of All Households in Census Tract

Nonfamily Households More than 30 Percent of All Households in Census Tract

Note: In 1970, married couples with children accounted for a majority of households in nearly 60 percent of the suburban census tracts in these fourteen metropolitan areas. Three decades later, only 12 percent of suburban census tracts had a majority of these "traditional families." Like central cities, suburbs increasingly had concentrations of female-headed and nonfamily households.

2000 census tracts in following metropolitan areas: Atlanta, Boston, Chicago, Dallas-Fort Worth, Detroit, Houston, Los Angeles, Miami, New York, Philadelphia, San Francisco, Seattle, St. Louis, and Washington, D.C. *Source*: Data from Geolytics, Inc. (2005).

made up 45 percent or more of all households went from 14 percent to 25 percent. A quarter of all the people in these suburbs now lived where, at a minimum, just under half the households were empty nests. This signaled an extraordinary departure from the original, postwar meaning of suburb. In the central cities, however, the share of residents living where empty nesters made up at least 45 percent of the households dropped from 30 percent to 21 percent.[82] There, immigration joined with the growth of nonfamily and female-headed households to dilute the impact of increased numbers of empty nests (see figures 3.9 and 3.10).

The emergence of this new domestic landscape rearranged the geography of inequality. In the postwar decades, the simultaneous movement

**Figure 3.9   Married Couple Families with Children as Percentage of All
Households, Chicago Metropolitan Area Census Tracts, 1970
and 2000**

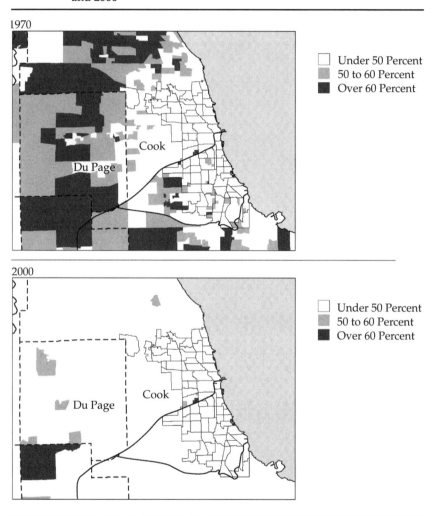

Note: In 1970, households consisting of married couples with children dominated
Chicago's suburbs while the city itself had relatively few. By 2000, this sharp split
was no longer evident. *Source*: Data from Geolytics, Inc. (2005).

of middle- and upper-income families to the suburbs, and the migration
of poor blacks from the South to the North and Midwest, drained older
cities of wealth and increased poverty within them. Poverty not only urbanized; it increasingly concentrated within districts of central cities.
This newly concentrated and isolated poverty, the intense focus of social
science research, intersected with the history of families because such a

Figure 3.10   Nonfamily Households as Percentage of All Households, Philadelphia Metropolitan Area Census Tracts, 1970 and 2000

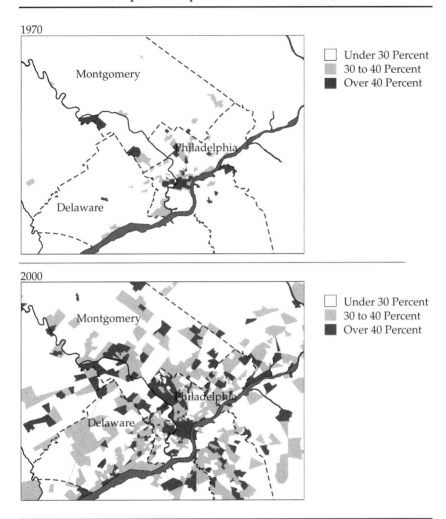

Note: In the 1970s, nonfamily households—usually composed of roommates or cohabiting couples—were concentrated in central city neighborhoods. As their numbers increased, however, they became more common throughout metropolitan areas. *Source*: Data from Geolytics, Inc. (2005).

large share of the poorest families were single mothers.[83] The increase in their numbers reshaped the geography of poverty. Although in a number of cities—especially in the Sunbelt—the concentration of poverty went down between 1990 and 2000, poverty remained far more highly concentrated than in 1970—and there was no sign that this situation would change any time soon. In fact, the concentration of poverty spread outward from city boundaries to inner-ring suburbs. Maps show that most of the suburban increase in concentrated poverty between 1970 and 2000 took place close to the borders of central cities. That is why the geography of inequality showed two simultaneous but, on the surface, contradictory trends: increased suburban wealth and poverty. An index of economic well-being developed by the sociologist John Logan and his colleagues shows suburbs with a clear and, for the most part, increasing advantage over central cities.[84] Yet, at the same time, suburban poverty concentration has increased. Suburbs, that is, are differentiating economically in ways masked by blanket generalizations that do not discriminate among them, especially between inner and outer suburbs.

The concentration of young adults and the movement of many empty nesters back to central cities brought new concentrations of wealth that redefined economic zones sharply. Indeed, the phenomenon referred to as "gentrification" is shorthand for the impact of shifting family and household forms on urban space. At the same time, immigration brought young working-class families back to cities—slowing the disappearance of traditional families. In the districts where they concentrated, immigrant families reshaped domestic landscapes, revived declining neighborhoods, and moderated the growing economic gulf that separated islands of gentrification from seas of concentrated poverty.[85]

In 2000, America's new domestic landscape embodied the immense changes in the life course and family during the century's last decades. The interruption of the standardized passage to independent adulthood—so common in mid-century—resulted in a new diversity that spread households of young women and men living by themselves or together everywhere. While they lived more often in cities, large numbers increasingly stayed in suburbs as well. At the same time, new ways of spending the years after 65—the slowed movement toward retirement, the diversity of activity, the withering of the ancient practice of living with one's children—combined with increased longevity to diffuse "empty nests" throughout suburbs and cities. The powerful surge in the number of single mothers—a result of the growing separation of marriage and parenthood as well as of divorce—proved a suburban as well as an inner-city phenomenon that left large numbers of mothers alone with children living in all sorts of places. The spread of all three of these family forms ate away at the numbers of married couples with children—traditional families—who became increasingly scarce in cities and suburbs. Cities had always been diverse, their social geographies shifting with waves of immigration and industrial change as well as with changing family forms. But for suburbs the new family landscape demanded nothing less than a redefinition of character and purpose. Although the need pfor change was clear, the product—the new definition of suburb—was not. Perhaps, even, the suburb was a concept whose time had passed.

Chapter 4

What America Is Becoming

B Y 2000, everything had changed. Where more than 50 percent of the population in 1900 had lived in places with at most one thousand residents, these small communities were home to only 2 percent in 2000. Roughly 50 percent now lived in towns and cities of at least twenty-five thousand and 27 percent in cities of one hundred thousand or more. The population, and with it the average population density, had just about tripled. Rather than on a farm, the modal American now lived in a suburb. Rather than in agriculture, she now worked in one of the service industries. Population had shifted southward and filled up some, though by no means all, of the vast empty spaces in the West. In 2000, California had the largest population of any state. At all levels—federal, state, local—government had grown immensely and assumed roles unimaginable earlier in the century. In 1901, the ratio of federal employees to population was 1 to 1,293; in 2000, it was 1 to 161.

Yet, for all the differences, similarities joined the two ends of the century. Both were periods of profound and discontinuous social and economic change. They were, to begin, the first and second eras of economic globalization, linking industries, finance, trade, and people in vast transnational networks whose cumulative impact worked its way into even the most intimate domestic matters. Massive industrialization and economic consolidation defined the first era. Although first-wave globalization was effectively over by 1920, America's great industrial era endured a few decades longer. Second-wave economic globalization, underway after World War II, gathered steam in the 1960s and barreled forward in the next decades. Linked, as was first-wave globalization, to technological change, its energy derived from information technology and new financial instruments rather than from the internal combustion engine and electricity, which had fueled revolutionary change a century earlier. Both globalization waves drew on immigrant labor. Around the world, disruptive economic reorganization drove women and men from their land and out of customary occupations, setting them loose in

171

search of new livelihoods. Many ended up in America, drawn by ethnic networks and economic opportunities. Central to both first- and second-wave globalization, thus, was diversity—the arrival of huge numbers of immigrants from parts of the world not previously well represented among the American population. How to assimilate these newcomers and anxiety over their impact were key public problems at both times. At both ends of the century, too, America's legacy of racial injustice and inequity remained stubborn reminders of democratic ideals still unrealized. Indeed, steep, enduring income and wealth pyramids were evidence of durable inequalities that persisted in the face of massive economic and social change.

As a consequence of this amalgam of change and continuity, familiar ideas lost their accustomed meanings. Work, city, inequality, race, gender, family, these concepts that frame thinking about public life suddenly had become problematic. Demographic, economic, and social change had overtaken old ideas, exploding intellectual frameworks. Here—in the urgency of recasting the conceptual basis of public life lay the most profound links between America at the start and end of the twentieth century.

It is misleading, however, to cast the explosion of old ideas as the result of vast, impersonal, irresistible forces. In every way, choices guided responses to economic development. The organization of work, the shape of cities, the opportunities open to blacks and women, the redefinition of life's stages all embodied the realization of some alternatives rather than others. Americans made many, although not all, these choices through their governments. Governments—federal, state, and local—enforced racial segregation and permitted lynching, for example. Urban renewal, federally backed mortgage underwriting policies, and highway construction profoundly reshaped the composition of cities and the very definition of city itself. But there was also a positive side to the story. The institutions of the state and labor market—social insurance, fair labor standards, minimum wage laws, trade unions—reduced economic inequality, raised living standards, increased economic security, and introduced health and retirement benefits. As a result, American workers enjoyed a historically unprecedented standard of living. Through the courts and civil rights legislation, the government helped reduce racial and gender inequities to historic lows. Through public and quasi-public employment, governments offered avenues of mobility that moved huge numbers of minorities and women into the middle class. This powerful and positive role of government has been a major theme in this book. Its erosion during the last quarter of the twentieth century underlies the story of recently increased inequality and insecurity and their sometimes lethal consequences, which is another theme in the stories this book has told.

How, then, do we think about the issues on the public agenda in the twenty-first century? This book offers no prescriptive answers. Rather, the histories it recounts point unambiguously only in one direction: the inadequacy of the old definitions that still largely frame public discussion. As they were a century ago, Americans are caught in the tension between what their nation was and what it is becoming, and, once again, if they are to respond with reason and realism, they need to recast the concepts that frame everyday life.

They might begin by asking just what is meant by public in the twenty-first century. Consider, first, one common meaning: universal accessibility or aid, as in public highway, public service, or public space.[1] In its historic sense, public space conjures images of places belonging to some level of government where individuals congregate and, within limits, conduct themselves as they please with, in the United States, their rights to free speech and assembly protected by the Constitution. Today, most new public spaces are legally private. Shopping malls serve as the prime example. The private owners of these new downtowns may restrict political speech and activity, ban solicitations, and enforce rules with their own police. One of America's greatest new spaces, the grounds and buildings of the Getty Museum in Los Angeles, throngs with families lolling in its garden, who enjoy free admission. They are there at the pleasure of the Getty, which can impose virtually whatever conditions of entrance and behavior it chooses. Furthermore, no level of government in America today would construct a space the size and quality of the Getty. What does public space mean in the twenty-first century?

Public has other historic meanings, which also demand reconsideration. Public "refers to activities that take place in full view of others as contrasted to those conducted in the family or other closed settings, that is, in private." It "refers to the whole rather than to a part; as in 'the' public or public opinion; it means everyone."[2] With personal information available in huge databases—with the capacity to trace and link an individual's finances, travel, credit, residences, criminal record, marital experience, and, perhaps soon, medical records—where does public end and private begin? With a nation deeply divided by political and social beliefs, diverse in its culture and demography, fractured by lifestyle, does it make any sense to speak in a singular sense of public opinion?

Public is also used in connection with institutions. Here, too, its meaning has a history full of implications for thinking about institutions today. We often define public institutions, such as schools, as owned and administered by government. In fact, however, public has had various definitions. Take the example of education. In the Colonial era, it meant education that took place in a school rather than in a private home. In the early nineteenth century, it referred to schools often owned and operated by private associations, such as the New York Public School Society, usually free, and open on a nonsectarian basis to a broad section of the population, though in practice attended primarily by the poor. As a result, public was equated with pauper. As they worked to break that association, the school promoters who built public education systems in the mid-nineteenth century introduced and solidified the definition of public as encompassing both finance and control—the definition still dominant today.[3] Even though the word public retains the administrative and legal meaning it acquired in the mid-nineteenth century, in big cities public education has reacquired its association with education for the poor. The once proud designation of other institutions as public also has worn off. Where Americans in the nineteenth and early twentieth centuries pointed with pride to the educational castles that housed city high schools, great new parks, and, even, the elaborate architecture of many poorhouses, by the late twentieth century they often used "public" as a synonym for shoddy, inefficient, and, with city schools or hospitals, for service to the poor.[4] Is the definition of public in place for the last one hundred and fifty years still appropriate? Is it possible to restore its luster? This is the question raised by advocates of school vouchers, who propose to de-link funding from ownership and control and return to an early nineteenth-century pattern when, for instance, the first policy for state supported secondary education was to allocate tax money to private academies. The point is not that voucher advocates are necessarily correct but that public is a historically contingent idea, not one frozen in time, and that the economic and demographic history of late twentieth-century American cities has undermined the conditions that sustained it.

Except for "the public," public as a term usually does not stand alone. It is, instead, attached to something else, as in public education, public opinion, public employment, or public life. Of these, public life, which encompasses the institutions, activities, and categories that shape everyday life, has the widest meaning. For the most part, our ideas about these—work, city, family, race, nationality, to take leading examples—rest on assumptions that remain largely unquestioned. As in public education, we think we know what they mean. These assumed meanings shape how we act—the decisions we make in everyday life, in the polling booth, and as neighbors and citizens in our communities. Every one of these assumptions, however, has become as problematic as public itself. With each of them, events on the ground—the history described in this book—has rendered existing assumptions and frameworks obsolete, inadequate guides to the twenty-first century. Each of them, therefore, requires interrogation. But before turning to the first—to work—one very important element needs to be added to the context within which change is assessed. That is economic globalization. Just as early twentieth-century economic globalization shaped the tensions between what

America was and what it was becoming, discussed in chapter 1, forcing a reconsideration of every idea underlying public life, its next great wave late in the century had the same result.

Economic Globalization

In the early twentieth century the internationalization of trade, finance, labor markets, and population defined economic globalization. The same features characterized it in the early twenty-first century as well. Economic globalization, according to the staff of the International Monetary Fund, "refers to the increasing integration of economies around the world, particularly through trade and financial flows. The term sometimes also refers to the movement of people (labor) and knowledge (technology) across international borders."[5]

Trade in goods and services increased not only because of the activity of the world's powerhouse economies but also from the entrance of new players. As a whole, developing countries increased their share of world trade between 1971 and 1999 from 19 percent to 29 percent, with the newly industrialized economies of Asia leading the way.[6] The flow of funds between nations followed the same upward trajectory.[7] In the United States, foreign direct investment soared 893 percent.[8] Converging wages, as we pointed out in chapter 1, indicate integration among labor markets. Tremendous international variation in wages, of course, remained in place early in the twenty-first century, but, as happened in the nation's first major era of economic globalization, with a few exceptions, differences were shrinking.[9] Converging wages, notably among developed and rapidly developing nations, however, do not signal increased income equality. Indeed, quite the opposite has been the case. Income inequality between rich and poor countries has been widening for decades.[10]

The flow of people, as well as goods and capital, across borders also marks economic globalization. In the late nineteenth and early twentieth centuries, massive capitalist industrialization uprooted women and men and forced them to move in search of employment and opportunity. In the late twentieth and early twenty-first centuries as capitalism has entered a new, disruptive phase migration again surged. Between 1965 and 1990, the share of foreign-born workers in labor forces around the world increased by half.[11] Adding the families of migrant as well as undocumented workers to the count underlines the scope of migration, the economist Ohtsu Sadayoshi observes.

> At the turn of the 21st century . . . there are some 30 to 40 million migrant workers in the world and, if we include their family members, the number rises to the order of 100 million people. If we include refugees and illegal

migrants, the number grows sharply to 150 million. . . . This is twice as big as it was two decades ago. Cross border migrants are now ubiquitous throughout the world.[12]

Whether or not they migrate, workers in different nations remain linked by the actions of international firms shifting production around the globe in search of cheap labor, a point underscored by Jefferson Cowie's powerful dissection of the links between workers in Bloomington, Indiana, and Ciudad Juarez, Mexico, in *Capital Moves*, his history of labor at RCA.[13]

Immigrants create a global workforce not only as a result of their movement but, also, because of the links they retain with their home countries. Global flows of money—in the form of remittances, information, and culture—also connect workers with the rest of the world.[14] Although international migration forms part of a chain stretching backward to link host and home countries, it also constitutes part of a chain that stretches forward to join international and domestic migration. In much of the world, notably developing countries, domestic migration results in massive urbanization. Many of these new urbanites will eventually find their way to other countries. Disruptive economic change drives women and men from the land, pushing them, as it did in Europe a century ago, into cities—a process often the first stage in international migration.[15] Extensive domestic migration also keeps population moving throughout the United States. In California, the U.S.-born population born in-state was 56 percent in 2000—in the nation's most populous state, this means that nearly half the native-born adults had moved in from elsewhere.[16] Migrants composed a much smaller share of the population of older northeastern and mid-Atlantic states. Around the world and within nations, individuals are on the move, linked in a vast flow across borders, oceans, and continents.

Globalization was a component in a set of discontinuous changes in technology, business practices, and financial markets that rearranged the production and distribution of goods and wealth with major consequences for everyday life—work and family—and for the composition of inequality. Together, these changes fueled a sharp rise in productivity, the single most important component of economic growth.[17]

An economic historian writing in the 1920s might have said much the same things, only the specific content would have been very different. Indeed, since the seventeenth century, the world has seen a number of "new" economies, each one fueling productivity, transforming work, and disrupting personal experience.[18] Steam and coal propelled the first industrial revolution, which gave way in the late nineteenth and early twentieth centuries to the era of electricity and the internal combustion engine, accompanied by new technologies, business practices, and finan-

Photograph 4.1   Worker Installing Power Supply at Dell Computer, 1994

By the late twentieth century, the flexible production of customized products suited the demands of an information economy. *Source:* © Ed Kashi/CORBIS.

cial markets that transformed America and much of the world—the subject of this book's first chapter. In the late twentieth century, the most recent of capitalism's unending cycles of "creative destruction" resulted in a configuration we are still struggling to label and understand. Whether we talk of a new economy or, with Manuel Castells, of an information age and network society, we confront a world that renders the customary frames through which we interpret and talk about public life obsolete.[19] That this is not the first moment of discontinuous change in American, or world, history makes it no less new or significant (see photograph 4.1).

The invention of the semiconductor made possible the extraordinary leap in computing technology and information management.[20] Like electricity early in the twentieth century, transistor-based technology grew slowly at first, disappointing its champions with its relatively small contribution to productivity. The slow initial adoption of both resulted from the time it took people to realize their potential and for companies to invest in new technologies and re-order their work processes. All this changed with remarkable speed after 1995. By the end of 2000, information technology and software accounted for about two-thirds of accelerating labor productivity after 1995.[21] Technical advances reduced the cost of processing information sevenfold in thirty years. [22] Both the development of information technology and productivity growth would have been impossible without active help from government.[23] The notion that free-market capitalism made the Internet possible is nothing but a fantasy. Funded by Cold War military needs, the research underlying the Internet was paid for with tax revenues and "carried out by giant corporations that existed in a state of cozy symbiosis with government and by universities that grew rich on research contracts."[24]

New business practices, as well as new technologies, define the new economy. The industrial era brought with it the reorganization of business often referred to as Fordism, after one of its most prominent pioneers, automobile maker Henry Ford. Fordism stands for the centralization of manufacturing in huge, hierarchically organized plants where the process of production is broken down into its constituent parts and labor is divided into repetitive actions performed over and over by the same workers on assembly lines. It is the system critically satirized by Charlie Chaplin in *Modern Times* and thought, as late as 1967 by John Kenneth Galbraith in *The New Industrial State,* to herald a collective future where capitalism shades into socialism.[25] Galbraith, however, was writing the epitaph for a dying era, not predicting the future. In recent decades, dissatisfaction with hierarchical, bureaucratic organizational forms has swept through education, government, the social services, and private enterprise. Firms pointing to a new paradigm have devolved authority, decentralized operations, and adopted just-in-time production.[26]

How many firms—what proportion of the total—have adopted lean, decentralized, computer-driven, collaborative practices is not known. Certainly, the exceptions, as critics of the "new economy" would be quick to point out, are legion.[27] The point, though, is not that all firms have adopted new business practices. Rather, firms like Dell and Toyota, new economy proponents argue, point toward the future, the direction that will become increasingly common in decades to come. For the present, American business remains between the age of manufacture and the age of information.

Transformed financial markets have joined new technologies and business practices as the third component of the emergent economy. A "complementary set of innovations in the financial sector," asserted Federal Reserve Vice Chairman Roger W. Ferguson, "have changed the financial landscape in ways that were especially appropriate to the predominate form of business organization in each period." In recent decades, with many start-up businesses looking for capital and the economic environment riskier, "financial intermediaries have expanded the range of financing alternatives . . . and have made marked improvements in quantifying and managing risks." The methods include junk bonds, venture capital, and leveraged buyouts.[28]

The impact of new technologies, business practices, and financial markets extended everywhere. They called into question the meaning of work, reconfigured inequality, rearranged urban landscapes, and invaded personal relationships. First, consider work.

Work

In 1900, work in the regular labor market was defined as an activity for men, and 82 percent of workers were male. It took a very long time for this definition to change. As late as 1940, men still made up some 75 percent of the labor force. By 2000, however, change was massive. Men's share had dropped to 52 percent, just over half. Many of the women now working were married, the story we told in chapter 2. In 1940, 49 percent of the women in the labor force were single, compared to 26 percent in 2000, and many more of them had young children at home. Between 1970 and 2000, the proportion of women with children under the age of one who worked nearly doubled from 31 percent to 57 percent.[29] In the same years, immigration began to shift the ethnic composition of the labor force. In 1900, white males made up 74 percent of the labor force and minorities about 14 percent. By the century's end, the white male fraction had declined to 40 percent and the minority share had risen to 25 percent. Even more dramatic changes lay ahead. New labor force entrants were 30 percent white male, 50 percent female, and 41 percent minority.[30]

Late in the twentieth century, the terms of work also changed. The "very concept of a job," writes Martin Carnoy, "is changing . . . [the] concept of secure, permanent work at rising wages for men and very little paid work for women is going by the boards." In the "economy of the future," he predicts, "the majority of workers will not have full-time, permanent, traditionally salaried jobs."[31] This trend marked a radical break with the trajectory of change throughout most of the twentieth century. Early in the century, employers often counted on men showing up at factory gates and hired them by the day. In turn, workers shifted from job to job, responding to small incentives. Labor market reformers tried to stem this extraordinarily high labor turnover in the nation's factories. High turnover, labor market reformers argued, served both industries and workers poorly by encouraging inefficiency and promoting insecurity.

The motley collection of programs referred to as "welfare capitalism," introduced in the 1910s and 1920s, was intended to partly address the labor turnover problem, as well as to stave off labor unions. At best a minority practice in American firms, welfare capitalism died under the weight of the Great Depression. Real change awaited the aftermath of World War II with mass unionization and the rapid introduction of employee benefits. Especially in the large manufacturing firms that dominated the Industrial Era, employment more often became long term, secure, and paternalistic. Employers funded and administered pension funds, which provided a defined set of benefits; offered health insurance at little, if any, cost to their employees; and encouraged workers to think of permanent careers in the same firms. The result was unprecedented security and compensation for the unionized working class.

In the 1980s, this trajectory began to reverse direction. By the 1990s, employers, openly advocating the end of paternalism, discouraged employees from thinking of permanent, or long-term, job tenure. By moving from defined benefit to defined contribution pensions, they encouraged them to take responsibility for their own future security. By increasing co-payments and premiums in health insurance, they were demanding that they share more of the cost of their medical expenses. As a consequence, job insecurity increased, turnover rose, and the temporary employment business boomed. Employment in the personnel services industries, which includes temporary work, skyrocketed from 247,000 in 1973 to 3, 532,000 in 2001, or from 0.3 percent to 3.2 percent of the workforce. Among thirty-five to forty-four-year-old men, the median years of job tenure declined from 7.6 in 1963 to 5.4 in 2000. A substantial fraction of this decline was attributable to involuntary job loss. Average wages for those who went from one full-time job to another dropped 13 percent, and 29 percent of those workers who had enjoyed health benefits on their previous job lost them in the transition to new employment.[32] The very notion of a job had changed.[33]

Much like early twentieth-century America, as we suggested in chapter 1, abrupt economic change—the introduction of new technologies and modes of organizing work—led in two quite different directions, toward a high and a low road to increased productivity: the high road of improving productivity by developing high-performance workplaces based on worker training, worker participation, wage incentives, and job security, the low road of reducing labor costs through outsourcing labor hires, fixed-term and part-time labor contracts, and pressuring government to reduce real minimum wages and the power of unions.[34]

The bifurcation of work along high and low roads did not, as some analysts—such as Jeremy Rifkin—predicted, lead to the "disappearance of work."[35] The number of jobs, in fact, increased and shows no signs of reversing direction. A disproportionate share of new jobs went to women and the number of middle-level jobs went down. What Barry Bluestone and Bennett Harrison called the "disappearing middle" consisted mainly of older workers, dropped from jobs that were deskilled or eliminated, who either left the workforce or ended up in lower-paying work. The higher-paying jobs that replaced the "disappearing middle" went to younger workers with more education.[36]

Carnoy sees the weight gradually tilting toward demand for highly skilled workers. Others are less certain. Economics writer Doug Henwood cites Bureau of Labor Statistics projections of the occupations that will grow fastest between 2000 and 2010. They do not point to a future full of "symbolic analysts," to use the phrase popularized by former U.S. Secretary of Labor Robert Reich. These are: combined food preparation and serving workers, including fast food; customer-service representatives; registered nurses; retail salespersons; computer support specialists; cashiers, except gaming; office clerks, general; security guards; computer-software engineers, applications; and waiters and waitresses. By Henwood's analysis, jobs in the lowest earnings quartile will account for about 40 percent of growth in the top thirty occupations.

Less than 25 percent of the top thirty jobs will require a bachelor's degree or higher; 54 percent will require short on-the-job training. Outside the top thirty, 25 percent of new jobs will require a bachelor's degree or more—but almost 50 percent will require no more than short-to-medium-term on-the-job training. Some 75 percent will require less than an associate's degree.[37]

Even the most technologically sophisticated industries include poorly paying, dead-end jobs that lack benefits. They include the stock clerks, maintenance workers, and office cleaners who work alongside the actuaries, systems analysts, and lawyers. The social structures of cities divide into vastly unequal formal and informal or contingent economies linked intimately to each other. Affluent symbolic analysts depend on armies of low-wage workers to supply personal services, staff specialty shops, and clean and maintain their offices and homes. David Cay Johnston, writing in *The New York Times*, called them the new servant class. Affluent urbanites, like corporations, outsource domestic tasks in the interests of economy and flexibility.[38]

The emergent transformation of work upset existing representations of occupational and industrial structures. But how to characterize and group occupations and industries in the new economy was by no means clear. The only thing certain was the inadequacy of existing classifications. The federal government recognized the problem in the 1990s when it adopted a new international classification of industries and decided to develop a new occupational classification.

Occupational and industrial classification sound like dry and technical subjects. But, in truth, they are freighted with important consequences. They shape the overall view of the economy and its subdivisions used by social scientists and in public policy. Different schemes obscure some trends and accentuate others. Furthermore, there is nothing automatic or inevitable about how classifications are developed. Instead, they express the underlying logic that analysts find in economic trends.[39]

Since the nineteenth century, census officials have worried about occupational classification, but modern occupational classification really began with Alba Edwards, who took over occupational statistics at the new Census Bureau in time for the 1910 census. Edwards remained influential throughout most of the first half of the twentieth century, writing the most important articles on the subject. For Edwards, occupational statistics underpinned progressive social reform with essential data, and he realized that older occupational classifications did not suit the new century. The advance of industrialization, with its attendant social problems, demanded a new way of categorizing the world of work.[40]

The problem was balancing the need for information about specific occupations with data on industries. Industrial location remained crucial to the social reform goals of occupational analysis, for example, to the comparative analysis of mortality in different industries. Occupational statistics should serve multiple purposes, classifying occupations' healthfulness, ranking individuals by skill, and dividing them by industrial position "as employer, employee, or working on his own account."[41] Edwards attempted to meet these goals in three ways. First, his occupational classification, which endured with minor modifications until 1940, combined occupation with industry. Second, he introduced a separate industry question in the census questionnaire: respondents were asked both their occupation and the industry in which they worked. Third, he gathered information on class with a new question asking whether individuals employed others, worked for themselves, or were employed by someone else. Implicitly, the new trio of census questions recognized that America had become a land of wage workers.

By 1917, Edwards had begun to stress the importance of grouping occupations by social and economic rank, but the Census Bureau did not follow his recommendations by adopting a new stratification-based classification of occupations until 1940.[42] By then, the data needs of social scientists newly engaged in the analysis of stratification and mobility had joined the needs of reformers and government officials for a classification that illuminated rank as well as location.

Edwards was a member of the Joint Committee on Occupational Classification, an interagency committee appointed in the 1930s by the Central Statistical Board and the American Statistical Association. Its task was to develop a standard occupational classification, and its work formed the basis of the scheme used in 1940, which remained, with minor revisions, in place until superseded by a new occupational classification in 2000. The Joint Committee resulted from the intersection of heightened data needs of the federal government's New Deal era programs with dissatisfaction at the inconsistencies and gaps in the uncoordinated gathering of statistics by government agencies. The Central Statistical Board was the new agency charged with pulling these scattered efforts together. With some minor changes, the Census Bureau adopted the Joint Committee's recommendations and put the new classification, with its nine socioeconomic groupings, into place in the 1940 census. With some modification in 1980, it remained the basis of occupational classification until the end of the century.[43]

By the 1990s, the "new economy" had exploded the old occupational classification. How to think about the new world of work emerged as a major problem for government statistical agencies, including the Census Bureau. As a result, in 1994, the Office of Management and Budget put together a committee, which produced a revised Standard Occupational Classification (SOC). The committee hoped to facilitate comparisons over time and among agencies by developing a system compatible with existing classifications "while mirroring the current occupational structure of the Nation." In practice, this meant, first, serving users whose main concern was workforce management and development. At the same time, the new scheme needed to reflect "advances in factory and office automation and information technology, the shift to a services-oriented economy, and increasing concern for the environment." The new classification met these goals by including "more professional, technical, and service occupations and fewer production and administrative support occupations."[44] But the change went beyond introducing new and growing occupations and consolidating declining ones, because the concept underlying the new scheme reverted to the production-oriented approach of the early twentieth century and deemphasized the focus on stratification dominant for the half century beginning in 1940.

The new classification dropped whatever vestiges remained of the social reformist goals of federal statistics and exchanged the long concern with status for a scheme directed toward promoting efficient labor markets. The treatment of professionals signaled the change of direction. Professional as such no longer existed in the new classification. Instead, professional occupations were scattered among the twenty-three major sectors or workplace-based groups into which occupations were divided. There were also no separate categories for laborers, operatives, or clerical occupations. The classification also collapsed many of the distinctions between supervisors and workers. "Supervisors of professional and technical workers usually have a background similar to the workers they supervise and are therefore classified with the workers they supervise. Likewise team leaders, lead workers, and supervisors of production workers who spend at least 20 percent of their time performing work similar to the workers they supervise, are classified with the workers they supervise." The new classification used a six-digit hierarchical code, which stretched from twenty-three major occupational groups to ninety-eight minor groups, 452 broad occupations, and 822 detailed occupations. Users concerned with status could still turn to the new classification to meet their data needs by reclassifying the detailed occupations into new groups. But official emphasis had clearly shifted.[45]

What lay behind the shift? Although the answer is not wholly clear, one potent influence was the reorganization of work. New organizational models devolve responsibility and decision making to teams which assume some of the "tasks previously performed by supervisors, engineers, and staff specialists." These changes in the organization of work increased the difficulty of differentiating supervisors from other workers. The "key point in current principles of classification," asserted another expert, is that, *an occupation should be classified on the basis of the work performed. . . .* It might include . . . classifying laborers, precision workers, and managers in the same group."[46]

The displacement of professionals, supervisors, and clerical work from major occupational categories was intended to mirror trends in the organization of work in the new economy. It also attempted to meet bureaucratic needs for standardization across government statistical agencies, especially those concerned with tracking the workforce and promoting efficient labor markets. Implicitly, it served another purpose as well. At the very time income inequality increased, the new scheme muted emergent trends in pay and rewards by merging workers on different rungs of the income hierarchy into single large categories. True, by dipping below the major categories, researchers could disentangle workers, supervisors, and professionals. But because the task took resources and work, the new occupational classification would leave trends in inequality less transparent.

In another way, also not mentioned by its advocates, the new classification reflected an important development: the expansion, feminization, and incipient proletarianization of managerial and professional work. The fraction of employees working in both kinds of jobs multiplied in the second half of the twentieth century. The last decades of the twentieth-century also witnessed the rapid movement of women into management and professions. The expansion and feminization of these occupations resulted in lowered pay for many who worked in them. In the last half of the century, the share of managers and officials in the top income quintile dropped from 63 percent to 47 percent as the share in the 20th to 60th (middle) percentile nearly doubled from 13 percent to 25 percent.[47] Working as a manager at McDonald's or Wal-Mart was not the same thing as at IBM. Even in banking, as we showed in chapter 2, a division opened among managers with the mainly women managers of small branches at the bottom. No longer a term that automatically and universally connoted independence from close supervision and high pay, "manager" ended the twentieth century as another commonly and often unreflectively used concept that had lost its grounding in practice. By eliminating manager and supervisor as separate categories and inserting them, instead, within functional and place-specific locations, the new classification preceded wider public recognition of a change in occupational structure pregnant with implications for the future of work.

The trends forcing a reclassification of occupations also provoked a new classification of industries. Modern industrial classification began in the United States with an interagency project sponsored by the Central Statistical Board (which subsequently became part of the Budget Bureau) in the 1930s. Previously, various agencies collecting data on industries had used their own classifications, and industries were grouped differently throughout the branches of government. The result undercut attempts to analyze industrial characteristics and trends. The 1939 Standard Industrial Classification (SIC), designed to overcome this problem, remained the basis of industrial classification for more than a half century, although it was occasionally modified and revised, notably in 1987.[48] The SIC based its classification on the kind of goods produced or services provided, and it emphasized manufacturing.[49] In the 1990s, almost half the one thousand and four industries recognized still represented manufacturing industries even though the manufacturing share of GDP had dipped to less than 20 percent. Service industries were underrepresented. Many of the fastest growing, in fact, were dumped into a residual category.

The new classification—the NAICS—remedied both these deficiencies while it also attempted to solve a problem that resulted from economic globalization. The integration of Mexican, U.S., and Canadian markets by the North America Free Trade Agreement (NAFTA) necessitated similar economic statistics.[50] The NAICS forced comparability on the classification systems of the three countries and shifted the principle of classification to grouping "producing units that use similar production processes." The goal was to facilitate "insights into the increasingly interrelated evolution of our economies." [51] The NAICS also paid "special attention to developing production-oriented classifications for (a) new and emerging industries, (b) service industries in general, and (c) industries engaged in the production of advanced technologies."[52] Thus, it recognized "nine new service sectors and 358 new industries . . . 250 of which are service industries." In the manufacturing sector, the most important change was a new computer and electronic product manufacturing subsector, and another new sector called information.[53]

Where occupational classification serviced domestic labor market development, industrial classification underpinned economic analysis and facilitated economic globalization. Customers for the new classification of occupations were primarily agencies concerned with training and employment and, secondarily, social scientists who studied stratification. Customers for the new classifications of industry, by contrast, would be economists tracking international economic trajectories and integration;

the new NAICS would prove useful to government officials defining trade policy and to investors making decisions about where to place capital. Both new sets of classifications, however, illustrated the same historic development: the relatively sudden inadequacy of existing ideas about the organization of work, the meaning of occupation, and the dynamics of economic growth. Discontinuous change had undermined the categories framing critical economic decisions; the new classifications pointed to ways of thinking about the economic dimensions of public life more suited to what America was becoming than to what it had been only a few decades earlier.[54]

City

In late nineteenth- and early twentieth-century America, the revolution in the size, organization, and technology of manufacturing resulted in the emergence of the industrial city. " 'Modern industry,' is almost equivalent to 'city life,' " observed University of Chicago sociologist Charles Henderson in 1909, "because the great industry, the factory system, builds cities around the chimneys of steam engines and electric plants."[55] How to define, understand, and guide this new industrial city and its attendant problems, as discussed in chapter 1, was the great conundrum for nascent social science as well as for reformers and public officials at the time. The late twentieth and early twenty-first century transition from an age of manufacture to an age of information poses similar and equally critical questions. In the second half of the twentieth century, American cities experienced major economic, demographic, and spatial transformations. The result was an urban form—or set of forms—unprecedented in history. How to characterize this new American city, however, remained unclear. None of the metaphors that attempted to capture its essence worked adequately, but, taken together, they illustrate both the collapse of older definitions of "city" and the urgency of arriving at new ones.

Despite their differences, late twentieth-century cities experienced common transformations of economy, demography, and space that have resulted in a new American urbanism shot through with inequalities, some long-standing, some new.[56] The economic transformation was as fundamental as the one that had emerged from the industrial revolution a century earlier. Even though deindustrialization accelerated in the 1960s, the process in fact had begun decades earlier. In the 1930s, for instance, some industries left the industrial heartland to move to the South, and signs of trouble appeared in older industrial cities during the 1950s. But the 1960s, 1970s, and 1980s were the decades of massive plant closings. This decimation of manufacturing resulted from both the growth of foreign industries, notably electronics and automobiles, and the corporate search for cheaper labor. Cities varied in their capacity to withstand the loss of industry. Those with economic sectors other than manufacturing—such as banking, commerce, medicine, government, and education—fared best, for example, New York, Miami, Los Angeles, the San Francisco Bay area, Chicago, Boston, and Houston. Those with no alternatives—Baltimore, Cleveland, Buffalo, St. Louis, Detroit—faced near collapse. Others teetered in between—Philadelphia, Pittsburgh, and the Twin Cities, for example. There were also newer urban economies based on entertainment, tourism, and retirement, such as Las Vegas, Phoenix, Albuquerque, and, in some ways, New Orleans. Everywhere, services replaced manufacturing, and office towers became the late twentieth century's urban factories. Service, of course, is a broad category. It embraces both demanding and rewarding jobs—Robert Reich's "symbolic analysts"—and low wage, non-unionized employment that offers few benefits. Cities' new economic functions, in the fortunate cities like Los Angeles, included the production of the financial and business services and products that served the emergent international economy. They also included, as, again, notably in Los Angeles, the reappearance of small-scale manufacturing drawing on inexpensive immigrant labor—a new manufacturing sector of grim sweatshops reminiscent of the early twentieth century.[57]

Various strands of social history twisted together to produce the demographic transformation of American cities. The first was the migration of blacks from the South to cities in the North, the Midwest, and even, to some extent, the West. In the second Great Migration between 1940 and 1970, five million blacks departed the South for cities elsewhere in the nation. As blacks moved into cities, many whites moved out. Between 1950 and 1970, seven million whites decamped central cities, mainly for the suburbs. Reasons other than racial change prompted their leaving: severe urban housing shortages; mass-produced suburban homes made affordable by federally insured, long-term, low interest mortgages; and the new interstate highway system were the most important. But fears of the consequences of racial change, fanned by aggressive and often unscrupulous realtors, played a role as well.[58] Because in the North and Midwest the number of African American newcomers did not equal the number of departing whites, city population size often went down. In the Sunbelt, in cities like Los Angeles, population trends went in the opposite direction. Economic opportunity and an inviting climate drew millions of migrants, boosting these cities' populations from 8.5 to 23 million between 1957 and 1990. (This urban population growth in the Sunbelt resulted from annexation as well as in-migration.) A great many of those who left central cities did not go very far, however. They moved instead to the suburbs, whose populations exploded during these decades. Between 1950 and 1970, overall, the population of American cities grew by 10 million and the population of suburbs by 85 million.

Two other developments transformed America's urban demography. One of these, of course, was the massive immigration that began following changes to federal law in 1965. These changes and immigration trends are discussed elsewhere in this book. Here it is important to remember that, with return migration taken into account, the 1980s was the decade of the greatest net immigration in American history—about six million people. The newcomers, who came predominantly from Asia and Latin America, altered the ethnic mix of America's population, most notably of its cities, and were the source of the growth that occurred during the 1990s in many of the nation's urban areas.[59] Hispanics, in fact, spread out faster than any other ethnic group in American history.[60] The other development that altered America's urban demography was the change in family patterns, as we have described elsewhere in this book. First among these was the growth in single-mother families, who composed a substantial share of city populations—in some areas a majority. In the 1990s, single women headed about 73 percent of African American families in extreme poverty zones. The other major urban demographic trend was the growth of nonfamily households, also discussed earlier, which resulted in clusters of young, unattached women and men fueling the development of new urban entertainment, retail, and cultural districts. Both these developments changed the family composition of suburbs as well as cities, as chapter 3 explained (see photograph 4.2).[61]

Suburbs linked demographic and spatial transformation. Although it began in the nineteenth century and accelerated in the early twentieth— the census bureau officially recognized suburbs for the first time in 1910— suburban growth in fact took off only in the years after World War II. In the 1950s, suburban population size increased ten times faster than city populations. Not only population but also retailing, services, and industry moved to the suburbs. Suburbs became the center of American manufacturing with industrial parks and warehouses dotted along highways. Shopping malls became a distinctive new quasi-urban form, in effect, privatized civic centers.[62] Suburbanization reinforced the other major spatial trend in American cities: racial segregation. Suburbs were predominantly white. Not until late in the twentieth century did African American suburbanization become an important trend, and, even then, blacks who moved to the suburbs lived often in reconstituted racial clusters.

Urban redevelopment also transformed urban space. In the decades after World War II, urban renewal displaced poor residents, usually without relocating them to alternate housing, and cleared away downtown land for reuse as offices, retailing, and homes for the affluent. Public housing, by and large, was confined to segregated districts and never

Photograph 4.2   Aerial Photograph, Levittown, New York, and Surrounding Fields in the Mid-Twentieth Century

In the last half of the twentieth century, real estate development transformed many rural communities into sprawling suburbs. *Source:* Tony Linck/Time & Life Pictures/Getty Images.

matched existing needs. As urban renewal cleared poor people out of districts adjacent to downtowns, gentrification drew the affluent in. Gentrification referred to rehabilitating working-class housing for use by a wealthier class. Although the size of the population attracted to gentrified neighborhoods did not reverse the trend toward segregation and inequality, it did transform visible components of cityscapes—drawing in, especially, young white professionals with above-average incomes and providing them with services such as restaurants, coffee shops, and health clubs.

By the end of the twentieth century, economic, demographic, and spatial transformations had undercut existing definitions of urban and city. New metaphors competed to replace them. The urban and city metaphors fall into two rough groups: those looking inward toward central cities and those looking outward to metropolitan areas, regions, and, indeed, the world. Urban metaphors are not mutually exclusive. Sometimes the same writers use different metaphors to capture the increasingly fractured reality of urban or city. All of them, however, try to make sense of the patterns of inequality that grew out of the economic, demographic, and spatial transformation of American cities in the second half of the twentieth-century. Consider, first, the inward-looking metaphor that still very often first springs to mind with the mention of urban—inner city. Since the 1960s, discussions of city and urban in public policy and the media have often focused on a bundle of problems—disorder, crime, drugs, poverty, homelessness, out-of-wedlock births—for which the term inner city has come to serve as an automatic and convenient shorthand reference, evoked as well by the rhetoric of urban crisis used widely in the media and elsewhere in the 1970s and 1980s. A search of the *New York Times* between 1970 and 1997 turned up three hundred articles with inner city in their titles. Almost all referred to problems of race, poverty, disorder, crime, housing, or jobs: "Many Post-riot Bus Projects to Carry Inner City Poor to Jobs Are Failing" (1970); "Abandonment of Federal Housing Blights Inner Cities" (1972); "Kennedy Warns of Threats of Unrest in Inner Cities" (1980); "U.S. Poverty Is Found Declining Everywhere But in Big Inner Cities" (1980); "Crack, Bane of Inner City, Is Now Gripping Suburbs" (1989); "Health Problems of Inner City Poor Reach Crisis Point" (1990); "5 Years After Los Angeles Riots, Inner City Still Cries Out for Jobs" (1997).[63] The reduction of city to inner city reflected class and racial population change. As a metaphor, inner city was colored poor and black. The term urban invoked images of concentrated minority poverty and its attendant problems. City residents, unless shown otherwise, were increasingly assumed to be poor, black, or Hispanic. So pervasive did the image become that it spawned a new genre of popular culture that diffused outward from inner cities to the American heartland. Urban music, a category that includes "funk, soul and hip hop, as well as R and B" became "the biggest selling genre in the United States."[64] Jameel Spencer, the president of Blue Flame Marketing and Entertainment, "not only helped P. Diddy's Bad Boy Entertainment bring in "$300 million last year, he did it by transforming urban America from a specific location into a state of mind. . . . 'Urban used to be a location,' says Spencer, referring to the euphemism used for people living in large cities and inner-city minority youth. 'But now, everyone has cable and internet, and can see Ashton Kutcher wearing a trucker hat. It's a philosophy. The coolest kid in Wichita is urban.' "[65]

"Post-industrial city," another inward looking metaphor, responded to the decline of manufacturing. In contrast to inner city, it focused on urban economics rather than demographics and social structures. With his widely discussed 1973 book, *The Coming of Post-Industrial Society*, the sociologist Daniel Bell injected the phrase postindustrial into the language of social science and public policy. For Bell, three features marked a postindustrial society: "a shift from manufacturing to services;" "the centrality of the new science-based industries;" and "the rise of new technical elites and the advent of a new principle of stratification."[66] In his 1988 study of planning and politics in New York, London, and Paris, *Post-Industrial Cities*, H. V. Savitch adopted Bell's definition and applied it to cities. Post-industrialism, he argued, embraced multiple dimensions. "It encompasses a change in *what* we do to earn a livelihood (processing or services rather than manufacture) as well as *how* we do it (brains rather than hands) and *where* we do it (offices rather than factories)."[67] In a similar usage, the political scientist John H. Mollenkopf identified a "profound transformation" that had "seriously eroded the nineteenth-century industrial city. For lack of a better term, it might be called 'the postindustrial revolution'. . . . The office building, not the factory, now provides the organizing institution of the central city."[68] The first step toward a new definition of city, postindustrial recognized the emergence of a new urban form, but its characterization was negative. Postindustrial defined city by what it was not rather than by what it had become. This negative definition—vivid though it was—limited the idea's usefulness as a guide to reinterpreting the emergent meaning of urban in the late twentieth and early twenty-first centuries. Indeed, recognizing this limitation, Bell later renamed the concept he had popularized the information society.[69]

A third inward-looking metaphor—"dual city"—focused on the intensification and configuration of inequality in the late twentieth century. Its focus was the social structure that had emerged from economic and demographic transformation. John Mollenkopf and Manuel Castells titled their 1991 book exploring new patterns of inequality in New York, *Dual City*. For them, dual city, a metaphor, embraced in journalism and fiction, captured the social structure that had emerged from the transition to postindustrial society. Dual city, they recognized, oversimplified a very complicated situation, but had its uses. Despite its flaws, the dual city metaphor had "the virtue of directing our attention to the new inequalities that define the postindustrial city, just as depictions of 'How the Other Half Lives' defined the emerging industrial city a century ago." In big cities, growing class polarization, a problem everywhere in the nation, appeared most vividly. Increasingly bereft of their middle class, city populations divided between rich and poor, the former buoyed by jobs in finance, information, and high end services, the latter barely sustained by low-end service jobs, the informal economy, or government assistance. The two worlds of the dual city, the gleaming office towers and condos and the rundown housing and public ghettos of the poor, were not two separate worlds. Dual city theorists wanted to show the linkages that joined them—how they produced and depended on one another.[70]

Outward-looking metaphors joined cities to their metropolitan areas, regions, and the world. Cities have never been islands, divorced from their surrounding hinterlands or regions. City and hinterland, rather, have joined in elaborate, mutually dependent networks, each essential to the other's survival. Chapter 1 explored the links between city and countryside early in the twentieth century. The character of those links changed dramatically in the twentieth century. The concentration and subsequent deconcentration of population reflected one of those changes. Early in the twentieth century, dynamic urban and industrial growth drew people from the countryside like a magnet. Population concentrated increasingly in cities. In the post–World War II years, as jobs and opportunities followed new housing to the suburbs, urban populations deconcentrated. "Although still separate legal jurisdictions, it no longer makes sense," writes Robert Geddes, "to talk of suburbs and cities as if they were separate; they are economically and ecologically joined in a new kind of human settlement, the city region."[71] City region, metropolitan area, and elastic-inelastic city are all metaphors intended to capture the inadequacy of definitions that limit cities to their legal boundaries.

Three urbanists have led the effort to substitute metropolitan definitions for narrowly bounded conceptions of contemporary cities. For David Rusk, Myron Orfield, and Bruce Katz the redefinition of city underlies policies needed to counteract the baneful effects of metropolitan political fragmentation. No less concerned with inequality than dual city theorists, they focus on economic and political disparities between jurisdictions—central cities and their suburbs—more than on income gaps among city residents. Grossly unequal public services and tax burdens, environmental degradation, sprawl, racial segregation, job growth: these problems, they argue, only can be mitigated through metropolitan-wide actions. In *Cities Without Suburbs*, David Rusk, former mayor of Albuquerque, New Mexico, divides cities into elastic and inelastic. By annexing or otherwise incorporating many of their wealthier suburbs, elastic Sunbelt cities such as Albuquerque, Charlotte, Phoenix, and, for much of the twentieth century, Los Angeles, acquired the resources with which to alleviate poverty, homelessness, substandard education and other urban problems. Inelastic older northeastern and midwestern cities such as Philadelphia and Chicago remained trapped within their boundaries by expanding suburbs. Increasingly segregated over time, their middle class lost to the suburbs, they cannot survive without outside aid. For Rusk, the racial and economic segregation that creates an "urban underclass in many inner cities" constitutes "America's true urban problem." To be effective, policies that address "this problem must treat suburb and city as indivisible parts of a whole—because the real city is not just what's inside the city limits, it's the whole metropolitan area."[72]

Like Rusk, Myron Orfield, a Minnesota state senator and adjunct professor at the University of Minnesota law school, stresses the harmful results of political fragmentation and destructive competition between cities and suburbs. With detailed maps and case studies, in *American Metropolitics* he shows both the diversity among suburbs and the common interests that should bind them with each other and with central cities. Only metropolitan-wide policies and politics, he argues, can reverse the devastating impact of sprawl, unequal resources, and racial segregation.[73] At the Brookings Institution's Center on Urban and Metropolitan Policy, which he directs, Bruce Katz also champions metropolitan coalitions and federal policies as the only effective response to urban problems.[74]

The redefinition of city in metropolitan terms is one side of the coin; the redefinition of suburb is the other. Where they rubbed up against each other, suburb and city were becoming more alike as conventionally urban problems spread outward. As distinctions lessened, the real differentiation separated older inner suburbs from those on the periphery of metropolitan areas. But they, too, were not immune from the urban problems attendant on growth. There was, as the sociologist Mark Baldassare presciently described in 1986, "trouble in paradise."[75] Just what a suburb was—what made it distinct—was no longer clear. In chapter 3, we argued that a new family landscape—the diffusion of a variety of family forms—has undermined the original meaning of suburb as a place for families with children. Others have deconstructed suburb from different starting points. The historian Robert Fishman proclaimed the end of the era of the suburb, defined as a sylvan residential enclave for affluent male-headed families, a "bourgeois utopia" of commuters. By the 1980s, he held, the classic suburb had been replaced by the "post-suburb" or technoburb.[76] Others reclassified suburbs differently. Orfield divided them into at-risk suburbs, bedroom-developing suburbs, and affluent job centers.[77] "Suburbia conceals as well as reveals its complexity," the historian Delores Hayden observes in *Building Suburbia*. "For years, when urban historians wrote about the 'city,' they meant the center, the skyline, downtown."[78] With a close look, she identifies seven suburban patterns. Although the earliest date from before the Civil War, vestiges of all still exist.

The most famous, or notorious, new suburban form is Joel Garreau's edge city. Edge cities represent "[a] new frontier being shaped by the free, in a constantly reinvented land," Garreau trumpets. When "full blown," edge cities—massive configurations of office towers and malls at the crossroads of exurban highways—have five defining features:

- Five million square feet of leasable office space or more
- Six hundred thousand square feet of retail space or more

- A population that increases at 9 a.m. on workdays—marking the location as primarily a work center, not a residential suburb
- A local perception as a single end destination for mixed use—jobs, shopping, and entertainment
- A history in which thirty years ago, the site was by no means urban; it was overwhelmingly residential or rural in character[79]

Fishman wrote with some nostalgia of the original bourgeois utopia; Hayden blasted modern suburban forms for their environmental degradation, aesthetic barbarism, and social atavism; Orfield warned of the environmental and economic disaster inherent in the competitive fragmentation underlying suburban differentiation; Garreau championed the edge city. All, however, recognized that economic and demographic growth and transformation had undermined the older idea of suburb. On just what should replace it, however, no consensus has emerged.

The metropolitan redefinition of city looked outward from central cities to their regions; the global city reached out to the world. Sasskia Sassen, whose work set the agenda for debate on global cities, connects patterns of urban development to economic globalization. Sassen identifies a set of global cities at the pinnacle of new urban hierarchies, detached from their regions, linked, instead, to the world of international finance and trade. The new global cities—New York, Tokyo, London, São Paulo, Hong Kong, Toronto, Miami, Sydney, among others—have become "transnational market 'spaces.' As such cities have prospered, they have come to have more in common with one another than with regional centers in their own nation-states, many of which have declined in importance." The "finance and producer services complex in each city," she asserts, "rests on a growth dynamic that is somewhat independent of the broader regional economy—a sharp change from the past, when a city was presumed to be deeply articulated with its hinterland." Global cities are not regional centers. Rather, they are "command points in the organization of the world economy." Contrary to predictions that the capacity for instant communication across great distances has undercut the need for business services to locate near each other, Sassen argues that proximity remains essential to the conduct of international business. Economic globalization has made great cities more relevant and important than ever. Within cities, she contends, economic globalization results in a bifurcated social structure divided between affluent beneficiaries of the best jobs in the global economy and those who service them— Sassen's global cities, thus, are also dual cities.[80] Although Sassen identifies only a limited number of truly global cities, the idea applies more widely. In one way or another, every city of any size links to the world; it cannot escape the reach of economic globalization. Its banks and brokerage houses, to take one example, are parts of a worldwide system of finance, impacted by currency fluctuations and commodity prices around the world. Many of its businesses are franchises of worldwide corporations. Its media are dominated by giant international conglomerates. To one extent or another, all cities, including the new edge cities, are global.

Another outward-looking metaphor defines modern cities by what they produce. For Manuel Castells, the late twentieth-century informational city replaces the early twentieth-century industrial city. "Each mode of production," the agricultural, industrial, and informational, he writes, "is defined by the element that is fundamental in fostering productivity in the production process. . . . In the new, informational mode of development the source of productivity lies in the technology of knowledge generation, information processing, and symbol communication."[81] Modes of production give rise to distinctive geographies. Thus the "Information Age is ushering in a new urban form, the informational city." Although the informational city takes different shapes in Silicon Valley, Europe, and Asia, "some common transnational features" underlie the differences. The new society's base in "knowledge, organized around networks, and made up of flows," means that the "informational city is not a form but a process," not adequately represented, as in Garreau's edge city, by a "primitive technological vision that sees the world through the simplified lenses of endless freeways and fiber-optic networks." Garreau's depiction of "the core of the new urbanization process" in the United States misses two key points. First is the interdependence of edge cities. Unlike Sassen, Castells finds "functional interdependence" among "different units and processes in a given urban system over very long distances." The second point that Garreau's metaphor misses is the multiple dependencies at the heart of America's distinctive informational city. "The profile of America's informational city is not fully represented by the edge city phenomenon, but by the relationship between fast ex-urban development, inner-city decay, and obsolescence of the suburban built environment."[82] Castells' informational city is better understood as a network than a place, a process rather than an object. America's informational cities, however, have given rise to a distinctive suburban form, what Margaret Pugh O'Mara identifies as "cities of knowledge," residential and high-tech industrial nodes built around major research universities.[83] As a process, the informational city assumes different forms around the world. Garreau's edge city is very American; European informational cities are quite different. Across nations, however, the processes defining informational cities have crystallized in a "new spatial form, which develops in a variety of social and geographical contexts: mega-cities," defined as "the nodes of the global economy, concentrating the directional, productive, and managerial upper functions all over the planet: the control of the media; the real politics of power; and the symbolic power to create and diffuse messages."[84]

Which metaphor—inner city, postindustrial city, dual city, city-region, edge city, global city, informational city, city of knowledge—best captures urban America's essential features at the start of the twenty-first century? One answer, surely, is that all are partial. The helpfulness of each depends on the angle of interest—inward vs. outward, national vs. global—and the concern—inequality, environmental degradation, aesthetic value, political fragmentation, the possibility of community, for example. But each demands exploration and evaluation in its own right, and they are not entirely consistent. Garreau's cheerful optimism about the role and future of edge cities and Hayden's withering attack is one example; Sassen's emphasis on the importance of place and contiguity in global cities and Castell's stress on a-geographic networks is another. The work of assessing and reconciling multiple metaphors for cities, and of exploring their implications, is a central and urgent task for an interdisciplinary twenty-first century urban studies. However the process shakes out, one point is certain. Economic, demographic, and spatial transformation have exploded old ideas of cities and suburbs, turning them into encumbrances to the reformulation of helpful public policies. A similar case may be made about old ideas of family.

Family

On November 18, 2003, the Supreme Judicial Court of Massachusetts ruled four to three that marriage should be redefined in state law as a "voluntary union of two persons as spouses." The divided court gave the legislature 180 days to change state marriage law. Even if the legislature failed to comply, gay marriage would become legal in May.[85] The decision touched off a firestorm. Massachusetts Governor Mitt Romney vowed to seek a constitutional amendment banning same-sex marriage. Gay couples eagerly awaited May. The court had placed a difficult and emotive question on the public agenda, where it could no longer be glossed over or evaded. Just what did marriage—and, by extension, family—mean? By its support for gay marriage, the court recognized that facts on the ground had altered. Deep changes had transformed marriage, family, and parenthood. The law had yet to catch up. As with work and city, late twentieth-century history had undermined the conventional definition of family. The emotional tie to the old meaning, however, held so firmly that the response was different. With work and city, the issue was not so much a reluctance to jettison old ways of thinking as an inability to reach consensus on a new meaning. With family, the problem ranged from a widespread refusal to admit the obsolescence of definitions to efforts to slow, or even reverse, the speed of change.

The future of the family—and the direction of family policy—had been a hot political issue since the 1960s when Daniel Patrick Moynihan's report on the black family aroused a fierce controversy.[86] In the 1970s, conflict over abortion and the Equal Rights Amendment added to growing anxieties about the erosion of the family as a bedrock institution of American society.[87] By 1976, as worry about family trends escalated, presidential candidate Jimmy Carter promised to call a conference on the American family. Carter kept his promise, but when he began to organize the conference, irreconcilable political differences surfaced in a conflict over the event's name. Advocacy groups, supported by many social scientists, argued that family no longer described the variety of domestic arrangements in which Americans lived. Rather, to signal recognition of the diversity that had emerged in recent decades, the object of the conference's concern should be labeled families. When Carter agreed to change the name to "White House Conference on Families," conservatives objected bitterly. Carter, they felt, had abandoned the singular model of family, which, in their view, existed outside history, representing the norm from which all other alleged family types diverged, with ruinous consequences for individuals and societies.[88] The conflict over the conference's title prefigured both the sharp divisions that marked its proceedings and the battle lines in the war over family-related issues in the decades that followed.

The battles resulted from the changes to family and life course we described in chapter 3. Early twentieth-century sociological jeremiads wrapped real changes in family and life course in a story of loss and decay. Their observations are less useful as a record of what was happening to families than as testimony to the anxiety provoked by massive economic and demographic change and emergent new family definitions. In the essence of their complaints—loss of parental authority, corrosive individuality, failure of socialization, permissive sexuality, family-unfriendly work, and urban culture—and ambivalent waffling between conservative reaction and modern adaptation, they prefigured commentators on family in the late twentieth and early twenty-first centuries. In both eras, public officials and cultural authorities tried to reverse the direction of change in family life and intimate behavior. In both eras, they failed. Early twentieth-century couples refused to give up birth control or to increase the number of their children, despite lamentations over "race suicide," the legal prohibition of contraception, or the jailing of birth control advocates. In the early twenty-first century, the pro-life, pro-family movement, even when supported by the president and reinforced by congressional legislation, could not reverse the disassociation of marriage and parenthood, the tendency of unmarried young people to live together, or the rate of divorce. When men and women, for their own reasons, decide to change how they live together in families and how they express their sexuality, public authorities, short of draconian or dictatorial measures, can make their lives more difficult, but, in the end, they do not prevail.

Events confounded the predictions of early twentieth-century family doomsayers. Ties among the immediate members of small families did not disintegrate; instead, they intensified, signaling the apotheosis of a new family ideal—call it the nuclear family—in the years around World War II. In these years, the anthropologist Peter George Murdock injected the term "nuclear family" into public conversation. Murdock first used the term in a journal article in 1941. Others used it sporadically in the 1940s. (It had been used earlier in psychoanalytic literature in a very different sense.) It gained prominence, however, with Murdock's 1949 book, *Social Structure*. The nuclear family, for Murdock, was the primary building block from which all other familial forms derived. As an anthropologist, Murdock certainly was cognizant of family variation around the world. Indeed, "composite families" prevailed in 140 of the 187 societies on which he had data.[89] His definition, however, seemed to universalize the modal post–World War II American family as the norm against which to evaluate families elsewhere and the standard with which to label other family forms as pathological.

By the late twentieth century, Murdock's nuclear family clearly no longer described America's diversifying family arrangements. "To attempt to define what is family in contemporary America," observed a January 2000 editorial in the *San Diego Union-Tribune*, "even if we limit the unit to one with children, is becoming more and more difficult. Is it, as in the days of 'Ozzie and Harriet,' a father, mother and two or three children? Is it a grandmother raising a grandchild? Is it a stepfather and mother, both with several children from previous marriages? Is it a single mom depending on a few girlfriends who share parental duties to raise their kids?"[90]

New definitions of family, as in Daniel Patrick Moynihan's 1965 report on the black family, included a language of pathology that stigmatized the growing number of mothers raising children on their own. Dressed up in the language of modern social science, the underlying message about the family life of the poor was not so very different than the one conveyed by reformers in the Progressive era. Worry about the family came from liberals as well as conservatives.[91] Critics combined out-of-wedlock births, teenage pregnancy, and single-parent families in a powerful, modern, racially-tinged jeremiad about the family and its implications—welfare dependence and crime—for the future of American society.

Other commentators—Leonore Weitzman and Barbara Defoe Whitehead—attacked the consequences of divorce.[92] Whitehead was one of the principal writers associated with The Institute for American Values

(IAV), the think tank, according to the sociologist Arlene Skolnick, "responsible for the sudden shift in the national debate on the family since 1992."[93] Together, according to Skolnick, these writers and the Institute promoted a clear message that underlay the emergent national concern with "family values": family change was "a catastrophe for the rest of society. . . .[a] direct cause of our worst individual and social problems: poverty, crime, violence, delinquency, drug and alcohol abuse, school failure, teenage pregnancy, welfare dependency."[94] Unlike Moynihan, for the writers associated with the IAV, family crisis did not refer primarily to poor African Americans. It was, rather, a dangerous trend cutting through the social structure from top to bottom and threatening the future of the nation.

Demographic trends supplied fertile soil for the institute's concerns. For the anxiety over divorce and single-parent families coincided with the declining marriage rates and disassociation of marriage and parenthood described in chapter 3. The meaning, not the existence, of these trends was the source of controversy. Feminists and many family researchers considered the trends deplored by family critics irreversible. In themselves, they did not harm either children or the wider society. The problem lay in the failure of public policy to adjust to change by offering adequate support to the single mothers who composed such a large share of the new families.[95] Despite their deep differences, both parties to the family debate agreed on one implication of demographic trends: nuclear was no longer an accurate label for a great many, perhaps most, American families. But what should replace it? Not surprisingly, one answer popularized by the writers associated with the Institute for American Values was "post-nuclear" family, a term that gained currency around the same time as post-industrial city. "In the early years of the divorce revolution," Whitehead claimed, "post-nuclear family households were defined according to their relationship to marriage. Single-parent families were broken because the marriage bond had been broken."[96] Despite its lack of precision, post-nuclear popped up in a variety of places.[97] The Institute for American Values writers used it to criticize family arrangements resulting from divorce and out-of-wedlock births. Some social scientists employed it descriptively as a label for changes in the emotional basis of family life as well as in actual family forms. Lawyers found it helpful in pointing out the need for specialized estate planning. Marketers deployed it to highlight new audiences for advertising and journalists to describe families with two working parents. Artists gave it their own idiosyncratic twists. Michael Cunningham, author of *The Hours*, told an interviewer, "I think my interest in the post-nuclear family, which might include, say, a biological mother, a same-sex lover and the drag queen who lives downstairs, probably comes from being a gay man living through the AIDS epidemic."[98]

Feminist scholars also advocated new definitions of family. Not only were they far more sympathetic toward single-parent families and divorce, their emphasis on shared responsibilities and symmetrical roles forced an internal redefinition of family membership. By 1980, their influence resulted in an important change in the way the U.S. Census Bureau defined family structures and roles. In 1940, for the first time, the census constructed family types: "(1) 'normal' families, that is, families with the head and his wife residing together, with or without other persons; (2) other families with a man as head of the family, including broken families with a widowed, divorced, or separated man as head, together with families having a single man as head; and (3) all families with a woman head of family."[99] In 1980, "householder" replaced "head of household"—a term used for more than a century—while the assumption that the head, or reference person, in a family was the man was jettisoned completely. The Census Bureau explained,

> Recent social changes have resulted in greater sharing of household responsibilities among the adult members and, therefore, have made the term "head" increasingly inappropriate in the analysis of household and family data. . . . in 1980, the Census Bureau discontinued its longtime practice of always classifying the husband as the reference person (head) when he and his wife are living together.[100]

Behind this quiet bureaucratic definition lay a revolution.

The trends that exploded existing definitions of family forced changes in family law. The key to the many judicial decisions on family matters was individualization: priority given to the rights of individuals over those of the family group.[101] In the 1971 Supreme Court case that invalidated Massachusetts' prohibition on prescribing or selling contraceptives to unmarried individuals, Justice William J. Brennan wrote, "The marital couple is not an independent entity with a mind and heart of its own, but an association of two individuals each with a separate intellectual and emotional makeup."[102] Changing divorce laws embodied the increased emphasis on individual rights and emergent contractual view of marriage. Although court decisions modified divorce law between the 1940s and 1970s, the most dramatic and consequential development was no-fault divorce, initiated in California in 1970. The new rules, Weitzman argues, shifted "the legal criteria for divorce—and thus for viable marriage—from fidelity to the traditional marriage to personal satisfaction. They thereby redefined marriage as a time-limited, contingent arrangement rather than a lifelong commitment."[103]

The shift of focus from the collective needs of the family to the rights of its individual members permeated family law. As a result, in the course of just one decade, the "legal structures that had sustained and directed the vision of family during the preceding century and a half were being dismantled," the legal scholar Janet Dolgin writes. Disputes between husbands and wives and, even, between children and parents increasingly found their way to the courts. In the late 1980s, questions of family law dominated nearly half of all civil cases in U.S. courts.[104]

The Supreme Court, however, waffled, recognizing the demographic transformation of "family," but hesitating to overturn long standing family law or to overturn conventional social mores. In Troxel v. Granville (2000), Justice Sandra Day O'Connor, writing for the majority, acknowledged the increased role of grandparents in cases of family breakup but refused to infringe on the absolute right of parents to limit the visits of grandparents with their children.[105]

> The demographic changes of the past century make it difficult to speak of an average American family. The composition of families varies greatly from household to household. While many children may have two married parents and grandparents who visit regularly, many other children are raised in single-parent households. . . . The nationwide enactment of nonparental visitation statutes is assuredly due, in some part, to the States' recognition of these changing realities of the American family. Because grandparents and other relatives undertake duties of a parental nature in many households, States have sought to ensure the welfare of the children therein by protecting the relationship those children form with such third parties.

State laws granting visiting rights to grandparents, nonetheless, conflicted with the ancient right of parents "to make decisions concerning the care, custody, and control of children."[106] The Troxel decision soon affected cases in other states. Across the country, state courts found unconstitutional statutes that permitted third parties—stepparents, guardians, aunts, uncles, for instance, as well as grandparents—to petition for custody or visitation when parents objected. The courts' tilt toward tradition—their reluctance in this instance to ratify demographic change as the basis for overturning centuries' worth of family law—was sufficiently narrow to avoid conflict with new family forms. The Lambda Legal Defense and Education Fund, representing gay interests, considered the decision a "middle ground recognizing changes in the American family" and "heralded the ruling for not making broad legal pronouncements with adverse consequences for lesbian, gay, and other nonbiological parents, such as stepparents and caregivers." But another 2000 decision, which did have adverse consequences for gays, showed the Supreme Court's reluctance to extend nondiscrimination law to sexuality: in that year, the Court sustained the rights of the Boy Scouts to expel gay members.[107]

As an issue, gay rights pushed questions of marriage, parenting, and family into the public spotlight. Gay marriage at once challenged and upheld conventional definitions of family. It upset traditional assumptions about the gendered basis of family structure, but, at the same time, reinforced the importance of a long-term, committed, monogamous relationship recognized by law. Its critics, however, saw only the first half of the equation. Benefits for domestic partners, for instance, proved even more controversial than visitation rights for grandparents. Did gay couples compose families? In light of proliferating family forms, on what grounds could employers or the state claim that the absence of marriage—a status denied them—meant that gay couples living together in long-term relationships were not families? When gay liberation began in the 1960s, homosexual activities remained largely illegal; gays faced widespread discrimination in hiring; as late as 1986, the Supreme Court had refused to strike down state sodomy laws, a decision reversed only in 2004 in Lawrence v. Texas. Within little more than a decade, the recognition of committed relationships between gay partners as family was spreading swiftly throughout the nation, winning ever increasing acceptance.

The Domestic Partners Benefits movement started in 1982 with the *Village Voice* newspaper in New York City. In 1985, the California cities of Berkeley and West Hollywood followed. By the fall of 1997, close to one of every four firms employing 5000 or more workers provided health benefits to nontraditional partners as did more than fifty cities and counties and four states. Between 1999 and 2004, employer-sponsored domestic partner programs grew at a rate of about 20 percent per year. Courts generally proved supportive.[108] William B. Rubenstein, attorney for the ACLU, who successfully argued an important case in New York regarding a gay partner's inheritance of a rent-controlled apartment, called it "the first opinion by a judicial body of this stature that confers legal recognition, and in this case, family member status, on gay or lesbian relationships. . . . The entire concept of family has changed nationwide, and gay/lesbian relationships are just a part of the non-traditional domestic scene that is now emerging." A number of state governments reinforced the trend with domestic partner legislation.[109]

Conservative opponents warned that domestic partnerships constituted the entering wedge to demands for same-sex marriage, a charge angrily denied by gay and lesbian spokespersons. In fact, in this instance, the conservative prediction proved correct. Over the opposition of leading gay and lesbian rights organizations, a movement for same-sex marriage, starting in Hawaii, emerged swiftly around the country. Gay and lesbian leaders at first opposed demands for same-sex marriage for two reasons. One was pragmatic. They feared it would arouse a backlash and block continued progress. The other was ideological. Many within the gay and lesbian movement viewed marriage as an oppressive

Photograph 4.3   A Gay Couple with Its Child, Late Twentieth Century

By the late twentieth century, gay couples with children signified the emergence of new definitions of family. *Source:* Scott Sherman.

institution. Their goal was not to assimilate into mainstream, heterosexual institutions but to challenge them. The eagerness with which ordinary gay men and women pursued domestic partnerships, parenthood, and marriage, however, revealed very different goals at the grassroots. From the start, writes Jonathan Rauch in *Gay Marriage*, pressure for gay marriage arose from the "homosexual rank and file, the man and woman in the street and in the pew."[110] Ironically, given conservative criticism, gay and lesbian couples sought to replicate and strengthen the most conventional ideas of family and marriage. In the midst of conservative counterattack and the terrible AIDS crisis, Chris Bull and John Gallagher point out in *Perfect Enemies*, "more and more gays were choosing to settle down, form relationships, and raise children." The debate among gays over assimilation "sounded increasingly outdated because it ignored the new reality of how gays and lesbians were living their lives."[111] (See photograph 4.3.)

In the early 1990s, three gay couples in Hawaii challenged the state's decision denying them a marriage license. When they decided to appeal, they received no help from national gay and lesbian associations, who believed they would lose and that the case would prove a public relations disaster. As everyone expected, the state court upheld the denial. At issue, claimed the court, was the very definition of family. The state law prohibiting gay marriage was "obviously designed to promote the general welfare interests of the community by sanctioning traditional man-woman family units and procreation." To everyone's surprise, however, the Hawaii Supreme Court overturned the lower court's ruling, arguing that denying marriage licenses to the couples violated the state constitution's equal protection clause prohibiting gender-based discrimination.[112] It remanded the case to a lower court for trial, scheduled for 1996.

The Hawaii decision aroused conservative fury throughout the nation even as it heartened gay and lesbian couples. The conservative national Christian legal group, the Rutherford Institute, based in Charlottesville, Virginia, was one of the outside groups that intervened. In his book, *Religious Apartheid*, the institute's founder, John Whitehead, wrote: "The family, once the bedrock of society, is under siege from state agencies and culture at large. . . . As new forms of family, such as homosexual liaisons, gain more acceptance, the traditional family is losing its authority."[113]

National opposition to gay marriage centered in Congress. In the 1996 Defense of Marriage Act, Congress provided "that no State shall be required to give effect to a law of any other State with respect to same-sex 'marriage.'" The Act also defined marriage and spouse in federal law: "marriage is a legal union of a man and a woman as husband and wife, and a spouse is a husband or wife of the opposite sex." The act passed with overwhelming support: 347-62 in the House and 85-14 in the Senate; President Bill Clinton signed the bill on September 21, 1996.[114] The act sanctioned the efforts of state legislatures around the country to shore up their marriage laws, which largely defined marriage as between a man and woman, by defending themselves from having to recognize same-sex marriages taking place in other states.

Although Vermont recognized civil unions in 2000, granting them many of the same benefits of marriage,[115] the 2003 Massachusetts Supreme Court decision legalizing gay marriage sparked the most controversy. In reaching its decision, the court relied on a wide array of arguments and precedents. Among them was the U.S. Supreme Court's reasoning in Troxel. The court quoted approvingly Justice O'Connor's observation: "The demographic changes of the past century make it difficult to speak of an average American family. The composition of families varies greatly from household to household." Massachusetts, the court pointed out, "has responded supportively to 'the changing realities of the American family' . . . and has moved vigorously to strengthen the modern family in its many variations."[116]

Neither the court's carefully reasoned arguments nor changing family realities persuaded opponents of gay marriage. In only one year, gay marriage reignited culture wars that had lost their intensity. Pro-family

Christian groups, Focus on the Family and the Family Research Council, which had concentrated their fury on Roe v. Wade, now directed their considerable resources to turning back gay marriage.[117] The battle was joined so quickly because the trenches had been dug three decades earlier in the abortion fight. The gay marriage war was fought along the same lines with parallel arguments and by armies with similar identities. *Washington Post* writer Alan Cooperman called gay marriage "the new abortion."[118]

Concerned that courts might invalidate the Defense of Marriage Act and force states to honor gay marriages contracted in other jurisdictions, President George W. Bush vigorously supported a constitutional amendment "defining and protecting marriage as a union of man and woman as husband and wife."[119]

The attempt to pass a federal constitutional amendment prohibiting gay marriage failed in the Senate, partly because some senators objected on principle, but, even more, because they considered it a question that should be left to individual states to decide. Nonetheless, polls showed that an overwhelming majority of Americans opposed granting marriage rights to gay and lesbian couples. Where the issue came to a popular vote, it usually lost. In November 1998, Hawaiians voted decisively to override their supreme court by amending the state's constitution to restrict marriage to same-sex partners. In Massachusetts, in March 2004, the state legislature voted to combine support for civil unions with a constitutional amendment banning same-sex marriage. The battle over the amendment, which required approval by the voters, promised to be intense: a poll showed 53 percent of the state's voters opposed to gay marriage and 60 percent in favor of civil unions. In August 2004, Missouri became the first state to bar gay marriage with a constitutional amendment—approved by 70 percent of voters. In the November 2004 election, eleven states passed constitutional amendments barring gay marriage.[120] In the eyes of most Americans, gay and lesbian couples, no matter how committed to one another, were not real families.

Another issue—assisted reproductive technologies—also posed fundamental questions about the definition of family. With these technologies, which include "egg donation, fetal ovary donation, or embryo micromanipulation," one scholar suggested, "women could arrange to give birth to their own siblings, aunts, and uncles." And they raised new and difficult questions for family law. "Which of two women—genetic contributor or gestational host—is a mother? Why are biological but unwed fathers treated differently from surrogate mothers? When two people produce embryos to further their parental ambitions, then change their minds, what is to be done with the embryos? Are they life, or property? Should courts enforce contracts involving these and other reproductive mechanisms that increasingly vary from the conventional model?" Already, in the late twentieth century, courts were being asked to decide the disposition of frozen embryos in divorce cases.[121] As technology joined with demography to explode older definitions of "family," courts—like the public—found themselves with no clear precedents or guidelines. With powerful passions—including strong opposition from religious conservatives—swirling around it, reproductive technology added to the contests over the meaning of sexuality and family aroused by gay marriage in the late twentieth and early twenty-first centuries.

Gay families, blended families, single-parent families, empty nest families, post-nuclear families were all terms in play to describe what American families had become. The confusion over the meaning of family in the early twenty-first century differed from the debates over the definition of work and city in one important way. With work and city, everyone recognized the irreversibility of change. The question was what it meant and how to respond. With family, a very large fraction of Americans refused to admit the permanency of change; they deplored new family forms and hoped, and believed it possible, to turn back the clock. They objected to the term families, wanting, instead, to talk of family. Public policies toward families therefore changed at an uneven pace. Divorce law moved fastest and furthest to recognize new realities. Court decisions touching on relations between parents, children, and third parties lurched uncertainly in different directions, although they did increasingly focus on the rights of the individual rather than the family unit. Measures affecting gays and lesbians also varied, opening up jobs, extending benefits, but threatening to make marriage impossible; policies toward reproductive technology were largely undeveloped. The federal government, however, sunk millions into an attempt to promote marriage.

The private sector responded most quickly to changing family definitions. Advertisers, for instance, tailored their appeals increasingly to working mothers and to two income and gay and lesbian families.[122] Developers and retailers redesigned suburban housing and shopping to cater to singles and empty nesters.[123] Most new day care facilities were developed by private providers. In the decade between 1987 and 1997 alone, the number of taxable day care businesses jumped from 26,809 to 43,955, an increase of 64 percent, and the nontaxable number rose only from 13,822 to 18,099, an increase of 31 percent.[124] Conservatives may have objected to new kinds of families, but the market, which they championed, found them an irresistible new source of profit.

An essentialist idea that placed family outside history often underlay reluctance to accept family change. The nuclear family of husband, wife, and children was primordial, an expression of human needs, the foundation of social stability and progress. In truth, however, not only were family forms historically contingent, they were also products of the state.[125] Throughout American history, relations between parents and children, marriage, divorce, inheritance, and other family matters were all subject to legislatures and courts. In fact, critics of family change now turn to law to reverse family trends. Only by using the power of the state aggressively can they hope to shift family history into reverse and enforce an idea of family that draws its authority from human nature and divine sanction. A similar turn to the state to enforce essentialist ideas has bedeviled the history of ideas of race.

Race

A 1997 *Time* article featuring Tiger Woods illustrates how immigration and intermarriage have undermined the language of race in America:

> The way Americans think and talk about race will have to catch up with the new reality. Just how anachronistic our racial vocabulary has become was made clear by Woods in an appearance last week on *The Oprah Winfrey Show*. When asked if it bothered him, the only child of a black American father and a Thai mother, to be called an African American, he replied, "It does. Growing up, I came up with this name: I'm a 'Cablinasian,'" which he explained is a self-crafted acronym that reflects his one-eighth Caucasian, one-fourth black, one-eighth American Indian, one-fourth Thai and one-fourth Chinese roots. . . . He said that when he was asked to check a box for racial background, he couldn't settle on just one. "I checked off 'African American' and 'Asian': Those are the two I was raised under."[126]

Wood's uncertainty about how to characterize his identity reflects the fluidity of race as an idea throughout American history. One moment of change occurred during the last decades of the twentieth century when events undermined the narrow biracial definition of race frozen in public discourse after World War I. What new definition would replace it remained contested. The politics of the debate reflected the painful ironies resulting from both centuries of oppression and the new, less visible form of inequality that, as discussed in chapter 2, replaced it.

How to word questions about racial identity in decennial censuses has occasioned contests over the definition of race since the nineteenth century. The answers arrived at by federal census officials profoundly shaped the national discourse of race.[127] By redrawing racial boundaries in the year 2000 census, the Census Bureau recognized the changing meaning of race in America reflected in Tiger Woods' uncertainty and pushed public discourse in new directions. Hard as it was for many people to recognize, the old idea of America as black and white—never an accurate reflection of the nation's demography—was gone forever.

For the first time, the 2000 census allowed individuals to choose more than one race. Simple and straightforward on the surface, this change was the culmination of a fierce political contest that heralded a new way of thinking about race in America. The new census rules, social scientists concur, mark a historic turning point in the meaning of race. "The greatest change in the measurement of race in the history of the United States occurred in the census of 2000," the preeminent census scholar Reynolds Farley asserted.[128] Former director of the Census Bureau responsible for conducting the 2000 census, Kenneth Prewitt, predicted: "when Census 2000 is interpreted from the vantage point of history, it will not be partisan politics or civic mobilization or coverage improvements or technical innovations that will command the most attention. It will be the multiple-race question on the census form."[129]

However, the full implications of the multirace option would remain obscure for years, Prewitt also observed.[130] For the Census Bureau had pulled back from injecting multiracial as a category in the official tabulations used for determining congressional representation or the allocation of money by race. Instead, it recategorized individual subjective responses into the old racial categories. Individuals who checked more than one racial box on the census form were officially counted as minorities if one category represented an official minority. (For instance, all those self-identified as white and African American were counted as African American in the official tabulations.)[131]

The intersection of four histories resulted in census 2000's new approach to the race question: the wording of census questions about race; ideas about race in the wider society; immigration and intermarriage; and the politics of civil rights. The problem of categorizing race emerged in 1850 with the first census that enumerated individuals. Racial "scientists"—as well as politicians—wanted evidence for their belief that black and white differences in longevity, mental health, and other characteristics reflected biological distinctions which marked whites as superior. Thus the census included three categories: white, black, and mulatto. (White was the default; race was entered according to enumerator's observations only for blacks and mulattos. Self-identification, a procedural shift with profound implications, began only with the 1970 census.) Indian was added in 1860, Chinese in 1870, Japanese and Quadroon and Octoroon in 1890.[132] These new categories reflected both immigration and the increased preoccupation with race in the late nineteenth century. In practice, census takers were unable to distinguish degrees of African American ancestry with accuracy, and quadroon and octoroon were dropped from subsequent censuses. Mulatto made its last appearance in 1920. The Census Bureau's rationale for dropping mulatto was bureaucratic: imperfections in the enumeration that seemed impossible to correct. There was, of course, more to the story.

Early in the twentieth century, the multiplicity of census categories reflected the capacious definition of race found in popular use. "In this moment of widespread social, economic, and cultural tumult," the historian Matthew Pratt Guterl explains, "a vast tide of racial categories washed over American culture" raising a host of crucial questions. "What, exactly, was a race? Where, precisely, should the boundary lines of racial difference be drawn?" With no clear answers, "Scientists, journalists, politicians, and cultural figures wavered between allegiance to one set of physical traits and to another, leaving a remarkable looseness of fit in the language of race." Americans used the term race to describe a wide array of peoples—southern and eastern Europeans, for instance, as well as African Americans and Asians. In the late nineteenth century, about fifty groups were recognized as races. Although this number was officially consolidated into five races by the 1900 census, race still was commonly used to refer to a wide number of groups: Celts, Jews, Slavs, and Italians, for example. Yet, by and large, Americans were racial essentialists, believing that race composed an inherited, unalterable, core identity. By the 1920s, "driven by the Great War, the Great Migration, the foreclosure of European immigration, and the emergence of a national culture obsessed with the 'the Negro,'" that identity had contracted to black or white.[133]

Census categories rested on the idea of blood quantas, which was both a scientific and legal concept. In science, it signified ancestry and the intergenerational transmission of racial traits. In the law, it cemented in place a view of race "as unchanging, natural, and ever-present, if not always visible." The color line, following southern practice, was set legally at "one drop" of black blood. In the technical language of the time, this was the "hypodescent" rule that increasingly governed Jim Crow and antimiscegenation laws. By removing the mulatto option, the Census Bureau implicitly recognized this rule and reinforced the growing tendency to think of race in America as black and white.[134]

Census racial categories changed only in minor ways between 1930 and 1960, even though science increasingly called into question the biological basis of race.[135] In 1970, the Census Bureau added a number of new categories.[136] These reflected minority group lobbying that led to what the historian David Hollinger labels the "ethno-racial pentagon," codified in the Office of Management and Budget's (OMB) 1977 Directive 15. The five-way classification, OMB stressed, was not "scientific or anthropological in nature." Rather, its purpose was bureaucratic: the demand "for the collection and use of compatible, nonduplicative, exchangeable racial and ethnic data by federal agencies." Directive 15 set the census racial categorization framework for the rest of the century. Its categories, based on group geographic origin, were American Indian or Alaskan Native, Asian or Pacific Islander, Black (later Black or African American), Hispanic, and Euro-American.[137] Individuals were to be assigned to only one category. Where their ancestry was mixed, they were to be put in the "category which most clearly reflects the individual's recognition in the community." The designation nonwhite was forbidden in federal government data.

These categories had consequences. They were to be used in civil rights reporting, which was why organized minority groups took them so seriously. The assessment of discrimination in employment, housing, and other arenas; political districting; and government funds: all depended on official categories. The census did not adopt these categories directly in its questions. Rather, it expanded the list of races to identify group members who could be aggregated into the ethno-racial pentagon. (By 2000, the list of races had been expanded to sixteen plus a residual but the Hispanic categories changed only slightly.)[138] Although the expanded list of races did not include Hispanic, which merited its own question and set of subdivisions, in practice, for purposes of civil rights and other federal tabulations, Hispanic was part of the pentagon. Although the OMB and Census Bureau were reactive, bowing to ethnic group pressure, they were also ahead of popular discourse because when Americans talked about race, they usually still meant black and white.

In the late twentieth century, two demographic trends—immigration and intermarriage—exploded whatever tenuous base had sustained America's biracial division into black and white.[139] The parallels with the situation a century earlier were profound. "Today, as the binary structure of racial identity—the white-black dyad—begins to give way before demographic trends . . . the despair over the 'disuniting' of the American community mirrors the fears and anxieties of the first thirty years of this century," the historian Matthew Guterl points out.[140] Population projections clearly showed that in the future blacks would not compose the largest minority and that whites no longer would be the majority. Just when those shifts would take place, and how large they would be, was not certain. Census Bureau estimates were not reliable because they excluded intermarriage. A group of distinguished demographers critical of the Census Bureau arrived at its own estimate: by 2050, about 15 percent of the population will be "multiple origin" and 55 percent "nonwhite." African Americans will be 15 percent of the population, Hispanics 24 percent, and Asians and Pacific Islanders 9 percent. At the beginning of the next century, they predict, the nonwhite fraction will have grown to 70 percent.[141]

This immense demographic shift results from both immigration and intermarriage. The immigration story has been outlined earlier in this book. Intermarriage deserves a closer look because it is the most accessible record of "amalgamation"—"a major theme in U.S. history."[142] Immigrants from eastern and southern Europe who arrived in the United States in the late nineteenth and early twentieth centuries did not intermarry very often. Their children and grandchildren did, however. The outcome was the attenuation of ethnic identity as immigrants increasingly became "white," blending into the "old stock" population, distinguishing themselves not only from African Americans but also from the new Hispanic and Asian arrivals.[143] Demographers predict that the children and grandchildren of recent immigrants will replicate the intermarriage patterns of earlier immigrant groups. The overall 30-percent intermarriage rate among Hispanics in 2000 masked generational differences: 8 percent for first, 32 percent for second, and 57 percent for the third generation. Similarly, the 20-percent intermarriage rate among Asian and Pacific Islanders combined 13 percent for the first, 34 percent for the second, and 54 percent for the third generation. Blacks, by contrast, intermarried much less often—10 percent—and whites, 8 percent, even less.[144] Nonetheless, black intermarriage rates had increased during the twentieth century. Consider thirty-year-old blacks born from 1906 to 1915, from 1936 to 1945, and from 1966 to 1975. The trends show an increase in intermarriage across the century, with the rate for men more than twice the fraction for women.[145] Virtually all this increase took place after World War II as racial barriers loosened.[146] The other important point about intermarriage is geographical. It did not take place to the same extent throughout the nation. Blacks intermarried much less often in the South, and rates for white as well as black intermarriage were highest in the Mountain and Pacific states (see figure 4.1).[147]

Married interracial couples and their children increasingly objected to forced labeling as members of only one race. Out of their objections in the 1980s and 1990s emerged organizations and publications that together formed the very loosely coordinated national multiracial movement.[148] One researcher, writing late in the twentieth century, discovered approximately eighty multiracial organizations founded since 1979 with forty still active. Although immigration and intermarriage propelled the multiracial movement, three other factors help account for the timing of its origins. First was state racial policy, which, through legislation such as the Civil Rights Act (1964), the Voting Rights Act (1965), and the Housing Act (1968), increased the occasions for racial self-classification and heightened its consequences. Second, the rise of identity politics—black power, the emergent pan-Asian movement, and heightened group consciousness among American Indians and Latinos, for instance—"provided a model along which demands for multiracial identity would be couched almost 25 years later." Third, the ascendance of identity group politics heightened the importance of official "ethno-racial identity" in America. Lacking an ethnic identity, people who claimed multiracial origin were "socially nonexistent." and required a "state category" to "recoup their social honor."[149]

Spokespersons for the multiracial movement did not ask the Census Bureau to allow individuals to check more than one race. Rather, they

Figure 4.1   Cross-Ethnic Marriages, Thirty- to Thirty-Nine-Year-Olds by Year of Birth

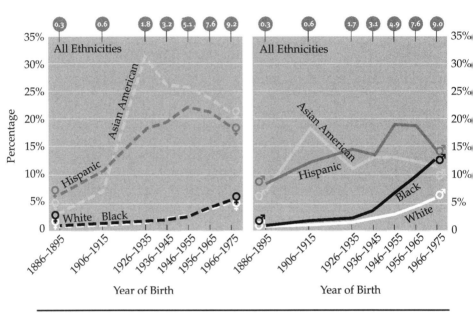

Note: Only one in a thousand white men and women born between 1866 and 1895 married someone from another ethnic group. Among those born between 1966 and 1975, nearly 10 percent intermarried. White women remained the least likely to be married to someone from another ethnic group, while 18 percent of Hispanic women and 21 percent of Asian American women had intermarried.
Source: Data from Ruggles et al. (2004).

wanted to add "mixed race" or "multiracial" as one racial option on the census.[150] The "mark more than one" option, they argued, perpetuated false essentialist notions of race, whereas the reaggregation of individual responses into a version of the old ethno-racial pentagon perpetuated the scientifically worthless and politically harmful one-drop rule. Some multiracial leaders wanted to do away with any racial questions on the census. Multiracial activists were not the first group to request special recognition on the census. Many ethnic groups had made similar demands. The multiracial advocates, however, were the first to claim "ethno-racial self-identification" as "a person's right."[151]

By the summer of 1993, civil rights organizations had concluded that a "multiracial" option on the census could shrink their demographic base, affecting the distribution of federal funds, the implementation of affirmative action, and congressional redistricting. The multiracial movement, they believed, threatened their political and legal interests by reducing their size. Opposing the addition of a multiracial census category, organizations representing African Americans, Hispanic Americans, Asian Americans, and American Indians found themselves in the odd position of defending classifications based on the odious one-drop rule.[152] (Ironically, the multiracial movement would not have been possible without the civil rights movement, which legitimized the advocacy of group rights and introduced tactics on which the multiracial movement drew.)[153] The multiracial option presented civil rights leaders with an excruciating dilemma. Essentialist definitions of race had legitimated centuries of overt, overlapping forms of oppression. Nonetheless, since the 1960s, minority group leaders had tried to preserve distinctions while transforming their associated stigmas into sources of pride and spurs to mobilization. Applied to group or individual attributes, as well as to schools, separate never had been equal. Yet, recognition of color-based differences, and the handicaps they imposed, lay at the heart of proposed remedies like affirmative action.

Leery of categories that threatened to dilute minority group numbers, advocates for minorities objected to a multiracial category on the census and, by and large, supported the status quo in racial identification. Like the multiracial advocates, they rejected biological views of race. However, they responded not by rejecting the idea of race but by defining it in contextual and social terms with a theory based on history. The African American legal scholar Christine Hickman, for example, highlighted the ironical results of the one-drop rule and argued for a definition of race rooted in social history. The one-drop rule, she contended, "created the African-American race as we know it today." Because it united blacks of disparate origins into one cohesive and politically influential group, the one-drop rule is an example of how "devil's work" can result in good. Hickman accepted the scientific deconstruction of race as biology. But, for her, it is beside the point. Race exists because it is there, part of our lived daily experience. Children of biracial couples are black because that is how they are perceived. Americans' instinctive response to them—that they are black not white—is the outcome of social history. Only by acknowledging the group identity that social history has created can blacks fight against discrimination and injustices it has imposed.[154]

Disputes over the multiracial option came to a head in 1993 when the Office of Management and Budget announced that it would consider modifying the old racial categories and invited recommendations—"a tremendous accomplishment for the multiracial movement," Farley observes.[155] Reviewing four years of work on the race question, in 1997 OMB grounded its recommendations in demographic change and bureaucratic imperative. "The multiracial population is growing, and the task of measuring this phenomenon will have to be confronted sooner or later. Adopting a method for reporting more than one race now means that the demographic changes in society can be measured more precisely with a smaller discontinuity in historical data series than would occur in the future."[156] After testing questions and reviewing evidence, OMB compromised. Instead of recommending a "multiracial" category, it proposed the "mark all that apply" option, a separate question for Hispanics, and reaggregation into a variant of the ethno-racial pentagon.

Neither the OMB in its 1997 guidelines nor the Census Bureau defined race explicitly. In practice, their definition blurred race and ethnicity, the boundaries of both of which seemed increasingly indistinct. OMB referred to the "fluid demarcation between the concepts of 'race' and 'ethnicity'" and encouraged "the search for a single question that satisfactorily captures both race and ethnicity."[157] Two elements together composed the official definition of race. First was geography: members of races shared a common geographic origin. Second was public opinion and political mobilization. As it derived its recommendations on racial categories, OMB surveyed a sample of public opinion through focus groups and other measures, and heard from representatives of racial and ethnic groups demanding recognition on the census and other government tabulations. Races, then, were groups of people with common, nonoverlapping, geographic origins identified as distinct by advocacy groups and public opinion. This definition did not pretend to grounding in biology, anthropology, or any other theory. It was developed, rather, to serve bureaucratic and political ends. But it served to reinforce essentialist notions of race, nonetheless.[158]

Scientists, who had demolished the biological basis of race, were not impressed. Commenting on the reception of the OMB guidelines by scientists, a writer in *Science* observed: "as far as geneticists are concerned, they're meaningless."[159] "Today, the majority of geneticists, evolutionary biologists, and anthropologists," the evolutionary biologist Joseph L. Graves, Jr., wrote, "agree that there are no biological races in the human species."[160] Yale University geneticist Kenneth Kidd claimed "the DNA samples he's examined show that there is 'a virtual continuum of genetic variation' around the world. 'There's no place where you can draw a line and say there's a major difference on one side of the line from what's on the other side. . . . there's no such thing as race in [modern] *Homo Sapiens*."[161]

Leaders of the multiracial movement were disappointed in the OMB, too, though they recognized its recommendations were a "major change." Some kept fighting for a true multiracial option or, better, abolition of the racial question altogether. Civil rights leaders also endorsed the OMB recommendations, first, because they recognized that only a small fraction of respondents would check more than one racial category and, second, because it would probably increase the number of minorities a bit by adding "people who primarily identify themselves as white but also knew that they had black, Asian, or Indian ancestors."[162]

Civil rights leaders' forecasts proved accurate. Only 2.4 percent of respondents marked more than one racial category on the 2000 census, but there were variations across groups: 2.5 percent of whites, 4.8 percent of African Americans, 13.9 percent of Asians, and 6 percent of self-identified Hispanics checked more than one box. The future, however, seemed clearly on the side of multiracial identification: 42 percent who checked more than one racial box were under the age of eighteen, compared to 25 percent who checked only one race; twenty-year-old black householders identified themselves as multiracial nine times more and twenty-year-old Asians twice as often as sixty-year-olds from the same backgrounds.[163]

Along with science, immigration and intermarriage had destabilized previously naturalized ideas of race and forced the Census Bureau to adopt a new category that broke sharply with past assumptions. No clear and agreed-upon alternative definition of race emerged, of course. One set of ideas fundamental to American politics, society, and law had been undermined without putting another in its place. There were, in fact, alternatives competing for attention: for example, the idea of race implicit in the census, the abolition of race proposed by the libertarian wing of the multiracial movement, the preservation of the status quo advocated, ironically, by some racial spokespersons, and the variants of "postethnicity," suggested by intellectuals such as David Hollinger.

Hollinger finds "the continued use of the word *race* to distinguish the groups of the [ethno-racial] pentagon, or indeed to distinguish any groups of people from one another in any context whatsoever . . . highly problematic." For Hollinger, victimization sets race apart from ethnicity in common usage. "When we now refer to a race, we most often mean to address the unequal treatment of people on the basis of biological ideas long discredited." The paradigm case, of course, is black people. But race is also used "to identify the one community of descent most responsible for these classifications and for the unequal treatment justified by them, the Caucasians or Europeans." Perceived victimization, he argues, also underlies the recent racialization of Latinos. The blocs that compose the ethno-racial pentagon, Hollinger contends, derive coherence not from science or culture but from "the dynamics of prejudice and oppression in U.S. history and from the need for political tools to overcome the legacy of that victimization." Hollinger wants to scuttle the term race and to replace it with ethno-racial blocs.[164] Immigration and intermarriage point toward an erosion of identifiable communities of descent and toward the possibility that persons now labeled black, Latino, or Asian, like white ethnics before them, will be able to choose their ethnic affiliation voluntarily. They will be postethnic: at once cosmopolitan citizens of the world and members of voluntarily chosen communities of descent. This, at any rate, is his hope.[165]

Aside from its service to real interests, the dilemmas and contradictions that the term and concept of race pose are so difficult and painful—so incapable of consistent and satisfactory resolution—that even most scholars, as well as writers for popular audiences, just avoid them. As an example, consider the excellent symposium in the June 2004 issue of *The Journal of American History* on the 1954 Brown v. Board of Education Supreme Court decision that declared racial segregation in education unconstitutional. The participating historians, all authors of important work, carefully contextualize the shifting meanings of integration and inequality. They do not, however, deconstruct ideas of race. In fact, race remains a given in their contributions, its meaning unchanged over time. Thus, while they attack racism and its consequences, they validate race's reality.[166] No easy way out of this dilemma exists. Although recognition is a first move, defining race will almost certainly remain as difficult and politicized in the twenty-first as in the twentieth century. In practical terms, the most workable response may turn out to be the Census Bureau's bureaucratic compromise.

The geographic, bureaucratic, multiracial, minority advocacy, and postethnic ideas of race surely do not exhaust the range of definitions current in early twenty-first century America.[167] But, in their variety, they underscore an important point. Despite their political and conceptual differences, all four start from a similar place: the realization that profound demographic and social change has undermined old definitions of race. America is not black and white; race is not a valid scientific idea; intermarriage is mingling women and men from all communities of descent. What vocabulary will best capture group identity in the twenty-first century? The answer remains far from clear. But two things are certain: it cannot be the same as in the twentieth century and it will have immense consequences that reverberate throughout every corner of public life.

Epilogue

What Does It Mean to
Be an American?

I F SCIENCE has undermined ideas of race, if intermarriage has blurred the meaning of ethnicity, if immigration has changed the geographic origins of the population, if America no longer can be described as black and white, if the vocabulary of group identity has been rendered obsolete, what, then, has happened to the idea of nationality? What does it mean to be an American? The term is actually very old. American was used in the sixteenth century to refer to the inhabitants of the North American continent.[1] Over time, its meaning became less, not more, precise, and since the early days of the republic it has always posed something of a puzzle. Americans, it has been said, are made, not born. In a technical sense, this is not true because anyone born in this nation automatically is a citizen. But in a looser sense it expresses something distinctive about the nation's identity. American did not emerge from ancient ties to place or reflect a singular ethnic or racial origin. As a political, rather than a geographic, identity American was constructed as a result of revolution and the act of creating a new nation. From the beginning, it designated women and men of diverse backgrounds. Some came from families resident on the North American continent for many decades; others had arrived in recent years. On this continent, they lived in colonies distinct in geography and economy; they thought of themselves as from Virginia or Massachusetts. It is telling that they called their creation, the United *States* of America. Until the Civil War, the United States was a plural noun—"The United States are," not "The United States is." The new nation's official motto—*E Pluribus Unum* translates to From Many, One—referred to the creation of one nation from thirteen independent colonies; on the Great Shield, thirteen arrows fill the quiver, thirteen stripes cross the flag, and thirteen stars dot the constellation.[2] It took weeks to travel between colonies or for information to circulate among them. Yet, at a point in the late eighteenth century,

217

these geographically dispersed colonists fought a revolutionary war together and in its course and afterwards called themselves Americans. What did they mean?

There was a protean quality to national identity. It was never static. Massive waves of immigration, internal migration, war, economic transformation, and the extension of civil and political citizenship forced continual renegotiation of its meaning. In the era with which this book starts—the early twentieth century—immigration, industrialization, and the acquisition of empire forced the question to the forefront of the public agenda; less than two decades later World War made it even more urgent. The same can be said for the late twentieth and early twenty-first centuries, and for similar reasons. Once again, events on the ground have shaken old certainties and demanded that we reformulate one of the principal ideas that structure thinking about public life.

For all the concern with the question, answers by and large have been partial and unsystematic. They have reflected the aspect of the term American of concern to individual observers—today, for instance, the obsession is multiculturalism—and a voice that looks outward or downward from positions of intellectual, cultural, or political authority. But American is a multivocal idea, one understood fully only as a collage of the view from various angles, the result of close attention paid to what the several parties to the conversation have to say. As a concept, in other words, American is multidimensional.

Four dimensions—source, voice, metric, and location—together constitute the elements necessary for understanding what it means to be an American at any particular moment in the nation's history. Source refers to what prompts concern with the question in the first place. In general, it is either large numbers of immigrants from new places or threat, usually war, homegrown "radicalism," or a combination of the two. Voice calls attention to whose definition is reported, insiders (authorities) or outsiders (immigrants, American Indians, for instance).

When a new immigration wave destabilizes the definition of American, the voice of insiders is sometimes generous, welcoming newcomers, expanding the idea of American to embrace multiple ethnicities; but sometimes it is hostile, drawing a tighter circle around an imagined idea of a pure America. Or, as happens most frequently, it may include both. When, however, the nation is threatened and authorities fear active and dangerous enemies, the definition is drawn in aggressively defensive ways that exclude many, natives as well as newcomers, on the basis of ideas, race, and ethnicity.

Outside voices are the ones about which we know least. What, at different points in the nation's past, has American meant to African Americans and American Indians? What did it mean to Southerners during and immediately after the Civil War? There are tantalizing clues, but no coherent history. For instance, despite slavery, hints abound that during the Civil War and early years of Reconstruction, blacks self-identified as patriotic Americans. In 1862, Corporal Prince Lambkin, a former slave from Florida, in an address to African American troops, scornfully pointed to slave masters' abandonment of the American flag, under which they "have grind us up, and put us in their pocket for money." At the first moment "they think that old flag mean freedom for us colored people, they pull it right down and run up the rag of their own. But we'll never desert the old flag, boys, never; we have lived under it for *eighteen hundred sixty-two years,* and we'll die for it now." For a brief period during Reconstruction, as they participated in writing new constitutions and elected officials to public office, Southern blacks felt themselves real Americans.[3] "At no other time during the nineteenth century," observes the historian Cecilia Elizabeth O'Leary, "would blacks consider themselves so fully American as they did during Reconstruction. . . . For the first time, the nation-state represented not just abstract American ideals but an institution obligated to correct historical injustices."[4] Of course, the grounds for identification with the ideals of the nation state soon collapsed. How blacks reformulated the meaning of American in the face of Jim Crow, lynching, and northern segregation and discrimination—or how they view it in the aftermath of Hurricane Katrina—remains a story to be written.

Metric describes the yardstick for determining whether someone is, indeed, an American. It may be objective (citizenship, language, even, as Lizabeth Cohen shows, consumption) or subjective (an individual's own sense of identity).[5] Insider and outsider voices, speaking at the same time, have often suggested different metrics, as with blacks or Asians. For much of American history, in fact, the metric was racial: only whites could be full Americans. Location refers to the geographic origin of the question, whether it is asked domestically, from inside the United States, or from elsewhere in the world. What does American mean, today, to the citizens of France or Iraq, for instance? How American has been defined elsewhere in the world remains a fascinating, intricate, neglected, and never more important subject for systematic study.

In the late twentieth and early twenty-first centuries, events similar to those a century earlier—massive immigration, war, the acquisition of empire, racial tension—again forced the question—what is an American?—to the forefront of public attention. The first source, of course, was the massive wave of immigration beginning in the mid-1960s, discussed earlier, that brought unprecedented numbers of newcomers from Latin America and Asia, tilting the country's demography in a new direction and promising a nonwhite majority in the future. For a nation whose identity had been bound up with race, where American, well into the twentieth century, had been colored white, the change was extraordinary. As earlier in the century, responses varied between optimism about the possibilities of assimilation and gloomy predictions about the transformation of national identity.

The 1997 report of the U.S. Commission on Immigration Reform to Congress echoed the earlier twentieth-century cultural pluralist tradition associated with philosopher Horace Kallen, now usually called multiculturalism. It illustrated the soft response to immigrants, which had reasserted itself in 1965 when Congress finally abolished nationality-based quotas and reopened the gates to immigration. When anti-immigrant sentiment periodically sweeps through the nation, it becomes difficult—but crucial—to recall the warm and welcoming response to immigrants that forms as vivid a thread in America's history as suspicion and hostility. Immigrants, the commission pointed out, had served the United States well through their contributions "to its vibrant and diverse communities; to its lively and participatory democracy; to its vital intellectual and cultural life; to its renowned job-creating entrepreneurship and marketplaces; and to its family values and hard work ethic." To be sure, there were costs as well as benefits, especially to low-wage workers, but these were manageable with intelligent policy. Overall, immigration had "created one of the world's most successful multiethnic nations." "American unity" depended on "a widely held belief in the principles and values embodied in the U.S. Constitution and their fulfillment in practice: equal protection and justice under the law; freedom of speech and religion; and representative government." Commitment to these principles constituted the metric that defined American identity. "Lawfully-admitted newcomers of any ancestral nationality—without regard to race, ethnicity, or religion—truly become Americans when they give allegiance to these principles and values," the commission claimed. Thus, the moment had arrived to reclaim Americanization, which had earned a "bad reputation when it was stolen by racists and xenophobes in the 1920s." To the commission, Americanization was a two-way street, not a one-way road: "the process of integration by which immigrants become part of our communities and by which our communities and the nation learn from and adapt to their presence."[6]

By the late twentieth century, the politics of immigration had grown complicated and contradictory. Supporters of expansive immigration policy included not only political progressives who championed diversity and America's role as a haven for the world's oppressed but, as well, conservative representatives of capital who looked to immigrants to supply cheap labor and act as a break on wages. Opponents of expansive policy included labor unions and African Americans worried the impact of massive immigration on low wage workers. But the harshest opponents reasserted classic nativist arguments.

Opponents of immigration, who harkened back to the 1920s xenophobic proponents of quotas, articulated a very different view of what it meant to be an American. Their anxiety found expressions in euphemisms more acceptable than racial fear. America would lack a common culture. Spanish would displace English. Loyalty would remain divided between the United States and the land of ethnic origin. In his apocalyptically titled book, *The Death of the West*, right-wing political commentator Patrick Buchanan warned that the "chasm in our country is not one of income, ideology, or faith, but of ethnicity and loyalty. . . . In 1960, only sixteen million Americans did not trace their ancestors to Europe. Today, the number is eighty million. . . . [N]o nation in history has gone through a demographic change of this magnitude in so short a time, and remained the same nation. . . . Uncontrolled immigration threatens to deconstruct the nation we grew up in and convert America into a conglomeration of peoples with almost nothing in common—not history, heroes, language, culture, faith, or ancestors."[7] For political scientist Samuel Huntington, the metric of American was commitment to "Anglo-Protestant culture," the core of American identity since the nation's founding. As never before in the nation's history, immigration threatened this national identity. "In the late twentieth century, developments occurred that, if continued, could change America into a culturally bifurcated Anglo-Hispanic society with two national languages." Immigration from Latin America, especially from Mexico, was driving this ominous change. "Mexican Americans," Huntington argued, "no longer think of themselves as members of a small minority who must accommodate the dominant group and adopt its culture. As their numbers increase, they become more committed to their own ethnic identity and culture." Clearly, the implication of his work pointed to the gloomy conclusion that Mexican immigrants and their children never would become real Americans.[8]

Two developments in particular worried the cassandras of American identity. The first was multiculturalism. As a movement, it had gone too far, reinforcing, even championing, non-American loyalties and roots, dividing the nation rather than uniting it. Scholars of immigration had made matters worse by scornfully tossing out the old assimilationist interpretation of ethnic history and replacing it with one that stressed the preservation of ethnicity. Immigration history had jettisoned its prevailing metaphor—the "uprooted," introduced by historian Oscar Handlin—for the "transplanted," the title of a widely cited book by the historian John Bodnar.[9] In this sense, critics held, multiculturalism distorts history, teaches false and dangerous ideas in the schools, and contributes to the disuniting of America. In the 1990s, multiculturalism came under attack from various quarters, with milder critics looking to restore what they believed to be a lost balance and harsher critics calling for a renewed patriotism.[10] In immigration scholarship, assimilation lost its negative,

chauvinistic loading as it reappeared in new, more nuanced interpretations that pulled back from the excesses that disturbed its earlier critics.[11]

The 1970s legalization of dual nationality constituted the other development that bred pessimism about the future of American nationality.
Would new citizens with dual nationalities really commit wholeheart-
edly to the United States? "Until the 1960s," points out sociologist
Nathan Glazer, "dual citizenship was seen as an anomaly to be eliminated as soon as possible so that each citizen owed allegiance to one
country only, and each country claimed the full allegiance of every citizen." Today, the situation is very different: "millions of new Americans
remain citizens or nationals of their countries of origin." For Glazer this
is more than a "technical anomaly that will rapidly be overcome by the
forces of assimilation." For today "dual citizenship is a . . . conscious and
deliberate matter" whose result makes "for a strikingly different attitude
towards assimilation among today's immigrants" than among early
twentieth-century newcomers.[12] It was difficult to know exactly how
dual nationality, the presence of many non-English speakers, or the persistence of ethnic loyalties would cause the sky to fall. (The grounds for
these fears, of course, as we have seen, were very shaky. Overwhelming
evidence points to the assimilation of the children and grandchildren of
immigrants on every measure.) The rhetoric was alarmist and not specific. But clear, and undoubtedly deeply troubling to many observers,
was that "American" had cast off its mooring in a shared identity and
culture. Where it would drift was unclear, but it would never be the
same.

Terror, of course, was the other source of renewed attention to the
meaning of American. The "long nineteenth century," historians often
argue, really ended only with World War I. The short twentieth century
ended on September 11, 2001. The attack was many things. One of them
was a prism refracting the transformative, late twentieth-century
changes described in this book. (In a different, but no less terrible, way so
was the impact of Hurricane Katrina, whose devastation lit up the inter-
secting histories of race, inequality, urban transformation, and government retreat from public service and protection.) Aside from military
and government targets, the object of attack was the World Trade Center,
as potent a symbol of the new economy as any that could be imagined.
Its construction, heavily subsidized by tax benefits, transformed urban
space by destroying an old economy business district. Within its towers,
the new economy rooted in information, services, and global finance—
from the brokerage firms high up to the shops below ground—flourished. The casualties, both those who died and those who lost their jobs,
reflected the divided social structure of the dual city. Not only did the attack kill firemen and policemen and highly educated, affluent employees
critical to the business services at the new economy's core. It also killed

those who serviced them and destroyed the livelihood of many others. An army of waitpersons, dishwashers, cleaners, and others, the underpaid foot soldiers of the new economy, surrounded the towers and lost their incomes. Many of them were immigrants, part of the wave of newcomers transforming New York City's demography.[13]

The response to the attack initiated the war on terror. As in wars, the response narrowed and hardened the definition of American. The major legislative response, known significantly as the "U.S. Patriot Act," included potential, and constitutionally questionable, threats to civil liberties.[14] The Patriot Act fell with special force on immigrants. It "permits indefinite detention of immigrants and other noncitizens. There is no requirement that those who are detained indefinitely be removed because they are terrorists." The weakening of civil liberties threatened the rights of U.S. citizens as well as immigrants. The government, the American Civil Liberties Union showed conclusively, was "using gag orders and secret evidence to keep the public in the dark about its use of the Patriot Act to investigate Americans."[15] At the same time, the administration of President George W. Bush, by asserting the right to hold American citizens without formal charges and to deny them legal counsel, stratified Americans into protected and unprotected classes with the boundary between the two uncertain. As an identity, American acquired a vulnerable, contingent quality. Because the attackers were foreign, it merged with the unease—ranging from anxiety to hostility—over immigrants. Entrance visas to the United States became much more time-consuming and difficult; Americans of Middle Eastern origin found themselves subject to surveillance and questioning; multiculturalism or hyphenated Americanism fell further into disfavor. In the early days following the attack, foreign sympathy poured spontaneously toward America. As viewed from other nations, images of Americans softened as they proved vulnerable, despite their nation's awesome power. The Iraq War, however, squandered goodwill and the internationalization of America's definition—the sense in Europe that Americans were more like us. Viewed from outside, America by and large appeared arrogant and dangerous. Even though most observers probably could differentiate between individual Americans and their government, in practice, it would be difficult to separate them completely.

In the late twentieth and early twenty-first centuries, events dislodged each of the components that made up the definition of American. Two sources, immigration and terrorist threat, provoked the need for new answers. The loudest response came from the insider *voice* of authority—critics, both in and out of government, of multiculturalism and enforcers of a new patriotism. Outsider voices, those of immigrants or blacks marginalized in the destroyed economies of the nation's inner cities, were harder to hear. Perhaps the most audible outsider challenge came from critics of the Iraq War, who called for a singular rather than stratified understanding of American grounded firmly in inviolable constitutional rights and an international focus that stressed the ties of Americans to people around the world rather than their exceptionalism. But, for many, the metric of Americanism became willingness to shed ethnic loyalties and to speak English even at home. At the same time, and in something of a contradiction, American could no longer be colored white; scary as this was for many observers, it could not be denied. As for location, by late 2004, the gap between the definition of American from inside and outside the nation may never have been greater. In an age of globalization, this was a potentially huge problem.

At the end of the twentieth century, what America had been seemed a lot clearer than what America was becoming. The look backward, of course, often reeked of nostalgia, especially in the culture wars, where the past itself became a battleground. But whether one saw earlier times as a lost golden age or a nightmare that had been partially escaped, almost no one denied that the future would be very different. Under pressure from transformative economic and social change, ideas thrown around unreflexively in everyday conversation—public, work, city, family, race, American—had lost their customary meanings. Everywhere, struggle and contention surrounded their new content. In some instances, as with work and city, antagonists disagreed over new terms to capture what all agreed were historic and irreversible changes. In others, as with family, race, and nationality, lines of conflict separated those who wanted to push ahead to find new definitions from others who wanted to restore the conditions that had sustained the old ones. Whatever definitions survived the Darwinian contest for wide public adoption, three threads ran through the century. One was diversity: America was a nation constructed by many people different from one another in almost every way. The mix constantly altered, but, continually renewed, it was never homogeneous or bland. The second thread was government. America was the land of the free market and frontier, but its every aspect was shaped in one way or another, for better or worse, by the hand of the state, which, to mention only one instance, through its immigration laws sculpted the texture of the nation's diversity. America was also, and this is the third thread, a land of multiple, durable, deeply rooted inequalities. Individuals and groups experienced dizzying mobility, up, down, and geographic. The way inequality worked underwent important change. But throughout the twentieth century America was, as it remains, one nation divisible, with liberty and justice for some.

Notes

Prologue

1. "'A Wonderful Year' and 'The Outlook,'" *New York Times*, January 1, 1900, 1.
2. Reynolds Farley. *The New American Reality: Who We Are, How We Got Here, Where We Are Going* (New York: Russell Sage Foundation, 1996).

Chapter 1

1. Walter LaFeber, *The New Empire: An Interpretation of American Expansion, 1860–1898*, 35th anniversary ed. (Ithaca, N.Y.: Cornell University Press, 1998).
2. Samuel Hays, *The Response to Industrialism* (Chicago: University of Chicago Press, 1957).
3. Gavin Wright, *Old South, New South: Revolutions in the Southern Economy Since the Civil War* (New York: Basic Books, 1986).
4. U.S. Bureau of the Census, *Thirteenth Census of the United States. Abstract of the Census* (Washington: U.S. Government Printing Office, 1913).
5. Robert A. Margo, "The Labor Force in the Nineteenth Century," in *The Cambridge Economic History of the United States. The Long Nineteenth Century*, edited by Stanley L. Engerman and Robert E. Gallman (Cambridge: Cambridge University Press, 2000), 207–43, 216.
6. Edmund deS. Brunner, *Village Communities* (New York: George H. Doran, 1927), 31–32.
7. D.W. Meinig, *The Shaping of America: A Geographical Perspective on 500 Years of History*, vol. 3: *Transcontinental America 1850–1915* (New Haven, Conn.: Yale University Press, 2000).
8. Ibid.
9. Alan L. Olmstead and Paul W. Rhode, "The Transformation of Northern Agriculture, 1910–1990," in *The Cambridge Economic History of the United States: The Twentieth Century* (see note 5), 693–742, 725–26.
10. U.S. Bureau of the Census, *Thirteenth Census of the United States. Abstract of the Census.* 43, 536.
11. Ibid., 265, 268; Robert E. Gallman, "Economic Growth and Structural Change in the Long Nineteenth Century," in *The Cambridge Economic History of the United States: The Long Nineteenth Century* (see note 5), 1–55; U.S. Bu-

reau of the Census, *Thirteenth Census of the United States Taken in the Year 1910*, vol. 5. *Agriculture*, 43.

12. Olmstead and Rhode, "The Transformation of Northern Agriculture, 1910–1990," 700; Jeremy Atack, F. Bateman, and William N. Parker, "Northern Agriculture and the Westward Movement," in *Cambridge Economic History of the United States: The Long Nineteenth Century* (see note 5), 259–61, 269–70, 285–325.

13. Olmstead and Rhode, "The Transformation of Northern Agriculture, 1910–1990," 696.

14. James L. Leloudis, *Schooling the New South* (Chapel Hill: University of North Carolina Press, 1996), 108; U.S. Bureau of the Census, *Thirteenth Census of the United States Taken in the Year 1910*, vol. 5, *Agriculture*, 173, table 5.

15. David B. Danbom, *The Resisted Revolution* (Ames: The Iowa State University Press, 1979), 33; Atack, Bateman, and Parker, "Northern Agriculture and the Westward Movement," 321–22.

16. Matthew Sobek, "A Century of Work: Gender, Labor Force Participation, and Occupational Attainment in the United States, 1880–1990" (Ph.D. diss., University of Minnesota, 1997).

17. U.S. Immigration Commission, *Abstracts of the Reports of the Immigration Commission* [Dillingham Commission], (Washington: U.S. Government Printing Office, 1911), 541.

18. U.S. Bureau of the Census, *Thirteenth Census of the United States Taken in the Year 1910*, vol. 11. *Mines and Quarries 1909* (Washington: U.S. Government Printing Office, 1913), 21, 24–25, 28, 212, 219, 237–38.

19. U.S. Bureau of the Census, *Abstract of the Twelfth Census of the United States 1900*, 3rd edition (Washington: U.S. Government Printing Office, 1904), 387, 407; Stanley L. Engerman and Kenneth L. Sokoloff, "Technology and Industrialization, 1790–1914," in *The Cambridge Economic History of the United States: The Long Nineteenth Century* (see note 5), 367–401, 386; David E. Nye, *Electrifying America: Social Meanings of a New Technology, 1880–1940* (Cambridge, Mass.: MIT Press, 1990); D. W. Meinig, *The Shaping of America*, 253, 293–94; Hal S. Barron, *Mixed Harvest: The Second Great Transformation in the Rural North, 1870–1930* (Chapel Hill: University of North Carolina Press, 1997). On the early introduction of telephones, and the adaptation of the technology by rural users, see Ronald R. Kline, *Consumers in the Country: Technology and Social Change in Rural America* (Baltimore, Md.: Johns Hopkins University Press, 2000), 23–54.

20. U.S. Bureau of the Census, *Abstract of the Thirteenth Census* (New York: Arno Press, 1976), 77. More immigrants still had been born in Germany than in any other country—27 percent in 1900 and 19 percent in 1910. The Irish, however, a major immigrant group in earlier years, had dropped to fifth place among the newcomers. Statistics on workforce and length of residence based on authors' calculations.

21. U.S. Immigration Commission, *Abstracts of the Reports of the Immigration Commission*, v. 1, 45.

22. Michael R. Haines, "The Population of the United States, 1790–1920," in *The Cambridge Economic History of the United States: The Long Nineteenth Century* (see note 5), 143–206, 198–99; Susan Cott Watkins, "Introduction," in *After*

Ellis Island: Newcomers and Natives in the 1910 Census, edited by Susan Cott Watkins (New York: Russell Sage Foundation, 1994); Mark Wyman, *Round-Trip to America: The Immigrants Return to Europe, 1880–1930* (Ithaca, N.Y.: Cornell University Press, 1993); U.S. Immigration Commission, *Abstracts of the Reports of the Immigration Commission*, vol. 1, 184.

23. U.S. Immigration Commission, *Abstracts of the Reports*, vol. 1, 23–24, 45, 181. Immigration historians have become critical of the conventional dichotomy between old and new immigration.

24. John Higham, *Strangers in the Land: Patterns of American Nativism, 1860–1925* (New Brunswick, N.J.: Rutgers University Press, 1955); Mai M. Ngai, *Impossible Subjects: Illegal Aliens and the Making of Modern America* (Princeton, N.J.: Princeton University Press, 2004); Desmond King, *Making Americans: Immigration, Race, and the Origins of the Diverse Democracy* (Cambridge, Mass.: Harvard University Press, 2000).

25. James Bryce, *The American Commonwealth*, 3rd ed, 2 vols. (New York: The MacMillan Company, 1894/1907, v. 1, 417.

26. Hal S. Barron, *Those Who Stayed Behind: Rural Society in Nineteenth-Century New England* (Cambridge: Cambridge University Press, 1984), 79–80; Stephan Thernstrom, *The Other Bostonians: Poverty and Progress in the American Metropolis, 1880–1970* (Cambridge, Mass.: Harvard University Press, 1973), 23.

27. U.S. Bureau of the Census, *Abstract of the Thirteenth Census*, 39–50; U.S. Bureau of the Census, *Abstract of the Twelfth Census of the United States 1900* (Washington: U.S. Government Printing Office, 1904), 32. Population density did not parallel settlement perfectly. Despite the dispersal of population in small villages, density in southern states generally was above average, over 30 per square mile. Frederick Jackson Turner, *The Frontier in American History* (New York: Henry Holt, 1920/1947).

28. Authors' calculations.

29. Wilbert L. Anderson, *The Country Town: A Study of Rural Evolution* (New York: Baker and Taylor, 1906), 247–48.

30. Atack, Bateman, and Parker, "Northern Agriculture and the Westward Movement," 324; Hope T. Eldgridge and Dorothy Swaine Thomas, *Population Redistribution and Economic Growth: United States, 1870–1950*, vol. III, *Demographic Analyses and Interrelations* (Philadelphia, Pa.: American Philosophical Society, 1964), 90, 251, table A1.11.

31. Authors' calculation.

32. Authors' calculation.

33. Eight of ten adult Jewish first and second generation immigrants were in cities of more than a million; Italians distributed themselves more evenly with about a quarter in cities over a million and another fifth in cities of 100,000 to 999,999. The distribution of Poles resembled the Italians. Jews here identified by parental mother tongue as Yiddish; Italians by father's mother tongue as Italian; Poles as Polish. The six major immigrant states were New York, New Jersey, Illinois, Pennsylvania, Massachusetts, and Michigan. See William H. Frey, "Census 2000 Reveals New Native-Born and Foreign-Born Shifts Across U.S," PSC Research Report 02-520 (Ann Arbor: Population Studies Center at the Institute for Social Research, University of

Michigan, 2002) and Theodore Saloutos, "The Immigrant in Pacific Coast Agriculture, 1880–1940," in *Immigrants on the Land: Agriculture, Rural Life, and Small Towns,* edited by George E. Pozzetta (New York: Garland, 1991), 308–27.

34. U.S. Bureau of the Census, *Abstract of the Thirteenth Census,* 200; authors' calculation from 63–64, 210.

35. Meinig, *The Shaping of America,* 227, 240; U.S. Bureau of the Census, *Abstract of the Twelfth Census of the United States 1900,* 330.

36. U.S. Bureau of the Census, *Abstract of the Twelfth Census of the United States,* 438; Engerman and Sokoloff, "Technology and Industrialization, 1790–1914," 380–82.

37. Ibid., 381. The shift of industry to the South and West occurred much later. Carol E. Heim, "Structural Changes: Regional and Urban," in *The Cambridge Economic History of the United States. The Twentieth Century* (see note 5), 93–190, 115.

38. U.S. Bureau of the Census, *Abstract of the Twelfth Census of the United States 1900,* 356; Walter Licht, *Industrializing America: The Nineteenth Century* (Baltimore, Md.: Johns Hopkins University Press, 1995); U.S. Bureau of the Census, *Abstract of the Thirteenth Census,* 451, table 8; Meinig, *The Shaping of America,* 240–42, Licht quote on 242.

39. Michael B. Katz, "Towards a Classification of Industries in 1910," America at the Millennium Project (Philadelphia, Pa.: University of Pennsylvania and the Russell Sage Foundation, 2001). The classification is based on the aggregate data for industries in the manufacturing census. The patterns should be considered as ideal types, or central trends, rather than descriptions of individual industries. Although some industries clearly fell into one of the three clusters, others showed evidence of more than one pattern. Nonetheless, these patterns do describe central trends in industrial development.

40. Authors' calculations.

41. Meinig, *The Shaping of America,* 243; U.S. Bureau of the Census, *Abstract of the Thirteenth Census,* 436.

42. Engerman and Sokoloff, "Technology and Industrialization, 1790–1914," 386–87. Black Americans are defined as native born blacks with American mothers. Watkins, "Introduction," 376–7, table b.1. The kind of work immigrants did often varied with the size of the place in which they lived.

43. Olmstead and Rhode, "The Transformation of Northern Agriculture, 1910–1990," 693.

44. William Bennett Munro, *The Government of American Cities* (New York: Macmillan Company, 1913), 26.

45. In the first decade of the twentieth century, Los Angeles grew 212 percent, Oakland 124 percent, Portland 129 percent, and Seattle 194 percent. Heim, "Structural Changes: Regional and Urban," 155.

46. Heim, "Structural Changes: Regional and Urban," 143–45, 177; Kenneth T. Jackson, *Crabgrass Frontier: The Suburbanization of the United States* (New York: Oxford University Press, 1985).

47. Meinig, *The Shaping of America,* 301; Heim, "Structural Changes: Regional and Urban," 95.

48. Meinig, *The Shaping of America*, 295–99.
49. William Jennings Bryan, "Cross of Gold" (Chicago, 1896).
50. Gretchen Ritter, *Goldbugs and Greenbacks: The Antimonopoly Tradition and the Politics of Finance in America* (New York: Cambridge University Press, 1997), 3.
51. Lawrence Goodwyn, *The Populist Moment: A Short History of the Agrarian Revolt in America* (New York: Oxford University Press, 1978).
52. U.S. Congress, Senate, "Report of the Country Life Commission and Special Message from the President of the United States" (Washington, D.C., 1909).
53. David B. Danbom, *The Resisted Revolution* (Ames: Iowa State University Press, 1979), 42– 47; see also William L. Bowers, *The Country Life Movement in America 1900–1920* (Port Washington, N.Y.: Kennikat Press, 1974); U.S. Congress, Senate, "Report of the Country Life Commission."
54. U.S. Congress, Senate, "Report of the Country Life Commission." Quotations from electronic version of report prepared by Cornell University.
55. Ibid.
56. Ibid.
57. In this, early twentieth-century critics of rural schools, whether they knew it or not, echoed a long tradition in American education. Antebellum era educational promoters who built common school systems in the Northeast fought against the district system—towns divided into small districts each running their tiny schools. Horace Mann and his allies struggled, for the most part successfully, to pull these largely autonomous little schools into professionally administered, age-graded school systems populated by trained teachers. Appalled by the civic and moral decay they believed to have accompanied the growth of cities and industry in Britain and elsewhere in Europe, they wanted to facilitate the technological transformation of American industry without paying its price in inequality, poverty, and immorality. A transformed, professionalized, systematized education—which started with abolition of the district system—they believed, would propel America into a modern economic future while checking the growth of crime, poverty, and immorality and preserving a cohesive and virtuous national culture. Like reformers in the early twentieth century, mid-nineteenth-century school promoters needed to win over skeptical, often hostile farmers and townspeople, reluctant to abandon democratic control of their institutions, fearful of change, unconvinced of the virtues of modernity or school systems. Michael B. Katz, *The Irony of Early School Reform: Educational Innovation in Mid-Nineteenth Century Massachusetts* (Cambridge, Mass.: Harvard University Press, 1968), Michael B. Katz, *Reconstructing American Education* (Cambridge, Mass.: Harvard University Press, 1987).
58. Barron, *Mixed Harvest*, 44.
59. David R. Reynolds, *There Goes the Neighborhood: Rural School Consolidation at the Grassroots in Early Twentieth-Century Iowa* (Iowa City: University of Iowa Press, 1999), 4, 14–16.
60. Ronald R. Kline, *Consumers in the Country: Technology and Social Change in Rural America* (Baltimore, Md.: Johns Hopkins University Press, 2000), 5–6; Barron, *Mixed Harvest*.

61. William M. Cronon, *Nature's Metropolis: Chicago and the Great West*. New York: Norton, 1991.
62. Anderson, *The Country Town: A Study of Rural Evolution*, 42, 44, 45, 36.
63. Ibid., 45, 53.
64. Ibid., 44; Naomi Lamoreaux, "Entrepreneurship, Organization, and Economic Concentration," in *The Cambridge Economic History of the United States*, vol. 2 (see note 5), 403–34. 433.
65. David B. Danbom, *Born in the Country: A History of Rural America* (Baltimore, Md.: Johns Hopkins University Press, 1995), 149–150; David Blanke, "A Comparison of the Catalogs Issued From Sears, Roebuck & Company and Montgomery Ward and Company 1893–1906," *Essays in Economic and Business History* 12 (1994): 319–34; Barron, *Mixed Harvest*, 155–91.
66. Wilcox, *The American City: A Problem in Democracy*, 14–15.
67. Haines, "The Population of the United States, 1790–1920," 189, table 4.4.
68. Hugh Rockoff, "Banking and Finance, 1989–1914," in *The Cambridge Economic History of the United States: The Twentieth Century* (see note 5), 643–684, 668.
69. Eric Helleiner, "Historicizing Territorial Currencies: Monetary Space and the Nation-state in North America," *Political Geography* 18, no. 3 (1999): 309–39; Viviana A. Zelizer, "Multiple Markets: Multiple Cultures," in *Diversity and its Discontents: Cultural Conflict and Common Ground in Contemporary American Society*, edited by Neil J. Smelser and Jeffrey C. Alexander (Princeton, N.J.: Princeton University Press, 1999), 194–212; Viviana A. Zelizer, *The Social Meaning of Money* (New York: Basic Books, 1994).
70. Alfred D. Chandler, Jr., "The Railroads: Pioneers in Modern Corporate Management," *Business History Review* 39:1 (Spring 1965), 40.
71. Harvey S. Perloff et al., *Regions, Resources, and Economic Growth* (Lincoln: University of Nebraska Press, 1960): 194–97.
72. Ibid., 192, 218.
73. Ibid., 220–21.
74. Joshua L. Rosenbloom, "The Extent of the Labor Market in the United States, 1870–1914," *Social Science History* 22, no. 3 (Fall) (1998): 287–318; Joshua L. Rosenbloom, "One Market or Many? Labor Market Integration in the Late Nineteenth-Century United States," *Journal of Economic History* 50, no. 1 (March) (1990): 85–107, 98. See also Joshua L. Rosenbloom, *Looking for Work; Searching for Workers* (Cambridge: Cambridge University Press, 2002).
75. Rosenbloom, "The Extent of the Labor Market," 289–90, 292, 299–300.
76. Wright, *Old South, New South*, 7; On black mobility in the late nineteenth- and early twentieth-century South, see William Cohen, *At Freedom's Edge: Black Mobility and the Southern White Quest for Racial Control, 1861–1915* (Baton Rouge: Louisiana State University Press, 1991); Rosenbloom, "The Extent of the Labor Market," 310.
77. Frank Norris, *The Octopus: A Story of California*, New York: Penguin Books, 1986 (New York: Doubleday, Page and Co, 1901), 53–54.
78. Kevin H. O'Rourke and Jeffrey G. Williamson, *Globalization and History: The Evolution of a Nineteenth-Century Atlantic Economy* (Cambridge, Mass.: MIT Press, 1999).
79. Jeffrey G. Williamson, "Globalization and Inequality Then and Now: The

Late 19th and Late 20th Centuries Compared" (Cambridge, Mass.: National Bureau of Economic Research, 1996).

80. Kevin H. O'Rourke and Jeffrey G. Williamson, "When Did Globalization Begin?" (March 2000); Robert E. Lipsey, "U.S. Trade and the Balance of Payments, 1800–1913," in *The Cambridge Economic History of the United States: The Long Nineteenth Century* (see note 5), 685–732. See also Michael D. Bordo, Barry Eichengreen, and Douglas A. Irwin, *Is Globalization Today Really Different Than Globalization A Hundred Years Ago?* (Cambridge, Mass.: National Bureau of Economic Research, 1999).

81. Lipsey, "U.S. Trade and the Balance of Payments, 1800–1913"; O'Rourke and Williamson, "When Did Globalization Begin?"

82. Richard E. Baldwin and Philippe Martin, "Two Waves of Globalization: Superficial Similarities, Fundamental Differences" (Cambridge, Mass.: National Bureau of Economic Research, 1999).

83. New World is defined as Argentina, Australia, Canada, and the United States, old world as Ireland, Great Britain, Denmark, Norway, Sweden, Germany, Belgium, Netherlands, France, Italy.

84. Jeffrey G. Williamson, "The Evolution of Global Labor Markets Since 1830: Background Evidence and Hypotheses," *Explorations in Economic History* 32, no. 2, April (1995): 141–96; Timothy J. Hatton and Jeffrey G. Williamson, *The Age of Mass Migration: Causes and Economic Impact* (New York: Oxford University Press, 1998), 210–11.

85. Hatton and Williamson, *The Age of Mass Migration*, 251–52.

86. Gunther Peck, *Reinventing Free Labor: Padrones and Immigrant Workers in the North American West* (Cambridge: Cambridge University Press, 2000), 47.

87. Hatton and Williamson, *The Age of Mass Migration: Causes and Economic Impact*, 161–73.

88. Stanley Lieberson, *A Piece of the Pie: Blacks and White Immigrants Since 1880* (Berkeley: University of California Press, 1980); Stewart E. Tolnay, "African Americans and Immigrants in Northern Cities: The Effects of Relative Group Size on Occupational Standing in 1920," *Social Forces* 80, no. 2 (2001): 573–604.

89. U.S. Immigration Commission, "Abstracts of the Reports," v. 1, 502–3.

90. Statistics of federal government growth and finance are taken from the following sources: U.S. Bureau of the Census, *Official Register of the United States 1921, Director* (Washington: U.S. Government Printing Office, 1922); U.S. Department of the Interior, Edward M. Dawson, *Official Register for the US Officers and Employees in the Civil Military and Naval Service,* vol. I, *Legislative, Executive, and Judicial* (1901, 1911); U.S. Bureau of the Census, *Statistics of Cities Having a Population of Over 30,000: Special Reports 1905* (1907), 302–3, 308; U.S. Bureau of the Census, *Thirteenth Census of the United States Taken in the Year 1910,* vol. IV, *Occupation Statistics* (1914), 106; Ibid., *Wealth, Debt, and Taxation 1913* (1915), 38–39, 42–43, 51; U.S. Bureau of Foreign and Domestic Commerce, *Statistical Abstract of the United States, 1920,* (1921); U.S. Census Office, *Report on Wealth, Debt, and Taxation at the Eleventh Census: 1890* (1895); Ibid., *Twelfth Census of the United States Taken in the Year 1900: Population* (1902), Part II, 510; Ibid., *Tenth Census of the United States* (1880), 736; Ibid., U.S. Department of Commerce, and Economics and Statistics Ad-

ministration, *Statistical Abstract of the United States: The National Data Book, 1920 Edition* (2000), 339, 354–355; U.S. Bureau of the Census, *Historical Statistics of the United States, Colonial Times to 1970* (1975), 1102, 1103, 1104, 1114.

91. Dana Frank, *Buy American: The Untold Story of Economic Nationalism* (Boston, Mass.: Beacon Press, 1999), 34–40; Sidney Ratner, *The Tariff in American History* (New York: Van Nostrand, 1972), 334–43; Judith Goldstein, *Ideas, Interests, and American Trade Policy* (Ithaca, N.Y.: Cornell University Press, 1993), 81–83.
92. On veterans' pensions, see Theda Skocpol, *Protecting Soldiers and Mothers: The Political Origins of Social Policy* (Cambridge, Mass.: Harvard University Press, 1992).
93. James Bryce, *The American Commonwealth*, 3rd ed., 2 vols. (1894; repr., New York: The MacMillan Company, 1907), v. 1, 64.
94. Ibid., 65.
95. Morton Keller, *Affairs of State: Public Life in Late Nineteenth Century America* (Cambridge, Mass.: Harvard University Press, 1977), 297–98.
96. Ibid., 299–300, Wilson quote, 299.
97. Keller, *Affairs of State*, 313, 318.
98. Bryce, *The American Commonwealth*, v. 1, 460.
99. Jon C. Teaford, *The Rise of the States: Evolution of American State Government* (Baltimore, Md.: Johns Hopkins University Press, 2002), 5.
100. Statistics about the growth and financing of state government are drawn from the following: Louis L. Emmerson. *Blue Book of the State of Illinois* (Springfield: Illinois State Journal Co, State Printers, 1923); Wm. J. Harris, *Wealth, Debt, and Taxation, 1913* (Washington: U.S. Government Printing Office, 1915), 484–85, 534–35, 582–83, 632–33; Roscoe C Martin, *The Growth of State Administration in Alabama* (Tuscaloosa: University of Alabama, Bureau of Public Administration, 1942); Herman P. Miller, *Smull's Legislative Hand Book and Manual of the State of Pennsylvania, 1920*, Harrisburg: J.L.L. Kuhn, Printer of the Commonwealth, 1920; James A. Rose, *Blue Book of the State of Illinois.* (Springfield, Ill.: Phillips Bros, State Printers, 1903); William P. Smull, *Smull's Legislative Hand Book, Rules and Decisions of the General Assembly of Pennsylvania* (Harrisburg: Lane S. Hart, State Printer, 1881); Harry Woods, *Blue Book of the State of Illinois* (Danville: Illinois Printing Company, 1914).
101. Teaford, *The Rise of the States*, 43, 55.
102. Keller, *Affairs of State*, 319–22; Teaford, *The Rise of the States*, 106.
103. Teaford, *The Rise of the States*, 70.
104. Bryce, *The American Commonwealth*, v. 1, 489; Keller, *Affairs of State*, 330–33; Delos F. Wilcox, *The American City: A Problem in Democracy* (New York: Macmillan, 1911), 276, 294.
105. Some cities, notably Chicago, relied more on special assessments than on property taxes. On the use of special assessments in Chicago, see Robin Einhorn, *Property Rules: Political Economy in Chicago, 1833–1872* (Chicago: University of Chicago Press, 1991).
106. Bryce, *The American Commonwealth*, v. 1, 637.
107. Wilcox, *The American City*, 7.

108. Ibid.; Charles A. Beard, *American City Government* (1912; repr. New York: Arno Press, 1970); Frederic C. Howe, *The City, the Hope of Democracy* (New York: C. Scribner's Sons, 1914); William Bennett Munro, *The Government of American Cities* (New York: Macmillan Company, 1913). Reference to urban dominance as new imperialism is from Wilcox.

109. Munro, *The Government of American Cities*, 21–23.

110. Statistics of city growth and finance are drawn from: Samuel H. Ashbridge, "Second Annual Message of Samuel H. Ashbridge, Mayor of the City of Philadelphia, with Annual Reports for the Year Ending December 31, 1900," vol. 1–3 (Philadelphia: Dunlap Printing Co, 1901); U.S. Bureau of the Census, *Statistics of Cities Having a Population of Over 30,000*, 302–3, 308; J. Hampton Moore, "First Annual Message of J. Hampton Moore, Mayor of Philadelphia for the Year Ending December 31, 1920" (Philadelphia, 1920), 876, 1011–14, 1017–22; John E. Reyburn, "Fourth Annual Message of John E. Reyburn, Mayor of the City of Philadelphia, for the year ending December 31, 1910," vol. 1 (Philadelphia, Pa.: Dunlap Printing Company, 1911); William S. Stokley, "Ninth Annual Message of William S. Stokley, March 31, 1881" (Philadelphia: E.C. Markley and Son, Printers, 1881).

111. Jon C. Teaford, *The Unheralded Triumph: City Government in America, 1870–1900* (Baltimore, Md.: Johns Hopkins University Press, 1984), Michael Willrich, *City of Courts: Socializing Justice in Progressive Era Chicago* (New York: Cambridge University Press, 2003).

112. Munro, *The Government of American Cities*, 24.

113. Families have been reconstructed for analysis using the IPUMS census sample for 1910.

114. Authors' calculations. The idea of calculating the length of the transition to adulthood in this matter is adapted from John Modell, Frank E. Furstenberg, Jr., and Theodore Hershberg, "Social Change and Transitions to Adulthood in Historical Perspective," *Journal of Family History* 1 (1976): 7–32.

115. Based on authors' calculations from manuscript census. On the history of Chelsea, Vermont, see Hal S. Barron, *Those Who Stayed Behind*.

116. On family structure in 1910, see the important essay, Andrew T. Miller, S. Phillip Morgan, and Antonio McDaniel, "Under the Same Roof: Family and Household Structure," in *After Ellis Island* (see note 22), 125–74.

117. Charles Franklin Thwing, *American Society: Interpretations of Educational and Other Forces* (New York: Macmillan, 1931), 52.

118. The rate at which fertility declined mirrored these occupational differences: for the three groups that composed the "educated classes" it dropped between 21 and 27 percent; for farmers and laborers, 13 percent; and for operatives and craftsmen, 16 percent and 18 percent.

119. Margaret F. Byington, *Homestead: The Households of a Mill Town* (1910; repr., Pittsburgh: University of Pittsburgh Press, 1974), 126.

120. Stewart E. Tolnay, *The Bottom Rung: African American Family Life on Southern Farms* (Urbana: University of Illinois Press, 1999), esp. 17–18; Mark J. Stern, *Society and Family Strategy: Erie County, New York, 1850–1920*, 93–114.

121. Wilcox, *The American City*, 138.

122. Byington, *Homestead: The Households of a Mill Town*, 142–43.

123. Steven Ruggles, "The Origins of African-American Family Structure," *American Sociological Review* 59, no. 1 (1994): 136–52.

124. Thwing, *American Society: Interpretations of Educational and Other Forces*, 46–47. Thwing's perception of increasing individualism as a force eroding family life was widely shared.

125. Michael B. Katz, "School Attendance in Philadelphia, 1850–1900," Working Paper No. 3; Michael B. Katz, et al., "The Organization of Work, Schooling, and Family Life in Philadelphia, 1838–1920," Final Report, NIE Grant No. 9-0173, May 1983.

126. Claudia Goldin and Lawrence F. Katz, "Education and income in the early twentieth century: Evidence from the prairies," *Journal of Economic History* 60, no. 3 (2000): 782–818.

127. Katz, "School Attendance in Philadelphia"; Ileen A. DeVault, *Sons and Daughters of Labor: Class and Clerical Work in Turn-of-the-Century Pittsburgh* (Ithaca, N.Y.: Cornell University Press, 1990).

Chapter 2

1. Charles Tilly, *Durable Inequality* (Berkeley: University of California Press, 1998).

2. Leslie McCall, *Complex Inequality: Gender, Class and Race in the New Economy* (London: Routledge, 2001).

3. Authors' calculation using IPUMS sample for all workers in labor force with real personal earnings greater than zero. The coefficient of variation is the standard deviation divided by the mean.

4. http://www.lraonline.org/charts.php?d=8.

5. Maria Cancian and Deborah Reed, "The Impact of Wives' Earnings on Income Inequality: Issues and Estimates," *Demography* 36, no. 2 (1999): 173–184. This figure is for all married couples with "prime age heads," other than farmers, students, and those in the military; Andrew Hacker, "The Underworld of Work," *The New York Review*, February 12, 2004, 38–40.

6. Joanna Slavins, "Credit Card Borrowing, Delinquency, and Personal Bankruptcy," *New England Economic Review* (2001): 15–30.

7. http://www.lraonline.org/charts.php?d=11.

8. W. Eliot Brownlee, *Federal Taxation in America: A Short History* (New York: Cambridge University Press, 1996); Jerry Tempalski, "Revenue Effects of Major Tax Bills" (U.S. Department of the Treasury, 1998); Joseph J. Thorndike, *The Price of Civilization: Taxation in Depression and War, 1933–1945* (Arlington, Va.: Tax History Project, 2002); Christopher Howard, *The Hidden Welfare State: Tax Expenditures and Social Policy in the United States* (Princeton, N.J.: Princeton University Press, 1997); Michael B. Katz, *The Price of Citizenship: Redefining the American Welfare State* (New York: Metropolitan Books, 2001), 12–13.

9. Robert S. McIntyre, "Avoiding a Fiscal Dunkirk," *The American Prospect Online Edition* 4, no. 12 (1993); Robert S. McIntyre and T. D. Coo Nyguyen. *Corporate Income Taxes in the 1990s* (Washington, D.C.: Institute on Taxation and Economic Policy, 2000); Citizens for Tax Justice, "Year-by-Year Analysis of

the Bush Tax Cuts Shows Growing Tilt to the Very Rich," (June 12, 2002); Citizens for Tax Justice, "Details on the Bush Tax Cuts So Far" (2003). Because of the way in which tax loopholes and exemptions allow rich individuals and corporations to evade paying taxes on much of their income, the situation is even more inequitable than these figures show; David Cay Johnston, *Perfectly Legal: The Covert Campaign to Rig Our Tax System to Benefit the Super Rich—and Cheat Everyone Else* (New York: Portfolio, 2003).

10. Dominic Vitiello, "Building the United States: Construction Labor and Laborers, 1880–1990" (Unpublished paper, University of Pennsylvania, 2002).

11. Rene Alvarez, "Carpenters and a 'Century of Change': An Occupation Research Project" (Unpublished paper, University of Pennsylvania, 2002).

12. Leah Gordon, "Analysis of Census Data on Textile Workers, 1880–1990" (Unpublished paper, University of Pennsylvania, 2002).

13. Andrew Heath, "Teamsters: History of an Occupation, 1880–1990" (Unpublished paper, University of Pennsylvania, 2002)

14. See also Nicole Maurantonio, "The Most Ancient of Crafts," (Unpublished paper, University of Pennsylvania, 2002); Miriam Cohen, *Workshop to Office: Two Generations of Italian Women in New York City, 1900–1950* (Ithaca, N.Y.: Cornell University Press, 1992); Samuel Cohn, *The Process of Occupational Sex–Typing* (Philadelphia: Temple University Press, 1985); Margery W. Davies, *Woman's Place Is at the Typewriter: Office Work and Office Workers 1870–1930* (Philadelphia: Temple University Press, 1982); Ileen A. DeVault, *Sons and Daughters of Labor: Class and Clerical Work in Turn–of–the–Century Pittsburgh* (Ithaca, N.Y.: Cornell University Press, 1990); Elyce J. Rotella, *From Home to Office: U.S. Women at Work, 1870–1930* (Ann Arbor: UMI Research Press, 1981).

15. Kim Gallon, "A History of the Stenographer in the United States" (Unpublished paper, University of Pennsylvania, 2002).

16. Elyse Carpenter, "Physicians as an Occupation, United States 1800–1990" (Unpublished paper, University of Pennsylvania, 2002).

17. Matthew Sobek, "Work, Status, and Income: Men in the American Occupational Structure Since the Late Nineteenth Century," *Social Science History* 20, no. 2 (1996): 169–207. See also Sobek, "A Century of Work: Gender, Labor Force Participation, and Occupational Attainment in the United States, 1880–1990" (Ph.D. diss., University of Minnesota, 1997).

18. Sobek, "Work, Status, and Income," 169–207; see also Sobek, "A Century of Work" (1997); Andrew Hacker, "The Underworld of Work," *New York Review*, February 12, 2004, 38–40.

19. Carl Abbott, *The New Urban America : Growth and Politics in Sunbelt Cities* (Chapel Hill: University of North Carolina Press, 1981); D. W. Meinig, *The Shaping of America: A Geographical Perspective on 500 Years of History*; vol. 3: *Transcontinental America 1850–1915* (New Haven, Conn.: Yale University Press, 2000); C. Van Woodward, *Origins of the New South, 1877–1913* (Baton Rouge: Louisiana State University Press, 1951); Gavin Wright, *Old South, New South: Revolutions in the Southern Economy since the Civil War* (New York: Basic Books, 1986); Bruce J. Schulman, *From Cotton Belt to Sunbelt: Federal Policy, Economic Development, and the Transformation of the South, 1938–1980* (New York: Oxford University Press, 1991); Margaret Pugh O'Mara, *Cities of*

Knowledge: Cold War Science and the Search for the Next Silicon Valley (Princeton, N.J.: Princeton University Press, 2005).

20. These figures exclude caring for boarders and lodgers and other forms of family-based work. Excluding these activities has a large impact on women's rates of labor force participation, especially before 1940. For more on measurement of women's participation, see Christine E. Bose, *Women in 1900: Gateway to the Political Economy of the 20th Century* (Philadelphia, Pa.: Temple University Press, 2001), 33–54; Claudia Goldin, *Understanding the Gender Gap: An Economic History of American Women* (New York: Oxford University Press, 1990); Sobek, "A Century of Work" (1997). The other measurement issue relates to the source of the data—the census itself. According to Goldin, the census measures labor force participation in different ways before and after 1940. The differences do not produce dramatic variations in the results, but it should be remembered that the rates for the two periods do not have exactly the same base. Some feminist historians, such as Bose, consider that all women living in farm households should be considered members of the labor force. The problem with this definition is that it loosens the boundaries of the idea of labor force to the point where they become almost nonexistent. As a consequence, it threatens to obscure important changes over time and to impede, rather than facilitate, analysis. In this book, we focus on domestic work, and the work that falls between home and market, as part of the analysis of family economies and strategies in chapter 3.

21. For a historical overview, see Alice Kessler-Harris, *Out to Work: A History of Wage-Earning Women in the United States* (New York: Oxford University Press, 1982).

22. Jacqueline Jones, *Labor of Love, Labor of Sorrow: Black Women, Work and the Family from Slavery to the Present* (New York: Basic Books, 1985) has pointed out that, for most of American history, work-on-account-of-necessity marked the experience of African American women. Similarly, for women employed in factories early in the twentieth century, the historian Leslie Tentler argues, wage work was a necessity, not the activity of choice [*Wage–Earning Women: Industrial Work and Family Life in the United States, 1900–1930* (New York: Oxford University Press, 1979)]. State mothers' pensions in the 1910s and 1920s and federal Aid to Families with Dependent Children in the 1930s, their promoters said, would permit women to remain at home with their children, see Joanne L. Goodwin, *Gender and the Politics of Welfare Reform: Mothers' Pensions in Chicago, 1911–1929* (Chicago: University of Chicago Press, 1997). Among women born in 1895, twenty-five-year-old married black women were about five times more likely than their white counterparts to work. Among those born in 1935, the difference had dropped to 13 percent and for those born in 1975 it was 7 percent.

23. Considering women of all ages together, the rate of labor force participation among black women-on-their-own declined from a high of 77 percent in 1910 to a low of 48 percent in 1970 before turning upward to 59 percent in 2000. The rate for white women was more erratic. See Lori Reid, "Occupa-

tional Segregation, Human Capital, and Motherhood: Black Women's Higher Exit Rates from Full-Time Employment," *Gender & Society*, 16, no. 5 (2002): 728–47.

24. Louise A. Tilly and Joan W. Scott, *Women, Work, and Family* (New York: Holt, Rinehart, and Winston, 1978) show how most of women's early paid employment grew out of conventional women's domestic tasks.

25. See Elyce J. Rotella, *From Home to Office: U.S. Women at Work, 1870–1930* (Ann Arbor: UMI Research Press, 1981); see Margery W. Davies, *Woman's Place Is at the Typewriter: Office Work and Office Workers 1870–1930* (Philadelphia, Pa.: Temple University Press, 1982).

26. For much of the background on clerical work, we found Rotella, *From Home to Office*, to be most useful.

27. Rotella, *From Home to Office*, 67–70; Davies, *Women's Place*, 9–27.

28. Samuel Cohn, *The Process of Occupational Sex–Typing* (Philadelphia: Temple University Press, 1985). See also Venus Green, *Race on the Line: Gender, Labor, and Technology in the Bell System, 1880–1980* (Durham, N.C.: Duke University Press, 2001). On another industry, see Angel Kwolek-Folland, "Gender, Self, and Work in the Life Insurance Industry, 1880–1930," in *Work Engendered: Toward a New History of American Labor*, edited by Ava Baron (Ithaca, N.Y.: Cornell University Press, 1991), 168–90.

29. Authors' calculations. Jerry A. Jacobs, "Women's Entry into Management: Trends in Earnings, Authority, and Values among Salaried Managers," in *Gender Inequality at Work,* edited by Jerry A. Jacobs (Thousand Oaks, Calif.: Sage Publications, 1995), 152.

30. Donald, Tomaskovic-Devey, "Sex Composition and Gendered Earnings Inequality," *Gender Inequality at Work* (see note 29).

31. Suzanne M. Bianchi, "Changing Economic Roles of Women and Men," in *State of the Union: America in the 1990s Volume One: Economic Trends,* edited by Reynolds Farley (New York: Russell Sage Foundation, 1995). Baunach also finds that two-thirds of women would have to change occupations to equalize distribution Dawn M. Baunach, "Trends in Occupational Sex Segregation and Inequality, 1950 to 1990," *Social Science Research* 31, no. 1 (2002): 77–98. The consensus among scholars studying women's occupational change is that most resulted from occupational desegregation rather than from structural shifts. See, for instance, David A. Cotter, Joanne M. DeFiore, Joan M. Hermsen, Brenda Marsteller Kowalewski, and Reeve Vanneman, "Occupational Gender Desegregation in the 1980s," *Work and Occupations* 22, no. 1 (1995): 3–21; Thomas Wells, "Changes in Occupational Sex Segregation During the 1980s and 1990s," *Social Science Quarterly* 80 (1999): 370–81.

32. On women in banking, see Chloe E. Bird, "High Finance, Small Change: Women's Increased Representation in Bank Management," in *Job Queues, Gender Queues: Explaining Women's Inroads into Male Occupations,* edited by Barbara F. Reskin and Patricia A. Roos (Philadelphia, Pa.: Temple University Press, 1990); Reskin and Roos, *Job Queues, Gender Queues: Explaining Women's Inroads into Male Occupations* (Philadelphia, Pa.: Temple University Press, 1990); and Michael B. Katz, Mark J. Stern, and Jamie J. Fader, "Women

and the Paradox of Inequality in Twentieth Century America," *Journal of Social History* (Fall 2005).

33. Barbara F. Reskin and Patricia A. Roos, *Job Queues, Gender Queues*, 302–3.

34. Ibid., 305. The most recent major reinterpretation of women's occupational segregation is Maria Charles and David B. Grusky, *Occupational Ghettos: The Worldwide Segregation of Women and Men* (Stanford: Stanford University Press, 2004).

35. "Something rather dramatic happened in the 1980s," Bianchi observes. "After at least two decades in which the ratio of women's to men's earnings fluctuated but remained at about the same level, there was a sizable increase in the ratio during the 1980s" (1995), 127; see also Reskin and Roos, *Job Queues, Gender Queues*, 1990. A number of researchers have highlighted the reduction in the earnings gender gap during the 1980s. The exact percentage change varies with the data set and method, but there is consensus on the trend. See, for example, Javed Ashraf, "Is Gender Pay Discrimination on the Wane? Evidence from Panel Data, 1968–1989," *Industrial and Labor Relations Review* 49, no. 3 (1996): 537–46; Annette Bernhardt, Martina Morris, and Mark S. Handcock, "Women's Gains or Men's Losses? A Closer Look at the Shrinking Gender Gap in Earnings," *American Journal of Sociology* 101, no. 2 (1995): 302–28; June O'Neill and Solomon Polachek, "Why the Gender Gap in Wages Narrowed in the 1980s," *Journal of Labor Economics* 11, no. 1 (1993): 205–28. On the interpretation of trends in women's earnings, see Reynolds Farley, *The New American Reality: Who We Are, How We Got Here, Where We Are Going* (New York: Russell Sage Foundation, 1996).

36. See Yvonne D. Newsome and F. Nii-Amoo Dodoo, "Reversal of Fortune: Explaining the Decline in Black Women's Earnings." *Gender & Society.* 16, no. 4 (2002): 442–64.

37. Income varied, as well, by ethnicity and labor markets. Black women and Latinas earned less than white women, whereas gender inequality among blacks and between blacks and whites varied with the concentration of blacks in metropolitan labor markets. See Cohen, 1998; David A. Cotter, Joan M. Hermsen, and Reeve Vanneman, "The Effects of Occupational Gender Segregation Across Race," *Sociological Quarterly* 44, no. 1 (2003): 17–36; Paula England, Karen Christopher, and Lori Reid. "Gender, Race, Ethnicity, and Wages," *Latinas and African American Women at Work: Race, Gender, and Economic Inequality,* edited by Irene Browne (New York: Russell Sage Foundation, 1999), 139–80.

38. Jane E. Prather, "When the Girls Move In: A Sociological Analysis of the Feminization of the Bank Teller's Job." *Journal of Marriage and the Family* 33, no. 4 (1971): 777–82.

39. See Bird, "High Finance, Small Change," 1990; Kessler-Harris, *Out to Work*, 1982.

40. Frances Fox Piven and Richard Cloward, *Poor People's Movements: Why They Succeed, How They Fail* (New York: Pantheon, 1977); Mary L. Dudziak, *Cold War Civil Rights: Race and the Image of American Democracy* (Princeton, N.J.: Princeton University Press, 2000). See also Martha F. Davis, *Brutal Need: Lawyers and the Welfare Rights Movement* (New Haven, Conn.: Yale University Press, 1993); John David Skrentny, *The Ironies of Affirmative Action: Poli-*

tics, Culture, and Justice in America (Chicago: University of Chicago, 1996). For an account of black wage growth by 1940, see Robert Higgs, "Black Progress and the Persistence of Racial Economic Inequalities," in *The Question of Discrimination: Racial Inequality in the U.S. Labor Market*, edited by Steven Shulman and William Darity (Middletown, Conn.: Wesleyan University Press, 1989), 9–31.

41. Andrew Hacker, *Two Nations: Black and White, Separate, Hostile, Unequal* (New York: Charles Scribner's, 1992); Stephan Thernstrom and Abigail Thernstrom, *America In Black and White: One Nation, Indivisible* (New York: Simon & Schuster, 1997). For an extended criticism of the Thernstroms as well as of others they term "racial realists," see Michael K. Brown et al., *Whitewashing Race: The Myth of a Color-Blind Society* (Berkeley: University of California Press, 2003). On the question of black progress as of 1990, see Reynolds Farley, *The New American Reality: Who We Are, How We Got Here, Where We Are Going* (New York: Russell Sage Foundation, 1996), 248–53; see also the essays in Shulman and Darity, ed., *The Question of Discrimination: Racial Inequality*; James Smith and Finis Welch, "Black Economic Progress After Myrdal," *Journal of Economic Literature* 27 (June) (1989): 519–64.

42. For another discussion that stresses the cumulative nature of racial inequality, see Brown et al., *Whitewashing Race*, 21–25. Brown and his co-authors also draw, as does this article, on Charles Tilly's notion of durable inequality. Their work is the best modern book-length account of current-day racial inequality.

43. African American women's economic experience has received surprisingly little analysis, a point made in Mary Corcoran, "The Economic Progress of African American Women," in *Latinas and African American Women at Work: Race, Gender, and Economic Inequality*, edited by Irene Browne (New York: Russell Sage Foundation, 1999), 35–60.

44. Frank Hobbs and Nicole Stoops, "Demographic Trends in the Twentieth Century," in *Census 2000 Special Reports* (Washington: U.S. Government Printing Office, 2002), 206, table 16.

45. Douglas S. Massey and Nancy A. Denton, *American Apartheid: Segregation and the Making of the Underclass* (Cambridge, Mass.: Harvard University Press, 1993). On the origins of black ghettos, see James Grossman, *Land of Hope: Chicago, Black Southerners, and the Great Migration* (Chicago: University of Chicago Press, 1989); Arnold R. Hirsch, *Making the Second Ghetto: Race and Housing in Chicago, 1940–1960* (New York: Cambridge University Press, 1983); Mumford Center, "Ethnic Diversity Grows, Neighborhood Integration Lags Behind" (Albany: State University of New York, 2001).

46. John F. Bauman, *Public Housing, Race, and Renewal: Urban Planning in Philadelphia, 1920–1974* (Philadelphia: Temple University Press, 1987); Hirsch, *Making the Second Ghetto*; Raymond A. Mohl, "Race and Space in the Modern City: Interstate–95 and the Black Community in Miami," in *Urban Policy in Twentieth–Century America*, edited by Arnold R. Hirsch and Raymond A. Mohl (New Brunswick, N.J.: Rutgers University Press, 1993), 100–58; Thomas J. Sugrue, *The Origins of the Urban Crisis: Race and Inequality in Postwar Detroit* (Princeton, N.J.: Princeton University Press, 1996).

47. It is possible that concentration is itself a source of inequality. On this, see

John J. Beggs, Wayne J. Villemez, and Ruth Arnold, "Black Population Concentration and Black-White Inequality: Expanding the Consideration of Place and Space Effects," *Social Forces* 76, no. 1 (1997): 65–91. On the impact of concentration on inequality, see also Samuel Cohn and Mark Fossett, "Why Racial Employment Inequality is Greater in Northern Labor Markets: Regional Differences in White-Black Employment Differentials," *Social Forces* 74, no. 2 (1995): 511–42.

48. Chinhui Juhn, "Black-White Employment Differential in a Tight Labor Market," in *Prosperity for All? The Economic Boom and African Americans*, edited by Robert Cherry and William M. Rodgers (New York: Russell Sage Foundation, 2000), 88–109. William E. Spriggs and Rhonda M. Williams, "What Do We Need to Explain About African American Unemployment?" in *Prosperity for All?*, 188–207. They write, "The fact that African American unemployment rates are consistently twice as high as white rates should be one of the greatest mysteries in labor economics, yet is among the least-researched dimensions of racial economic inequality." (203)

49. A useful review of the issue of labor force attachment, including its measurement, is Monica D. Castillo, "Persons Outside the Labor Force Who Want a Job," *Monthly Labor Review* 121, no. 7 (1998): 34–42. See also John P. Blair and Rudy H. Fichtenbaum, "Changing Black Employment Patterns," in *The Metropolis in Black and White: Place, Power, and Polarization*, edited by George Galster and Edward Hill (New Brunswick, N.J.: Center for Urban Policy Research, 1992). For a discussion of black men's nonparticipation in the labor force, see James J. Heckman, "The Impact of Government on the Economic Status of Black Americans," in *The Question of Discrimination: Racial Inequality in the U.S. Labor Market*, edited by Steven Shulman and William Darity (Middletown, Conn.: Wesleyan University Press, 1989), 50–80.

50. Many writers have commented on the complicated lives led by working mothers. A good discussion is Daphne Spain and Suzanne M. Bianchi, *Balancing Act: Motherhood, Marriage, and Employment Among American Women* (New York: Russell Sage Foundation, 1996).

51. On the history of black women's work, see Jacqueline Jones, *Labor of Love, Labor of Sorrow: Black Women, Work and the Family from Slavery to the Present* (New York: Basic Books, 1985). On the history of women's work see also Alice Kessler–Harris, *Out to Work: A History of Wage–Earning Women in the United States* (New York: Oxford University Press, 1982). The question of public assistance raises the issue of the impact of changes in family structure on the economic situation of black women; we discuss this issue in chapter 3. Lawrence M. Mead, *The New Politics of Poverty: The Nonworking Poor in America* (New York: Basic Books, 1992); William Julius Wilson, *The Truly Disadvantaged: The Inner City, the Underclass, and Public Policy* (Chicago: University of Chicago Press, 1987); William Julius Wilson, *When Work Disappears: The World of the New Urban Poor* (New York: Alfred A. Knopf, 1996).

52. A trenchant look at the rise in incarceration is Christian Parenti, *Lockdown America: Police and Prisons in an Age of Crisis* (New York: Verso, 1999). In the argument suggested here, labor force nonparticipation should not be confounded with official unemployment. There appears to have been little relation between unemployment rates and incarceration. In other words, the

economic boom of the 1990s did not reduce the imprisonment of black men, which had other sources, particularly state policy. See William A. Darity, Jr., and Samuel L. Myers, Jr., "The Impact of Labor Market Prospects on Incarceration Rates," in *Prosperity for All?* (see note 48), 279–307. On the labor market impact of incarceration, see Bruce Western, Jeffrey R. Kling, and David F. Weiman, "The Labor Market Consequences of Incarceration," *Crime & Delinquency* 47, no. 3 (2001): 410–27; Devah Pager, "The Mark of a Criminal Record," *American Journal of Sociology* 108, no. 5 (2003): 937–75. "U.S. Prison Populations—Trends and Implications" (Washington, D.C.: The Sentencing Project, 2003); Marc Mauer, "The Crisis of the Young African American Male and the Criminal Justice System" (Washington, D.C.: The Sentencing Project, 1999). Another consequence of incarceration for inequality is the reduction in the number of marriageable men.

53. Jacqueline Jones, "Southern Diaspora: Origins of the Northern 'Under-class'," in *The "Underclass" Debate: Views from History*, edited by Michael B. Katz (Princeton, N.J.: Princeton University Press, 1993).

54. The literature on employer preferences is summarized in Philip Moss and Chris Tilly, "How Labor–Market Tightness Affects Employer Attitudes and Actions Toward Black Job Applicants: Evidence from Employer Surveys," in *Prosperity for All?* (see note 48), 129–59.

55. An important issue we have not discussed here is black self-employment, which has remained relatively low. Good discussions of trends and reasons are Robert L. Boyd, "A Contextual Analysis of Black Self-Employment in Large Metropolitan Areas, 1970–1980," *Social Forces* 70, no. 2 (1991): 409–29, Robert W. Fairlie and Bruce D. Meyer, "Trends in Self-Employment among White and Black Men during the Twentieth Century," *The Journal of Human Resources* 35, no. 4 (2000): 643–69.

56. The increasing sex differentiation within municipal employment is shown for New Orleans in Joshua Behr, "Black and Female Municipal Employ-ment: A Substantive Benefit of Minority Political Incorporation?" *Journal of Urban Affairs* 22, no. 3 (2002): 243–64.

57. Authors' calculations.

58. Among black women, technician jobs became important. In 1940, techni-cians were 1.8 percent of white women employed in professional and tech-nical work and 0.0 percent of black women; in 2000, they were 9.9 percent of white and 13.4 percent of black women. What is most striking, though, about the comparison between black and white women is their convergence within professional and technical occupations. By 2000, the differences among them were minor.

59. Myrdal describes the tenuous presence of blacks in public employment be-fore World War II. The contrast with the post-1960 years is striking. Gunnar Myrdal, *An American Dilemma: The Negro Problem and Modern Democracy*, 2 vols. (New Brunswick, N.J.: Transaction Books, 2002). The role of public em-ployment in African American history deserves much more attention from historians. Some useful social science articles on the subject are: Peter K. Eisinger, "The Economic Conditions of Black Employment in Municipal Bureaucracies," *American Journal of Political Science* 26, no. 4 (1982): 754–71;

Kevin M. O'Brien, "The Determinants of Minority Employment in Police and Fire Departments," *Journal of Socio–Economics* 32, no. 2 (2003): 183–95; Behr, "Black and Female Municipal Employment" (see note 56); Marlese Durr and John R. Logan, "Racial Submarkets in Government Employment: African American Managers in New York State," *Sociological Forum* 12, no. 3 (1997): 353–70; Philip Harvey, *Securing the Right to Employment: Social Welfare Policy and the Unemployed in the United States* (Princeton, N.J.: Princeton University Press, 1989); Margaret Weir, *Politics and Jobs: The Boundaries of Employment Policy in the United States* (Princeton, N.J.: Princeton University Press, 1992); Eisinger, "The Economic Conditions of Black Employment in Municipal Bureaucracies." On the role and characteristics of black public employment in a large city in 1940, see St. Clair Drake and Horace Cayton, *Black Metropolis: A Study of Negro Life in a Northern City*, rev. ed. (Chicago: University of Chicago Press, 1993); R. L. Boyd, "Differences In The Earnings of Black Workers In the Private and Public Sectors," *Social Science Journal* 30, no. 2 (1993): 133–42; Martin Carnoy, *Faded Dreams: The Politics and Economics of Race in America* (New York: Cambridge University Press, 1994). See also *A Common Destiny: Blacks and American Society* (Washington, D.C.: National Academy Press, 1989) and Suzanne Model, "The Ethnic Niche and the Structure of Opportunity: Immigrants and Minorities in New York City," in *The "Underclass" Debate: Views from History*, ed. Michael B. Katz (Princeton, N.J.: Princeton University Press, 1993), 161–93; Roger Waldinger, *Still the Promised City? African-Americans and New Immigrants in Post–Industrial New York* (Cambridge, Mass.: Harvard University Press, 1996).

60. John F. Zipp, "Government Employment and Black-White Earnings Inequality, 1980–1990," *Social Problems* 41, no. 3 (1994): 363–82.

61. Eisinger, "The Economic Conditions of Black Employment in Municipal Bureaucracies." A study based on 1980 data found that African Americans in the public sector were more protected and earned higher incomes. Boyd, "Differences in the Earnings of Black Workers in the Private and Public Sectors." Declining black incomes in the 1980s resulted in part from reductions in government employment, see Carnoy, *Faded Dreams: The Politics and Economics of Race in America*. Carnoy also points to higher wages for blacks in public employment. Peter Eisinger, "Local Civil Service Employment and Black Socio-Economic Mobility," *Social Science Quarterly* 67, no. 2 (1986): 171–75. See also M. V. Lee Badgett, "The Impact of Affirmative Action on Public-Sector Employment in California, 1970–1990," in *Impacts of Affirmative Action: Policies and Consequences in California*, edited by Paul Ong (Walnut Creek, Calif.: Sage Publications, 1999), 83–102.

62. For more detail on these points, see Michael B. Katz and Mark J. Stern, "Poverty Since 1940," in Gwendolyn Mink and Alice O'Connor, *Encyclopedia of Poverty and Social Welfare* (Santa Barbara: ABC–CLIO, 2004), 2 vol., I, 33–47.

63. Louis Harlan, *Separate and Unequal: Public School Campaigns and Racism in the Southern Seaboard States, 1901–1915* (Chapel Hill: University of North Carolina Press, 1958). An excellent study of education in the South after the Civil War is James L. Leloudis, *Schooling the New South: Pedagogy, Self, and Society in North Carolina, 1880–1920* (Chapel Hill: University of North Car-

olina Press, 1996). On the education of blacks in the South, the best overview is James D. Anderson, *The Education of Blacks in the South, 1860–1935* (Chapel Hill: University of North Carolina Press, 1988).

64. The best source on the expansion of high school enrollment is Claudia Goldin and Lawrence F. Katz, "Human and Social Capital: The Rise of Secondary Schooling in the United States, 1890 to 1940," *Journal of Economic Perspectives* 13, no. Winter (1999): 37–62.

65. The Education Trust, "Telling the Whole Truth (Or Not) About High School Graduation Rates: New State Data" (Washington, D.C.: The Education Trust, 2003); U.S. Department of Health and Human Services, "Trends in the Well-Being of America's Children and Youth, 1997 Edition" (Washington: U.S. Government Printing Office, 1997), EA1.5; David Boesel, Nabeel Alsalam, and Thomas M. Smith, "Educational and Labor Market Performance of GED Recipients" (Washington: U.S. Government Printing Office, 1998); Jay Greene, *The GED Myth* (Austin: Texas Education Review, 2002).

66. On the commitment of African Americans to education in the early twentieth century, see Grossman, *Land of Hope*; Timothy L. Smith, "Native Blacks and Foreign Whites: Varying Responses to Educational Opportunity in America, 1880–1950," *Perspectives in American History* VI (1972): 309–335. An excellent discussion of educational attainment trends among African Americans from 1940 to 1990 is Farley, *The New American Reality,* 228–38.

67. This conclusion about the relative influence of race and education is based on a regression analysis, which is described in Michael Katz, Mark J. Stern, and Jamie L. Fader, "New African American Inequality," *Journal of American History* 92(1) (2005): 75–108.

68. John Bound and Laura Dresser, "Losing Ground: The Erosion of the Relative Earnings of African American Women During the 1980s," in *Latinas and African American Women at Work: Race, Gender, and Economic Inequality*, edited by Irene Browne (New York: Russell Sage Foundation, 1999), 61–104. Relative incomes of black and white women, it should be noted, differed by region. Corcoran, "The Economic Progress of African American Women."

69. A discussion of the different pathways from marriage and employment to economic security for black and white women is, Andrea E. Willson, "Race and Women's Income Trajectories: Employment, Marriage, and Income Security over the Life Course," *Social Problems* 50 (February) (2003): 87–110.

70. For a superb exposition of the declining economic prospects of young white men, see Annette Bernhardt, et al., *Divergent Paths: Economic Mobility in the New American Labor Market* (New York: Russell Sage Foundation, 2001). On the decline in black men's incomes and labor market position in the 1980s, see John Bound and Richard B. Freeman, "What Went Wrong? The Erosion of the Relative Earnings and Employment of Young Black Men in the 1980s," *Quarterly Journal of Economics* 107, no. 1 (1992): 201–32; Carnoy, *Faded Dreams: The Politics and Economics of Race in America*; Richard B. Freeman, "Black Economic Progress After 1964: Who Has Gained and Why?" in *Studies in Labor Markets*, edited by Sumner Rosen (Chicago: University of Chicago Press, 1981). In the 1990s boom, black income started to rise once again—the decline in unemployment had more impact on their prospects than on whites. Cordelia W. Reimers, "The Effect of Tighter Labor Markets

on Unemployment of Hispanics and African Americans: The 1990s Experience," in *Prosperity for All?* (see note 48), 3–49. For the non–college educated, the impact of the boom was greatest on young men; among older men there were no similar gains. Richard B. Freeman and William M. Rodgers III, "Area Economic Conditions and the Labor Market Outcomes of Young Men in the 1990s Expansion," in *Prosperity for All?* (see note 48), 50–87. See also Bennett Harrison and Lucy Gorham, "What Happened to African-American Wages in the 1980s?" in *The Metropolis in Black and White,* ed. George Galster and Edward Hill (New Brunswick, N.J.: Center for Urban Policy Research, 1992), 56–71.

71. Melvin L. Oliver, and Thomas M. Shapiro. *Black Wealth/White Wealth: A New Perspective on Racial Inequality.* (New York: Routledge, 1997); Dalton Conley, *Being Black, Living in the Red: Race, Wealth, and Social Policy in America* (Berkeley: University of California Press, 1999). See also Francine D. Blau and John W. Graham, "Black–White Differences in Wealth and Asset Composition," *Quarterly Journal of Economics* 105, no. 2 (1990): 321–39.

72. A further "screen" was incarceration, which lowers the subsequent earnings opportunities of black men. Pager, "The Mark of a Criminal Record." An argument for the cumulative deficits acquired by young black men as a result of job instability is Marta Tienda and Haya Stier, "Generating Labor Market Inequality: Employment Opportunities and the Accumulation of Disadvantage," *Social Problems* 43, no. 2 (1996): 147–65. Another "screen," hard to see and not visible with just the census, consists of the "glass ceilings" that have remained in occupations. On this see, Heather Boushey and Robert Cherry, "Exclusionary Practices and Glass-Ceiling Effects Across Regions: What Does the Current Expansion Tell Us?" in *Prosperity for All?* (see note 48), 160–87.

73. For a similar argument about the bifurcation of black social structure in Los Angeles, see, David M. Grant, Melvin L. Oliver, and Angela D. James, "African Americans: Social and Economic Bifurcation," in *Ethnic Los Angeles,* edited by Roger Waldinger and Mehdi Bozorgmehr (New York: Russell Sage Foundation, 1996), 379–411. Bifurcation is also discussed in Heckman, "Impact of Government on the Economic Status of Black Americans." On the black middle class, see Thomas J. Durant, Jr., and Joyce S. Louden, "The Black Middle Class in America: Historical and Contemporary Perspectives," *Phylon* 47 (1986), 253–63. See also Harrison, "What Happened to African-American Wages?"; Bart Landry, *The New Black Middle Class* (Berkeley: University of California Press, 1987); William Julius Wilson, *The Declining Significance of Race: Blacks and Changing American Institutions* (Chicago: University of Chicago, 1978); Wilson, *Truly Disadvantaged.*

74. George J. Borjas, *Heaven's Door: Immigration Policy and the American Economy* (Princeton, N.J.: Princeton University Press, 1999); Thomas Espenshade and Gregory A. Huber, "Fiscal Impacts of Immigrants and the Shrinking Welfare State," in *The Handbook of International Migration: The American Experience,* edited by Charles Hirschman, Philip Kasinitz, and Josh DeWind (New York: Russell Sage Foundation, 1999), 360–70, Reynolds Farley and Richard D. Alba, "The New Second Generation in the United States," *International Migration Review* 36, no. 13 (Fall) (2002): 669–701; Christopher Jencks, "Who

Should Get In?" *New York Review of Books*, November 29, 2001; Christopher Jencks, "Who Should Get In? Part II," *New York Review of Books*, December 20 2001; Nelson Lim, "On the Back of Blacks? Immigrants and the Fortunes of African Americans," in *Strangers at the Gates: New Immigrants in Urban America*, edited by Roger Waldinger (Berkeley: University of California Press, 2001), 186–227; Alejandro Portes and Ruben G. Rumbaut, *Legacies: The Story of the Immigrant Second Generation* (Berkeley: University of California Press and Russell Sage Foundation, 2001); James P. Smith and Barry Edmonston, *The New Americans: Economic, Demographic, and Fiscal Effects of Immigration* (Washington, D.C.: National Academy Press, 1997); Roger Waldinger, *Still the Promised City? African-Americans and New Immigrants in Post-Industrial New York* (Cambridge, Mass.: Harvard University Press, 1996); Roger Waldinger and Jennifer Lee, "New Immigrants in Urban America," in *Strangers at the Gates*, 80–116. David E. Lopez and Ricardo D. Stanton-Salazar, "Mexican Americans: A Second Generation at Risk," in *Ethnicities: Children of Immigrants in America*, ed. Ruben G. Rumbaut and Alejandro Portes (Berkeley and New York: University of California Press and Russell Sage Foundation, 2001), 57–90, is an example of a pessimistic historical comparison of Mexicans to earlier immigrants.

75. This argument is made in terms somewhat different than ours in Richard Alba and Victor Nee, *Remaking the American Mainstream: Assimilation and Contemporary Immigration* (Cambridge, Mass.: Harvard University Press, 2003); Franklin Bean and Gillian Stevens, *America's Newcomers and the Dynamics of Diversity* (New York: Russell Sage Foundation, 2003); and Joel Perlmann and Roger Waldinger, "Immigrants, Past and Present: A Reconsideration," in *The Handbook of International Migration* (see note 74), 223–38.

76. Waldinger for one recognizes this problem with the literature. Borjas in *Heaven's Door* bases his analysis entirely on men, or on men and women together. He tries unsuccessfully to justify this in footnote 3, 214–15. Bean and Stevens (*America's Newcomers*, 216–19) take him to task for this omission and discuss some of the literature pointing to gender differences among migrants.

77. A convenient source for an overview of immigration trends in American history is Mary M. Kritz and Douglas T. Gurak, *Immigration and a Changing America* (New York and Washington, D.C.: Russell Sage Foundation and Population Reference Bureau, 2004).

78. Campbell J. Gibson and Emily Lemmon, *Historical Census Statistics on the Foreign–born Population of the United States: 1850–1900* (Washington: U.S. Census Bureau, 1999).

79. Jeffrey S. Passel, "Estimates of the Size and Characteristics of the Undocumented Population," (Washington, D.C.: Pew Hispanic Center, 2005); B. Lindsay Lowell and Robert Suro, "How Many Undocumented: The Numbers Behind The U.S.–Mexican Immigration Talks" (Washington, D.C.: Pew Hispanic Center, 2002).

80. Borjas, *Heaven's Door*, 8.

81. John Higham, *Strangers in the Land: Patterns of American Nativism, 1860–1925* (New Brunswick, N.J.: Rutgers University Press, 1955) is the classic account; Stan Vittoz, "World War I and the Political Accommodation of Transitional

Market Forces: The Case of Immigration Restriction," *Politics and Society* 8, no. 1 (1978): 49–78, persuasively offers a revision of his argument. The most important recent works are Mai M. Ngai, *Impossible Subjects: Illegal Aliens and the Making of Modern America* (Princeton, N.J.: Princeton University Press, 2004) and Daniel J. Tichenor, *Dividing Lines: The Politics of Immigration Control in America* (Princeton, N.J.: Princeton University Press, 2002).

82. John W. Briggs, *An Italian Passage: Immigrants to Three American Cities, 1890–1930* (New Haven, Conn.: Yale University Press, 1978); Victor Greene, "Poles," in *Harvard Encyclopedia of American Ethnic Groups*, edited by Stephan Thernstrom (Cambridge, Mass.: Harvard University Press, 1980), 787–803; Simon Kuznets, "Immigration of Russian Jews to the United States: Background and Structure," *Perspectives in American History* IX (1975): 35–126; Humbert S. Nelli, "Italians," in *Harvard Encyclopedia of American Ethnic Groups*, edited by Stephan Thernstrom (Cambridge, Mass.: Harvard University Press, 1980), 545–60.

83. Briggs, *Italian Passage*, 37–38.

84. Stanley Lieberson, *A Piece of the Pie: Blacks and White Immigrants Since 1880* (Berkeley: University of California Press, 1980).

85. Caroline Golab, *Immigrant Destinations* (Philadelphia, Pa.: Temple University Press, 1977). The classic work on Polish immigrants is William Isaac Thomas and Florian Znaniecki, *The Polish Peasant in Europe and America*, 5 vols. (Boston, Mass.: Richard D. Badger, 1920). A superb study of east central Europeans in a small American industrial city is Ewa Morawska, *For Bread With Butter* (New York: Cambridge University Press, 1986). For the Polish background to immigration, see also, Pacyga, *Polish Immigrants and Industrial Chicago: Workers on the South Side, 1880–1922*, 17–24, 125.

86. Lieberson, *Piece of the Pie*, 208.

87. Golab, *Immigrant Destinations*, 74.

88. Golab, *Immigrant Destinations*, 74–75. Greene, "Poles," 796.

89. Kuznets, "Immigration of Russian Jews," 121. "After the assassination of Tsar Alexander II in 1881," observes the historian Arthur Goren, "the new regime introduced policies that encouraged mob violence. Pogroms in 1881 and 1882 struck over 200 Jewish communities and ushered in three decades of anti–Jewish outbursts. An economic policy of pauperization. . . included the expulsion of the Jews from villages and rural centers and severe restrictions on their trade in the cities." Arthur A. Goren, "Jews," in *Harvard Encyclopedia of Ethnic Groups*, edited by Stephan Thernstrom (Cambridge, Mass.: Harvard University Press, 1980), 571–98.

90. Kuznets, "Immigration of Russian Jews," 80–82; Lieberson, *Piece of the Pie*, 280.

91. Kuznets, "Immigration of Russian Jews," 107, 112.

92. By selecting cohorts we are able to control for historical time and age. In the rest of this chapter, when we refer to the first generation of Poles, Italians, and Russian Jews, it should be understood that we mean individuals born between 1885 and 1894, and when we write of the second generation, we mean individuals born between 1905 and 1914, unless we specify otherwise.

93. Take the Polish as an example: 58 percent of first generation forty- to forty-nine-year-old men worked forty-eight weeks in the year prior to the census compared to 77 percent of the second generation; for fifty- to fifty-nine-

year-olds, the percentages were 59 percent and 81 percent. Similar distinctions held among both the Russian Jews and Italians. Thus, it was in the ability to find steady work that the second generation advantage showed.

94. E. P. Hutchinson, *Immigrants and Their Children, 1850–1950* (New York: John Wiley & Sons, 1956).

95. On the movement of Italian women into clerical work see Miriam Cohen, *Workshop to Office: Two Generations of Italian Women in New York City, 1900–1950* (Ithaca, N.Y.: Cornell University Press, 1992).

96. Two principal sets of statistics are useful for examining earnings. One is the median earnings; the other is the distribution of earnings into quintiles. Unfortunately, because the census only started to report earnings in 1940, it is not possible to track earnings growth in the first generation. In fact, we pick up its members only near the end of their working lives in 1950—the first year the census reported total personal earnings, which includes earnings from self-employment. (In 1940, the census reports only earnings from wages and salaries.) The statistics here are for male earnings only. Unless otherwise noted, earnings are given in 1990 dollars.

97. This analysis is based on blue collar employment in twelve industries: coal mining, blast furnaces, steel works and rolling mills, construction, fabricated steel products, electrical machinery, equipment and supplies, motor vehicle equipment, aircraft and parts, meat products, apparel and accessories, rubber products, railroad and railway, and trucking services. There is no direct data on unionization by ethnicity in this period. The figures here compare ethnic employment by industry as listed in the census with union density reported in other sources: H. G. Lewis, *Unionism and Relative Wages in the United States, An Empirical Inquiry* (Chicago: The University of Chicago Press, 1963), p. 250, and David Brody, *Workers in Industrial America: Essays on the 20th Century Struggle,* 2nd ed. (New York: Oxford University Press, 1993), 82–119.

98. This is an inference from the data. Russian Jews, as well, more often with an urban background, did not have as strong an attachment to land as first generation immigrant groups with more ties to peasant origins. One thing does seem certain. Russian Jews did not forgo property ownership in order to send their children to school longer. There is no negative association between homeownership and school attendance.

99. Here poverty is measured using the IPUMS variable which applies the post-1960 federal poverty standard to individual earnings. Poverty here consists of earnings below 100 percent of the poverty line.

100. In 1950, 16 percent for Poles, 17 percent for both Italians and Russian Jews.

101. Among households headed by native whites in 1970, 13 percent of the 1905 to 1914 cohort had poverty earnings, which, again, highlights the relative economic success of the second generation ethnics.

102. "History of Korean Immigration to the United States," no author, no date, http://www.columbia.edu/itc/sipa/U6210/ik105/history.html (accessed August 2003).

103. Reynolds Farley and Richard D. Alba, "The New Second Generation in the United States," *International Migration Review* 36, no. 13 (Fall 2002): 669–701.

104. This discussion is drawn from the following books: Illsoo Kim, *The New Urban Immigrants* (Princeton, N.J.: Princeton University Press, 1981); Ivan Light and Edna Bonacich, *Immigrant Entrepreneurs: Koreans in Los Angeles, 1965–1982* (Berkeley: University of California Press, 1988); Pyong Gap Min, *Caught in the Middle: Korean Communities in New York and Los Angeles* (Berkeley: University of California Press, 1996).

105. Because the census did not specify parental birthplace after 1970, it is not possible to accurately distinguish between second and subsequent generation individuals of Korean ancestry. Because there were so few Korean immigrants—50,000—in the United States in 1970, most with Korean ancestry born in the United States and listed in the next three censuses were, almost entirely, second generation.

106. Earnings figures for first generation Korean women are so suspiciously low that they are not used here.

107. This discussion of the background to contemporary Mexican immigration draws mainly on Franklin D. Bean and Gillian Stevens, *America's Newcomers and the Dynamics of Diversity* (New York: Russell Sage Foundation, 2003); Douglas S. Massey, Jorge Durand, and Nolan J. Malone, *Beyond Smoke and Mirrors: Mexican Immigration in an Era of Economic Integration* (New York: Russell Sage Foundation, 2002); Enrique Dussel Peters, "Recent Structural Changes in Mexico's Economy: A Preliminary Analysis of Some Sources of Mexican Migration to the United States," in *Crossings: Mexican Immigration in Interdisciplinary Perspectives*, edited by Marcelo Suarez–Orozco (Cambridge, Mass.: Harvard University Press, 1998), 55–74.

108. For an excellent discussion of repatriation see George J. Sanchez, *Becoming Mexican American: Ethnicity, Culture, and Identity in Chicano Los Angeles, 1900–1945* (New York: Oxford University Press, 1993).

109. Massey et al., *Beyond Smoke and Mirrors*, 69–70.

110. These statistics are based on the sample in the Mexican Migration Project directed by Massey.

111. Franklin D. Bean, "Unauthorized Migration," in *The New Americans*, edited by Mary Waters and Reed Ueda (Cambridge, Mass.: Harvard University Press, forthcoming); Massey et al., *Beyond Smoke and Mirrors*, 6; Fernando Lozano-Ascencio, Bryan R. Robert, and Frank D. Bean, "The Interconnections of Internal and International Migration: The Case of the United States and Mexico," in *Migration and Transnational Social Spaces*, edited by L. Preis (Aldershot, Hampshire: Ashgate Publishing); Enrico Marcelli and Wayne Cornelius, "The Changing Profile of Mexican Migrants to the United States: New Evidence from California and Mexico," *Latin American Research Review* 36, 2001: 105–31.

112. Massey et al. 2002

113. Victor Zúñiga and Rubén Hernández-León, "Introduction," and Jorge Durand, Douglas S. Massey, and Chiara Capoferro, "The New Geography of Mexican Migration," in *New Destinations: Mexican Immigrants in the United States*, edited by Victor Zúñiga and Rubén Hernández-León (New York: Russell Sage Foundation, 2005), xvi, 11–12.

114. Zúñiga and Hernández-León, "Introduction," xxvii. More of the Mexican-

origin population moved to Illinois, Michigan, and Wisconsin. Demographers predict this deconcentration will continue. James H. Johnson, Jr., Karen D. Johnson-Webb, and Walter C. Farrell, Jr., "Newly Emerging Hispanic Communities in the United States: A Spatial Analysis of Settlement Patterns, In-Migration Fields, and Social Receptivity," in *Immigration and Opportunity: Race, Ethnicity, and Employment in the United States*, edited by F. D. Bean and S. Bell-Rose (New York: Russell Sage Foundation, 1999), 263–310.

115. Passel, "Estimates of the Size"; Susan Gonzales Baker, Frank Baker, Escobar Latapi, and Sidney Weintraub, "U.S. Immigration Policies and Trends: The Growing Importance of Migration from Mexico," in *Crossings* (see note 107), 82–105.

116. Massey et al., *Beyond Smoke and Mirrors*, 136.

117. There is little consensus about the impact of immigrants on native workers. Some scholars argue the impact is nil; others find considerable displacement. An excellent discussion that starts to reconcile these views—the product of econometrics and ethnography, respectively—is Michael J. Rosenfeld and Marta Tienda, "Mexican Immigration, Occupational Niches, and Labor Market Competition: Evidence from Los Angeles, Chicago, and Atlanta, 1970–1990," in *Immigration and Opportunity* (see note 114), 64–105.

118. Jon Gjerde, *The Minds of the West: Ethnocultural Evolution in the Rural Middle West, 1830–1917* (Chapel Hill: University of North Carolina Press, 1997).

119. Using the Current Population Surveys of 1999 through 2001, if second generation is defined as having two foreign-born parents, the figures are 7 percent for the second generation and 35 percent for other U.S.-born Mexicans. We would like to do a strict test of the second-generation hypothesis, but this is not permitted by the census data. Fortunately, using the Current Population Survey, we found that the difference between second-generation Mexican Americans and those whose parents had been born in the United States were small. For example, the median total personal income of Mexican Americans with foreign parents was $27,000 for men and $19,000 for women, whereas the figures for those with U.S.-born parents were $28,600 and $17,000 respectively. The comparable figures for Mexican immigrants were $18,350 and $11,000. The educational achievement differences between those with U.S. parents and those with Mexican parents were small as well. Among Mexican American men born between 1945 and 1954, for example, 15 percent of those with foreign parents and 17 percent of those with U.S. parents had four or more years of college, compared to only 7 percent of Mexican immigrants. Authors' calculations from Miriam King, Steven Ruggles, and Matthew Sobek, Integrated Public Use Microdata Series, Current Population Survey: Preliminary Version 0.1. (Minneapolis: Minnesota Population Center, University of Minnesota, 2003).

120. For an explanation of why women do better than men in education, see Dowell Myers and Cynthia Cranford, "Temporal Differences in the Occupational Mobility of Immigrant and Native-born Latina Workers," *American Sociological Review*, 63 (1998): 68–93 and Robert C. Smith, "Gender, Eth-

nicity, and Race in School and Work Outcomes of Second-Generation Mexican Americans," in *Latinos in the Twenty-First Century*, edited by Marcelo Suarez–Orozco and Mariela Paez (Berkeley: University of California Press, 2002), 110–25.

121. The emergence of the gender gap among both African Americans and Mexicans requires its own historian to sort out the reasons, which are beyond the scope of this discussion. Certainly, they involve a variety of factors: the greater availability of jobs in sex-segregated occupations, the willingness of young women to stay longer in school than young men, and the preferences of employers undoubtedly have been important factors.

122. Part of the perceived Mexican disadvantage stems from the census questions. During the early twentieth century, the census asked about English language skills as a yes/no question. Any level of ability earned a yes. Late twentieth-century questions were more precise. They asked the respondent to rate how well the person being enumerated spoke English. Following guidelines in IPUMS, this analysis collapses the late twentieth-century categories to a yes/no variable, which should be equivalent to the early twentieth-century question.

123. Jack Citrin, Beth Reingold, Evelyn Walters, Donald P. Green, "The 'Official English' Movement and the Symbolic Politics of Language in the United States," *Western Political Quarterly* 43, no. 3 (1990): 535; Kathryn A. Woolard, "Sentences in the Language Prison: the Rhetorical Structuring of an American Language Policy Debate," *American Ethnologist* 16, no. 2 (May 1989): 268.

124. Alba and Nee, *Remaking the American Mainstream*, 217–30, summarizes the large literature on Mexican immigration and language.

125. The Mexican figure may underestimate entrepreneurship by missing a substantial number who operated informal businesses, if Raijman's and Tienda's findings from Chicago's Little Village can be generalized. Rebeca Raijman and Marta Tienda, "Training Functions of Ethnic Economies: Mexican Entrepreneurs in Chicago," *Sociological Perspectives* 43, no. 3 (Fall 2000): 439.

126. This conclusion is based on representation in earnings percentiles. The percentiles are based on the entire adult income-earning population in both 1970 and 2000.

127. Tilly, *Durable Inequality*.

Chapter 3

1. U.S. Bureau of the Census, *Thirteenth Census of the United States. Abstract of the Census* (Washington: U.S. Government Printing Office, 1913), 121.

2. Howard P. Chudacoff, *How Old Are You? Age Consciousness in American Culture* (Princeton, N.J.: Princeton University Press, 1989), 10, 65.

3. Lawrence K. Frank, "Childhood and Youth," in *Recent Social Trends in the United States: Report of the President's Research Committee on Social Trends* (New York: McGraw-Hill, 1933), 751–800. On changing ideas of childhood, see Viviana A. Zelizer, *Pricing the Priceless Child: The Changing Social Value of Children* (New York: Basic Books, 1985).

4. John Modell, *Into One's Own: From Youth to Adulthood In The United States*

1920–1975 (Berkeley: University of California Press, 1989), 26, makes the
point that the life course of youth in the twentieth century has been "quite
malleable." On the history of childhood and youth, see Harvey J. Graff, *Conflicting Paths: Growing Up in America* (Cambridge, Mass.: Harvard University Press, 1995).

5. Chudacoff, *How Old Are You?* 29–38. Leonard P. Ayers, *Laggards In Our Schools: A Study of Retardation and Elimination in City School Systems* (New York: Charities Publication Committee, 1913); Michael B. Katz, *The Irony of Early School Reform: Educational Innovation in Mid-Nineteenth Century Massachusetts* (Cambridge, Mass.: Harvard University Press, 1968), 55–56.

6. Matilda White Riley was the pioneer in the study of age stratification. See, for instance, Matilda White Riley, "Age Strata in Social Systems," in *Handbook of Aging and the Social Sciences*, edited by Robert H. Binstock and Ethel Shanas (New York: Van Nostrand Reinhold, 1976), 189–217. The literature on age of consent shows especially well the interaction of public policy with the emerging precision about age—and just how much confusion remained in the early twentieth century. Edith Houghton Hooker, *The Laws of Sex* (Boston, Mass.: Richard D. Badger, 1921); Ann Garlin Spencer, "The Age of Consent and its Significance," *Forum* 49 (1913): 406–13.

7. Tamar Lewin, "Financially-Set Grandparents Help Keep Families Afloat, Too," *New York Times*, July 14, 2005. In 1900, women's life expectancy at age sixty-five exceeded men's by 5.9 percent, in 1940 by 15 percent, and in 1990 by 21 percent. In 2000, it had dropped back (and this was an estimate) to 15 percent. Marilyn J. Field, "When Children Die," *Issues in Science and Technology Online* (Spring 2003); Federal Interagency Forum on Aging-Related Statistics, "Older Americans 2000: Key Indicators of Well-Being" (2000), table 12A. Percentage changes computed by authors.

8. Personal communication from Samuel Preston, February 18, 2004.

9. National Center for Health Statistics, "Health, United States 2003" (Washington: U.S. Government Printing Office), updated trend tables, tables 22 and 35.

10. Donald J. Bogue, *The Population of the United States: Historical Trends and Future Projections* (New York: Free Press, 1985), 44. For an interesting and provocative discussion of the growing share of the very elderly, see Susan Dominus, "Life in the Age of Old, Old Age," *New York Times*, February 22, 2004.

11. Irene B. Taeuber and Conrad Taeuber, *People of the United States in the Twentieth Century* (Washington: U.S. Census Bureau, 1971).

12. Ibid., 142–43.

13. U.S. Commission on Population Growth and the American Future, *Population Growth and the American Future* (Washington: U.S. Government Printing Office, 1971), 19, 22.

14. Michael B. Katz, *The Price of Citizenship: Redefining the American Welfare State* (New York: Metropolitan Books, 2001), 242–43.

15. Ibid. For a discussion of the importance of studying the life course, see Modell, *Into One's Own*; Michael J. Shanahan, "Pathways to Adulthood in Changing Societies: Variability and Mechanisms in Life Course Perspective," *American Sociological Review* 62 (2000): 667–92.

16. Peter Laslett, "Age of Menarche in Europe Since the Eighteenth Century," in *The Family in History*, edited by Theodore K. Rabb and Robert I. Rotberg (New York: Harper and Row, 1973), 28–47.

17. Elizabeth Fussell and Frank E. Furstenberg, Jr., "The Transition to Adulthood during the Twentieth Century: Race, Nativity, and Gender," in *On the Frontier of Adulthood: Theory, Research, and Public Policy*, edited by Frank E. Furstenberg, Jr., Ruben G. Rumbaut, and Richard A. Settensten, Jr. (Chicago: University of Chicago Press, 2005). Alan Booth, Ann C. Crouter, and Michael J. Shanahan, *Transitions to Adulthood in a Changing Economy: No Work, No Family, No Future?* (London: Praeger, 1999).

18. For other discussions of the transition to adulthood, whose interpretations are consistent with the one presented here, see Marlis Buchmann, *The Script of Life in Modern Society: Entry Into Adulthood in a Changing World* (Chicago: University of Chicago Press, 1989); Frances Goldscheider and Calvin Goldscheider, *The Changing Transition to Adulthood: Leaving and Returning Home* (Thousand Oaks, Calif.: Sage Publications, 1999); Frances Goldscheider and Calvin Goldscheider, *Leaving Home Before Marriage: Ethnicity, Familism, and Generational Relationships* (Madison: University of Wisconsin Press, 1993); Myron Gutmann, Sara M. Pullum-Piñón, and Thomas Pullum, "Three Eras of Young Adult Home Leaving in Twentieth-Century America," *Journal of Social History* 35, no. 3 (2002): 533–76.

19. Frank E. Furstenberg, Jr., et al., "Growing Up Is Harder to Do," *Contexts* 3, no. 3 (2004): 33–41. The approach here draws on, and was inspired by, John Modell, Frank E. Furstenberg, Jr., and Theodore Hershberg, "Social Change and Transitions to Adulthood in Historical Perspective," *Journal of Family History* 1 (1976): 7–32. With the census data, it is possible to examine systematically the relations among the first five. It is not possible to know the age at the birth of the first child exactly, though it is feasible to make a rough estimate of the onset of parenthood by noting the age at which women and men live with children of their own. For most men and women, for most of the century, determining the initial age of parenthood does not matter greatly. Parenthood usually followed marriage, which, along with a household of one's own could be taken as the terminus of the road to independence from parents (although of course many couples have received some support from their parents after marriage).

20. Kathryn Edin and Maria Kefalas, *Promises I Can Keep: Why Poor Women Put Motherhood before Marriage* (Berkeley: University of California Press, 2005), chap. 1; Furstenberg et al., "Growing Up Is Harder to Do."

21. The stage might be called "semiautonomy." We discuss and illustrate semiautonomy in the nineteenth-century in Michael B. Katz, Michael J. Doucet, and Mark J. Stern, *The Social Organization of Early Industrial Capitalism* (Cambridge: Harvard University Press, 1982), 244–52. See also Joseph Kett, *Rites of Passage: Adolescence in America, 1790 to the Present* (New York: Basic Books, 1977). The periodization and data on the transition to adulthood are drawn primarily from Jordan Stanger-Ross, Christina Collins, and Mark J. Stern, "Falling Far From the Tree: Three Reinventions of the Transition to Adulthood in 20th Century America," *Social Science History* (forthcoming).

22. Robert Schoeini and Karen F. Ross, "Material Aid Received from Families

during the Transition to Adulthood," in *On the Frontier of Adulthood* (see note 17); Lewin, "Financially-Set Grandparents."

23. Fussell and Furstenberg, "The Transition to Adulthood"; Peg Tyre, Karen Springen, and Julie Scelfo, "Bringing Up Adultolescents," *Newsweek*, March 25, 2002, 34; Buchmann, *The Script of Life in Modern Society*.

24. David T. Ellwood and Christopher Jencks, "The Growing Differences in Family Structure: What Do We Know? Where Do We Look for Answers?" (Russell Sage Foundation, 2001).

25. On the impact of the Great Depression on marriage age in a supposedly representative community, see Robert S. Lynd and Helen Merrell Lynd, *Middletown in Transition: A Study in Cultural Conflicts* (New York: Harcourt, Brace, and World, 1937), 149–50.

26. Buchmann, *The Script of Life in Modern Society* and Furstenberg et al., "Growing Up Is Harder to Do" find similar patterns.

27. Especially early in the century, there also were differences between regions of the country that reflected their distinctive demographies. These largely disappeared over the course of the century.

28. Between 1970 and 1980, the fraction of married African American twenty-five-year-old women dropped from 76 percent to 59 percent and then plunged further to 32 percent in 1990, declining only a little more in the next decade

29. Of black women born in 1910, 92 percent had married, compared to 86 percent born in 1940, and 71 percent born in 1960. At age thirty, the decline across cohorts was even steeper.

30. Edin and Kefalas, *Promises I Can Keep;* Furstenberg et al., "Growing Up Is Harder to Do"; see also the similar finding in Buchmann, *The Script of Life in Modern Society*. Despite these trends, pathways to independent adulthood varied. Two researchers found that the ways in which most women combined marriage and childbearing fit one of fourteen common patterns. But they identified hundreds of other patterns as well—with the most variety among black women. To take just one cohort, women born between 1945 and 1954: the fraction of women's histories falling outside the fourteen common patterns varied from 31.6 percent for whites to 49.5 percent for blacks, and 35.6 percent for Hispanics. Lawrence L. Wu and Jui-Chung Allen Li, "Marital and Childbearing Trajectories of American Women: 50 Years of Social Change," in *On the Frontier of Adulthood* (see note 17), table 5.

31. Robert S. Lynd and Helen Merrell Lynd, *Middletown: A Study in Modern American Culture* (New York: Harcourt, Brace, and World, 1929), 187.

32. For a summary of child labor laws by the 1920s, see Frank, "Childhood and Youth," 777; G. Stanley Hall, *Adolescence, Its Psychology and Its Relations to Physiology, Anthropology, Sociology, Sex, Crime, Religion, and Education* (London: Sidney Appleton, 1904), xiii–xviii.

33. Modell, *Into One's Own*; Lynd and Lynd, *Middletown: A Study in Modern American Culture*, 111.

34. Sherman J. Dorn, *Creating the Dropout: An Institutional and Social History of School Failure* (Westport, Conn.: Praeger, 1992).

35. Robert J. Havighurst and J. Stiles Lindley, "National Policy for Alienated Youth," *Phi Delta Kappan* XLII (1960–1961): 286–88.

36. "The Challenge of Jobless Youth" (Washington: U.S. President's Committee on Youth Employment, 1963).

37. Kenneth Clark, "Present Threats to Children and Youth," in *National Committee on the Employment of Youth* (1957) quoted in Robert H. Bremmer, ed., *Children and Youth in America: A Documentary History*, vol. III: *1933–1973*, Parts 1–4 (Cambridge, Mass.: Harvard University Press, 1974), 163–64.

38. From the distinguished African American sociologist, E. Franklin Frazier, to Daniel Patrick Moynihan's 1965 report to President Lyndon Johnson on the black family, to Nicholas Lemann's widely read 1991 popular history of the urban black experience, *The Promised Land*, observers have attributed the high rate of out-of-wedlock births among African American women to the destruction of black families under slavery. Nicholas Lemann, *The Promised Land: The Great Black Migration and How It Changed America* (New York: Alfred A. Knopf, 1991); U.S. Department of Labor, *The Negro Family: The Case for National Action* (Washington: U.S. Government Printing Office, 1965). Stewart E. Tolnay, *The Bottom Rung: African American Family Life on Southern Farms* (Urbana: University of Illinois Press, 1999), 113–16, 154, refutes this assumption.

39. Lizabeth Cohen, *A Consumers' Republic: The Politics of Mass Consumption in Postwar America* (New York: Knopf, 2003), 167–73.

40. In General Dynamics Land Systems, Inc. v. Cline et al., No. 02-1080, decided February 24, 2004, the Supreme Court ruled that employers may reduce benefits for younger workers, thus opening another door to increased inequality.

41. Henry Fairlie, "Talkin 'bout My Generation: Government Assistance to Those over 65 and the Pampered Lifestyle," *New Republic*, March 28, 1988, 9; Theodore R. Marmor, Fay Lomax Cook, and Stephen Scher, "Social Security Politics and the Conflicts between Generations: Are We Asking the Right Questions?" in *Social Security in the 21st Century*, edited by Eric R. Kingson and James H. Schulz (New York: Oxford University Press, 1977), 204; Samuel H. Preston, "Children and the Elderly in the U.S," *Scientific American* 251, no. 6 (1984): 44–49.

42. Susan B. Carter and Richard Sutch, "Myth of the Industrial Scrapheap: A Revisionist View of Turn-of-the-Century American Retirement," *Journal of Economic History* 56, no. 1 (1996): 5–38; Richard Ransom and Richard Sutch, "The Labor of Older Americans: Retirement of Men On and Off the Job, 1870–1937," *Journal of Economic History* 46, no. 1 (1986): 1–20.

43. Authors' calculations. See Michael B. Katz and Mark J. Stern, "1940s to the Present" in *Poverty in the United States: An Encyclopedia of History, Politics, and Poverty,* edited by Gwendolyn Mink and Alice O'Connor (Santa Barbara, Calif.: ABC-CLIO, 2004), v. 1, 33–47.

44. Quoted in Carole Haber, *Beyond Sixty-Five: The Dilemma of Old Age in America's Past* (Cambridge: Cambridge University Press, 1983), 86; see also Michael B. Katz, *In the Shadow of the Poorhouse: A Social History of Welfare in America*, 10th anniversary ed. (New York: Basic Books, 1996), 90–91.

45. At first, it appears that black men age sixty-five and over remained household heads more often whites—87 percent to 81 percent. But this was because African American men worked longer. With work controlled, the dif-

ferences disappeared. Black and white women were equally likely to be the spouse of household heads, or household heads themselves.

46. Haber, *Beyond Sixty-Five: The Dilemma of Old Age in America's Past*, 71; Osler (1910) quoted in William Graebner, *A History of Retirement: The Meaning and Function of an American Institution, 1885–1978* (New Haven, Conn.: Yale University Press, 1980), 4, 18–35; David Hackett Fischer, *Growing Old in America* (New York: Oxford University Press, 1978), 140–42.

47. Lynd and Lynd, *Middletown: A Study in Modern American Culture*, 33–35.

48. There are many sources on the beginnings of social insurance. Three particularly good ones are: Roy Lubove, *The Struggle for Social Security 1900–1935* (Pittsburgh: University of Pittsburgh Press, 1986); Daniel T. Rodgers, *Atlantic Crossings: Social Politics in a Progressive Age* (Cambridge, Mass.: Harvard University Press, 1998); Theda Skocpol, *Protecting Soldiers and Mothers: The Political Origins of Social Policy* (Cambridge, Mass.: Harvard University Press, 1992). On saving, see Rohit Daniel Wadhwani, "Citizen Savers: The Family Economy, Financial Institutions, and Social Policy in the Northeastern U.S. from the Market Revolution to the Great Depression," *Enterprise & Society* 5, no. 4 (2004).

49. The literature on the origins and history of Social Security, and on the crisis of the 1930s, is very large. Four different perspectives can be found in Arthur J. Altmeyer, *The Formative Years of Social Security* (Madison: University of Wisconsin Press, 1968); Edward Berkowitz, *America's Welfare State: From Roosevelt to Reagan* (Baltimore, Md.: Johns Hopkins University Press, 1991); Michael K. Brown, *Race, Money, and the American Welfare State* (Ithaca, N.Y.: Cornell University Press, 1999); Jerry Cates, *Insuring Inequality* (Ann Arbor: University of Michigan Press, 1983).

50. Authors' calculations.

51. As with most major family developments, change occurred most dramatically after the World War II. After 1970, the fraction reached a plateau (Authors' calculations).

52. Eric Klinenberg, *Heat Wave: A Social Autopsy of Disaster in Chicago* (Chicago: University of Chicago Press, 2002).

53. "Report Suggests National Assisted Living Center Is Needed To Manage Growth," *Contemporary Long Term Care* 26, no. 7 (2003): 14.

54. U.S. Department of Labor, "The Older American Worker: Age Discrimination in Employment," (Washington: U.S. Government Printing Office, 1965). The legislation was a response to a report of the secretary of labor ordered by the Civil Rights Act of 1964. "Questioning Age-Old Wisdom: The Legacy of Mandatory Retirement," *Harvard Law Review* 105 (1991–1992): 889–907; Kenneth Noble, "End of Forced Retirement Means a Lot to a Few," *New York Times*, October 26, 1986, 5; Albert Rees and Sharon P. Smith, "The End of Mandatory Retirement for Tenured Faculty," *Science* 253, no. 5022 (1991): 838; Steven V. Roberts, "House Votes to End Mandatory Retirement," *New York Times*, October 18, 1986, 33; Barbara Vobeda, "Congress Voted To End Mandatory Retirement," *Washington Post*, October 18, 1986, A3.

55. A representative of the AARP made a similar point: "Medical studies demonstrate that chronological age is a poor determinant of ability and that

capability varies greatly with the individual, regardless of age." The chairman emphasized that "mandatory retirement costs the United States very much. Besides being a drag on the economy, removing from the workforce persons who could be contributing to their own economic support as well as to the U.S. Treasury and to Social Security retirement funds, it wastes human potential" and damages individual emotional and physical health. Subcommittee on Employment Health and Long-Term Care of the Select Committee on Aging, "The Removal of Age Ceiling Cap Under the Age Discrimination in Employment Act," 99th Congr., 2d sess., March 12, 1986.

56. Kenneth S. Apfel, "Commissioner of Social Security, Praises Senate Action and Announces Implementation Plan for the Repeal of the Retirement Earnings Test," *Social Security News Release,* March 24, 2000.

57. On this shift, see Katz, *The Price of Citizenship.*

58. There are many compelling criticisms of privatization, or individual retirement accounts, in Social Security along with clear explanations of the lack of crisis in the system. For a particularly trenchant, short example, see Paul Krugman, "Social Security Scares," *New York Times,* March 5, 2004.

59. For an excellent overview of the history of American family structure, see Steven Ruggles, "The Transformation of American Family Structure," *American Historical Review* 99, no. 1 (1994): 103–28.

60. The speed of the decline and its implications are dealt with in Mark J. Stern, *Society and Family Strategy: Erie County, New York, 1850–1920* (Albany: State University of New York Press, 1987). The measure here is the number of own children per one thousand women aged fifteen to forty-nine.

61. Jacques Henripin, *Trends and Factors of Fertility in Canada* (Ottawa: Statistics Canada, 1972), 237–62.

62. Maris Vinovskis, *An "Epidemic" of Adolescent Pregnancy? Some Historical and Policy Considerations* (New York: Oxford University Press, 1988); National Center for Health Statistics, "Health, United States 2003."

63. Edin and Kefalas, *Promises I Can Keep.*

64. James Reed, *From Private Vice to Public Virtue: The Birth Control Movement and American Society since 1830* (New York: Basic Books, 1978).

65. Geraldo C. Arnas, "Record Number of Women Childless," *Philadelphia Inquirer,* October 25, 2003.

66. These gaps amounted to 14 percent for whites, 25 percent for blacks, and 28 percent for Latinos.

67. An indeterminate number of women listed as widows were either separated or unmarried; they reported themselves as widows to avoid stigma. This, however, does not change the overall trend. On the fluidity of marital designations in the late nineteenth century, see Beverly Schwartzberg, "Lots Of Them Did That": Desertion, Bigamy, and Marital Fluidity in Late-Nineteenth Century America," *Journal of Social History* 37, no. 3 (2004): 573–600.

68. In 1900, the fraction with nonfamily members was 40 percent to 31 percent of male-headed families and in 2000, 22 percent to 15 percent.

69. On the struggle for survival among single mothers, see Kathryn Edin and Laura Lein, *Making Ends Meet: How Single Mothers Survive Welfare and Low-Wage Work* (New York: Russell Sage Foundation, 1997).

70. Lynne M. Casper and Suzanne M. Bianchi, *Continuity and Change in the American Family* (Thousand Oaks, Calif.: Sage Publications, 2002); Frank E. Furstenberg, Jr., "History and Current Status of Divorce in the United States," *Children and Divorce* 4, no. 1 (1994): 29–43; Rose M. Kreider and Jason M. Fields, *Number, Timing, and Duration of Marriages and Divorces 1996* (Washington, D.C.: U.S. Census Bureau, 2002).
71. For an overview of the EITC, see Katz, *The Price of Citizenship*.
72. Caspar and Bianchi, *Continuity and Change in the American Family*, 39. For a good overview of research on cohabitation that stresses its variety, see Lynette F. Hoelter and Dawn E. Stauffer, "What Does it Mean to Be 'Just Living Together' in the New Millennium? An Overview," in *Just Living Together: Implications of Cohabitation on Families, Children, and Social Policy*, edited by Alan Booth and Ann C. Crouter (Mahwah, N.J.: Lawrence Erlbaum, 2002), 255–72.
73. Milton B. Hunt, "The Housing of Non-Family Groups of Men in Chicago," *American Journal of Sociology* 16, no. 2 (1910): 145–70, quotations 145 and 147.
74. The increase was from 5 percent for high school and 11.1 percent for college graduates. Men still lived in nonfamily households more often than women, but the differences between sexes had shrunk.
75. This is what all researchers who study cross-sectional populations find. For example, see the data on homelessness and poverty in, respectively, Dennis Culhane et al., "Assessing Homeless Population Size Through the Use of Emergency and Transitional Shelter Services in 1998: Results from the Analysis of Administrative Data from Nine US Jurisdictions," *Public Health Reports* 116, no. 4 (2001): 344–54; and Greg J. Duncan and Richard Coe, *Years of Poverty, Years of Plenty: The Changing Fortunes of American Workers and Families* (Ann Arbor: University of Michigan Press, 1984).
76. In 1995, for instance, nearly 50 percent of thirty- to thirty-nine-year-old women reported having "cohabited" at least once. J. Smock and Sanjiv Gupta, "Cohabitation in Contemporary North America," in *Just Living Together* (see note 72), 53–84.
77. This classification excludes institutions.
78. It is surprisingly hard to give exact proportions for these household and family types. Part of the difficulty relates to manipulating the census data. But more arises from the different assumptions that may be made (should the population be restricted to those age eighteen and over, for instance?). How are families living with other families (married couples with married children, women with children with the mother's parents, for instance?) to be considered? Should there be age cutoffs for nonfamily households to capture the early adulthood phenomenon? The way these questions are answered affects the precise numbers. Nonetheless, whatever the answers, the quantities are not very different and, what is most important, the trends are the same.
79. On the growth of suburbs, see Cohen, *A Consumers' Republic*; Robert Fishman, *Bourgeois Utopias: The Rise and Fall of Suburbia* (New York: Basic Books, 1987); Herbert J. Gans, *Levittowners: Ways of Life and Politics in a New Suburban Community* (New York: Vintage Books, 1969); Kenneth T. Jackson, *Crabgrass Frontier: The Suburbanization of the United States* (New York: Oxford

University Press, 1985); Delores Hayden, *Building Suburbia: Green Fields and Urban Growth, 1820–2000* (New York: Pantheon, 2003). On the role of realtors in promoting both suburbanization and segregation, see Kevin Fox Gotham, *Race, Real Estate, and Uneven Development: The Kansas City Experience, 1900–2000* (Albany: State University of New York Press, 2002).

80. From 2 percent to 8 percent in suburbs and from 2 percent to 28 percent in central cities.

81. Linda S. Kadaba, "Singles on the move? Yes, to the Suburbs," *Philadelphia Inquirer*, April 13, 2004, 1.

82. In some cities—Atlanta, Boston, Seattle—the share went up; in the other eleven, it declined. The decline was especially steep in Miami and Los Angeles, where the fraction living with a high concentration of empty nesters also went down in the suburbs. There, trends reflected the immigration of young families from Latin America. (In Miami's suburbs the Hispanic share of the population went from .4 percent to 29 percent and in the city itself from 16 percent to 59 percent in these three decades; in Los Angeles the suburban increase was from 4 percent to 18 percent and the city rise was from 6 percent to 29 percent.)

83. The book that called attention to, and aroused interest in, concentrated poverty was William Julius Wilson, *The Truly Disadvantaged: the Inner City, the Underclass, and Public Policy* (Chicago: University of Chicago Press, 1987). On the phenomenon of concentration, see also Paul A. Jargowsky, *Poverty and Place: Ghettos, Barrios, and the American City* (New York: Russell Sage Foundation, 1997). Concentrated poverty was the major impetus behind the formation of a Social Science Research Council committee for research on the urban underclass. This episode, and much else of relevance, is analyzed in Alice O'Connor, *Poverty Knowledge: Social Science, Social Policy, and the Poor in Twentieth-Century U.S. History* (Princeton, N.J.: Princeton University Press, 2001).

84. Paul A. Jargowsky, *Stunning Progress, Hidden Problems: The Dramatic Decline of Concentrated Poverty in the 1990s,* (Washington, D.C.: Brookings Institution Press, 2003); University of Texas at Dallas Bruton Center, *Windows on Urban Poverty*; John Logan, "Regional Divisions Dampen '90s Prosperity" (Albany: State University of New York, 2002); John Logan, "Separate and Unequal: The Neighborhood Gap for Blacks and Hispanics in Metropolitan America" (Albany: State University of New York, 2002).

85. For an overview of gentrification, see the essays in Neil Smith and Peter Williams, eds., *Gentrification and the City* (Boston, Mass.: Allen and Unwin, 1986). For examples of how immigration revived decaying cities, see Richard Higgins, "Older Cities See Large Growth in Population," *Boston Globe*, March 25, 1991, A1.

Chapter 4

1. Michael B. Katz and Christoph Sachsse, "Introduction," in *The Mixed Economy of Social Welfare*, edited by Michael B. Katz and Christoph Sachsse (Baden-Baden: Nomos, 1996), 12.

2. Ibid.

3.   Michael B. Katz, *Improving Poor People: the Welfare State, the "Underclass," and Urban Schools as History* (Princeton, N.J.: Princeton University Press, 1995), 131.

4.   Eric H. Monkkonen, "Nineteenth-Century Institutions: Dealing with the Urban 'Underclass,'" in *The "Underclass" Debate: Views from History*, edited by Michael B. Katz (Princeton, N.J.: Princeton University Press, 1993), 334–65.

5.   International Monetary Fund, "Globalization: Threat or Opportunity?" (Washington, D.C., 2000, corrected 2002).

6.   Ibid.; OECD, *Year To Year Percentage Changes In Selected Economic Variables*, U.S. Census Bureau, "U.S. Trade in Goods—Balance of Payments (BOP) Basis vs. Census Basis Value in Millions of Dollars 1960 thru 2003" (Washington: U.S. Government Printing Office, 2004).

7.   International Monetary Fund, "Globalization: Threat or Opportunity?"

8.   U.S. Census Bureau, "Flow of Funds Account—Financial Assets and Liabilities of Foreign Sector: 1980–2000" (Washington: U.S. Government Printing Office, 2001); U.S. Census Bureau, "U.S. Banking Office of Foreign Banks—Summary: 1980 to 2000," in *Statistical Abstract of the United States: 2001* (Washington: U.S. Government Printing Office, 2001), 731.

9.   U.S. Department of Labor, Bureau of Labor Statistics, "International Comparisons of Hourly Compensation Costs for Production Workers in Manufacturing, revised data for 2002" (Washington: U.S. Government Printing Office, 2004), table 1.

10. However, another measure, the United Nations' Human Development Indicators (HDI), which includes education and life expectancy, shows improvement—"judged by their HDIs, today's poor countries are well ahead of where the leading countries were in 1870. This is largely because medical advances and improved living standards have brought strong increases in life expectancy." International Monetary Fund, "Globalization: Threat or Opportunity?" On inequality among nations, see Branko Milanovic, *Worlds Apart: Measuring International and Global Inequality* (Princeton, N.J.: Princeton University Press, 2005).

11. Milanovic, *Worlds Apart*.

12. Ohtsu Sadayoshi, "Changing Characteristics of International Labor Migration in Northeast Asia: With a Focus on the Russo-Chinese Border," *Slavic Eurasian Studies* 2 (2004); John Salt, "Current Trends In International Migration in Europe (1999): Social Cohesion and Quality of Life" (London: Council of Europe, 1999).

13. Jefferson Cowie, *Capital Moves: RCA's Seventy-Year Quest for Cheap Labor* (Ithaca, N.Y.: Cornell University Press, 1999).

14. Manuel Castells, *The Rise of the Network Society*, in *The Information Age: Economy, Society, and Culture,* vol. I, 2nd ed. (Oxford: Blackwell Publishers, 2000), 131.

15. Population Reference Bureau, *Human Populations: Fundamentals of Growth Patterns of World Urbanization* (2004).

16. Authors' calculations. For discussions of domestic migration, see Rachel S. Franklin, "Domestic Migration Across Regions, Divisions, and States: 1995–2000," in *Census 2000 Special Reports* (Washington: U.S. Census Bureau,

2003); William H. Frey, "Census 2000 Reveals New Native-Born and For-
eign-Born Shifts Across U.S." (Ann Arbor: Population Studies Center at the
Institute for Social Research, University of Michigan, 2002); Marc J. Perry,
"Migration and Geographic Mobility in Metropolitan and Non-Metropoli-
tan America," and "State-to-State Migration Flows," in *Census 2000 Special
Reports* (U.S. Census Bureau, 2003).

17.   A sober case for the new economy is made in Roger Alcaly, *The New Economy* (New York: Farrar, Straus, & Giroux, 2003). Alcaly stresses the role of
productivity growth. A similar discussion is Roger W. Ferguson Jr.,
"Lessons From Past Productivity Booms" (paper, Meetings of the American
Economic Association, January 4, 2004).

18.   Jeff Madrick, *Why Economies Grow: The Forces That Shape Prosperity and How
We Can Get Them Working Again* (New York: Basic Books, 2002), 17–19.

19.   Castells, *The Rise of the Network Society*.

20.   Alcaly, *The New Economy*.

21.   Other statistics also highlight its rapid spread. Only five years after its introduction to the public—in 1999—Netscape Navigator Web Browser
reached 120 million Americans, of whom 60 percent claimed to use it regularly. It took less time for the Internet than for any previous technology to
find fifty million users.

22.   Alcaly, *The New Economy*, 56–58.

23.   Madrick, *Why Economies Grow*, 189; Alcaly, *New Economy*, 103, 237.

24.   Godfrey Hodgson, *More Equal Than Others: American From Nixon To The New
Century* (Princeton, N.J.: Princeton University Press, 2004), 65–66; Margaret
Pugh O'Mara, *Cities of Knowledge: Cold War Science and the Search for the Next
Silicon Valley* (Princeton, N.J.: Princeton University Press, 2005); Madrick,
Why Economies Grow, 21, 25, 120–21. Alcaly, *The New Economy*, 20–21; Hodgson, 106–7, points out that underestimation of the effects of innovation,
among other factors, caused the CPI to significantly overstate inflation in
the 1970s and 1980s. The result of this underestimation, he contends, led to
an exaggeration of productivity growth in the 1990s; U.S. Department of Labor, Bureau of Labor Statistics, "Productivity and Costs, First Quarter 2004,
Revised 2004" (Washington: U.S. Government Printing Office).

25.   John Kenneth Galbraith, *The New Industrial State* (Boston: Houghton Mifflin,
1967). We are indebted to Alcaly for this point.

26.   Alcaly, *The New Economy*, 132–33.

27.   Ibid., 46–47; Henwood, *After the New Economy*, 64–67; Deborah Fink, *Cutting
Into the Meat Packing Line: Workers and Change in the Rural Midwest* (Chapel
Hill: University of North Carolina Press, 1998).

28.   New junk bonds ballooned from $11 billion in 1984 to $100 billion in 2001,
and the par value of outstanding junk bonds jumped from less than $100
billion in the mid-1980s to almost $700 billion early in the twenty-first cen-
tury. Negligible in the early 1980s, venture capital investments skyrocketed
to more than $100 billion in 2000, before retreating. Ferguson, "Lessons
from Past Productivity Booms."

29.   For data on women in the labor force, see chapter 3. The massive surge in
women's role in the regular labor force resulted from a variety of sources,
but one of the most important was the emergence of the "new economy,"
whose features they, in turn, helped define. The shift toward service and

technical occupations favored women, who clustered disproportionately in them. On this point, see Martin Carnoy, *Sustaining the New Economy* (New York and Cambridge, Mass.: Russell Sage Foundation and Harvard University Press, 2000), 31–32.

30. Angela Bayer and Joshua Bonilla, "Executive Summary: Our Changing Nation" (Washington, D.C.: Population Resource Center, 2001).

31. Carnoy, *Sustaining the New Economy*, 64–65, 78.

32. Lawrence Mishel, Jared Bernstein, and Heather Boushey, *The State of Working America 2002/2003* (Ithaca, N.Y.: ILR Press, 2003), 260–75.

33. The story of the change in employer behavior, the end of paternalism, is told in Michael B. Katz, *The Price of Citizenship: Redefining the American Welfare State* (New York: Metropolitan Books, 2001), chap. 7.

34. Carnoy, *Sustaining the New Economy*, 69.

35. Jeremy Rifkin, *The End of Work: The Decline of the Global Labor Force and the Dawn of the Post-Market Era* (New York: G. Putnam's and Sons, 1995).

36. Carnoy, *Sustaining the New Economy*, 39, 46.

37. Henwood, *After the New Economy*, 72–73.

38. David Cay Johnston, "The Servant Class Is at the Counter," *New York Times*, August 28 1995; Saskia Sassen, *Cities in a World Economy* (Thousand Oaks, Calif.: Pine Forge Press, 1994); Saskia Sassen, *Global City: New York, London, and Tokyo* (Princeton, N.J.: Princeton University Press, 1991), 245–83.

39. This section on occupational and industrial classification draws on the research of Daniel Amsterdam who produced an excellent summary of the history of these classifications.

40. Alba M. Edwards, "Classification of Occupations: The Classification of Occupations, with Special Reference to the United States and the Proposed New Classification for the Thirteenth Census Report on Occupations," *Publications of the American Statistical Association* 12, no. 94 (1911): 618–46.

41. Ibid., 621, 636.

42. Alba M. Edwards, "Social-Economic Groups of the United States," *Publications of the American Statistical Association* 15, no. 118 (1917): 643–61. Edwards continued his advocacy for a stratification-based system and, in 1933, put forth a concrete plan. Alba M. Edwards, "A Social-Economic Grouping of the Gainful Workers of the United States," *Journal of the American Statistical Association* 28, no. 184 (1933): 377–87.

43. Gladys L. Palmer, "The Convertibility List of Occupations and the Problems of Developing It," *Journal of the American Statistical Association* 34, no. 208 (1939): 693–708. On the relation between the work of the Joint Committee and the census, see P. K. Whelpton and Edward Hollander, "A Standard Occupational and Industrial Classification of Workers," *Social Forces* 18, no. 4 (1940): 488–94; Thomas Scopp and John Priebe, "Census Occupational Classification System and the Standard Occupational Classification" (paper, Proceedings of the International Occupational Classification Conference, Washington, D.C., September 1993).

44. Chester Levine, Laurie Salmon, and Daniel H. Weinberg, "Revising the Standard Occupational Classification System," *Monthly Labor Review* (1999): 36–45. See also "Federal Register Notice" (1999).

45. Levine, Salmon, and Weinberg, "Revising the Standard Occupational Classification System," 38–40.

46. Peter Capelli, "Conceptual Issues in Developing a System of Occupational Classification" (paper, Seminar on Research Findings, April 11, 1995), 20–21; Seymour L. Wolfbein, "Uses of an Occupational Classification System" (paper, International Occupational Classification Conference, Washington, D.C., September 1993), 116–23.

47. Authors' calculations.

48. Vladimir S. Kolesnikoff, "Standard Classification of Industries in the United States," *Journal of the American Statistical Association* 35, no. 209 (1940): 65–73; Esther Pearce, "History of the Standard Industrial Classification" (Washington: U.S. Government Printing Office, 1957).

49. Its eight major groups—the top of a four-digit coding system—were agricultural, forestry, and fishing industries; mining; construction; manufacturing; wholesale and retail trade; finance, insurance, and real estate; transportation, communication, and other public utilities; transportation; and services.

50. John B. Murphy, "Introducing the North American Industry Classification System," *Monthly Labor Review* (1998): 43–47.

51. The alternative to this supply side principle was a demand side approach that groups together "commodities or services that have similarities in use, that belong together or are used together for some purpose, or that define market groupings." U.S. Census Bureau, "Issues Paper No. 1 Conceptual Issues" (Washington: U.S. Government Printing Office, 1993).

52. U.S. Office of Management and Budget, "1997 North American Industry Classification System—1987 Standards Industrial Classification Replacement" (Washington: U.S. Government Printing Office, 1997).

53. Carol A. Ambler, "NAICS and U.S. Statistics" (paper, Annual Meeting of the American Statistical Association, Dallas, Texas, August 9–13, 1998).

54. For an alternative industrial classification designed to capture change in the economy, see James K. Galbraith, *Created Unequal: The Crisis in American Pay* (New York: Free Press, 1998), chap. 7.

55. Charles Richmond Henderson, "Are Modern Industry and City Life Unfavorable to the Family?" *American Journal of Sociology* 14, no. 5 (1909): 668–80.

56. Historian Alice O'Connor describes how the production of urban inequality works:

> In major cities nationwide, overall economic growth is accompanied by higher than average rates of unemployment and poverty, concentrated especially in low-income, working-class minority neighborhoods that have only recently begun to show signs of recovery following decades of steady decline. Still, the low-skilled urban workforce, greatly expanded by the "end of welfare," has little access to local jobs that provide living wages, employment security, and adequate benefits. For the past several years job creation has been faster in the suburbs, where minority workers encounter greater racial discrimination in hiring. Meanwhile, despite gradually rising rates of nonwhite suburbanization, racial residential segregation remains the norm—laying the basis for racial and class segregation in education, transportation systems, access to public services, and political representation. Yet, the commitment to deliberate policies of integration, on the metropolitan as well as the national level, is in open retreat.

Alice O'Connor, "Understanding Inequality in the Late Twentieth-Century Metropolis: New Perspectives on the Enduring Racial Divide," in *Urban Inequality: Evidence from Four Cities*, edited by Alice O'Connor, Chris Tilly, and Lawrence D. Bobo (New York: Russell Sage Foundation, 2001), 1–33.

57. This discussion of economic, demographic, and spatial transformation is based on Katz, *The Price of Citizenship: Redefining the American Welfare State*, chap. 2.

58. Kevin Fox Gotham, *Race, Real Estate, and Uneven Development: The Kansas City Experience, 1900–2000* (Albany: State University of New York Press, 2002) provides a vivid account of how realtors promoted racial segregation.

59. Edward L. Glaeser and Jesse M. Shapiro, "City Growth: Which Places Grew and Why," in *Redefining Urban and Suburban America: Evidence From Census 2000*, edited by Bruce Katz and Robert E. Lang (Washington, D.C.: Brookings Institution, 2003), 13–32.

60. Roberto Suro and Audrey Singer, "Changing Patterns of Latino Growth in Metropolitan America," in *Redefining Urban and Suburban America* (see note 59), 181–210.

61. For another discussion of the changing family and household composition of suburbs, see William H. Frey and Alan Berube, "City Families and Suburban Singles: An Emerging Household Story," in *Redefining Urban and Suburban America* (see note 59), 257–89.

62. Stephanie Dyer, "Markets in the Meadows: Department Stores and Shopping Centers in the Decentralization of Philadelphia" (Ph.D. dissertation, University of Pennsylvania, 2000).

63. The search was carried out by Leah Gordon using Proquest in the course of her excellent research for material for this section.

64. "The Urban Beat," *Maclean's*, July 19, 1999, p. 2.

65. Melanie Shortman, "Spencer Spreads Urban Sensibility Beyond the City," *PR Week*, August 25, 2003, p. 11.

66. Daniel Bell, *The Coming of Post-Industrial Society: A Venture in Social Forecasting* (New York: Basic Books, 1973).

67. H. V. Savitch, *Post-Industrial Cities: Politics and Planning in New York, Paris, and London* (Princeton, N.J.: Princeton University Press, 1988), 5.

68. John H. Mollenkopf, *The Contested City* (Princeton, N.J.: Princeton University Press, 1983), 12–13; William J. Stull and Janice Fanning Madden, *Post-Industrial Philadelphia: Structural Changes in the Metropolitan Economy* (Philadelphia: University of Pennsylvania Press, 1990), 126–27.

69. Daniel Bell, "The Social Framework of the Information Society," in *The Computer Age: A 20 Year View*, edited by M. L. Dertoozos and J. Moses (Cambridge, Mass.: MIT Press, 1979), 500–49.

70. John Hull Mollenkopf and Manuel Castells, eds., *Dual City: Restructuring New York* (New York: Russell Sage Foundation, 1991), 8, 16–17.

71. Robert Geddes, "Metropolis Unbound: The Sprawling American City and the Search for Alternatives," *American Prospect*, no. 35 (1997): 40–47.

72. David Rusk, *Cities Without Suburbs* (Baltimore, Md.: Johns Hopkins University Press, 1996). For some discussions of Rusk's book see, Bill Barnes, "Cities Without Suburbs (1993)," *Nation's Cities Weekly* 16, no. 34 (1993): 10; Harold Henderson, "Cities Without Suburbs (book review)," *Planning* 59,

no. 7 (1993): 36–37; Glenna Matthews, "Cities Without Suburbs (review),"
Journal of Urban History 25, no. 1 (1998): 94–102.

73. Myron Orfield, *American Metropolitics: The New Suburban Reality* (Washing-
    ton: Brookings Institution Press, 2002), 172.

74. Bruce Katz, "Reviving Cities: Think Metropolitan," (Washington, D.C.:
    Brookings Institution Center on Urban and Metropolitan Policy, 1988).

75. Mark Baldassare, *Trouble in Paradise: The Suburban Transformation in America*
    (New York: Columbia University Press, 1986).

76. Robert Fishman, *Bourgeois Utopias: The Rise and Fall of Suburbia* (New York:
    Basic Books, 1987). For a criticism of the concept that the traditional suburb
    had been replaced by a new urban form, see the stimulating, if not wholly
    convincing, William Sharpe and Leonard Wallock, "Bold New City or Built-
    Up 'Burb? Redefining Contemporary Suburbia," *American Quarterly* 46, no.
    1 (1994): 1–30.

77. Orfield, *American Metropolitics: The New Suburban Reality*.

78. Delores Hayden, *Building Suburbia: Green Fields and Urban Growth,
    1820–2000* (New York: Pantheon, 2003), 14.

79. Joel Garreau, *Edge City: Life on the New Frontier* (New York: Doubleday, 1991),
    414, 425. Useful discussions of Garreau include Kenneth T. Jackson, "The
    View From the Periphery," *New York Times*, September 22, 1991, p. BR11; Jane
    Holz Kay, "Edge City: Life on the New Frontier (book review)," *The Nation*,
    October 14, 1991, p. 454–55; Ross Miller, "Edge City: Life on the New Fron-
    tier (book review)," *The Journal of the Society of Architectural Historians* 52, no.
    3 (1993): 349–51. A variant of the edge city is the "Boomburb," defined "as
    places with more than 100,000 residents that are *not* the largest cities in their
    respective metropolitan areas and that have maintained double-digit rates of
    population growth in recent decades." Robert E. Lang and Patrick A. Sim-
    mons, "'Boomburbs': The Emergence of Large, Fast-Growing Suburban Cities,"
    in *Redefining Urban and Suburban America* (see note 59), 101–15.

80. Sassen, *Cities in a World Economy*, 1, 65, 107–8.

81. Castells, *The Rise of the Network Society*, 16–17.

82. Ibid., 430–31.

83. O'Mara, *Cities of Knowledge* (Princeton, N.J.: Princeton University Press,
    2004).

84. Castells, *The Rise of the Network Society*, 434.

85. Kathleen Burge, "Gays Have Right To Marry, SJC Says in Historic Ruling,"
    Boston.com, November 19, 2003. Leah Gordon provided invaluable research
    assistance for this section.

86. Lee Rainwater and William Yancey, *The Moynihan Report and the Politics of
    Controversy* (Cambridge, Mass.: MIT Press, 1967).

87. For a chronology of the E.R.A., see National Organization for Women,
    "Chronology of the Equal Rights Amendment, 1923–1996" (2004). For a his-
    tory of the E.R.A. written by an opponent, see The Phyllis Schlafly Report,
    "A Short History of the E.R.A." (September 1986).

88. John Leo, "Sneer Not At 'Ozzie and Harriet,'" *U.S. News and World Report*
    [online edition], September 14, 1992.

89. George Peter Murdock, "Anthropology and Human Relations," *Sociometry*
    4, no. 2 (1941): 140–49; John Dollard, "Review of J. Steward Lincoln, *The*

Dream in Primitive Cultures," *American Anthropologist* New Series, 39, no. 3 (1937): 547–48; George Peter Murdock, *Social Structure* (New York: MacMillan, 1949); Kingsley Davis, "Review of *Social Structure*," *American Sociological Review* 15, no. 1 (1950): 138–40.

90. "Extended families; Courts should let states put child's needs first," *San Diego Union-Tribune,* January 12, 2000, p. B-8, B-10.

91. Rainwater and Yancey, *The Moynihan Report and the Politics of Controversy;* Andrew Hacker, "Family and Nation," *Fortune* 113 (1986): 131(2); Andrew Hacker, "The Myths of Racial Division: Blacks, Whites—And Statistics," *The New Republic* 206, no. 12 (1992): 21–4.

92. Leonore J. Weitzman, *The Divorce Revolution: The Unexpected Social and Economic Consequences for Women and Children in America* (New York: Free Press, 1985); Frank E. Furstenberg, Jr., "Children and Family Change: Discussion Between Social Scientists and the Media," *Contemporary Sociology* 28, no. 1 (1999): 10–17; Barbara Dafoe Whitehead, "Dan Quayle Was Right," *The Atlantic* 271, no. 4 (1993): 47–67; Barbara Dafoe Whitehead, *The Divorce Culture* (New York: Alfred A. Knopf, 1997).

93. Others were Maggie Gallagher, *The Abolition of Marriage;* David Popenoe, *Life Without Father;* and Jean Bethke Elshtain and David Blankenhorn, eds., *Promises to Keep.*

94. Arlene Skolnick, "Family Values: The Sequel," *The American Prospect*, May-June 1997, 86–94. See Institute for American Values, http://www.american-values.org/index.html.

95. Steven Mintz and Susan Kellogg, *Domestic Revolutions: A Social History of American Family Life* (New York: Free Press, 1988).

96. Whitehead, *The Divorce Culture,* 132.

97. A search of Lexis-Nexis major English language papers by Leah Gordon found the term used more frequently in the 1990s: there were only six hits for post-nuclear family between 1985 and 1990 and 76 from 1990 to 2004.

98. David Popenoe, *Disturbing the Nest: Family Change and Decline in Modern Societies* (New York: Aldine de Gruyter, 1988); David Popenoe, *Life Without Father: Compelling New Evidence that Fatherhood and Marriage are Indispensable for the Good of Children and Society* (New York: Free Press, 1996); "Sunnyvale: The Rise and Fall of a Silicon Valley Family (Book Review)," *Publisher's Weekly* 247, no. 23 (2000): 80; Mary Kay Blakely, "Thoughts for Father's Gift," *New York Times,* June 8, 1985, C10; Michael Coffey, "Michael Cunningham: New Family Outing (Interview)," *Publisher's Weekly*, November 2, 1998, 53; Janet L. Dolgin, "The Fate of Childhood: Legal Models of Children and the Parent-Child Relationship," *Albany Law Review* 61, no. 2 (1997): 345–431; Howard Hampton, "Ultraviolent Movies: From Sam Peckinpah to Quentin Tarantino (Book Review)," *Artforum International* 35, no. 3 (1996): S12–13; Ruth Nicholas, "Speaking Out On Women's Real Needs," *Marketing*, April 14, 1994, 18–19; Peggy Knee Sheahan, "Estate Planning for the Post-Nuclear Family," *New Jersey Law Journal* 137, no. 4 (1994): S6; Skolnick, "Family Values: The Sequel"; Corinna Vallianatos, "The Divorce Culture (Book Review)," *Washington Monthly* 29, no. 4 (1997): 52–53.

99. Paul C. Glick, "Types of Families: An Analysis of Census Data," *American Sociological Review* 6, no. 6 (1941): 830–38.

100. U.S. Census Bureau, "Current Population Survey definitions. Head versus Householder" (Washington: U.S. Government Printing Office, 2004).

101. "The idea that couples could redefine marriage on their own terms re-sounded appealingly through the 1970s," writes historian Nancy Cott. "To reinvent marriage, why not make it a malleable arrangement—extend its founding principle of consent between the couple to all terms of the rela-tionship, allowing the contractual side of the hybrid institution to bloom." Nancy Cott, *Public Vows: A History of Marriage and the Nation* (Cambridge, Mass.: Harvard University Press, 2000).

102. Quoted in ibid.

103. Weitzman, *The Divorce Revolution: The Unexpected Social and Economic Con-sequences for Women and Children in America*. For a devastating criticism of Weitzman's major statistical finding, and, hence, of the uses to which her book was put, see Richard Peterson, "An Evaluation of the Economic Con-sequences of Divorce," *American Sociological Review* 61, no. 3 (1996): 523–36; Richard Peterson, "Statistical Errors, Faulty Conclusions, Misguided Pol-icy: Reply to Weitzman," *American Sociological Review* 61, no. 3 (1996): 539–40. No-fault divorce overturned traditional law by eliminating the need for grounds (adultery or physical cruelty) for family dissolution and abandoning gender-based assumptions in the calculation of alimony and the division of property.

104. Dolgin, "The Fate of Childhood;" Mintz and Kellogg, *Domestic Revolutions*.

105. "Extended families; Courts should let states put child's needs first," *San Diego Union-Tribune* (Texas), January 12, 2000.

106. Troxel et vir. v. Granville (U.S. Supreme Court, 2000).

107. Sara Hoffman Jurand, "Courts Expand Troxel Precedent Beyond Grand-parent Cases," *Trial* 39, no. 2 (2003): 83(2); Rebecca Porter, "Supreme Court Delivers Narrow Ruling On Grandparents' Visitation Rights," *Trial* 36, no. 8 (2000): 84.

108. Jonathan Rauch, *Gay Marriage* (New York: Times Books: Henry Holt, 2004).

109. Charles-Edward Anderson, "The New Nuclear Family: N.Y. Court Says Gays Are Family Under Rent-Control Laws," *ABA Journal* 75 (1989): 20; "Christine A. Tanner et al. v. Oregon Health Sciences University and Pub-lic Employees' Benefit Board," (Court of Appeals of the State of Oregon, 1998); "Steve Tyma et al. v. Montgomery County of Maryland," (Court of Appeals of Maryland, 2001); Lambda Legal Defense and Education Fund, "Basic Facts About Domestic Partner Benefits," (1997); Lambda Legal De-fense and Education Fund, "Details About Domestic Partner Benefits," (1997); Law Office of David C. Codell, Lambda Legal Defense and Educa-tion Fund, National Center for Lesbian Rights, "Brief of Amici Curiae In Opposition To Motion For Preliminary Injunction" ("Thomasson v. Davis," case no. BC 302928, Superior Court of the State of California for the County of Los Angeles, 2003).

110. For an exceptionally lucid and thoughtful analysis of gay marriage as an is-sue, see Rauch, *Gay Marriage*. For an excellent analysis of why gay mar-riage emerged as an issue, see George Chancey, *Why Marriage? The History Shaping Today's Debate Over Gay Equality* (New York: Basic Books, 2004).

111. Chris Bull and John Gallagher, *Perfect Enemies: The Battle between the Reli-*

gious Right and the Gay Movement, updated ed. (Lanham, New York, Oxford: Madison Books, 2001).

112. Ibid., 198–99.
113. Quoted in ibid., 212.
114. Lectlaw.com, "Defense of Marriage Act. 1996. H.R. 3396: Summary/Analysis" (1996). The constitutionality of the act was not certain. On the surface, at least, it appeared to violate Article V of the Constitution, requiring states to give full faith and credit to each others' actions.
115. Vermont CivilUnion.com, "Civil Union Resource Guide" (2000).
116. "Hillary Goodridge and Others v. Department of Public Health and Another" (Supreme Judicial Court of Massachusetts, 2003). The decision was written by Justice C. J. Marshall.
117. See, for example, Family Research Council, "Human Sexuality" (2004).
118. Alan Cooperman, "Gay Marriage as 'the New Abortion,'" *Washington Post*, July 6, 2004, p. A03.
119. Executive Office of the President, Office of the Press Secretary, "President Calls For Constitutional Amendment Protecting Marriage: Remarks by the President" (Washington: U.S. Government Printing Office, 2004). In August 2004, the California Supreme Court ruled that the many same-sex marriages in San Francisco violated state law and had no standing. The Court did not rule on the validity of the state marriage law itself, which was under appeal. Dean Murphy, "California Supreme Court Rules Gay Unions Have No Standing," *New York Times*, August 13, 2004, online edition.
120. Susan Milligan, "Senate Rejects Move to Ban Gay Marriage: Amendment Vote Comes Up Short," *Boston.com*, July 15, 2004. Before the Massachusetts amendment could become law, the legislature would need to vote on it once more in the 2005–2006 session and, then, to put it on a ballot in a general election. Paul Axel-Lute, "Same-Sex Marriage" (Newark: Rutgers, the State University of New Jersey School of Law, 2002); Rick Klein, "Vote Ties Civil Unions to Gay-Marriage Ban," *Boston.com*, March 30, 2004; Monica Davey, "Message of Voters in Missouri Against Gay Marriage Leaves Backers Discouraged," *New York Times*, August 5, 2004; Monica Davey, "Missourians Back Ban on Same-Sex Marriage," *New York Times*, August 4, 2004; Adam Liptak, "Caution in Court for Gay Rights Groups," *New York Times*, November 12, 2004.
121. Cynthia B. Cohen, "Children of Choice: Freedom and the New Reproductive Technologies," *Women and Health* 26, no. 2 (1997): 97–100; Patricia Novotny, "Review of *Defining the Family: Law, Technology and Reproduction in an Uneasy Age*," *Signs* 26, no. 2 (2001): 565; Janet L. Dolgin, "Embryonic Discourse: Abortion, Stem Cells And Cloning," *Issues in Law and Medicine* 19, no. 3 (2004): 203–61.
122. Packaged Facts, "The Gay and Lesbian Market: New Trends, New Opportunities" (New York: Packaged Facts, 2002); Salary.com, "Right on Target—Reaching Minorities Through Ads" (New York: Vault, 2000).
123. Linda S. Kadaba, "Singles on the move? Yes, to the Suburbs," *Philadelphia Inquirer*, April 13, 2004, p. 1.
124. U.S. Census Bureau, "Businesses Classified as Providing Child Care Ser-

vice, by Income Tax Status for State. 1987" (Washington: U.S. Government Printing Office, 2001).

125. This is a major theme of Cott, *Public Vows: A History of Marriage and the Nation*.

126. Jack E. White, "I'm Just Who I Am," *Time*, May 5, 1997, p. 32.

127. Melissa Nobles, *Shades of Citizenship: Race and the Census in Modern Politics* (Stanford, Calif.: Stanford University Press, 2000), xi.

128. The debate over the census question on race, the historian David A. Hollinger observes, was "only the most visible aspect of an unprecedented discursive episode in the history of American engagement" with race. "A society that often has policed the black-white color line with terror now registers a more relaxed fascination with the crossing of that line, even widespread acceptance of the crossings." David A. Hollinger, "Amalgamation and Hypodescent: The Question of Ethnoracial Mixture in the History of the United States," *American Historical Review* 108, no. 5 (2003): 1363–90; Reynolds Farley, "Racial Identities in 2000: The Response to the Multiple-Race Response Option," in *The New Race Question: How The Census Counts Multiracial Individuals*, edited by Joel Perlmann and Mary C. Waters (New York: Russell Sage Foundation, 2002), 33–61. Racial issues linked to the census always have had major political consequences. Before the Civil War, one racially based class was especially important: the number of slaves; by the infamous compromise in the Constitution, a slave counted as three-fifths of a white person for purposes of apportioning congressional representation.

129. Kenneth Prewitt, "Race in The 2000 Census: A Turning Point," in *The New Race Question* (see note 128), 354–61. The political scientist Jennifer L. Hochschild observed, "Led, ironically, by the Census Bureau, which used to be seen as a stodgy data collector, the United States is embarking on a dramatic experiment that will change the way our government counts races and recognizes multiracials. This experiment will have repercussions on a wide range of attitudes and activities, from individual self-identification through corporate advertising budgets to allocations of billions of tax-payers' dollars and millions of people into voting districts." Jennifer Hochschild, "Multiple Racial Identifiers in the 2000 Census, and Then What?" in *The New Race Question* (see note 128), 340–53.

130. Prewitt, "Race in the 2000 Census," 355.

131. Sonya Tafoya, Hans Johnson, and Laura Hill, *Who Chooses to Choose Two?* edited by Reynolds Farley and John Haaga (New York and Washington: Russell Sage Foundation and Population Reference Bureau, 2004), 3–4.

132. The instruction to enumerators read, "The word 'black' should be used to distinguish between blacks, mulattoes, quadroons, and octoroons. The word 'black' should be used to describe those persons who have three-fourths or more black blood; 'mulatto,' those persons who have from three-eighths to five-eighths black blood; 'quadroon,' those persons who have one-fourth black blood; and 'octoroons,' those persons who have one-eighth or any trace of black blood."

133. Matthew Pratt Guterl, *The Color of Race in America* (Cambridge, Mass.: Harvard University Press, 2001), 16, 70, 155. The 1924 federal legislation re-

stricting immigration and basing it on quotas also played a key role in the racialization of groups and the hardening of the line between black and white. On this see Mae M. Ngai, "The Architecture of Race in American Immigration Law," *Journal of American History* 86, no. 1 (1999): 67–92.

134. James F. Davis, *Who Is Black?* (University Park: Pennsylvania State University Press, 1991); Nobles, *Shades of Citizenship*.

135. Nobles, *Shades of Citizenship*, 74–75.

136. These were Filipino, Korean, Hawaiian, and Other, and, for the first time, included Hispanic ethnicity, divided into six subcategories, as a separate question.

137. David A. Hollinger, *Postethnic America* (New York: Basic Books, 1995), 23–24, 36–39, 48; U.S. Office of Management and Budget, "Directive No. 15 Race and Ethnic Standards for Federal Statistics and Administrative Reporting" (Washington: U.S. Government Printing Office, 1977).

138. Population Reference Bureau, "Race and Ethnicity in the Census: 1860 to 2000," (Washington, D.C.: Population Reference Bureau, 2000).

139. The tendency to think of race in terms of black and white has obscured the geographic variation in the racialization of Asians and Mexicans, notable on the Pacific Coast and in the Southwest. Henry Yu, "Tiger Woods Is Not the End of History: or, Why Sex across the Color Line Won't Save Us All," *American Historical Review* 108, no. 5 (2003): 1406–14.

140. Guterl, *The Color of Race in America*, 5.

141. Barry Edmonston, Sharon M. Lee, and Jeffrey S. Passel, "Recent Trends in Intermarriage and Immigration and Their Effects on the Future Racial Composition of the U.S. Population," in *The New Race Question* (see note 128), 227–55.

142. Hollinger, "Amalgamation and Hypodescent," 1386.

143. For a stunning case study of this process, see Russell A. Kazal, *Becoming Old Stock: The Paradox of German-American Identity* (Princeton, N.J.: Princeton University Press, 2004); Joel Perlmann, "Census Bureau Long-Term Racial Projections: Interpreting Their Results And Seeking Their Rationale," in *The New Race Question* (see note 128), 215–26; Stanley Lieberson and Mary Waters, *From Many Strands: Ethnic and Racial Groups in Contemporary America* (New York: Russell Sage Foundation, 1988), 162–246, 251.

144. Edmonston, Lee, and Passel, "Recent Trends in Intermarriage," table 9.6, 241.

145. Among men, intermarriage increased from 1.3 to 3.6 to 13.3 percent and among women from 1.2 to 1.3 to 5.6 percent.

146. Rates for non-Hispanic whites also increased, although they still were quite low, between 5 and 6 percent. Other major groups—Hispanics and Asians—showed little change, with, in fact, some decline between the postwar and more recent cohorts, undoubtedly a result of massive immigration. It was among their children and grandchildren that intermarriage spiked.

147. In 2000, in the three southern census divisions, intermarriage rates for African American men ranged between 4 and 7 percent compared to 16 percent in New England, 11 percent in the middle Atlantic division, and 24

percent in the Pacific. Rates for black women, though lower, followed the same distribution.

148. These included the Association of Multiethnic Americans (AMEA), Project RACE (Reclassify All Children Equally), APFU (A Place for Us), and multiracial organizations on many college and university campuses. Kimberly McClain DaCosta, "New Faces, Old Faces: Counting the Multiracial Population Past and Present," in *Multiracial Identity: From Personal Problem to Public Issue*, edited by Herman L. DeBose and Loretta I. Winters (Thousand Oaks, Calif.: Sage Publications, 2003), 68–84.

149. Kim M. Williams, "From Civil Rights to the Multiracial Movement," in *New Faces in a Changing America* (see note 148), 85–98.

150. Farley, "Racial Identities in 2000," 34–35. The multiracial movement has had its own complicated internal politics. See Nathan Douglas, "The Multiracial Movement: An Uncomfortable Political Fit" (October/November 2003).

151. "The Mission," *The Multiracial Advocate*, July 10, 2004, p. 69.

152. For a harsh criticism of the multiracial movement from an African American perspective, see Mary Thierry Texeira, "The New Multiracialism: An Affirmation of or an End to Race as We Know It?" in *New Faces in a Changing America* (see note 148), 21–37.

153. Williams, "From Civil Rights to the Multiracial Movement," 88–93.

154. Christine B. Hickman, "The Devil and the One Drop Rule: Racial Categories, African Americans, and the U.S. Census," *Michigan Law Review* 95 (1996–1997): 1161–265.

155. Farley, "Racial Identities in 2000," 40.

156. U.S. Office of Management and Budget, "Recommendations from the Interagency Committee for the Review of the Racial and Ethnic Standards to the Office of Management and Budget Concerning Changes to the Standards for the Classification of Federal Data on Race and Ethnicity," *Federal Register*, Part II (1997), 36873–946.

157. Ibid., 136873–946.

158. Hollinger, "Amalgamation and Hypodescent," 1378.

159. Eliot Marshall, "DNA Studies Challenge the Meaning of Race," *Science* 282, no. 5389 (1998): 654–55.

160. Joseph L. Graves, Jr., *The Emperor's New Clothes: Biological Theories of Race at the Millennium* (New Brunswick, N.J.: Rutgers University Press, 2001), 5.

161. Marshall, "DNA Studies Challenge the Meaning of Race."

162. Farley, "Racial Identities in 2000," 36–37.

163. Nicholas A. Jones and Amy Symens Smith, "The Two or More Race Population: 2000" (Washington: U.S. Census Bureau, 2001); Tafoya, Johnson, and Hill, *Who Chooses to Choose Two?* 16.

164. Hollinger, *Postethnic America*.

165. Ibid.

166. The discussion of race in chapter 2 of this book does exactly the same thing. It traces the transformation in the nature of African American inequality but assumes a static definition of race.

167. See, for instance, Barbara J. Fields, "Of Rogues and Geldings," *American Historical Review* 108, no. 5 (2003): 1397–405.

Epilogue

1. *Oxford English Dictionary Online*, American, *a.* and *n.* (Oxford University Press, 1989). A wise meditation on this theme is Michael Walzer, *What It Means To Be An American: Essays on the American Experience* (New York: Marsilio Publishers, 1992). For assistance with the research on this section, we are indebted to Daniel Amsterdam.

2. U.S. Department of State, "Frequently Asked Historical Questions," http://www.state.gov/r/pa/ho/faq/.

3. Steven Hahn, *A Nation Under Our Feet: Black Political Struggles in the Rural South from Slavery to the Great Migration* (Cambridge, Mass.: Harvard University Press, 2003), 110.

4. Cecilia Elizabeth O'Leary, *To Die For: The Paradox of American Patriotism* (Princeton, N.J.: Princeton University Press, 1999).

5. Lizabeth Cohen, *A Consumers' Republic: The Politics of Mass Consumption in Postwar America* (New York: Alfred A. Knopf, 2003).

6. U.S. Commission on Immigration Reform, "Becoming an American: Immigration and Immigration Policy" (1997).

7. Patrick J. Buchanan, *The Death of the West* (New York: Thomas Dunne Books, St. Martin's Press, 2002).

8. Samuel P. Huntington, *Who Are We? The Challenges to America's National Identity* (New York: Simon & Schuster, 2004).

9. John Bodnar, *The Transplanted: A History of Immigrants in Urban America* (Bloomington: University of Indiana Press, 1985); Oscar Handlin, *The Uprooted: The Epic Story of the Great Migrations that Made the American People* (Boston, Mass.: Little, Brown, 1951).

10. Multiculturalism, the noted historian Arthur M. Schlesinger observed, had in recent years "emerged not alone as a word but as an ideology and mystique." Schlesinger sympathized with its "mild form," which called "attention to neglected groups, themes, and viewpoints" and redressed "a shameful imbalance in the treatment of minorities both in the actualities of life and in the judgments of history." In its inclusive and generous form, multiculturalism stayed "within a conception of a shared culture." Schlesinger strongly supported immigration but deplored identity politics. Multiculturalism, he observed, also appeared in "a militant form, in which it opposes the idea of a common culture, rejects the goals of assimilation and integration, and celebrates the immutability of diverse and separate ethnic and racial communities." Arthur M. Schlesinger, Jr., *The Disuniting of America: Reflections on a Multicutural Society*, rev. ed. (New York: W. W. Norton, 1998). For a useful collection of viewpoints on multiculturalism in the early twenty-first century, see Tamar Jacoby, ed., *Reinventing the Melting Pot: The New Immigrants and What It Means To Be An American* (New York: Basic Books, 2004). There is a very large literature on multiculturalism. A collection of essays with a thoughtful and scholarly approach to the issues is Neil J. Smelser and Jeffrey C. Alexander, eds., *Diversity and Its Discontents* (Princeteon, N.J.: Princeton University Press, 1999).

11. The best statement of this more balanced position is Russell A. Kazal's "Revisiting Assimilation: The Rise, Fall, and Reappraisal of a Concept in Amer-

ican Ethnic History," *American Historical Review* 100 (1995): 437-471. See also the excellent discussion of the issue throughout Richard Alba and Victor Nee, *Remaking the American Mainstream: Assimilation and Contemporary Immigration* (Cambridge, Mass.: Harvard University Press, 2003).

12. Nathan Glazer, "Assimilation Today: Is One Identity Enough?" in *Reinventing the Melting Pot: The New Immigrants and What It Means To Be An American*, ed. Tamar Jacoby (New York: Basic Books, 2004), 61–73.

13. "The terrorists who attacked the World Trade Center may have been trying to crush American capitalism and its masters of the universe on Wall Street," the *New York Times* noted. "But the economic impact of the attack is felling a very different group of people: cooks, cabdrivers, sales clerks and seamstresses." Leslie Eaton and Edward Wyatt, "Attacks Hit Low-Pay Jobs The Hardest," *New York Times*, November 6, 2001, B1; Daniel Mont, Virginia Reno, and Catherine Hill, "Social Insurance for Survivors: Family Benefits from Social Security and Workers' Compensation" (Washington, D.C.: National Academy of Social Insurance, 2002).

14. U.S. Congress, Senate, "USA Patriot Act," 107th Congress (2001); Electronic Privacy Information Center, *The USA Patriot Act*, (Washington, D.C., 2004), http://www.epic.org/privacy/terrorism/usapatriot/.

15. American Civil Liberties Union, *How the Anti-Terrorism Bill Permits Indefinite Detention of Immigrants Who Are Not Terrorists* (2001); American Civil Liberties Union, "Through Gag Orders and Secret Evidence, Government Is Suppressing Information About Controversial Patriot Act Powers, ACLU Charges" (August 19, 2004); available at: http://www.aclu.org/SafeandFree/SafeandFree.cfm?ID=16723&c=262.

References

Abbott, Carl. 1981. *The New Urban America: Growth and Politics in Sunbelt Cities.* Chapel Hill: University of North Carolina Press.

Abramovitz, Moses, and Paul A. David. 2000. *American Macroeconomic Growth in the Era of Knowledge-Based Progress: The Long-Run Perspective."* In *The Cambridge Economic History of the United States,* edited by S. L. Engerman and R. E. Gallman. Cambridge and New York: Cambridge University Press.

Adema, Willem, and Marcel Einerhand. 1998. "The Growing Role of Private Social Benefits." Labor Market and Social Policy Occasional Papers, Number 32. Paris: OECD Directorate for Education, Employment, Labour, and Social Affairs.

Alba, Richard D. 1985. *Italian Americans: Into the Twilight of Ethnicity.* Englewood Cliffs, N.J.: Prentice-Hall.

Alba, Richard D., and Victor Nee. 1999. "Rethinking Assimilation Theory for a New Era of Immigration." In *The Handbook of International Migration: The American Experience,* edited by C. Hirschman, P. Kasinitz, and J. DeWind. New York: Russell Sage Foundation.

———. 2003. *Remaking the American Mainstream: Assimilation and Contemporary Immigration.* Cambridge, Mass.: Harvard University Press.

Alcaly, Roger. 2003. *The New Economy.* New York: Farrar, Straus, & Giroux.

Altmeyer, Arthur J. 1968. *The Formative Years of Social Security.* Madison: University of Wisconsin Press.

Alvarez, Rene. 2002. "Carpenters and a 'Century of Change': An Occupation Research Project." Unpublished paper. University of Pennsylvania.

Ambler, Carol A. 1998. "NAICS and U.S. Statistics." Paper read at Annual Meeting of the American Statistical Association. Dallas, Texas (August 9–13).

Amenta, Edward. 1998. *Bold Relief: Institutional Politics and the Origins of Modern American Social Policy.* Princeton, N.J.: Princeton University Press.

American Association of Housing and Services for the Aging. 2004. "Types of Facilities and Services." Available at: http://www.aasha.org.

American Civil Liberties Union. 2001. *How the Terrorism Bill Permits Indefinite Detention of Immigrants Who Are Not Terrorists.* New York: ACLU. Available at: http://www.aclu.org/NationalSecurity/NationalSecurity.cfm?ID=9153&c=111 (accessed October 26, 2005).

———. "Through Gag Orders and Secret Evidence, Government is Suppressing Information about Controversial Patriot Act Powers, ACLU Charges." Press

Release (August 19, 2001). Available at: http://www.aclu.org/SafeandFree/
SafeandFree.cfm?ID=16273&c=262 (accessed October 26, 2005).

Amott, Teresa, and Julie A. Matthaei. 1991. *Race, Gender and Work: A Multicultural
Economic History of Women in the United States.* Boston, Mass.: South End Press.

Anderson, Charles-Edward. 1989. "The New Nuclear Family: N.Y. Court Says
Gays Are Family Under Rent-Control Laws." *ABA Journal* 75: 20.

Anderson, Claud. 1994. *Black Labor, White Wealth: The Search for Power and Economic Justice.* Edgewood, Md.: Duncan and Duncan.

Anderson, James D. 1988. *The Education of Blacks in the South, 1860–1935.* Chapel
Hill: University of North Carolina Press.

Anderson, Wilbert L. 1906. *The Country Town: A Study of Rural Evolution.* New
York: Baker and Taylor.

Angle, John. 1986. "The Surplus Theory of Social Stratification and the Size Distribution of Personal Wealth." *Social Forces* 65(2): 293–326.

anonymous. 2003. "Is Housing Discrimination Diminishing? New Research Ex-
amines Unequal Treatment Today." *Urban Research Monitor* 8(7): 1–2.

Anthony, Susan B. 1902. "Woman's Half Century of Evolution." *The North American Review* 175(December): 800–10.

Apfel, Kenneth S. 2000. "Commissioner of Social Security, Praises Senate Action
and Announces Implementation Plan for the Repeal of the Retirement Earnings Test." Social Security News Release Washington, D.C. (March 24).

Armor, David J. 1992. "Why is Black Educational Achievement Rising?" *Public
Interest* 108(summer): 65–80.

Arnas, Geraldo C. 2003. "Record Number of Women Childless." *Philadelphia Inquirer.*

Aronson, Karen W. 2003. "Colleges Struggle To Help Black Men Stay Enrolled."
New York Times, December 30, 2003, p. A1.

Ashbridge, Samuel H. 1901. "Second Annual Message of Samuel H. Ashbridge,
Mayor of the City of Philadelphia, with Annual Reports for the Year Ending
December 31, 1900." Philadelphia: Dunlap Printing Co.

Ashraf, Javed. 1996. "Is Gender Pay Discrimination on the Wane? Evidence from
Panel Data, 1968–1989." *Industrial and Labor Relations Review* 49(3): 537–46.

Association of MultiEthnic Americans. 2002. "Fact Sheet." Available at:
http://www.ameasite.org/factsheet.pdf (accessed October 26, 2005).

———. "About AMEA 1997–2003." Available at: http://www.ameasite.org/
about.asp (accessed October 26, 2005).

Atack, Jeremy, F. Bateman, and William N. Parker. 2000. "Northern Agriculture
and the Westward Movement." In *Cambridge Economic History of the United
States,* edited by S. L. Engerman and R. E. Gallman. New York: Cambridge
University Press.

Atkinson, A. T., ed. 1980. *Wealth, Income, and Inequality,* 2nd ed. New York: Oxford
University Press.

Axel-Lute, Paul. 2002. *Same-Sex Marriage, A Selective Bibliography.* Newark: Rutgers, the State University of New Jersey School of Law. Available at:
http://www.rci.rutgers.edu/~axellute/ssm.htm (accessed October 24, 2005).

Ayers, Leonard P. 1913. *Laggards in Our Schools: A Study of Retardation and Elimination in City School Systems.* New York: Charities Publication Committee.

Badgett, Lee. 1994. "Rising Black Unemployment: Changes in Job Stability or In Employability." *Review of Black Political Economy* 22(3): 55–75.

———. 1999. "The Impact of Affirmative Action on Public-Sector Employment in California, 1970–1990." In *Impacts of Affirmative Action: Policies and Consequences in California,* edited by P. Ong. Walnut Creek, Calif.: Sage Publications.

Badgett, Lee, and Rhonda Williams. 1994. "The Changing Contours of Discrimination: Race, Gender, and Structural Economic Change." In *Understanding American Economic Decline,* edited by Michael A. Bernstein and David E. Adler. New York: Cambridge University Press.

Bailey, Thomas. 1990. "Black Employment Opportunities." In *Setting Municipal Priorities,* edited by C. Brecher and R. H. Horton. New York: New York University Press.

Baker, Therese L. and William Velez. 1996. "Access to and Opportunity in Postsecondary Education in the United States." *Sociology of Education* 69(2): 82–101.

Baldassare, Mark. 1986. *"Trouble in Paradise: The Suburban Transformation in America.* New York: Columbia University Press.

Baldwin, Marjorie L. and William G. Johnson. 1996. "The Employment Effects of Wage Discrimination Against Black Men." *Industrial and Labor Relations Review* 49(2): 302–16.

Baldwin, Richard E., and Philippe Martin. 1999. *"Two Waves of Globalization: Superficial Similarities, Fundamental Differences.* NBER Working Paper 6904. Cambridge, Mass.: National Bureau of Economic Research.

Barnes, Bill. 1993. "Cities Without Suburbs (1993)." *Nation's Cities Weekly* 16(34): 10.

Baron, James N. and Andrew E. Newman. 1990. "For What It's Worth: Organizations, Occupations, and the Value of Work Done by Women and Nonwhites." *American Sociological Review* 55(2): 155–75.

Barron, Hal S. 1984. *Those Who Stayed Behind: Rural Society in Nineteenth-Century New England.* Cambridge: Cambridge University Press.

———. 1997. *Mixed Harvest: The Second Great Transformation in the Rural North, 1870–1930.* Chapel Hill: University of North Carolina Press.

Baskerville, Peter, and Eric W. Sager. 1998. *Unwilling Idlers: The Urban Unemployed and Their Families in Late Victorian Canada.* Toronto: University of Toronto Press.

Bauman, John F. 1987. *Public Housing, Race, and Renewal: Urban Planning in Philadelphia, 1920–1974.* Philadelphia, Pa.: Temple University Press.

Bauman, Kurt J. 1998. "Schools, Markets, and Family in the History of African-American Education." *American Journal of Education* 106(4): 500–31.

Baunach, Dawn M. 2002. "Trends in Occupational Sex Segregation and Inequality, 1950 to 1990." *Social Science Research* 31(1): 77–98.

Bayard, Kimberly, Judith Hallerstein, David Neumark, and Kenneth Troske. 1999. "Why Are Racial and Ethnic Wage Gaps Larger for Men Than for Women? Exploring the Role of Segregation Using the New Worker-Establishment Characteristics Database." In *The Creation and Analysis of Employer-Employee Matched Data,* edited by J. C. Haltiwanger, Julia I. Lane, James R. Spletzer, Jules J. M. Theeuwes, and Kenneth R. Troske. Amsterdam: Elsevier.

276   References

Bayer, Angela, and Joshua Bonilla. 2001. *Executive Summary: Our Changing Nation.* Washington, D.C.: Population Resource Center.

Bean, Franklin D., and Stephanie Bell-Rose. 1999. *Immigration and Opportunity: Race, Ethnicity, and Employment in the United States.* New York: Russell Sage Foundation.

Bean, Franklin D., and Gillian Stevens. 2003. *America's Newcomers and the Dynamics of Diversity.* New York: Russell Sage Foundation.

Bean, Franklin D., Jennifer Van Hook, and Mark A. Fossett. 1999. "Immigration, Spatial and Economic Change, and African American Employment." In *Immigration and Opportunity: Race, Ethnicity, and Employment in the United States,* edited by Frank D. Bean and Stephanie Bell-Rose. New York: Russell Sage Foundation.

Beard, Charles A. 1912/1970. *American City Government.* New York: Arno Press.

Bebchuck, Lucian Ayre, Jesse M. Fried, and David I. Walker. 2001. *Executive Compensation in America: Optimal Contracting or Extraction of Rents.* Washington, D.C.: National Bureau of Economic Research.

Beggs, John J., Wayne J. Villemez, and Ruth Arnold. 1997. "Black Population Concentration and Black-White Inequality: Expanding the Consideration of Place and Space Effects." *Social Forces* 76(1): 65–91.

Behr, Joshua G. 2000. "Black and Female Municipal Employment: A Substantive Benefit of Minority Political Incorporation?" *Journal of Urban Affairs* 22(3): 243–64.

Beijbom, Ulf. 1980. "Swedes." In *Harvard Encyclopedia of American Ethnic Groups,* edited by Stephen Thernstrom. Cambridge, Mass.: Harvard University Press.

Bell, Daniel. 1973. *The Coming of Post-Industrial Society: A Venture in Social Forecasting.* New York: Basic Books.

———. 1979. "The Social Framework of the Information Society." In *The Computer Age: A 20 Year View,* edited by M. L. Dertoozos and J. Moses. Cambridge, Mass.: MIT Press.

Bell, Earl H. 1942. *Culture of a Contemporary Rural Community: Sublette, Kansas.* Washington: U.S. Department of Agriculture, Bureau of Agricultural Economics.

Belz, Herman. 1991. *Equality Tranformed: A Quarter-Century of Affirmative Action.* New Brunswick, N.J.: Transaction Publishers.

Bennett, Neil G., Jiali Li, Younghwan Song, and Keming Yang. 1999. " Young Children in Poverty: A Statistical Update." A Fact Sheet, June 1999 edition. New York: National Center for Children in Poverty. Available at: http://www.nccp.org/pub_ycp99.html (accessed October 24, 2005).

Berkowitz, Edward. 1991. *America's Welfare State: From Roosevelt to Reagan.* Baltimore, Md.: Johns Hopkins University Press.

Berkowitz, Edward, and Kim Mcquaid. 1988. *Creating the Welfare State: The Political Economy of Twentieth-Century Reform.* New York: Praeger.

Berlin, Gordon L. 2002. *What Works in Welfare Reform: Evidence and Lessons to Guide TANF Reauthorization.* New York: Manpower Demonstration Research Corporation.

Bernhardt, Annette, Martina Morris, and Mark S. Handcock. 1995. "Women's Gains or Men's Losses? A Closer Look at the Shrinking Gender Gap in Earnings." *American Journal of Sociology* 101(2): 302–28.

Bernhardt, Annette, Martina Morris, Mark S. Handcock, and Marc A. Scott. 2001. *"Divergent Paths: Economic Mobility in the New American Labor Market.* New York: Russell Sage Foundation.

Bianchi, Suzanne M. 1995. "Changing Economic Roles of Women and Men." In *State of the Union: America in the 1990s,* vol. 1: *Economic Trends,* edited by Reynolds Farley. New York: Russell Sage Foundation.

———. 1996. *Balancing Act: Motherhood, Marriage, and Employment Among American Women.* New York: Russell Sage Foundation.

———. 1999. "Feminization and Juvenilization of Poverty: Trends, Relative Risks, Causes, and Consequences." *Annual Review of Sociology* 25: 307–33.

Bird, Chloe E. 1990. "High Finance, Small Change: Women's Increased Representation in Bank Management." In *Job Queues, Gender Queues: Explaining Women's Inroads Into Males Occupations,* edited by B. F. Reskin and P. A. Roos. Philadelphia, Pa.: Temple University Press.

Birnbaum, Howard, and Rafael Weston. 1974. "Home Ownership and the Wealth Position of Black and White Americans." *Review of Income and Wealth* 20(1): 103–18.

Blackwell, James E. 1991. "Graduate and Professional Education for Blacks." In *The Education of African-Americans,* edited by C. V. Willie, Antoine M. Garibaldi, and Wornie L. Reed. New York: Auburn House.

Blair, John P., and Rudy H. Fichtenbaum. 1992. "Changing Black Employment Patterns." In *The Metropolis in Black and White: Place, Power, and Polarization,* edited by George Galster and Edward Hill. New Brunswick, N.J.: Center for Urban Policy Research.

Blakely, Mary Kay. 1985. "Thoughts for Father's Gift." *New York Times.* June 8, p. C10.

Blank, Rebecca M. 1995. "The Employment Strategy: Public Policies to Increase Work and Earnings." In *Confronting Poverty: Prescriptions for Change,* edited by Sheldon Danziger, G. D. Sandefur and D. H. Weinberg. Cambridge, Mass.: Harvard University Press.

Blanke, David. 1994. "A Comparison of the Catalogs Issued From Sears, Roebuck & Company and Montgomery Ward and Company 1893–1906." *Essays in Economic and Business History* 12: 319–34.

Blau, Francine D., and Andrea H. Beller. 1992. "Black-White Earnings Over the 1970s and 1980s: Gender Differences in Trends." *Review of Economics and Statistics* 74(2): 276–86.

Blau, Francine D., and John W. Graham. 1990. "Black-White Differences in Wealth and Asset Composition." *Quarterly Journal of Economics* 105(2): 321–39.

Blessing, Patrick. 1980. "Irish." In *Harvard Encyclopedia of American Ethnic Groups,* edited by Stephen Thernstrom. Cambridge, Mass.: Harvard University Press.

Bluestone, Barry, and Bennett Harrison. 1982. *The Deindustrialization of America: Plant Closings, Community Abandonment, and the Dismantling of Basic Industry.* New York: Basic Books.

Boas, Franz. 1925. "What Is Race?" *The Nation* 120: 89–95.

Bodnar, John. 1985. *The Transplanted: A History of Immigrants in Urban America.* Bloomington: University of Indiana Press.

Boesel, David, Nabeel Alsalam, and Thomas M. Smith. 1998. *Educational and La-*

bor Market Performance of GED Recipients. U.S. Department of Education, Office of Educational Research and Improvement. Washington: U.S. Government Printing Office.

Bogardus, Emory S. 1923. *Essentials of Americanization.* Los Angeles: University of California Press.

Bogue, Donald J. 1985. *The Population of the United States: Historical Trends and Future Projections.* New York: Free Press.

Bonacich, Edna. 1976. "Advanced Capitalism and Black/White Race Relations in the United States: A Split Labor Market Interpretation." *American Sociological Review* 41(1): 34–51.

Bond, Horace Mann. 1934/1966. *The Education of the Negro in the American Social Order.* New York: Octagon Books.

Booth, Alan, Ann C. Crouter, and Michael J. Shanahan. 1999. *Transitions to Adulthood in a Changing Economy: No Work, No Family, No Future?* London: Praeger.

Bordo, Michael D., Barry Eichengreen, and Douglas A. Irwin. 1999. *Is Globalization Today Really Different Than Globalization A Hundred Years Ago?* NBER Working Paper 7195. Cambridge, Mass.: National Bureau of Economic Research.

Borjas, George J. 1985. "Assimilation, Changes in Cohort Quality, and the Earnings of Immigrants." *Journal of Labor Economics* 3: 463–89.

———. 1987. "Self-selection and the Earnings of Immigrants." *American Economic Review* 77: 531–53.

———. 1994. "Long-Run Convergence of Ethnic Skill Differentials: The Children and Grandchildren of the Great Migration." *Industrial and Labor Relations Review* 47(4): 553–73.

———. 1995. "The Economic Benefits of Immigration." *Journal of Economic Perspectives* 9(2): 3–22.

———. 1999. *Heaven's Door: Immigration Policy and the American Economy.* Princeton, N.J.: Princeton University Press.

Bose, Christine E. 2001. *Women in 1900: Gateway to the Political Economy of the 20th Century.* Philadelphia, Pa.: Temple University Press.

Bound, John, and Laura Dresser. 1999. "Losing Ground: The Erosion of the Relative Earnings of African American Women During the 1980s." In *Latinas and African American Women at Work: Race, Gender, and Economic Inequality,* edited by I. Browne. New York: Russell Sage Foundation.

Bound, John, and Richard B. Freeman. 1992. "What Went Wrong? The Erosion of the Relative Earnings and Employment of Young Black Men in the 1980s." *Quarterly Journal of Economics* 107(1): 201–32.

Bound, John, and George Johnson. 1991. "Wages in the United States during the 1980s and Beyond." In *Workers and Their Wages: Changing Patterns in the United States,* edited by M. H. Kosters. Washington, D.C.: American Enterprise Institute Press.

Boushey, Heather, and Robert Cherry. 2000. "Exclusionary Practices and Glass-Ceiling Effects Across Regions: What Does the Current Expansion Tell Us?" In *Prosperity for All? The Economic Boom and African Americans,* edited by R. Cherry and W. M. Rodgers. New York: Russell Sage Foundation.

Bowers, William L. 1974. *The Country Life Movement in America 1900–1920.* Port Washington, N.Y.: Kennikat Press.

Bowler, Mary. 1999. "Women's Earnings: An Overview." *Monthly Labor Review* 122(12): 13–21.

Boyd, Robert L. 1990. "Black and Asian Self-Employment in Large Metropolitan Areas: A Comparative Analysis." *Social Problems* 37(2): 258–73.

———. 1991. "A Contextual Analysis of Black Self-Employment in Large Metropolitan Areas, 1970–1980." *Social Forces* 70(2): 409–29.

———. 1993. "Differences in the Earnings of Black Workers in the Private and Public Sectors." *Social Science Journal* 30(2): 133–42.

Braun, Denny. 1991. *The Rich Get Richer: The Rise of Income Inequality in the United States and the World.* Chicago: Nelson-Hall.

Breckinridge, Sophonisba P. 1933. *Women in the Twentieth Century: A Study of Their Political, Social, and Economic Activities.* New York and London: McGraw-Hill.

Bremmer, Robert H., ed. 1974. *Children and Youth in America: A Documentary History.* Vol. III: *1933–1973.* Parts One through Four. Cambridge, Mass.: Harvard University Press.

Brewer, Rose M. 1996. "Black Women's Economic Inequality: The Intersection of Race, Gender and Class." *International Policy Review* 6(1): 46–50.

Briggs, John W. 1978. *An Italian Passage: Immigrants to Three American Cities, 1890–1930.* New Haven, Conn.: Yale University Press.

Brimmer, Andrew F. 1988. "Income, Wealth, and Investment Behavior in the Black Community." *American Economic Review* 78(2): 151–55.

Brody, David. 1960. *Steelworkers in America: the Nonunion Era.* Cambridge, Mass.: Harvard University Press.

———. 1993. *Workers in Industrial America: Essays on the 20th Century Struggle,* 2nd ed. New York: Oxford University Press.

Brown, Michael K. 1999. *Race, Money, and the American Welfare State.* Ithaca, N.Y.: Cornell University Press.

Brown, Michael K., Martin Carnoy, Elliott Currie, Troy Duster, David B. Oppenheimer, Marjorie M. Schultz, and David Wellman. 2003. *Whitewashing Race: The Myth of a Color-Blind Society.* Berkeley and Los Angeles: University of California Press.

Brown, Michael K., and Steven P. Erie. 1981. "Blacks and the Legacy of the Great Society: The Economic and Political Impact of Federal Social Policy." *Public Policy* 29(3): 299–330.

Brown, Nancy G., and Ramona E. Douglas. 2003. "Evolution of Multiracial Organizations: Where We Have Been and Where We Are Going." In *New Faces in a Changing America: Multiracial Identity in the 21st Century,* edited by H. L. DeBose and L. I. Winters. Thousand Oaks, Calif.: Sage Publications.

Browne, Irene. 1997. "Explaining the Black-White Gap in Labor Force Participation Among Women Headed Households." *American Sociological Review* 62(2): 236–52.

———. 1999. "Latinas and African American Women in the U.S. Labor Market." In *Latinas and African American Women at Work: Race, Gender, and Economic Inequality,* edited by I. Browne. New York: Russell Sage Foundation.

Browne, Irene, Cynthia Hewitt, Leann Tigges, and Gary Green. 2001. "Why Does Job Segregation Lead to Wage Inequality among African Americans? Person, Place, Sector, or Skills? *Social Science Research* 30(3): 473–95.

Brownlee, W. Eliot. 1996. *Federal Taxation in America: A Short History.* New York: Cambridge University Press.

Brunner, Edmund deS. 1927. *Village Communities.* New York: George H. Doran Company.

Brush, B. L. 1999. "Has Foreign Nurse Recruitment Impeded African American Access to Nursing Education and Practice?" *Nursing Outlook* 47(4): 175–80.

Bruton Center. "Windows on Urban Poverty." University of Texas at Dallas and the Brookings Institute. Available at: http://www.urbanpoverty.net (accessed October 24, 2005).

Bryan, William Jennings. 1896. "Cross of Gold." Speech given at the Democratic National Convention, Chicago, July 9. Available at: http://historymatters.gmu.edu/d/5354/ (accessed October 24, 2005).

Bryant, Alyssa N. 2001. "The Economic Outcomes of Community College Attendance." ERIC Digest ED467981. Los Angeles: ERIC Clearinghouse for Community Colleges.

Bryce, James. 1888/1907. *The American Commonwealth,* 3rd ed., vol. 2. New York: The Macmillan Company.

Buchanan, Patrick J. 2002. *The Death of the West.* New York: Thomas Dunne Books, St. Martin's Press.

Buchmann, Marlis. 1989. *The Script of Life in Modern Society: Entry Into Adulthood in a Changing World.* Chicago: University of Chicago Press.

Budig, Michelle J. 2002. "Male Advantage and the Gender Composition of Jobs: Who Rides the Glass Escalator?" *Social Problems* 49(2): 258–77.

Bull, Chris, and John Gallagher. 2001. *Perfect Enemies: The Battle Between the Religious Right and the Gay Movement,* rev. ed. Lanham, New York, Oxford: Madison Books.

Burge, Kathleen. 2003. "Gays Have Right To Marry, SJC Says in Historic Ruling." *Boston.com,* November 19.

Burr, Clinton Stoddard.1922. *America's Race Heritage.* New York: The National Historical Society.

Burstein, Paul, ed. 1994. "Equal Employment Opportunity: Labor Market Discrimination and Public Policy." In *Sociology and Economics: Controversy and Integration,* edited by P. S. England, George Farkas, and Kevin Lang. New York: Aldine de Gruyter.

Burtless, G. 1994. "Public Spending on the Poor: Historical Trends and Economic Limits." In *Confronting Poverty: Prescriptions for Change,* edited by Sheldon H. Danziger, Gary D. Sandefur, and Daniel H. Weinburg. Cambridge, Mass.: Harvard University Press.

Burtless, Gary. 1993. "The Contribution of Employment and Hours Changes to Family Income Inequality." *The American Economic Review* 83(2): 131–35.

Button, James W., and Barbara A. Rienzo. 2003. "The Impact of Affirmative Action: Black Employment in Six Southern Cities." *Social Science Quarterly* 84(1): 1–14.

Byington, Margaret F. 1974. *Homestead: The Households of a Mill Town.* Pittsburgh, Pa.: University of Pittsburgh Press. First published 1910 by Russell Sage Foundation.

Cain, Glen G., and Finnie E. Ross. 1990. "The Black-White Difference in Youth

Employment: Evidence for Demand-Side Factors." *Journal of Labor Economics* 8(1): S364–95.

Cancian, Maria, Sheldon Danziger, and Peter Gottschalk. 1993. "Working Wives and Family Income Inequality Among Married Couples." In *Uneven Tides: Rising Inequality in America,* edited by Sheldon Danziger and Peter Gottschalk. New York: Russell Sage Foundation.

Cancian, Maria, Thomas Kaplan, and Daniel R. Meyer. 1999. "Outcomes for Low-Income Families Under the Wisconsin AFDC Programs: Understanding the Baseline So That We Can Estimate the Effects of Welfare Reform." IRP Special Report #75. Madison, Wisc.: Institute for Research on Poverty.

Cancian, Maria, and Deborah Reed. 1999. "The Impact of Wives' Earnings on Income Inequality: Issues and Estimates." *Demography* 36(2): 173–84.

Cancio, A. Silvia, T. David Evans, and David J. Maume, Jr. 1997. "The Declining Significance of Race Reconsidered: Racial Differences in Early Career Wages." *American Sociological Review* 61(4): 541–56.

Capelli, Peter. 1995. "Conceptual Issues in Developing a System of Occupational Classification." Paper read at Seminar on Research Findings, Standard Occupational Classification Revision Policy Committee. Washington, D.C. (April 11).

Carnevale, Anthony P. 2000. *Community Colleges and Career Qualifications. New Expeditions: Charting the Second Century of Community Colleges.* Washington, D.C.: American Association of Community Colleges.

Carnoy, Martin. 1994. *Faded Dreams: The Politics and Economics of Race in America.* New York: Cambridge University Press.

———. 2000. *Sustaining the New Economy.* New York and Cambridge, Mass.: Russell Sage Foundation and Harvard University Press.

Carpenter, Elyse. 2002. "Physicians as an Occupation: United States 1800–1990." Unpublished paper. University of Pennsylvania History 580, Philadelphia.

Carrington, William J., Kristin McCue, and Brooks Pierce. 1996. "Black/White Wage Convergence: The Role of Public Sector Wages and Employment." *Industrial and Labor Relations Review* 49(3): 456–71.

Carroll, C. D., B. K. Rhee, and C. Rhee. 1994. "Are There Cultural Effects on Saving? Some Cross-Sectional Evidence." *Quarterly Journal of Economics* 109: 695–99.

Carter, Susan B., and Richard Sutch. 1996. "Myth of the Industrial Scrapheap: A Revisionist View of Turn-of-the-Century American Retirement. *Journal of Economic History* 56(1): 5–38.

———. 1999. "Historical Perspectives on the Economic Consequences of Immigration into the United States." In *The Handbook of International Migration: The American Experience,* edited by C. Hirschman, P. Kasinitz, and J. DeWind. New York: Russell Sage Foundation.

Casper, Lynne M., and Suzanne M. Bianchi. 2002. *Continuity and Change in the American Family.* Thousand Oaks, Calif.: Sage Publications.

Castells, Manuel. 1997. "The Power of Identity." In *The Information Age: Economy, Society, and Culture,* vol. II. Oxford: Blackwell Publishers.

———. 1998. "End of Millennium." In *The Information Age: Economy, Society, and Culture,* vol. III. Oxford: Blackwell Publishers.

———. 2000. *The Rise of the Network Society*. In *The Information Age: Economy, Society, and Culture*, vol. I, 2nd ed. Oxford: Blackwell Publishers.

Castillo, Monica D. 1998. "Persons Outside the Labor Force Who Want a Job." *Monthly Labor Review* 121(7): 34–42.

Catanzarite, Lisa. 2003. "Race-Gender Composition and Occupational Pay Degradation." *Social Problems* 50(1): 14–37.

Cates, Jerry. 1983. *Insuring Inequality*. Ann Arbor: University of Michigan Press.

Cayer, N. Joseph, and Lee Siegelman. 1980. "Minorities and Women in State and Local Government: 1973–1975." *Public Administration Review* 4: 443–50.

Challenge of Jobless Youth, The. 1963. Washington: U.S. President's Committee on Youth Employment.

Chandler, Alfred D., Jr. 1965. "The Railroads: Pioneers in Modern Corporate Management." *Business History Review* 39: 16–40.

Chauncey, George. 2004. *Why Marriage? The History Shaping Today's Debate Over Gay Equality*. New York: Basic Books.

Cherry, Robert. 1999. "Black Male Employment and Tight Labor Markets. *The Review of Black Political Economy* 27(1): 31–45.

Cherry, Robert, and William M. Rodgers, ed. 2000. *Prosperity for All? The Economic Boom and African Americans*. New York: Russell Sage Foundation.

Chiswick, Barry. 1977. "Sons of Immigrants: Are They at an Earnings Disadvantage?" *American Economic Review* 67(February): 376–80.

———. 1978. "The Effect of Americanization on the Earnings of Foreign-born Men." *Journal of Political Economy* 86: 897–921.

Christopher, Karen. 1996. "Explaining the Recent Employment Gap Between Black and White Women." *Sociological Focus* 29(3): 263–80.

Chudacoff, Howard P. 1989. *How Old Are You? Age Consciousness in American Culture*. Princeton, N.J.: Princeton University Press.

Chudacoff, Howard, and Judith E. Smith. 1988. *The Evolution of American Urban Society*. Englewood Cliffs, N.J.: Prentice-Hall.

Church, Robert L. 1976. *Education in the United States: An Interpretive History*. New York: Free Press.

Citizens for Tax Justice. 2002. "Year-by-Year Analysis of the Bush Tax Cuts Show Growing Tilt to the Very Rich." Washington, D.C. Available at: http://www.ctj.org/html/gwb0602.htm (accessed October 24, 2005).

———. 2003. "Details on the Bush Tax Cuts So Far." Washington, D.C. Available at: http://www.ctj.org/pdf/gwbdata.pdf (accessed October 24, 2005).

Clague, Christopher K. 1977. "Effects of Marital and Fertility Patterns on the Transmission and Distribution of Wealth." *The Journal of Human Resources* 12(2): 220–41.

Clark, William A. V. 2001. "The Geography of Immigrant Poverty: Selective Evidence of an Immigrant Underclass." In *Strangers at the Gates: New Immigrants in Urban America*, edited by Roger Waldinger. Berkeley: University of California Press.

Clignet, Remi. 1988. "Ethnicity and Inheritance." In *Inheritance and Wealth in America*, edited by J. Robert, K. Miller, and S. J. McNamee. New York: Plenum Press.

———. 1992. *Death, Deeds, and Descendants: Inheritance in Modern America, Social Institutions and Social Change*. New York: Aldine de Gruyter.

Clinton, Hillary Rodham. 2004. "Now Can We Talk About Health Care?" *New York Times Magazine*, April 18, pp. 26–31, 56.

Coffey, Michael. 1998. "Michael Cunningham: New Family Outing(Interview)." *Publisher's Weekly*, November 2, 1998, p. 53.

Cohen, Cynthia B. 1997. "Children of Choice: Freedom and the New Reproductive Technologies." *Women and Health* 26(2): 97–100.

Cohen, Lizabeth. 2003. *A Consumers' Republic: The Politics of Mass Consumption in Postwar America.* New York: Alfred A. Knopf.

Cohen, Miriam. 1992. *Workshop to Office: Two Generations of Italian Women in New York City, 1900–1950.* Ithaca, N.Y.: Cornell University Press.

Cohen, Philip N. 1998. "Black Concentration Effects on Black-White and Gender Inequality: Multilevel Analysis for U.S. Metropolitan Areas." *Social Forces* 77(1): 207–229.

Cohen, Philip N., and Matt L. Huffman. 2003. "Individuals, Jobs, and Labor Markets: The Devaluation of Women's Work." *American Sociological Review* 68: 443–63.

Cohen, William. 1991. *At Freedom's Edge: Black Mobility and the Southern White Quest for Racial Control, 1861–1915.* Baton Rouge: Louisiana State University Press.

Cohn, Samuel. 1985. *The Process of Occupational Sex-Typing.* Philadelphia, Pa.: Temple University Press.

Cohn, Samuel, and Mark Fossett. 1995. "Why Racial Employment Inequality is Greater in Northern Labor Markets: Regional Differences in White-Black Employment Differentials." *Social Forces* 74(2): 511–42.

Coley, Richard J. 2001. *Differences in the Gender Gap: Comparisons across Racial/Ethnic Groups in Education and Work.* Princeton, N.J.: Educational Testing Service.

Collins, Sharon. 1983. "The Making of the Black Middle Class." *Social Problems* 30(4): 369–82.

Collins-Lowry, Sharon M. 1997. *Black Corporate Executives: The Making and Breaking of a Black Middle Class, Labor and Social Change.* Philadelphia, Pa.: Temple University Press.

Collins, William J., and Jeffrey G. Williamson. 1999. *Capital Goods, Prices, Global Capital Markets and Accumulation: 1870–1950.* Working Paper 7145. Cambridge, Mass.: National Bureau of Economic Research.

———. 1999. *Capital Goods, Prices, Global Capital Markets and Accumulations: 1870–1950.* Cambridge, Mass.: National Bureau of Economic Research.

Conk, Margo A. 1978. *The United States Census and Labor Force Change: A History of Occupation Statistics, 1870–1940.* Ann Arbor, Mich.: UMI Research Press.

Conley, Dalton. 1999. *Being Black, Living in the Red: Race, Wealth, and Social Policy in America.* Berkeley: University of California Press.

Conzen, Kathleen Neils. 1980. "Germans." In *Harvard Encyclopedia of American Ethnic Groups,* edited by Stephen Thernstrom. Cambridge, Mass.: Harvard University Press.

Cooperman, Alan. 2004. "Gay Marriage as 'the New Abortion.'" *Washington Post.* July 6, p. AO3.

Corazzini, Arthur J. 1972. "Equality of Employment Opportunity in the Federal White-Collar Civil Service." *Journal of Human Resources* 7(3): 424–45.

Corbett, Thomas. 2001. "Evaluating Welfare Reform in an Era of Transition: Are We Looking in the Wrong Places?" *Focus* 21(1): 1–5.

Corcoran, Mary. 1999. "The Economic Progress of African American Women." In *Latinas and African American Women at Work: Race, Gender, and Economic Inequality,* edited by Irene Browne. New York: Russell Sage Foundation.

Cornelius, Wayne A. 1998. "The Structural Embeddedness of Demand for Mexican Immigrant Labor: New Evidence from California." In *Crossings: Mexican Immigration in Interdisciplinary Perspectives,* edited by M. Suarez-Orozco. Cambridge, Mass.: Harvard University Press.

Cose, Ellis, and Allison Samuels. 2003. "The Black Gender Gap." *Newsweek,* March 3, 2003, p. 46.

Costa, Dora L. 1998. *The Evolution Of Retirement: An American Economic History, 1880–1990.* NBER series on long-run factors in economic development. Chicago: University of Chicago Press.

Cott, Nancy. 2000. *Public Vows: A History of Marriage and the Nation.* Cambridge, Mass.: Harvard University Press.

Cotter, David A., Joanne M. DeFiore, Joan M. Hermsen, Brenda Marsteller Kowalewski, and Reeve Vanneman. 1995. "Occupational Gender Desegregation in the 1980s." *Work and Occupations* 22(1): 3–21.

Cotter, David A., Joan M. Hermsen, and Reeve Vanneman. 2003. "The Effects of Occupational Gender Segregation Across Race." *Sociological Quarterly* 44(1): 17–36.

Cotton, Jeremiah. 1989. "Opening the Gap: The Decline in African American Economic Indicators in the 1980s." *Social Science Quarterly* 70(4): 803–35.

———. 1990. "The Gap at the Top: Relative Occupational Earnings Disadvantages of the Black Middle Class." *The Review of Black Political Economy* 18: 21–38.

Cowie, Jefferson. 1999. *Capital Moves: RCA's Seventy-Year Quest for Cheap Labor.* Ithaca, N.Y.: Cornell University Press.

Crichton, Judy. 1998. *America 1900: The Turning Point.* New York: Henry Holt.

Critzer, John W. 1998. "Racial and Gender Income Inequality in the American States. *Race & Society* 1(2): 159–76.

Cronon, William M. 1991. *"Nature's Metropolis: Chicago and the Great West.* New York: W. W. Norton.

Cross, Theodore. 1994. "What If There Was No Affirmative Action in College Admission? A Further Refinement of Our Calculations. *Journal of Blacks in Higher Education* 5: 55.

Cross, Theodore, and Robert Bruce Slater. 1997. "The Commanding Wealth Advantage of College-Bound White Students." *The Journal of Blacks in Higher Education* 15: 80–90.

Culhane, Dennis, et al. 2001. "Assessing Homeless Population Size Through the Use of Emergency and Transitional Shelter Services in 1998: Results from the Analysis of Administrative Data from Nine US Jurisdictions." *Public Health Reports* 116(4): 344–54.

Cummings, Scott. 1987. "Vulnerability to the Effects of Recession: Minority and Female Workers." *Social Forces* 65: 834–57.

Cunningham, James S., and Nadja Zalokar. 1992. "The Economic Progress of

Black Women, 1940–1980: Occupational Distribution and Relative Wages." *Industrial and Labor Relations Review* 45(3): 540–55.

Curry, G.E., ed. 1996. *The Affirmative Action Debate*. Reading, Mass.: Addison-Wesley.

DaCosta, Kimberly McClain. 2003. "New Faces, Old Faces: Counting the Multiracial Population Past and Present." In *Multiracial Identity: From Personal Problem to Public Issue,* edited by H. L. DeBose and L. I. Winters. Thousand Oaks, Calif.: Sage Publications.

Danbom, David B. 1979. *The Resisted Revolution*. Ames: The Iowa State University Press.

———. 1995. *Born in the Country: A History of Rural America*. Baltimore, Md.: Johns Hopkins University Press.

Danziger, Sheldon H., and Peter Gottschalk, ed. 1993. *Uneven Tides: Rising Inequality in America*. New York: Russell Sage Foundation.

———. 1995. *America Unequal*. New York and Cambridge, Mass.: Russell Sage Foundation and Harvard University Press.

———. 2004. *Diverging Fortunes: Trends in Poverty and Inequality, The American People: Census 2000 Series*. New York and Washington: Russell Sage Foundation and Population Reference Bureau.

Danziger, Sheldon, and Daniel H. Weinberg, eds. 1986. *Fighting Poverty: What Works and What Doesn't*. Cambridge, Mass.: Harvard University Press.

———. 1995. "The Historical Record: Trends in Family Income, Inequality, and Poverty." In *Confronting Poverty: Prescriptions for Change,* edited by S. Danziger, G. D. Sandefur and D. H. Weinberg. Cambridge, Mass.: Harvard University Press.

Darity, William A., Jr., and Samuel L. Myers, Jr. 1998. *Persistent Disparity: Race and Economic Inequality in the United States Since 1945*. Northampton, Mass.: Edward Elgar.

———. 2000. "The Impact of Labor Market Prospects on Incarceration Rates." In *Prosperity for All? The Economic Boom and African Americans,* edited by Robert Cherry and William M. Rodgers. New York: Russell Sage Foundation.

———. 2001. "Racial Economic Inequality in the USA." In *The Blackwell Companion to Sociology,* edited by J. R. Blau. Malden, Mass.: Blackwell.

Davey, Monica. 2004. "Missourians Back Ban on Same-Sex Marriage." *New York Times*. August 4, online edition.

———. 2004. "Message of Voters in Missouri Against Gay Marriage Leaves Backers Discouraged." *New York Times.* August 5, online edition.

Davies, Margery W. 1982. *Woman's Place Is at the Typewriter: Office Work and Office Workers 1870–1930*. Philadelphia, Pa.: Temple University Press.

Davis, James F. 1991. *Who Is Black?* University Park, Pa.: Pennsylvania State University Press.

Davis, Kingsley. 1950. "Review of Social Structure." *American Sociological Review* 15(1): 138–140.

Davis, Lance, et al. 1972. *American Economic Growth: An Economist's History of the United States*. New York: Harper and Row.

Davis, Martha F. 1993. *"Brutal Need: Lawyers and the Welfare Rights Movement.* New Haven, Conn.: Yale University Press.

Davis, Theodore J., Jr. 1995. "The Occupational Mobility of Black Men Revisited: Does Race Matter?" *Social Science Journal* 32(2): 121–35.

Dawley, Alan. 1976. *Class and Community: The Industrial Revolution in Lynn*. Cambridge, Mass.: Harvard University Press.

DeBose, Herman L. 2003. "Introduction." In *New Faces in a Changing America: Multiracial Identity in the 21st Century*, edited by H. L. DeBose and L. I. Winters. Thousand Oaks, Calif.: Sage Publications.

Debs, Eugene. 1908. "The Issue." Speech after being named Socialist candidate for the presidency, at Girard, Kansas, May 23, 1908. Available at: http://douglassarchives.org/debs_a80.htm (accessed October 24, 2005).

Defreitas, Gregory E. 2000. "Urban Racial Unemployment Differentials: The New York Case." In *Prosperity for All? The Economic Boom and African Americans*, edited by Robert Cherry and William M. Rogers III. New York: Russell Sage Foundation.

DeNavas-Walt, Carmen, Bernadette D. Proctor, and Robert J. Mills. 2004. *Income, Poverty, and Health Insurance Coverage in the United States: 2003*. U.S. Census Bureau, Current Population Reports, P60–226. Washington: U.S. Government Printing Office.

DeVault, Ileen A. 1990. *Sons and Daughters of Labor: Class and Clerical Work in Turn-of-the-Century Pittsburgh*. Ithaca, N.Y.: Cornell University Press.

———. 1991. "'Give the Boys a Trade': Gender and Job Choice in the 1890s." In *Work Engendered: Toward a New History of American Labor*, edited by A. Baron. Ithaca, N.Y.: Cornell University Press.

DiPrete, Thomas A., and Whitman T. Soule. 1986. "The Organization of Career Lines: Equal Employment Opportunity and Status Advancement in a Federal Bureaucracy." *American Sociological Review* 51(3): 295–309.

Dobbin, Frank R. 1992. "The Origins of Private Social Insurance: Public Policy and Fringe Benefits in America, 1920–1950." *American Journal of Sociology* 97(5): 1424.

Dohm, Arlene. 2000. "Gauging the Labor Force Effects of Retiring Baby-Boomers." *Monthly Labor Review* 127(7): 17–25.

Dolgin, Janet L. 1997. "The Fate of Childhood: Legal Models of Children and the Parent-Child Relationship." *Albany Law Review* 61(2): 345–431.

———. 2004. "Embryonic Discourse: Abortion, Stem Cells and Cloning." *Issues in Law and Medicine* 19(3): 203–62.

Dollard, John. 1937. "Review of J. Steward Lincoln. The Dream in Primitive Cultures." *American Anthropologist. New Series* 39(3): 547–48.

Dominus, Susan. 2004. "Life in the Age of Old, Old Age." *New York Times*, February 22, 2004. Available at: http://query.nytimes.com/gst/health/article-page.html?res=9C05E6D9173DF931A15751C0A9629C8B63 (accessed October 24, 2005).

Dorn, Sherman J. 1992. *Creating the Dropout: An Institutional and Social History of School Failure*. Westport, Conn.: Praeger.

Dougherty, Kevin. 1987. "The Effects of Community Colleges: Aid or Hindrance to Socioeconomic Attainment?" *Sociology of Education* 60(2): 86–103.

———. 1994. *The Contradictory College: The Conflicting Origins, Impacts, and Futures of the Community College*. SUNY series, Frontiers in Education. Albany: State University of New York Press.

Douglas, Nathan. 2003. "The Multiracial Movement: An Uncomfortable Political Fit." *The Multiracial Activist* (October/November).

Drake, St. Clair, and Horace Cayton. 1945/1993. *"Black Metropolis: A Study of Negro Life in a Northern City,* rev. ed. Chicago: University of Chicago Press.

Drake, W. Avon, and Robert D. Holsworth. 1996. *Affirmative Action and the Stalled Quest for Black Progress.* Chicago: University of Illinois Press.

Dreier, Peter, John Mollenkopf, and Todd Swanstrom. 2005. *Place Matters: Metropolitics for the Twenty-first Century,* 2d ed. rev. Lawrence: University Press of Kansas.

Du Bois, W. E. B. 1995. "The Color Line Belts The World." In *W. E. B. Du Bois: A Reader,* edited by D. L. Lewis. New York: Henry Holt.

Dubester, Henry J. 1948/1969. *State Censuses: An Annotated Bibliography of Censuses of Population taken after the Year 1790 by States and Territories of the United States,* reprint ed. New York: Burt Franklin.

———. 1950. *Catalog of United States Census Publications 1790–1945.* Washington: U.S. Government Printing Office.

Dudziak, Mary L. 2000. *Cold War Civil Rights: Race and the Image of American Democracy.* Princeton, N.J.: Princeton University Press.

Duncan, Greg J., and Richard Coe. 1984. *Years of Poverty, Years of Plenty: The Changing Fortunes of American Workers and Families.* Ann Arbor: University of Michigan Press.

Duncan, Otis Dudley. 1961. "A Socioeconomic Index for All Occupations." In *Occupations and Social Status,* edited by A. Reiss et al. New York: Free Press.

Durant, Thomas J., Jr., and Joyce S. Louden. 1986. "The Black Middle Class in America: Historical and Contemporary Perspectives." *Phylon* 47(4): 253–63.

Durr, Marlese, and John R. Logan. 1997. "Racial Submarkets in Government Employment: African American Managers in New York State." *Sociological Forum* 12(3): 353–70.

Dyer, Stephanie. 2000. "Markets in the Meadows: Department Stores and Shopping Centers in the Decentralization of Philadelphia." Ph.D. Dissertation: University of Pennsylvania.

Eaton, Judith S., ed. 1988. *Colleges of Choice: The Enabling Impact of the Community College.* Macmillan Series on Higher Education. New York: American Council on Higher Education.

Eaton, Leslie, and Edward Wyatt. 2001. "Attacks Hit Low-Pay Jobs the Hardest." *New York Times.* November 6, 2001, p. B1.

Edin, Kathryn, and Maria Kefalas. 2005. *Promises I Can Keep: Why Poor Women Put Motherhood before Marriage.* Berkeley: University of California Press.

Edin, Kathryn, and Laura Lein. 1997. *Making Ends Meet: How Single Mothers Survive Welfare and Low-Wage Work.* New York: Russell Sage Foundation.

Edmonston, Barry, Sharon M. Lee, and Jeffrey S. Passel. 2002. "Recent Trends in Intermarriage and Immigration and their Effects on the Future Racial Composition of the U.S. Population." In *The New Race Question: How the Census Counts Multiracial Individuals,* edited by Joel Perlmann and Mary C. Waters. New York: Russell Sage Foundation.

Edmonston, Barry, and Jeffrey S. Passel. 1999. "How Immigration and Intermarriage Affect the Racial and Ethnic Composition of the U.S. Population." In *Immigration and Opportunity: Race, Ethnicity, and Employment in the United States,* edited by Frank D. Bean and Stephanie Bell-Rose. New York: Russell Sage Foundation.

Education Trust, The. 2003. "Telling the Whole Truth (Or Not) About High School Graduation Rates: New State Data." Washington, D.C.: The Education Trust.

Edwards, Alba M. 1911. "Classification of Occupations: The Classification of Occupations, with Special Reference to the United States and the Proposed New Classification for the Thirteenth Census Report on Occupations." *Publications of the American Statistical Association* 12(94): 618–46.

———. 1917. "Social-Economic Groups of the United States." *Publications of the American Statistical Association* 15(118): 643–61.

———. 1933. "A Social-Economic Grouping of the Gainful Workers of the United States." *Journal of the American Statistical Association* 28(184): 377–87.

———. 1941. "Occupation and Industry Statistics." *Journal of the American Statistical Association* 36(215): 387–92.

Einhorn, Robin. 1991. *Property Rules: Political Economy in Chicago, 1833–1872.* Chicago: University of Chicago Press.

Eisinger, Peter K. 1982. "Affirmative Action in Municipal Employment: The Impact of Black Political Power." *American Political Science Review* 76(2): 380–92.

———. 1982. "The Economic Conditions of Black Employment in Municipal Bureaucracies." *American Journal of Political Science* 26(4): 754–71.

———. 1986. "Local Civil Service Employment and Black Socio-Economic Mobility." *Social Science Quarterly* 67(2): 171–75.

Eldridge, Hope T., and Dorothy Swaine Thomas. 1964. "Population Redistribution and Economic Growth: United States, 1870–1950." *Demographic Analyses and Interrelations*, vol. III. Philadelphia, Pa.: American Philosophical Society.

Electronic Privacy Information Center. 2005. *The USA Patriot Act.* Washington, D.C.: EPIC. Available at: http://www.epic.org/privacy/terrorism/usapatriot (accessed October 24, 2005).

Ellis, Mark. 2001. "A Tale of Five Cities? Trends in Immigrant and Native-Born Wages." In *Strangers at the Gates: New Immigrants in Urban America,* edited by Roger Waldinger. Berkeley: University of California Press.

Ellwood, David T., and Christopher Jencks. 2001. *The Growing Differences in Family Structure: What Do We Know? Where Do We Look for Answers?* New York: Russell Sage Foundation.

Elshtain, Jean Bethke, and David Blankenhorn, eds. 1996. *Promises to Keep: Decline and Renewal of Marriage in America.* Lanham, Md.: Rowman and Littlefield.

Emmerson, Louis L. 1923. *Blue Book of the State of Illinois.* Springfield: Illinois State Journal Co.

Engel, Cynthia. 1999. "Health Services Industry: Still A Job Machine?" *Monthly Labor Review* 122(3): 3–14.

Engerman, Stanley L., and Robert E. Gallman, eds. 2000. *The Cambridge Economic History of the United States: The Long Nineteenth Century,* vol. II. Cambridge: Cambridge University Press.

———, eds. 2000. *The Cambridge Economic History of the United States: The Twentieth Century,* vol. III. Cambridge: Cambridge University Press.

———. 2000. "Technology and Industrialization, 1790–1914." In *The Cambridge*

Economic History of the United States. The Long Nineteenth Century, edited by S. L. Engerman and R. E. Gallman. Cambridge: Cambridge University Press.

England, Paula, Karen Christopher, and Lori Reid. 1999. "Gender, Race, Ethnicity, and Wages." In *Latinas and African American Women at Work: Race, Gender, and Economic Inequality,* edited by I. Browne. New York: Russell Sage Foundation.

Epstein, Richard A. 1992. *Forbidden Grounds: The Case Against Employment Discrimination Laws.* Cambridge, Mass.: Harvard University Press.

Ericksen, Eugene P. 1988. "A Review: Estimating the Concentration of Wealth in America." *Public Opinion Quarterly* 52(2): 243–53.

Espenshade, Thomas, and Gregory A. Huber. 1999. "Fiscal Impacts of Immigrants and the Shrinking Welfare State." In *The Handbook of International Migration: The American Experience,* edited by C. Hirschman, P. Kasinitz and J. DeWind. New York: Russell Sage Foundation.

ESRI BIS. 2003. "Census 2000 Detailed Race Profile." Redlands, Calif.: ESRI Business Information Solutions. Available at: http://www.esribis.com/reports/census2000.html (accessed October 25, 2005).

Executive Office of the President. Office of the Press Secretary. 2004. "President Calls for Constitutional Amendment Protecting Marriage: Remarks by the President." White House Press Briefings. February 24, 2004. Washington: U.S. Government Printing Office. Available at: http://www.whitehouse.gov/news/releases/2004/02/20040224-2.html (accessed October 25, 2005).

"Extended Families: Courts Should Let States Put Child's Needs First." 2000. *San Diego Union-Tribune,* January 12, 2000, pp. B-8, B-10.

Fain, J. R. 1999. "Ranking the Factors that Affect Occupational Outcomes." *Industrial Relations* 38(1): 92–105.

Fairlie, Henry. 1988. "Talkin 'bout My Generation: Government Assistance to Those over 65 and the Pampered Lifestyle." *New Republic,* March 28, 1988, p. 9.

Fairlie, Robert W., and Bruce D. Meyer. 2000. "Trends in Self-Employment among White and Black Men during the Twentieth Century." *Journal of Human Resources* 35(4): 643–69.

Falk, William W., and Bruce H. Rankin. 1992. "The Cost of Being Black in the Black Belt." *Social Problems* 39: 299–313.

Family Research Council. 2004. "The Slippery Slope of Same-Sex Marriage." Washington, D.C.: Family Research Council. Available at: http://www.frc.org/get.cfm?i=BC04C02 (accessed October 25, 2005).

Farley, Reynolds, ed. 1995. *State of the Union: America in the 1990s,* 2 vols. New York: Russell Sage Foundation.

———. 1996. *The New American Reality: Who We Are, How We Got Here, Where We Are Going.* New York: Russell Sage Foundation.

———. 2002. "Racial Identities in 2000: The Response to the Multiple-Race Response Option." In *The New Race Question: How The Census Counts Multiracial Individuals,* edited by Joel Perlmann and Mary C. Waters. New York: Russell Sage Foundation.

Farley, Reynolds, and Richard D. Alba. 2002. "The New Second Generation in the United States." *International Migration Review* 36(13): 669–701.

Farley, Reynolds, and Walter R. Allen. 1987. *The Color Line and the Quality of Life in America.* New York: Russell Sage Foundation.

Federal Interagency Forum on Aging-Related Statistics. 2000. *Older Americans 2000: Key Indicators of Well-Being.* Washington: Federal Interagency Forum on Aging-Related Statistics.

Felony Disenfranchisement Laws in the United States. 2003. "The Sentencing Project." Available at: http://www.sentencingproject.org/pdfs/1046.pdf (accessed October 25, 2005).

Ferguson, Roger W., Jr. 2004. "Lessons from Past Productivity Booms." Paper read at Meetings of the American Economic Association. San Diego, Calif. (January 4).

Field, Marilyn J. 2003. "When Children Die." *Issues in Science and Technology Online* 19 (3, spring). Available at: http://www.issues.org/issues/19.3/realnumbers.htm (accessed October 25, 2005).

Fields, Barbara J. 2003. "Of Rogues and Geldings." *American Historical Review* 108(5): 1397–405.

Fink, Deborah. 1998. *Cutting into the Meat Packing Line: Workers and Change in the Rural Midwest.* Chapel Hill: University of North Carolina Press.

Fink, Leon, and Brian Greenberg. 1989. *Upheaval in the Quiet Zone: A History of Hospital Workers' Union, Local 1199.* Urbana: University of Illinois Press.

Fischer, David Hackett. 1978. *Growing Old in America.* New York: Oxford University Press.

Fishman, Robert. 1987. *Bourgeois Utopias: The Rise and Fall of Suburbia.* New York: Basic Books.

Fitzgerald, Deborah. 2001. "Accounting for Change: Farmers and the Modernizing States." In *The Countryside in the Age of the Modern State: Political Histories of Rural America,* edited by C. M. Stock and R. D. Johnston. Ithaca, N.Y.: Cornell University Press.

Fitzpatrick, David. 1999. "Emigration: 1801–1921." In *The Encyclopedia of the Irish in America,* edited by M. Glazier. Notre Dame, Ind.: University of Notre Dame Press.

Forest, B. 2002. "Hidden Segregation? The Limits of Geographically Based Affirmative Action." *Political Geography* 21(7): 855–80.

Forster, M. F. 1994. *The Effects of Net Transfers on Low Income Families Among Non-Elderly Families.* OECD Economic Study No. 22. Paris: Organization for Economic Cooperation and Development.

Fossett, Mark A., Omer R. Galle, and Jeffrey A. Burr. 1989. "Racial Occupational Inequality, 1940–1980: A Research Note on the Impact of Changing Regional Distribution of the Black Population." *Social Forces* 68(2): 415–27.

Fossett, Mark A., Omer R. Galle, and William R. Kelly. 1986. "Racial Occupational Inequality, 1940–1980: National and Regional Trends." *American Sociological Review* 51(3): 421–29.

Fosu, Augustin Kwasi. 1995. "Occupational Mobility and Post-1964 Earnings Gains by Black Women." *The American Economic Review* 85(2): 143–47.

Fountain, John W., and Edward L. Andrews. 2002. "750,000Americans Lose Jobless Benefits." *New York Times,* December 28, 2002. Available at: http://select.nytimes.com/gst/abstract.html?res=F50E16FE3D5B0C7B8ED-DAB0994DA404482 (accessed October 24, 2005).

Frank, Dana. 1999. *Buy American: The Untold Story of Economic Nationalism.* Boston, Mass.: Beacon Press.

Frank, Lawrence K. 1933. Childhood and Youth." In *Recent Social Trends in the*

United States: Report of the President's Research Committee on Social Trends. New York: McGraw-Hill.

Franklin, Rachel S. 2003. "Domestic Migration Across Regions, Divisions, and States: 1995–2000." In *Census 2000 Special Reports.* Washington: U.S. Government Printing Office.

Freeman, Richard B. 1976. *Black Elite: The New Market for Highly Educated Black Americans.* New York: McGraw-Hill.

———. 1981. "Black Economic Progress After 1964: Who Has Gained and Why?" In *Studies in Labor Markets,* edited by Sumner Rosen. Chicago: National Bureau of Economic Research, University of Chicago Press.

———. 1996. "Labor Market Institutions and Earnings Inequality." *New England Economic Review* 157(12).

Freeman, Richard B., and Harry J. Holzer. 1986. *The Black Youth Employment Crisis, National Bureau of Economic Research Project Report.* Chicago: University of Chicago Press.

Freeman, Richard B., and William M. Rodgers III. 2000. "Area Economic Conditions and the Labor Market Outcomes of Young Men in the 1990s Expansion." In *Prosperity for All? The Economic Boom and African Americans,* edited by Robert Cherry and William M. Rodgers. New York: Russell Sage Foundation.

Frey, William H. 1999. "New Black Migration Patterns in the United States: Are They Affected by Recent Immigration?" In *Immigration and Opportunity: Race, Ethnicity, and Employment in the United States,* edited by Frank D. Bean and Stephanie Bell-Rose. New York: Russell Sage Foundation.

———. 2002. "Census 2000 Reveals New Native-Born and Foreign-Born Shifts across U.S." PSC Research Report 02-520. Ann Arbor: Population Studies Center at the Institute for Social Research, University of Michigan.

Frey, William H., and Alan Berube. 2003. "City Families and Suburban Singles: An Emerging Household Story." In *Redefining Urban and Suburban America: Evidence From Census 2000,* edited by B. Katz and R. E. Lang. Washington, D.C.: Brookings Institution.

Frye, John H. 1992. *The Vision of the Public Junior College, 1900–1940: Professional Goals and Popular Aspirations, Contributions to the Study of Education.* New York: Greenwood Press.

Furstenberg, Frank E., Jr. 1994. "History and Current Status of Divorce in the United States." *Children and Divorce* 4(1): 29–43.

———. 1999. "Children and Family Change: Discussion between Social Scientists and the Media." *Contemporary Sociology* 28(1): 10–17.

Furstenberg, Frank E., Jr., Sheela Kennedy, Vonnie C. McLoyd, Ruben G. Rumbaut, and Richard A. Settersten, Jr. 2004. "Growing Up Is Harder to Do." *Contexts* 3(3): 33–41.

Furstenberg, Frank E., Jr., Ruben G. Rumbaut, and Richard A. Settersten, Jr. 2005. *On the Frontier of Adulthood: Theory, Research, and Public Policy.* Chicago: University of Chicago Press.

Fussell, Elizabeth, and Frank E. Furstenberg, Jr. 2005. The Transition to Adulthood during the Twentieth Century: Race, Nativity, and Gender." In *On the Frontier of Adulthood: Theory, Research, and Public Policy,* edited by Frank E. Furstenberg, Jr., Ruben G. Rumbaut and Richard A. Settersten, Jr. Chicago: University of Chicago Press.

Galbraith, James K. 1998. *Created Unequal: The Crisis in American Pay*. New York: Free Press.

Galbraith, James K., Michael Kerlin, Richard D. Alba, and Christopher Jencks. 2002. "'Who Should Get In?' An Exchange." *New York Review of Books*, May 23, 2002. Available at: http://www.nybooks.com/articles/15423 (accessed October 24, 2005).

Galbraith, John Kenneth. 1967. *The New Industrial State*. Boston, Mass.: Houghton Mifflin.

Gallagher, Maggie. 1996. *The Abolition of Marriage: How We Destroy Lasting Love*. Washington, D.C.: Regnery.

Gallman, Robert E. 2000. "Economic Growth and Structural Change in the Long Nineteenth Century." In *The Cambridge Economic History of the United States: The Long Nineteenth Century*, edited by S. L. Engerman and R. E. Gallman. Cambridge: Cambridge University Press.

Gallon, Kim. 2002. "A History of the Stenographer in the United States." Unpublished paper. University of Pennsylvania History 580, Philadelphia.

Gans, Herbert J. 1969. *Levittowners: Ways of Life and Politics in a New Suburban Community*. New York: Vintage Books.

Gardecki, Rosella. 2001. "Racial Differences in Youth Employment." *Monthly Labor Review* 124(8): 51–67.

Garibaldi, Antoine M. 1991. "Blacks in College." In *The Education of African-Americans*, edited by C. V. Willie, Antoine M. Garibaldi, and Wornie L. Reed. New York: Auburn House.

Garreau, Joel. 1991. *Edge City: Life on the New Frontier*. New York: Doubleday.

Geddes, Robert. 1997. "Metropolis Unbound: The Sprawling American City and the Search for Alternatives." *American Prospect* 35: 40–47.

Geiger, Shirley M. 1998. "Employment of Black and White Women in State and Local Government, 1973–1995." *NWSA Journal* 10(3): 151–59.

Geolytics, Inc. 2005. Neighborhood Change Database. Long form release 2.0. East Brunswick, N.J.: Geolytics, Inc.

George, Henry. 1883. *Social Problems*. Online edition. New York: The Robert Schalkenbach Foundation. Available at: http://www.schalkenbach.org/library/george.henry/spcont.html (accessed October 25, 2005).

Gibson, Campbell J., and Emily Lemmon. 1999. "*Historical Census Statistics on the Foreign-born Population of the United States: 1850–1900*. Washington: U.S. Census Bureau.

Gil, Andrew M., and Duane E. Leigh. 2000. "Community College Enrollment, College Major, and the Gender Wage Gap." *Industrial and Labor Relations Review* 54(1): 163–81.

Gjerde, Jon. 1985. *From Peasants to Farmers: the Migration From Balestrand, Norway, to the Upper Middle West*. New York: Cambridge University Press.

———. 1997. *The Minds of the West: Ethnocultural Evolution in the Rural Middle West, 1830–1917*. Chapel Hill: University of North Carolina Press.

Glaeser, Edward L., and Jesse M. Shapiro. 2003. "City Growth: Which Places Grew and Why." In *Redefining Urban and Suburban America: Evidence From Census 2000*, edited by B. Katz and R. E. Lang. Washington, D.C.: Brookings Institution.

Glaeser, Edward L., and Jacob L. Vigdor. 2003. "Racial Segregation: Promising

News." In *Redefining Urban and Suburban America: Evidence From Census 2000,* edited by B. Katz and R. E. Lang. Washington, D.C.: Brookings Institution.

Glazer, Nathan. 2004. "Assimilation Today: Is One Identity Enough?" In *Reinventing the Melting Pot: The New Immigrants and What It Means to Be an American,* edited by Tamar Jacoby. New York: Basic Books.

Glenn, Evelyn Nakano. 1992. "From Servitude to Service Work: Historical Continuities in the Racial Division of Paid Reproductive Labor." *Signs: Journal of Women in Culture and Society* 18(1): 1–43.

———. 2002. *Unequal Freedom: How Race and Gender Shaped American Citizenship and Labor.* Cambridge, Mass.: Harvard University Press.

Glick, Paul C. 1941. "Types of Families: An Analysis of Census Data." *American Sociological Review* 6(6): 830–38.

Golab, Caroline. 1977. *Immigrant Destinations.* Philadelphia, Pa.: Temple University Press.

Goldin, Claudia. 1990. *Understanding the Gender Gap: An Economic History of American Women.* New York: Oxford University Press.

———. 1998. "Now hiring: The feminization of work in the United States, 1900–1995." *Journal of Interdisciplinary History* 29(2): 318–19.

———. 1999. "Egalitarianism and the returns to education during the great transformation of American education." *Journal of Political Economy* 107(6): S65–S94.

———. 2000. "Meritocracy and economic inequality." *Journal of Interdisciplinary History* 31(3): 431–33.

———. 2000. "Labor Markets in the Twentieth Century." In *Cambridge Economic History of the United States,* vol. III, *The Twentieth Century,* edited by S. L. Engerman and R. E. Gallman. New York: Cambridge University Press.

Goldin, Claudia, and Lawrence F. Katz. 1999. "Human capital and social capital: The rise of secondary schooling in America, 1910–1940." *Journal of Interdisciplinary History* 29(4): 683–723.

———. 1999. "Human and Social Capital: The Rise of Secondary Schooling in the United States, 1890 to 1940." *Journal of Economic Perspectives* 13(winter): 37–62.

———. 2000. "Education and income in the early twentieth century: Evidence from the prairies." *Journal of Economic History* 60(3): 782–818.

Goldscheider, Frances K., and Calvin Goldscheider. 1991. "The Intergenerational Flow of Income: Family Structure and the Status of Black Americans." *Journal of Marriage and the Family* 53(2): 499–508.

———. 1993. *Leaving Home Before Marriage: Ethnicity, Familism, and Generational Relationships.* Madison: University of Wisconsin Press.

———. 1999. *The Changing Transition to Adulthood: Leaving and Returning Home.* Thousand Oaks, Calif.: Sage Publications.

Goldstein, Joshua R., and Ann J. Morning. 2002. "Back In The Box: The Dilemma Of Using Multiple-Race Data for Single-Race Laws." In *The New Race Question: How the Census Counts Multiracial Individuals,* edited by Joel Perlmann and Mary C. Waters. New York: Russell Sage Foundation.

Goldstein, Judith. 1993. *Ideas, Interests, and American Trade Policy.* Ithaca, N.Y.: Cornell University Press.

Gonzales Baker, Susan, Frank Baker, Augustin Escobar Latapi, and Sidney Wein-braub. 1998. "U.S. Immigration Policies and Trends: The Growing Importance of Migration from Mexico." In *Crossings: Mexican Immigration in Interdisciplinary Perspectives*, edited by M. Suarez-Orozco. Cambridge, Mass.: Harvard University Press.

Goodwin, Joanne L. 1997. *Gender and the Politics of Welfare Reform: Mothers' Pensions in Chicago, 1911–1929*. Chicago: University of Chicago Press.

Goodwyn, Lawrence. 1978. *The Populist Moment: A Short History of the Agrarian Revolt in America*. New York: Oxford University Press.

Gordon, David M. 1996. *Fat and Mean: The Corporate Squeeze of Working Americans and the Myth of Managerial "Downsizing."* New York: Free Press.

Gordon, Leah. 2002. *Analysis of Census Data on Textile Workers, 1880–1990*. Unpublished manuscript in authors' possession.

Gordon, Linda. 1994. *Pitied but Not Entitled: Single Mothers and the History of Welfare, 1890–1935*. New York: Free Press.

Goren, Arthur A. 1980. "Jews." In *Harvard Encyclopedia of Ethnic Groups*, edited by Stephen Thernstrom. Cambridge, Mass.: Harvard University Press.

Gossett, Thomas F. 1965. *Race: The History of an Idea in America*. New York: Schocken Books.

Gotham, Kevin Fox. 2002. *Race, Real Estate, and Uneven Development: The Kansas City Experience, 1900–2000*. Albany: State University of New York Press.

Gould, Charles W. 1922. *America: A Family Matter*. New York: Charles Scribner's Sons.

Graebner, William. 1980. *A History of Retirement: The Meaning and Function of an American Institution, 1885–1978*. New Haven, Conn.: Yale University Press.

Graham, Hugh David. 2002. "The Origins of Official Minority Designation." In *The New Race Question: How The Census Counts Multiracial Individuals*, edited by Joel Perlmann and Mary C. Waters. New York: Russell Sage Foundation.

Grant, David M., Melvin L. Oliver, and Angela D. James. 1996. "African Americans: Social and Economic Bifurcation." In *Ethnic Los Angeles*, edited by Roger Waldinger and M. Bozorgmehr. New York: Russell Sage Foundation.

Graves, Joseph L., Jr. 2001. *The Emperor's New Clothes: Biological Theories of Race at the Millennium*. New Brunswick, N.J.: Rutgers University Press.

Greedy Pay Chase. 2002. *St. Petersburg Times*, December 2, 2002, p. 8A.

Green, Venus. 2001. *Race on the Line: Gender, Labor, and Technology in the Bell System, 1880–1980*. Durham, N.C.: Duke University Press.

Greene, Jay. 2002. *The GED Myth*. Austin: Texas Education Review. Available at: http://www.educationreview.homestead.com/2002GreeneGEDMyth.html (accessed October 25, 2005).

Greene, Victor. 1980. "Poles." In *Harvard Encyclopedia of American Ethnic Groups*, edited by Stephen Thernstrom. Cambridge, Mass.: Harvard University Press.

Greider, William. 1997. *One World, Ready or Not*. New York: Simon & Schuster.

Grimshaw, William. 1992. *Bitter Fruit: Black Politics and the Chicago Machine*. Chicago: University of Chicago Press.

Grossman, James. 1989. *Land of Hope: Chicago, Black Southerners, and the Great Migration*. Chicago: University of Chicago Press.

Grubb, Norton W. 1999. *Learning and Earning in the Middle: The Economic Benefits of Sub-Baccalaureate Education.* New York: Community College Research Center, Columbia University.

Grubb, W. Norton, and Robert H. Wilson. 1992. "Trends in Wage and Salary Inequality, 1967–88." *Monthly Labor Review* 115(6): 23–39.

Guinier, Lani. 2004. "From Racial Liberalism to Racial Literacy: Brown v. Board of Education and the Interest-Divergence Dilemma." *Journal of American History* 91(1): 92–118.

Guterl, Matthew Pratt. 2001. *The Color of Race in America.* Cambridge, Mass.: Harvard University Press.

Gutierrez, David G. 1998. "Ethnic Mexicans and the Transformation of 'American' Social Space: Reflections on Recent History." In *Crossings: Mexican Immigration in Interdisciplinary Perspectives,* edited by M. Suarez-Orozco. Cambridge, Mass.: Harvard University Press.

Gutmann, Myron, Sara M. Pullum-Piñón, and Thomas Pullum. 2002. "Three Eras of Young Adult Home Leaving in Twentieth-Century America." *Journal of Social History* 35(3): 533–76.

Haber, Carole. 1983. *Beyond Sixty-Five: The Dilemma of Old Age in America's Past.* Cambridge and New York: Cambridge University Press.

Hacker, Andrew. 1986. "Family and Nation." *Fortune* 113: 131–33.

———. 1992. "The Myths of Racial Division: Blacks, Whites—And Statistics." *The New Republic* 206(12): 21–25.

———. 1992. *Two Nations: Black and White, Separate, Hostile, Unequal.* New York: Charles Scribner's.

———. 2003. *Mismatch: The Growing Gulf Between Women and Men.* New York: Charles Scribner's.

———. 2004. "The Underworld of Work." *The New York Review of Books.* February 12, 2002, pp. 38–40.

Hagerty, James J. 1909. "How Far Should Members of the Family Be Individualized." *American Journal of Sociology* 14(6): 797–802.

Hahamovitch, Cindy. 1997. *Fruits of their Labor: Atlantic Coast Farmworkers and the Making of Migrant Poverty, 1870–1945.* Chapel Hill: University of North Carolina Press.

Hahn, Steven. 2003. *A Nation Under Our Feet: Black Political Struggles in the Rural South from Slavery to the Great Migration.* Cambridge, Mass.: Harvard University Press.

Haines, Michael R. 2000. "The Population of the United States, 1790–1920." In *The Cambridge Economic History of the United States,* edited by S. L. Engerman and R. E. Gallman. Cambridge: Cambridge University Press.

Hall, G. Stanley. 1904. *Adolescence, Its Psychology and Its Relations to Physiology, Anthropology, Sociology, Sex, Crime, Religion, and Education.* London: Sidney Appleton.

Hampton, Howard. 1996. "Ultraviolent Movies: From Sam Peckinpah to Quentin Tarantino (Book Review)." *Artforum International* 35(3): S12–14.

Handlin, Oscar. 1951. *The Uprooted: The Epic Story of the Great Migrations that Made the American People.* Boston, Mass.: Little, Brown.

Hansen, Marcus Lee. 1942. *The Immigrant in American History.* Cambridge, Mass.: Harvard University Press.

Hao, Lingxin. 1996. "Family Structure, Private Transfers, and the Economic Well-Being of Families with Children." *Social Forces* 75(1): 269–92.

Harlan, Louis. 1958. *Separate and Unequal: Public School Campaigns and Racism in the Southern Seaboard States, 1901–1915.* Chapel Hill: University of North Carolina Press.

Harrington, Michael. 1962. *The Other America: Poverty in the United States.* New York: Macmillan.

Harris, David R. 2002. "Does It Matter How We Measure? Racial Classification And The Characteristics Of Multiracial Youth." In *The New Race Question: How The Census Counts Multiracial Individuals,* edited by Joel Perlmann and Mary C. Waters. New York: Russell Sage Foundation.

Harris, William J. 1915. *Wealth, Debt, and Taxation, 1913.* Washington: U.S. Government Printing Office.

Harrison, Bennett, and Barry Bluestone. 1988. *The Great U-Turn: Corporate Restructuring and the Polarizing of America.* New York: Basic Books.

Harrison, Bennett, and Lucy Gorham. 1992. "What Happened to African-American Wages in the 1980s?" In *The Metropolis in Black and White,* edited by George C. Galster and Edward H. Hill. New Brunswick, N.J.: Center for Urban Policy Research.

Hartley, William B. 1969. *Estimation of the Incidence of Poverty in the United States, 1870–1914.* Madison: University of Wisconsin.

Harvey, Philip. 1989. *Securing the Right to Employment: Social Welfare Policy and the Unemployed in the United States.* Princeton, N.J.: Princeton University Press.

Hatton, Timothy J., and Jeffrey G. Williamson. 1998. *The Age of Mass Migration: Causes and Economic Impact.* New York: Oxford University Press.

Hauser, Robert M. 1993. "The Decline in College Entry Among African-Americans: Findings In Search of Explanations." In *Prejudice, Politics, and the American Dilemma,* edited by Paul M. Sniderman, Philip E. Tetlock, and Edward G. Carmines. Stanford, Calif.: Stanford University Press.

Havighurst, Robert J., and J. Stiles Lindley. 1960–1961. "National Policy for Alienated Youth." *Phi Delta Kappan* XLII: 286–88.

Hayden, Delores. 2003. *Building Suburbia: Green Fields and Urban Growth, 1820–2000.* New York: Pantheon.

Hays, Samuel. 1957. *The Response to Industrialism.* Chicago: University of Chicago Press.

He, Wan. 2002. *The Older Foreign-Born Population in the United States: 2000.* Washington: U.S. Census Bureau.

Heath, Andrew. 2002. "Teamsters: History of an Occupation, 1880–1990." Unpublished paper, University of Pennsylvania History 580, Philadelphia.

Hecker, Daniel E. 1998. "Earnings of College Graduates: Women Compared With Men. *Monthly Labor Review* 121(3): 62–71.

———. 1998. "How Hours of Work Affect Occupational Earnings." *Monthly Labor Review* 121(10): 8–18.

———. 2001. "Occupational Employment Projections to 2010." *Monthly Labor Review* 124 (11): 57–84.

Heckman, James J. 1989. "The Impact of Government on the Economic Status of Black Americans." In *The Question of Discrimination: Racial Inequality in the U.S. Labor Market,* edited by Steven Shulman and William Darity, Jr. Middletown, Conn.: Wesleyan University Press.

Heckman, James, and Brook Payner. 1989. "Determining the Impact of Federal

Anti-Discrimination Policy on the Economic Status of Blacks: A Study of South Carolina." *American Economic Review* 79(1): 138–77.

Heflin, Colleen M., and Mary Pattillo. 2002. "Kin Effects on Black-White Account and Home Ownership." *Sociological Inquiry* 72(2): 220–39.

Heim, Carol E. 2000. "Structural Changes: Regional and Urban." In *The Cambridge Economic History of the United States. The Twentieth Century,* edited by S. L. Engerman and R. E. Gallman. Cambridge: Cambridge University Press.

Helleiner, Eric. 1999. "Historicizing Territorial Currencies: Monetary Space and the Nation-state in North America." *Political Geography* 18(3): 309–39.

Henderson, Charles Richmond. 1909. "Are Modern Industry and City Life Unfavorable to the Family?" *American Journal of Sociology* 14(5): 668–80.

Henderson, Harold. 1993. "Cities Without Suburbs" (Book Review). *Planning* 59(7): 36–37.

Henretta, John C., and Richard T. Campbell. 1978. "Net Worth as an Aspect of Status." *American Journal of Sociology* 83(5): 1204–23.

Henripin, Jacques. 1972. *Trends and Factors of Fertility in Canada.* Ottawa: Statistics Canada.

Henwood, Doug. 2002. "Not Such a Good Year, 2001." *Left Business Observer* 103 (December 18): 4. Available at: http://www.leftbusinessobserver.com/IncPov01.html (accessed October 25, 2005).

———. 2003. *After the New Economy.* New York: New Press.

Herideen, Penelope E. 1998. *Policy, Pedagogy, and Social Inequality: Community College Student Realities in Post-Industrial America.* Critical Studies in Education and Culture. Westport, Conn.: Bergin & Garvey.

Hershberg, Theodore. 1981. *Philadelphia: Work, Space, Family, and Group Experience in the Nineteenth Century: Toward an Interdisciplinary History of the City.* New York: Oxford University Press.

Hickman, Christine B. 1996–1997. "The Devil and the One Drop Rule: Racial Categories, African Americans, and the U.S. Census." *Michigan Law Review* 95: 1161–265.

Higginbotham, Elizabeth. 1994. "Black Professional Women: Job Ceilings and Employment Sectors." In *Women of Color in U.S. Society*, edited by Maxine Baca Zinn and Bonnie Thornton Dill. Philadelphia, Pa.: Temple University Press.

———. 2001. *Too Much to Ask: Black Women in the Era of Integration.* Chapel Hill: University of North Carolina Press.

Higginbotham, Elizabeth and Lynn Weber. 1992. "Moving Up with Kin and Community: Upward Social Mobility for Black and White Women." *Gender & Society* 6(3): 416–40.

Higgins, Richard. 1991. "Older Cities See Large Growth in Population." *Boston Globe,* March 25, p. A1.

Higgs, Robert. 1989. "Black Progress and the Persistence of Racial Economic Inequalities." In *The Question of Discrimination: Racial Inequality in the U.S. Labor Market,* edited by Steve Shulman and William Darity, Jr. Middletown, Conn.: Wesleyan University Press.

Higham, John. 1955. *Strangers in the Land: Patterns of American Nativism, 1860–1925.* New Brunswick, N.J.: Rutgers University Press.

Hiles, David R. H. 1992. "Health Services: The Real Job Machine. "*Monthly Labor Review* 115(11): 3–16.

Hill, Herbert. 1989. "Black Labor and Affirmative Action: An Historical Perspective." In *The Question of Discrimination: Racial Inequality in the U.S. Labor Market*, edited by Steve Shulman and William Darity, Jr. Middletown, Conn.: Wesleyan University Press.

Hine, Darlene Clark. 1982. "The Ethel Johns Report: Black Women in the Nursing Profession, 1925." *The Journal of Negro History* 67(3): 212–28.

———. 1989. *Black Women in White: Racial Conflict and Cooperation in the Nursing Profession, 1890–1950*. Bloomington: Indiana University Press.

Hirsch, Arnold R. 1983. *Making the Second Ghetto: Race and Housing in Chicago, 1940–1960*. New York: Cambridge University Press.

Hirsch, B., and E. Schumacher. 1992. "Labor Earnings, Discrimination, and the Racial Composition of Jobs." *Journal of Human Resources* 27: 602–28.

Hirschman, Charles, Philip Kasinitz, and Josh DeWind, eds. 1999. *The Handbook of International Migration*. New York: Russell Sage Foundation.

Hirschman, Charles, and Ellen Kraly. 1988. "Immigrants, Minorities, and Earnings in the United States in 1950." *Ethnic & Racial Studies* 11(3): 332–65.

Hobbs, Frank, and Nicole Stoops. 2002. "Demographic Trends in the Twentieth Century." In *Census 2000 Special Reports*. Series CENSR–4. U S. Census Bureau. Washington: U.S. Government Printing Office.

Hochschild, Jennifer. 2002. "Multiple Racial Identifiers In The 2000 Census, And Then What? In *The New Race Question: How The Census Counts Multiracial Individuals*, edited by Joel Perlmann and Mary C. Waters. New York: Russell Sage Foundation.

Hodgson, Godfrey. 2004. *More Equal Than Others: America From Nixon To The New Century*. Princeton, N.J.: Princeton University Press.

Hoelter, Lynette F., and Dawn E. Stauffer. 2002. "What Does it Mean to Be 'Just Living Together' in the New Millennium? An Overview." In *Just Living Together: Implications of Cohabitation on Families, Children, and Social Policy*, edited by A. Booth and A. C. Crouter. Mahwah, N.J.: Lawrence Erlbaum Associates.

Hogan, Dennis P., David I. Eggebeen, and Clifford C. Clogg. 1993. "The Structure of Intergenerational Exchange in American Families." *American Journal of Sociology* 98(6): 1428–58.

Hogan, Richard, Meesook Kim, and Carolyn Perrucci. 1997. "Racial Inequality in Men's Employment and Retirement Earnings." *Sociological Quarterly* 38(3): 431–38.

Hollinger, David A. 1995. *Postethnic America*. New York: Basic Books.

———. 2003. "Amalgamation and Hypodescent: The Question of Ethnoracial Mixture in the History of the United States." *American Historical Review* 108(5): 1363–90.

Holzer, Harry. 1996. *What Employers Want: Job Prospects for Less-Educated Workers*. New York: Russell Sage Foundation.

Hooker, Edith Houghton. 1921. *The Laws of Sex*. Boston, Mass.: Richard D. Badger.

Horton, Hayward Derrick. 1992. "Race and Wealth: A Demographic Analysis of Black Ownership." *Sociological Inquiry* 62(4): 480–89.

———. 1995. "Population Change and the Employment Status of College Educated Blacks." *Research in Race & Ethnic Relations* 8: 99–114.

Hout, Michael. 1997. "Inequality at the Margins: The Effects of Welfare, the Minimum Wage, and Tax Credits on Low-Wage Labor." *Politics & Society* 25(4): 513–24.

Howard, Christopher. 1997. *The Hidden Welfare State: Tax Expenditures and Social Policy in the United States*. Princeton, N.J.: Princeton University Press.

Howe, Frederic C. 1914. *The City, the Hope of Democracy*. New York: Charles Scribner's Sons.

Hsueh, Sheri, and Marta Tienda. 1995. "Earnings Consequences of Employment Instability among Minority Men. *Research in Social Stratification & Mobility* 14: 39–69.

Hunt, Milton B. 1910. "The Housing of Non-Family Groups of Men in Chicago." *American Journal of Sociology* 16(2): 145–70.

Hunter, Robert. 1904. *Poverty*, reprint ed. New York: Harper and Row. First published 1904 by Macmillan

Huntington, Samuel P. 2004. "The Hispanic Challenge." *Foreign Policy* 141 (March/April).

———. 2004. "*Who Are We? Challenges to America's National Identity*. New York: Simon & Schuster.

Hutchinson, E. P. 1956. *Immigrants and Their Children, 1850–1950*. New York: John Wiley & Sons.

Hvidt, Kristian. 1975. *Flight to America: The Social Background of 300,000 Danish Emigrants*. New York: Academic Press.

———. 1976. *Danes Go West: A Book About Emigration to America*. Skorping, Denmark: Rebild National Park Society.

Idson, Todd L., and Hollis F. Price. 1992. "An Analysis of Wage Differentials by Gender and Ethnicity in the Public Sector." *The Review of Black Political Economy* 20: 75–97.

Ihlanfeldt, Keith R., and David L. Sjoquist. 1991. "The Role of Space in Determining the Occupations of Black and White Workers." *Regional Science and Urban Economics* 21(2): 295–315.

Ilg, Randy E., and Steven E. Haugen. 2000. "Earnings and Employment Trends in the 1990s." *Monthly Labor Review* 123(3): 21–33.

Inhaber, Herbert, and Sidney Carroll. 1992. *How Rich is Too Rich? Income and Wealth in America*. New York: Praeger.

Institute for American Values. Available at: http://www.americanvalues.org/index.html (accessed October 25, 2005).

International Monetary Fund. April 12, 2000 (corrected January 2002). "Globalization: Threat or Opportunity?" Issue Brief. Washington, D.C.: International Monetary Fund. Available at: http://www.imf.org/external/np/exr/ib/2000/041200.htm (accessed October 25, 2005).

Inter-University Consortium for Political and Social Research (ICPSR). 197-. "Historical, Demographic, Economic, and Social Data: The United States [computer file]." Ann Arbor, Mich.: ICPSR.

Jackman, Mary R., and Robert W. Jackman. 1980. "Racial Inequalities in Home Ownership." *Social Forces* 58(4): 1221–33.

Jackson, Kenneth T. 1985. *Crabgrass Frontier: The Suburbanization of the United States*. New York: Oxford University Press.

———. 1991. "The View From the Periphery." *New York Times*, September 22, BR11.

Jackson, Monica. 1990. "And We Still Rise: African-American Women and the U.S. Labor Market." *Feminist Issues* 10(2): 55–63.

Jacobs, Jerry A. 1995. "Women's Entry Into Management: Trends in Earnings, Authority, and Values Among Salaried Managers." In *Gender Inequality at Work*, edited by J. A. Jacobs. Thousand Oaks, Calif.: Sage Publications.

———. 1996. "Gender Inequality and Higher Education." *Annual Review of Sociology* 22: 153–85.

Jacobs, Jerry A., and Ronnie J. Steinberg. 1995. "Further Evidence on Compensating Differentials and the Gender Wage Gap." In *Gender Inequality at Work*, edited by J. A. Jacobs. Thousand Oaks, Calif.: Sage Publications.

Jacobson, Jonathan, Cara Olsen, Jennifer King Rice, and Stephen Sweetland. 2001. *Educational Achievement and Black-White Inequality*. Washington, D.C.: National Center for Education Statistics.

Jacobson, Matthew Frye. 1998. *Whiteness of a Different Color: European Immigrants and the Alchemy of Race*. Cambridge, Mass.: Harvard University Press.

———. 2002. "History, Historicity, And The Census Count By Race." In *The New Race Question: How The Census Counts Multiracial Individuals*, edited by Joel Perlmann and Mary C. Waters. New York: Russell Sage Foundation.

Jacoby, Tamar, ed. 2004. *Reinventing the Melting Pot: The New Immigrants and What it Means To Be An American*. New York: Basic Books.

Jargowsky, Paul A. 1997. *Poverty and Place: Ghettos, Barrios, and the American City*. New York: Russell Sage Foundation.

———. 2003. *Stunning Progress, Hidden Problems: The Dramatic Decline of Concentrated Poverty in the 1990s*. Washington, D.C.: Brookings Institution Press.

Jaynes, David Gerald, and Robin M. Williams, Jr., eds. 1989. *A Common Destiny: Blacks and American Society*. Washington, D.C.: National Academy Press.

Jaynes, Gerald D. 1990. "The Labor Market Status of Black Americans: 1939–1985." *Journal of Economic Perspectives* 4(4): 9–24.

Jencks, Christopher. 1987. "The Politics of Income Measurement." In *The Politics of Numbers*, edited by W. Alonso and P. Starr. New York: Russell Sage Foundation.

———. 2001a. "Who Should Get In?" *New York Review of Books*, November 29, 2001. Available at: http://www.nybooks.com/articles/14868 (accessed October 24, 2005).

———. 2001b. "Who Should Get In?" Part II. *New York Review of Books*, December 20, 2001. Available at: http://www.nybooks.com/articles/14942 (accessed October 24, 2005).

Jencks, Christopher, and Paul E. Peterson, eds. 1991. *The Urban Underclass*. Washington, D.C.: Brookings Institution.

Jennings, James. 1991. "Persistent Poverty in the United States: Review of Theories and Explanations." In *A New Introduction to Poverty: The Role of Race, Power, and Politics*, edited by L. Kushnick and J. Jennings. New York: New York University Press.

Jensen, Leif. 2001. "The Demographic Diversity of Immigrants and Their Children." In *Ethnicities: Children of Immigrants in America*, edited by R. G. Rumbaut and A. Portes. Berkeley and New York: University of California Press and Russell Sage Foundation.

Jensen, Leif, David J. Eggebeen, and Daniel T. Lichter. 1993. "Child Poverty and the Ameliorative Effects of Public Assistance." *Social Science Quarterly* 74(3): 542–59.

Johnson, James H., Jr., Karen D. Johnson-Webb, and Walter C. Farrell, Jr. 1999. "Newly Emerging Hispanic Communities in the United States: A Spatial Analysis of Settlement Patterns, In-Migration Fields, and Social Receptivity." In *Immigration and Opportunity: Race, Ethnicity, and Employment in the United States,* edited by F. D. Bean and S. Bell-Rose. New York: Russell Sage Foundation.

Johnston, David Cay. 1995. "The Servant Class Is at the Counter." *New York Times,* August 28, 1995. Available at: http://select.nytimes.com/gst/abstract .html?res=F60616FD3F5A0C748EDDA10894DD494D81 (accessed October 24, 2005).

———. 2003. *Perfectly Legal: The Covert Campaign to Rig Our Tax System to Benefit the Super Rich—and Cheat Everyone Else.* New York: Portfolio.

Jones, Barbara A. P. 1986. "Black Women and Labor Force Participation: An Analysis of Sluggish Growth Rates." In *Slipping Through the Cracks: The Status of Black Women,* edited by Margaret C. Simms and Julianne Malveaux. New Brunswick: Transaction Press.

Jones, Jacqueline. 1985. *Labor of Love, Labor of Sorrow: Black Women, Work and the Family from Slavery to the Present.* New York: Basic Books.

———. 1993. "Southern Diaspora: Origins of the Northern 'Underclass.'" In *The "Underclass" Debate: Views from History,* edited by M. B. Katz. Princeton, N.J.: Princeton University Press.

———. 1998. *American Work: Four Centuries of Black and White Labor.* New York: W. W. Norton.

Jones, Nicholas A., and Amy Symens Smith. 2001. "The Two or More Race Population: 2000" Washington: U.S. Census Bureau. Available at: http://www.census.gov/prod/2001pubs/c2kbr01-6.pdf (accessed October 25, 2005).

Juhn, Chinhui. 2000. "Black-White Employment Differential in a Tight Labor Market." In *Prosperity for All? The Economic Boom and African Americans,* edited by Robert Cherry and William M. Rodgers. New York: Russell Sage Foundation.

Juhn, Chinhui, Kevin M. Murphy, and Brooks Pierce. 1993. "Wage Inequality and the Rise in Returns to Skill." *The Journal of Political Economy* 101(3): 410–42.

Jurand, Sara Hoffman. 2003. "Courts Expand Troxel Precedent Beyond Grandparent Cases." *Trial* 39(2): 83–85.

Kadaba, Linda S. 2003. "Retirees Altering Life in Suburbs." *Philadelphia Inquirer,* July 21, 2003.

———. 2004. "Singles on the Move? Yes, to the Suburbs." *Philadelphia Inquirer,* April 13, 2004, p. 1.

Kahlenberg, R. D. 1996. *The Remedy: Class, Race, and Affirmative Action.* New York: Basic Books.

Kallen, Horace M. 1998. *Culture and Democracy in the United States.* New Brunswick and London: Transaction Books. First published 1924 by Boni and Liveright.

Katz, Bruce. 1988. "Reviving Cities: Think Metropolitan." Policy Brief 33. Washington, D.C.: Brookings Institution.

Katz, Bruce, and Robert E. Lang. 2003. "Introduction." In *Redefining Urban and Suburban America,* edited by B. Katz and R. E. Lang. Washington, D.C.: Brookings Institution Press.

———, eds. 2003. *Redefining Urban and Suburban America: Evidence From Census 2000*. Washington, D.C.: Brookings Institution Press.

Katz, Lawrence F., and Kevin M. Murphy. 1992. "Changes in Relative Wages, 1963–1987: Supply and Demand Factors." *Quarterly Journal of Economics* 107(1): 35–78.

Katz, Michael B. 1968. *The Irony of Early School Reform: Educational Innovation in Mid-Nineteenth Century Massachusetts*. Reissued with a new introduction by Teachers College Press, 2001 ed. Cambridge, Mass.: Harvard University Press.

———, et al. 1983. "School Attendance in Philadelphia, 1850–1900." Working Paper No. 3. "The Organization of Work, Schooling, and Family Life in Philadelphia, 1838–1920." Final Report. NEI Grant No. 9-0173.

———. 1987. *Reconstructing American Education*. Cambridge, Mass.: Harvard University Press.

———, ed. 1993. *The "Underclass" Debate: Views from History*. Princeton, N.J.: Princeton University Press.

———. 1995. *Improving Poor People: the Welfare State, the "Underclass," and Urban Schools as History*. Princeton, N.J.: Princeton University Press.

———. 1996. *In the Shadow of the Poorhouse: A Social History of Welfare in America*. Tenth Anniversary ed. New York: Basic Books.

———. 2001. *The Price of Citizenship: Redefining the American Welfare State*. New York: Metropolitan Books.

———. 2001. "Towards a Classification of Industries in 1910." America at the Millennium Project. Working Paper 5. Philadelphia: University of Pennsylvania. Available at: http://www.sp2.upenn.edu/america2000.

Katz, Michael B., Michael J. Doucet, and Mark J. Stern. 1982. *The Social Organization of Early Industrial Capitalism*. Cambridge, Mass.: Harvard University Press.

Katz, Michael B., and Yansong Lu. 2001. "Property Ownership in the Early Twentieth Century: America at the Millennium Project." Philadelphia: University of Pennsylvania. Available at: http://www.sp2.upenn.edu/america2000.

Katz, Michael B., and Christoph Sachsse. 1996. "Introduction." In *The Mixed Economy of Social Welfare*, edited by M. B. Katz and C. Sachsse. Baden-Baden: Nomos.

Katz, Michael, and Mark J. Stern. 2000. "Comparing the socio-economic standing of early and late 20th century immigrants: occupation, property ownership, and English ability among Italians, Poles, Russians, Jews, Mexicans, and other Latin Americans, and Koreans, 1900–2000." America at the Millennium Project. Philadelphia: University of Pennsylvania. http://www.sp2.upenn.edu/america2000.

———. 2002. *Technical Notes on the Measurement of Poverty Since 1940: America at the Millennium Project*. Philadelphia: University of Pennsylvania.

———. 2004. "1940s to the Present." In *Poverty in the United States: An Encyclopedia of History, Politics, and Poverty*, edited by Gwendolyn Mink and Alice O'Connor. Santa Barbara, Calif.: ABC-CLIO.

Katz, Michael B., Mark J. Stern, and Jamie L. Fader. 2005. "The New African American Inequality." *Journal of American History* 92(1): 75–108.

———. 2005. "Women and the Paradox of Inequality in Twentieth Century America." *Journal of Social History* 39(1): 65–88.

Kaufman, Robert L. 2001. "Race and Labor Market Segmentation." In *Sourcebook of Labor Markets: Evolving Structures and Processes,* edited by Ivar Berg aand Arne L. Kalleberg. New York: Kluwer Academic/Plenum.

———. 2002. "Assessing Alternative Perspectives on Race and Sex Employment Segregation." *American Sociological Review* 67(4): 547–72.

Kay, Jane Holz. 1991. "Edge City: Life on the New Frontier (book review)." *The Nation,* October 14, 454–55.

Kazal, Russell A. 1995. "Revisiting Assimilation: The Rise, Fall, and Reappraisal of a Concept in American Ethnic History." *American Historical Review* 100(April): 437–71.

———. 2004. *Becoming Old Stock: The Paradox of German-American Identity.* Princeton, N.J.: Princeton University Press.

Keister, Lisa A. 2000. "Race and Wealth Inequality: The Impact of Racial Differences in Asset Ownership on the Distribution of Household Wealth." *Social Science Research* 29(4): 477–502.

———. 2000. *Wealth in America: Trends in Wealth Inequality.* New York: Cambridge University Press.

Keller, Morton. 1977. *Affairs of State: Public Life in Late Nineteenth Century America.* Cambridge, Mass.: Harvard University Press.

Kellor, Frances A. 1918. "What is Americanization?" *Yale Review* 8: 32–48.

Kellough, J. Edward. 1990. "Federal Agencies and Affirmative Action for Blacks and Women." *Social Science Quarterly* 71(1): 83–92.

Kellough, J. Edward, and Euel Elliott. 1992. "Demographic and Organizational Influences on Racial/Ethnic and Gender Integration in Federal Agencies." *Social Science Quarterly* 73(1): 1–11.

Kessler-Harris, Alice. 1982. *Out to Work: A History of Wage-Earning Women in the United States.* New York: Oxford University Press.

———. 2001. *In Pursuit of Equity: Women, Men, and the Quest for Economic Citizenship in 20th-Century America.* New York: Oxford University Press.

Kett, Joseph. 1977. *Rites of Passage: Adolescence in America, 1790 to the Present.* New York: Basic Books.

Keyssar, Alexander. 1986. *Out of Work: The First Century of Unemployment in Massachusetts.* New York: Cambridge University Press.

Kim, Illsoo. 1981. *The New Urban Immigrants.* Princeton, N.J.: Princeton University Press.

King, Desmond. 1995. *Separate and Unequal: Black Americans and the U.S. Federal Government.* New York: Oxford University Press.

———. 2000. *Making Americans: Immigration, Race, and the Origins of the Diverse Democracy.* Cambridge, Mass.: Harvard University Press.

King, Mary C. 1992. "Occupational Segregation by Race and Sex, 1940–88." *Monthly Labor Review* 115(4): 30–37.

King, Mary C., and Todd Easton. 2000. "Should Black Women and Men Live in the Same Place? An Intermetropolitan Assessment of Relative Labor Market Success." *The Review of Black Political Economy* 27(3): 9–34.

King, Miriam, Steven Ruggles, and Matthew Sobek. 2003. Integrated Public Use Microdata Series, Current Population Survey: Preliminary Version 0.1. Minneapolis: Minnesota Population Center, University of Minnesota. Available at: www.ipums.org/cps (accessed October 25, 2005).

Klein, Rick. 2004. "Vote Ties Civil Unions to Gay-Marriage Ban." *Boston.com* [*Boston Globe*], March 30, 2004.

Kleppner, Paul. 1985. *Chicago Divided: The Making of a Black Mayor.* DeKalb: Northern Illinois University Press.

Kline, Ronald R. 2000. *Consumers in the Country: Technology and Social Change in Rural America.* Baltimore, Md.: Johns Hopkins University Press.

Klinenberg, Eric. 2002. *Heat Wave: A Social Autopsy of Disaster in Chicago.* Chicago: University of Chicago Press.

Kmec, Julie A. 2003. "Minority Job Concentration and Wages." *Social Problems* 50(1): 38–59.

Kolchin, Peter. 2002. "Whiteness Studies: The New History of Race in America." *Journal of American History* 89(1): 154–73.

Kolesnikoff, Vladimir S. 1940. "Standard Classification of Industries in the United States." *Journal of the American Statistical Association* 35(209): 65–73.

Kollmann, Wolfgang, and Peter Marschalck. 1973. "German Emigration to the United States." *Perspectives in American History* VII: 499–556.

Koretz, Daniel. 1990. *Trends in Postsecondary Enrollment.* Santa Monica, Calif.: Rand Corporation.

Kotlikoff, Laurence, and Lawrence Summers. 1981. "The Role of Intergenerational Transfers in Aggregate Capital Accumulation." *Journal of Political Economy* 89(4): 706–32.

Kovar, Lillian Cohen. 1996. *Here to Complete Dr. King's Dream: The Triumphs and Failures of a Community College.* Lanham, Md.: University Press of America.

Kreider, Rose M., and Jason M. Fields. 2002. *Number, Timing, and Duration of Marriages and Divorces: 1996.* Current Population Reports, P70-80. Washington: U.S. Census Bureau.

Krislov, Samuel. 1967. The Negro in Federal Employment: The Quest for Equal Opportunity. Minneapolis: University of Minnesota Press.

Kritz, Mary M. and Douglas T. Gruak. 2004. "Immigration and a Changing America. The American People: Census 2000 Series. New York and Washington, D.C. : Russell Sage Foundation and Population Reference Bureau.

Kronus, Sidney. 1971. *The Black Middle Class.* Columbus, Ohio: Merrill.

Krugman, Paul. 2004. "Social Security Scares." *New York Times*, March 5, 2004. Available at: http://select.nytimes.com/gst/abstract.html?res=F00D15F93B5B0C768CDDAA0894DC404482 (accessed October 24, 2005).

Kull, Andrew. 1992. *The Color-Blind Constitution.* Cambridge, Mass.: Harvard University Press.

Kuttner, Robert. 1997. *Everything for Sale: The Virtues and Limits of Markets.* New York: Knopf.

Kuznets, Simon. 1955. "Economic Growth and Income Inequality." *American Economic Review* 45(1): 1–28.

———. 1975. "Immigration of Russian Jews to the United States: Background and Structure." *Perspectives in American History* IX: 35–126.

Kuznets, Simon, Ann R. Miller, and Richard A. Easterlin. 1960. "Population Redistribution and Economic Growth: United States, 1870–1950." *Analyses of Economic Change*, vol. II. Philadelphia, Pa.: American Philosophical Society.

Kwolek-Folland, Angel. 1991. "Gender, Self, and Work in the Life Insurance Industry, 1880–1930." In *Work Engendered: Toward a New History of American Labor*, edited by A. Baron. Ithaca, N.Y.: Cornell University Press.

Labor Research Online. 2003. Labor Research Associates. Available at: http://www.lraonline.org (cited and accessed January 2, 2003).

LaFeber, Walter. 1998. *The New Empire: An Interpretation of American Expansion, 1860–1898*, 35th anniversary ed. Ithaca, N.Y.: Cornell University Press.

Lamoreaux, Naomi. 2000. "Entrepreneurship, Organization, and Economic Concentration." In *The Cambridge Economic History of the United States*, edited by S. L. Engerman and R. E. Gallman. Cambridge and New York: Cambridge University Press.

Land, Kenneth C., and Stephen T. Russell. 1996. "Wealth Accumulation Across the Life Course: Stability and Change in Sociodemographic Covariate Structures of Net Worth Data in the Survey of Income and Program Participation." *Social Science Research* 25(4): 423–62.

Landry, Bart. 1987. *The New Black Middle Class*. Berkeley: University of California Press.

Landry, Bart, and Margaret Platt Jendrek. 1978. "The Employment of Wives in Middle-Class Black Families." *Journal of Marriage and the Family* 40(4): 787–97.

Lang, Robert E., and Patrick A. Simmons. 2003. "'Boomburbs': The Emergence of Large, Fast-Growing Suburban Cities." In *Redefining Urban and Suburban America: Evidence From Census 2000*, edited by B. Katz and R. E. Lang. Washington, D.C.: Brookings Institution.

Lapidus, Jane, and Deborah M. Figart. 1998. "Remedying 'Unfair Acts': U.S. Pay Equity by Race and Gender." *Feminist Economics* 4(3): 7–28.

Laslett, Peter. 1973. "Age of Menarche in Europe Since the Eighteenth Century." In *The Family in History*, edited by Theodore K. Rabb and Robert I. Rothberg. New York: Harper and Row.

Law Office of David C. Codell, Lambda Legal Defense and Education Fund, National Center for Lesbian Rights. 2003. "Brief of Amici Curiae In Opposition To Motion For Preliminary Injunction." "Thomasson v. Davis," case no. BC 302928. Los Angeles: Superior Court of the State of California for the County of Los Angeles. Available at: http://www.lambdalegal.org/binary-data/LAMBDA_PDF/pdf/259.pdf (accessed October 24, 2005).

Lazear, Edward P,. and Sherwin Rosen. 1990. "Male-Female Wage Differentials in Job Ladders. *Journal of Labor Economics* 8(1): S106–S123.

Lectlaw.com. 1996. "Defense of Marriage Act. 1996. H.R. 3396: Summary/Analysis." http://www.lectlaw.com/files/leg23.htm.

Lee, Jennifer. 1998. "Cultural Brokers: Race-Based Hiring in Inner-City Neighborhoods." *American Behavioral Scientist* 41(7): 927–37.

Lee, Valerie E., and Kenneth A. Frank. 1990. "Students' Characteristics that Facilitate the Transfer from Two-Year to Four-Year Colleges." *Sociology of Education* 63(3): 178–93.

Leloudis, James L. 1996. *Schooling the New South: Pedagogy, Self, and Society in North Carolina, 1880–1920*. Chapel Hill: University of North Carolina Press.

Lemann, Nicholas. 1991. *The Promised Land: The Great Black Migration and How It Changed America*. New York: Alfred A. Knopf.

Leo, Joe. 1992. "Sneer Not at 'Ozzie and Harriet.'" *U.S. News and World Report.* September 14, online edition.

Leonard, Jonathan S. 1990. "The Impact of Affirmative Action Regulation and Equal Employment Law on Black Employment." *Journal of Economic Perspectives* 4(4): 47–63.

Lescohier, Don D. 1923. *The Labor Market.* New York: The Macmillan Company.

Levine, Chester, Laurie Salmon, and Daniel H. Weinberg. 1999. "Revising the Standard Occupational Classification System." *Monthly Labor Review* 122(5): 36–45.

Levy, Frank. 1995. "Incomes and Income Inequality." In *State of the Union: America in the 1990s.* vol. I: *Economic Trends,* edited by R. Farley. New York: Russell Sage Foundation.

———. 1998. "Occupational Change: Can the Economy Still Produce Good Jobs and, If So, Who Gets Them? In *The New Dollars and Dreams: American Incomes and Economic Change.* New York: Russell Sage Foundation.

Levy, Frank and Richard Murnane. 1992. "U.S. Earnings Levels and Earnings Inequality: A Review of Recent Trends and Proposed Explanations." *Journal of Economic Literature* 30(3): 1333–81.

Lewin, Tamar. 2005. "Financially-Set Grandparents Help Keep Families Afloat, Too." *New York Times.* July 14. Available at: http://www/nytimes.com/2205/07/14/national/14grandparents.html.

Lewis, Gregory B. 1988. "Progress Toward Racial and Sexual Equality in the Federal Civil Service?: *Public Administration Review* 48: 700–7.

Lewis, H. G. 1963. *Unionism and Relative Wages in the United States: An Empirical Inquiry.* Chicago and London: University of Chicago Press.

———. 1996. "Gender Integration of Occupations in the Federal Civil Service: Extent and Effects on Male-Female Earnings." *Industrial and Labor Relations Review* 49(3): 472–83.

Liberman, Myron. 1993. *Public Education: An Autopsy.* Cambridge, Mass.: Harvard University Press.

Licht, Walter. 1995. *Industrializing America: The Nineteenth Century.* Baltimore, Md.: Johns Hopkins University Press.

Lichtenstein, Nelson. 2002. *State of the Union: A Century of American Labor.* Princeton, N.J.: Princeton University Press.

Lichter, Daniel.T. 1988. "Racial Differences in Underemployment in American Cities." *American Journal of Sociology* 93(4): 771–92.

Lieberman, Robert C. 1988. *Shifting the Color Line: Race and the American Welfare State.* Cambridge, Mass.: Harvard University Press.

Lieberson, Stanley. 1963. *Ethnic Patterns in American Cities.* New York: Free Press of Glencoe.

———. 1980. *A Piece of the Pie: Blacks and White Immigrants Since 1880.* Berkeley: University of California Press.

Lieberson, Stanley, and Mary Waters. 1988. *From Many Strands: Ethnic and Racial Groups in Contemporary America.* New York: Russell Sage Foundation.

Light, Ivan, and Edna Bonacich. 1988. *Immigrant Entrepreneurs: Koreans in Los Angeles, 1965–1982.* Berkeley: University of California Press.

Light, Ivan, and Carolyn Rosenstein. 1995. *Race, Ethnicity, and Entrepreneurship in Urban America.* New York: Aldine de Gruyter.

Lim, Nelson. 2001. "On the Back of Blacks? Immigrants and the Fortunes of African Americans." In *Strangers at the Gates: New Immigrants in Urban America*, edited by Roger Waldinger. Berkeley: University of California Press.

Lin, Yangjing, and W. Paul Vogt. 1996. "Occupational Outcomes for Students Earning Two-Year College Degrees: Income, Status, and Equity. *Journal of Higher Education* 67(4): 446–75.

Lipset, Seymour Martin. 1992. "Affirmative Action and the American Creed." *Wilson Quarterly.* Winter: 52–62.

Lipsey, Robert E. 2000. "U.S. Trade and the Balance of Payments, 1800–1913." In *The Cambridge Economic History of the United States,* edited by S. L. Engerman and R. E. Gallman. Cambridge: Cambridge University Press.

Liptak, Adam. 2004. "Caution in Court for Gay Rights Groups." *New York Times.* November 12, 2004, p. A16. Available at: http://query.nytimes.com/gst/abstract.html?res=F50C17FF3D5B0C718DDDA80994DC404482 (accessed October 25, 2005).

Logan, John. 2001. "The New Ethnic Enclaves in America's Suburbs." Lewis Mumford Center for Comparative Urban and Regional Research. Albany: State University of New York.

———. 2002. "Regional Divisions Dampen '90s Prosperity." Lewis Mumford Center for Comparative Urban and Regional Research. Albany: State University of New York.

———. 2002. "Separate and Unequal: The Neighborhood Gap for Blacks and Hispanics in Metropolitan America." Lewis Mumford Center for Comparative Urban and Regional Research. Albany: State University of New York.

Logan, John, and Richard D. Alba. 1999. "Minority Niches and Immigrant Enclaves in New York and Los Angeles: Trends and Impacts." In *Immigration and Opportunity: Race, Ethnicity, and Employment in the United States,* edited by Frank D. Bean and Stephanie Bell-Rose. New York: Russell Sage Foundation.

Lomotey, Kofi, ed. 1990. *Going to School: The African-American Experience.* Albany: State University of New York Press.

Long, James E. 1976. Employment Discrimination in the Federal Sector. *Journal of Human Resources* 11(1): 86–97.

Long, James E. and Steven B. Caudill. 1992. "Racial Differences in Homeownership and Housing Wealth, 1970–1986." *Economic Inquiry* 30(January): 83–100.

Lopez, David E. 1999. "Social and Linguistic Aspects of Assimilation Today." In *The Handbook of International Migration: The American Experience,* edited by C. Hirschman, P. Kasinitz and J. DeWind. New York: Russell Sage Foundation.

Lopez, David E., and Ricardo D. Stanton-Salazar. 2001. "Mexican Americans: A Second Generation at Risk." In *Ethnicities: Children of Immigrants in America,* edited by Ruben G. Rumbaut and Alejandro Portes. Berkeley and New York: University of California Press and Russell Sage Foundation.

Lorence, Jon. 1992. "Service Sector Growth and Metropolitan Occupational Sex Segregation." *Work and Occupations* 19(2): 128–56.

Lowell, B. Lindsay, and Robert Suro. 2002. *How Many Undocumented: The Numbers Behind The U.S.–Mexican Immigration Talks.* Washington, D.C.: The Pew Hispanic Center.

Lozano-Ascencio, Fernando, Bryan R. Robert, and Frank D. Bean. 1999. "The Interconnections of Internal and International Migration: The Case of the United

States and Mexico." In *Migration and Transnational Social Spaces*, edited by L. Preis. Aldershot, Hampshire: Ashgate Publishing.

Lubove, Roy. 1986. *The Struggle for Social Security 1900–1935*. Pittsburgh: University of Pittsburgh Press.

Luebke, Frederick C. 1991. "Ethnic Group Settlement on the Great Plains." In *Immigrants on the Land: Agriculture, Rural Life, and Small Towns*, edited by G. E. Pozzetta. London: Garland.

Luxembourg Income Study (LIS) Key Figures. 2004. "Poverty Rates for Children by Family Types 2000." Syracuse, N.Y.: Luxembourg Income Study. Available at: http://www.lisproject.org/keyfigures.htm (accessed October 25, 2005).

Lynd, Robert S., and Helen Merrell Lynd. 1929. *Middletown: A Study in Modern American Culture*. New York: Harcourt, Brace, and World.

———. 1937. *Middletown in Transition: A Study in Cultural Conflicts*. New York: Harcourt, Brace, and World.

MacDonagh, Oliver. 1976. "The Irish Famine Emigration to the United States." *Perspectives in American History* X: 357–448.

MacGregor, Morris J., and Bernard C. Nalty, ed. 1994. *Blacks in the U.S. Armed Forces*. Wilmington, Del.: Scholarly Resources.

Madrick, Jeff. 2002. *Why Economies Grow: The Forces That Shape Prosperity and How We Can Get Them Working Again*. New York: Basic Books.

Mailman, Stanley. 1995. "California's Proposition 187 and Its Lessons." *New York Law Journal*, January 3, 1995, 3.

Marcelli, Enrico, and Wayne Cornelius. 2001. ""The Changing Profile of Mexican Migrants to the United States: New Evidence from California and Mexico." *Latin American Research Review* 36: 105–31.

Margo, Robert A. 1990. *Race and Schooling in the South, 1880–1950: An Economic History*. Chicago: University of Chicago Press.

———. 2000. "The Labor Force in the Nineteenth Century." In *The Cambridge Economic History of the United States. The Long Nineteenth Century*. Cambridge: Cambridge University Press.

Marini, Margaret M., and Pi-ling Fan. 1997. "The Gender Gap in Earnings at Career Entry." *American Sociological Review* 62(4): 588–604.

Markham, William T., Scott J. South, Charles M. Bonjean, and Judy Corder. 1985. "Gender and Opportunity in the Federal Bureaucracy." *American Journal of Sociology* 91(1): 129–50.

Marks, Carole C. 1995. "Separate Societies: Negotiating Race and Class in the '90s." *Sociological Focus* 28(1): 49–61.

Marmor, Theodore R., Fay Lomax Cook, and Stephen Scher. 1977. "Social Security Politics and the Conflicts between Generations: Are We Asking the Right Questions?" In *Social Security in the 21st Century*, edited by E. R. Kingson and J. H. Schulz. New York: Oxford University Press.

Marshall, C.J. 2003. Decision for "Hillary Goodridge and Others v. Department of Public Health and Another," case no. SJC-08860. Boston: Supreme Judicial Court of Massachusetts.

Marshall, Eliot. 1998. "DNA Studies Challenge the Meaning of Race." *Science* 282(5389): 654–55.

Marshall, T. H. 1992. "Citizenship and Social Class [1950]." In *Citizenship and So-*

cial Class, edited by T. H. Marshall and T. Bottomore. Concord, Mass.: Pluto Press.

Martellone, Anna Maria. 1984. "Italian Mass Emigration to the United States, 1876–1930: A Historical Survey." *Perspectives in American History* 1(New Series): 379–423.

Martin, Roscoe C. 1942. *The Growth of State Administration in Alabama.* Tuscaloosa: University of Alabama, Bureau of Public Administration.

Massey, Douglas S., and Nancy A. Denton. 1993. *American Apartheid: Segregation and the Making of the Underclass.* Cambridge, Mass.: Harvard University Press.

Massey, Douglas S., Jorge Durand, and Nolan J. Malone. 2002. *Beyond Smoke and Mirrors: Mexican Immigration in an Era of Economic Integration.* New York: Russell Sage Foundation.

Matthews, Glenna. 1998. "Cities Without Suburbs (review)." *Journal of Urban History* 25(1): 94–102.

Mauer, Marc. April 15–16, 1999. "The Crisis of the Young African American Male and the Criminal Justice System." Washington, D.C.: The Sentencing Project.

Maume, David. 1985. "Government Participation in the Local Economy and Race- and Sex-Based Earnings Inequality." *Social Problems* 32(3): 285–99.

Maurantonio, Nicole. 2002. "The Most Ancient of Crafts." Unpublished paper. University of Pennsylvania History 580, Philadelphia.

Mays, William E. 1968. *Sublette Revisited: Stability and Change in a Rural Kansas Community After a Quarter Century.* New York: Florham Park Press.

McCall, Leslie. 2001. *Complex Inequality: Gender, Class and Race in the New Economy.* New York and London: Routledge.

McDonald, Katrina Bell, and Thomas A. LaVeist. 2001. "Black Educational Advantage in the Inner City. *The Review of Black Political Economy* 29(1): 25–47.

McIntyre, Robert S. 1993. "Avoiding a Fiscal Dunkirk" (June 1, 1993). *The American Prospect Online Edition* 4(12). Available at: http://www.prospect.org/print/V4/12/mcintyre-r.html (accessed October 25, 2005).

McIntyre, Robert S., and T. D. Coo Nyguyen. 2000. "Corporate Income Taxes in the 1990s." Washington, D.C.: Institute on Taxation and Economic Policy.

McLafferty, Sara, and Valerie Preston. 1992. "Spatial Mismatch and Labor Market Segmentation for African-American and Latina Women." *Economic Geography* 68(4): 406–31.

McNamee, Stephen J., and Robert K. Miller, Jr. 1998. "Inheritance and Stratification." In *Inheritance and Wealth in America,* edited by Robert Miller and Stephen McNamee. New York: Plenum Press.

McSeeney, Edward F. 1924. "The Racial Contributions to the United States." In *The Jews and the Making of America,* edited by George Cohen. Boston, Mass.: Stratford.

Mead, Lawrence M. 1992. *The New Politics of Poverty: The Nonworking Poor in America.* New York: Basic Books.

Meinig, D. W. 2000. *The Shaping of America: A Geographical Perspective on 500 Years of History,* vol. 3. *Transcontinental America, 1850–1915.* New Haven, Conn.: Yale University Press.

Menchik, Paul L., and Nancy Ammon Jianakoplos. 1997. "Black-White Wealth Inequality: Is Inheritance the Reason?" *Economic Inquiry* 35: 428–42.

Mettler, Suzanne. 1998. *Dividing Citizens: Gender and Federalism in New Deal Public Policy.* Ithaca, N.Y.: Cornell University Press.

Milanovic, Branko. 2005. *Worlds Apart: Measuring International and Global Inequality.* Princeton, N.J.: Princeton University Press.

Miller, Andrew T., S. Phillip Morgan, and Antonio McDaniel. 1994. "Under the Same Roof: Family and Household Structure." In *After Ellis Island: Newcomers and Natives in the 1910 Census,* edited by S. C. Watkins. New York: Russell Sage Foundation.

Miller, Ann R. 1994. "The Industrial Affiliation of Workers: Differences by Nativity and Country of Origin." In *After Ellis Island: Newcomers and Natives in the 1910 Census,* edited by S. C. Watkins. New York: Russell Sage Foundation.

Miller, Herman P. 1920. *Smull's Legislative Hand Book and Manual of the State of Pennsylvania, 1920.* Harrisburg, Pa.: J. L. L. Kuhn, State Printers.

Miller, Ross. 1993. "Edge City: Life on the New Frontier (book review)." *The Journal of the Society of Architectural Historians* 52(3): 349–51.

Milligan, Susan. 2004. "Senate Rejects Move to Ban Gay Marriage: Amendment Vote Comes Up Short." *Boston.com [Boston Globe],* July 15.

Millman, Marcia. 1991. *Warm Hearts and Cold Cash: The Intimate Dynamics of Families and Money.* New York: Free Press.

Min, Pyong Gap. 1996. *Caught in the Middle: Korean Communities in New York and Los Angeles.* Los Angeles: University of California Press.

Minino, A. M., et al. 2002. "Deaths: Final Data for 2000." *National Vital Statistics Reports* 50, no. 15. Hyattsville, Md.: National Center for Health Statistics.

Mink, Gwendolyn. 1995. *The Wages of Motherhood: Inequality in the Welfare State, 1917–1942.* Ithaca, N.Y.: Cornell University Press.

Mintz, Steven, and Susan Kellogg. 1988. *Domestic Revolutions: A Social History of American Family Life.* New York: Free Press.

Mishel, Lawrence, Jared Bernstein, and Heather Boushey. 2003. *The State of Working America 2002/2003.* An Economic Policy Institute Book. Ithaca, N.Y.: ILR Press.

"The Mission." 2004. *The Multiracial Advocate,* July 10. Available at: http://www.multiracial.com (accessed August 2004).

Model, Suzanne. 1993. "The Ethnic Niche and the Structure of Opportunity: Immigrants and Minorities in New York City." In *The "Underclass" Debate: Views from History,* edited by Michael B. Katz. Princeton, N.J.: Princeton University Press.

Modell, John. 1989. *Into One's Own: From Youth to Adulthood In The United States 1920–1975.* Berkeley and Los Angeles: University of California Press.

Modell, John, Frank E. Furstenberg, Jr., and Theodore Hershberg. 1976. "Social Change and Transitions to Adulthood in Historical Perspective." *Journal of Family History* 1: 7–32.

Moffit, Robert. 1992. "Incentive Effects of the U.S. Welfare System: A Review." *Journal of Economic Literature* 30(1): 1–61.

Mohl, Raymond A. 1993. "Race and Space in the Modern City: Interstate-95 and the Black Community in Miami." In *Urban Policy in Twentieth-Century America,* edited by A. R. Hirsch and R. A. Mohl. New Brunswick, N.J.: Rutgers University Press.

Mollenkopf, John H. 1983. *The Contested City.* Princeton, N.J.: Princeton University Press.

Mollenkopf, John H., and Manuel Castells, eds. 1991. *Dual City: Restructuring New York.* New York: Russell Sage Foundation.

Monk-Turner, Elizabeth. 1990. "The Occupational Achievements of Community and Four-Year College Entrants." *American Sociological Review* 55(5): 719–25.

Monkkonen, Eric H. 1993. "Nineteenth-Century Institutions: Dealing with the Urban 'Underclass.'" In *The "Underclass" Debate: Views from History,* edited by M. B. Katz. Princeton, N.J.: Princeton University Press.

Mont, Daniel, Virginia Reno, and Catherine Hill. 2002. "Social Insurance for Survivors: Family Benefits from Social Security and Workers' Compensation." *Social Security Briefs,* no 12. Washington, D.C.: National Academy of Social Insurance.

Moore, J. Hampton. 1920. "First Annual Message of J. Hampton Moore, Mayor of Philadelphia, Containing the Reports of the Various Departments of the City of Philadelphia for the Year ending December 31, 1920." Philadelphia.

Morawska, Ewa. 1986. *For Bread With Butter.* New York: Cambridge University Press.

Morenoff, Jeffrey M., and Marta Tienda. 1997. "Underclass Neighborhoods in Temporal and Ecological Perspective: An Illustration from Chicago." *The Annals of the American Academy of Political and Social Science* 551(May): 59–72.

Moro, Andrea and Peter Norman. 2003. "Affirmative Action in a Competitive Economy." *Journal of Public Economics* 87(3): 567–94.

Moss, Philip I. 1988. "Employment Gains by Minorities, Women in Large City Government." *Monthly Labor Review:* 111.

Moss, Philip, and Chris Tilly. 1991. *Why Black Men Are Doing Worse in the Labor Market.* New York: Social Science Research Council.

———. 1996. "'Soft' Skills and Race: An Investigation of Black Men's Employment Problems." *Work and Occupations* 23(3): 252–76.

———. 2000. "How Labor-Market Tightness Affects Employer Attitudes and Actions Toward Black Job Applicants: Evidence from Employer Surveys." In *Prosperity for All? The Economic Boom and African Americans,* edited by Robert Cherry and William M. Rodgers. New York: Russell Sage Foundation.

Moulton, Brent R. 1990. "A Reexamination of the Federal-Private Wage Differential in the United States." *Journal of Labor Economics* 8(2): 270–93.

The Multiracial Activist. "About." Available at: http://www.multiracial.com/about.html (accessed October 25, 2005).

Mumford Center. 2001. "Ethnic Diversity Grows, Neighborhood Integration Lags Behind." Lewis Mumford Center. Albany: State University of New York. Available at: http://mumford.albany.edu/census/WholePop/WPreport/page1.html (accessed October 25, 2005).

Munch, Peter A. 1980. "Norwegians." In *Harvard Encyclopedia of American Ethnic Groups,* edited by Stephen Thernstrom. Cambridge, Mass.: Harvard University Press.

Munro, William Bennett. 1913. *The Government of American Cities.* New York: The Macmillan Company.

Murdock, George Peter. 1941. "Anthropology and Human Relations." *Sociometry* 4(2): 140–49.

————. 1949. *Social Structure*. New York: Macmillan.

Murphy, Dean. 2004. "California Supreme Court Rules Gay Unions Have No Standing." *New York Times*. August 13, 2004, online edition.

Murphy, John B. 1998. "Introducing the North American Industry Classification System." *Monthly Labor Review*: 43–47.

Murray, Charles. 1980. *Losing Ground: American Social Policy, 1950–1980*. New York: Basic Books.

Myers, Dowell. 1998. "Dimensions of Economic Adaptation by Mexican-Origin Men." In *Crossings: Mexican Immigration in Interdisciplinary Perspectives*, edited by M. Suarez-Orozco. Cambridge, Mass.: Harvard University Press.

Myers, Dowell, and Cynthia Cranford. 1998. "Temporal Differences in the Occupational Mobility of Immigrant and Native-born Latina Workers." *American Sociological Review* 63: 68–93.

Myers, Dowell, and Seong Woo Lee. 1998. "Immigrant Trajectories into Homeownership: a Temporal Analysis of Residential Assimilation." *International Migration Review* 32(3): 593–625.

Myrdal, Gunnar. 2002. *An American Dilemma: The Negro Problem and Modern Democracy*, 2 vols. New Brunswick, N.J.: Transaction Books [First published by Harper and Row 1944].

National Center for Health Statistics. 2003. "Health, United States 2003." Washington: U.S. Government Printing Office. http://www.cdc.gov/nchs/data/hus/hus03.pdf.

National Organization for Women. 2004. "Chronology of the Equal Rights Amendment, 1923–1996." Available at: http://www.now.org/issues/economic/cea/history.html (accessed October 25, 2005).

Neal, Derek A., and William R. Johnson. 1996. "The Role of Pre-Market Forces in Black-White Wage Differences." *Journal of Political Economy* 104(5): 869–95.

Neckerman, Kathryn M., and Joleen Kirschenman. 1991. "Hiring Strategies, Racial Bias, and Inner-city Workers." *Social Problems* 38(4): 433–47.

Nelli, Humbert S. 1980. "Italians." In *Harvard Encyclopedia of American Ethnic Groups*, edited by Stephan Thernstrom. Cambridge, Mass.: Harvard University Press.

Nettles, Michael T., A. Robert Theony, and Erica J. Gosman. 1986. "Comparative and Predictive Analyses of Black and White Students' College Achievement and Experiences." *The Journal of Higher Education* 57(3): 289–318.

News and Views. 1995. "Higher Education: So Far the Only Proven Force for Closing the Black-White Unemployment Gap." *The Journal of Blacks in Higher Education* 7(Fall): 18.

————. 1996. "The Racial Wealth Advantage in Access to Higher Education." *The Journal of Blacks in Higher Education* 11(fall): 34–36.

————. 1999a. "A College Diploma Adds Large Sums to Black Incomes but Makes Only Small Inroads in the Black-White Unemployment Gap." *The Journal of Blacks in Higher Education* 23(spring): 43.

————. 1999b. "Black Women Far Outdistance Black Men in Doctoral Degree Awards: But How are They Doing Compared to White Women?" *The Journal of Blacks in Higher Education* 26(winter): 69.

Newsome, Yvonne D., and F. Nii-Amoo Dodoo. 2002. "Reversal of Fortune: Explaining the Decline in Black Women's Earnings." *Gender & Society* 16(4): 442–64.

Ngai, Mae M. 1999. "The Architecture of Race in American Immigration Law." *Journal of American History* 86(1): 67–92.

———. 2004. *Impossible Subjects: Illegal Aliens and the Making of Modern America.* Princeton, N.J.: Princeton University Press.

Nicholas, Ruth. 1994. "Speaking Out On Women's Real Needs." *Marketing.* April 14, 1994, pp. 18–20.

Noble, Kenneth. 1986. "End of Forced Retirement Means a Lot to a Few." *New York Times*, October 26, 1986, p. 5.

Nobles, Melissa. 2000. *Shades of Citizenship: Race and the Census in Modern Politics.* Stanford, Calif.: Stanford University Press.

Nord, Stephen, John J. Phelps, and Robert G. Sheets. 1988. "An Analysis of the Economic Impact of the Service Sector on Underemployment in Major Metropolitan Areas in the United States." *Urban Studies* 25(5): 418–32.

Norris, Frank. 1901/1986. *The Octopus: A Story of California.* New York: Penguin Books. First published 1901 by Doubleday, Page, and Co.

Novotny, Patricia. 2001. "Review of Defining the Family: Law, Technology and Reproduction in an Uneasy Age." *Signs* 26(2): 565.

Nye, David E. 1990. *Electrifying America: Social Meanings of a New Technology, 1880–1940.* Cambridge, Mass.: MIT Press.

O'Brien, Kevin M. 2003. "The Determinants of Minority Employment in Police and Fire Departments." *Journal of Socio-Economics* 32(2): 183–95.

O'Connor, Alice. 2001. *Poverty Knowledge: Social Science, Social Policy, and the Poor in Twentieth-Century U.S. History.* Princeton, N.J.: Princeton University Press.

———. 2001. "Understanding Inequality in the Late Twentieth-Century Metropolis: New Perspectives on the Enduring Racial Divide." In *Urban Inequality: Evidence from Four Cities*, edited by A. O'Connor, C. Tilly, and L. D. Bobo. New York: Russell Sage Foundation.

O'Connor, Alice, Chris Tilly, and Lawrence D. Bobo, eds. 2001. *Urban Inequality: Evidence from Four Cities.* New York: Russell Sage Foundation.

O'Leary, Cecilia Elizabeth. 1999. *To Die For: The Paradox of American Patriotism.* Princeton, N.J.: Princeton University Press.

O'Mara, Margaret Pugh. 2004. *Cities of Knowledge: Cold War Science and the Search for the Next Silicon Valley.* Princeton, N.J.: Princeton University Press.

O'Neill, June, and Solomon Polachek. 1993. "Why the Gender Gap in Wages Narrowed in the 1980s." *Journal of Labor Economics* 11(1): 205–28.

O'Rourke, Kevin H., and Jeffrey G. Williamson. 1999. *Globalization and History: The Evolution of a Nineteenth-Century Atlantic Economy.* Cambridge, Mass.: MIT Press.

———. 2000. "When Did Globalization Begin?" NBER Working Paper No. 7632 (April 2000). Available at: http://www.nber.org/papers/w7632 (accessed October 25, 2005).

OECD. *Year To Year Percentage Changes in Selected Economic Variables.* Available at: http://oecdnt.ingenta/OECD/eng/TableViewer/wdsview/print.asp.

Ogbu, John U. 1978. *Minority Education and Caste: the American System in Cross-Cultural Perspective.* New York: Academic Press.

Oggen, Christopher, and Jeff Manza. 2003. "They've Paid Their Debts; Let Them Vote": Berkeley, Calif.: Rockridge Institute.

Oliver, Melvin L., and Thomas M. Shapiro. 1989. "Race and Wealth." *Review of Black Political Economy* 17: 5–25.

———. 1990. "Wealth of a Nation: At Least One-Third of Households are Asset Poor." *American Journal of Economics and Sociology* 49: 129–51.

———. 1997. *Black Wealth/White Wealth: A New Perspective on Racial Inequality.* New York: Routledge.

Olmstead, Alan L., and Paul W. Rhode. 2000. "The Transformation of Northern Agriculture, 1910–1990." In *The Cambridge Economic History of the United States: The Twentieth Century,* edited by S. L. Engerman and R. E. Gallman. Cambridge: Cambridge University Press.

Ong, Paul, and Eugeune Grigsby III. 1988. "Race and Life Cycle Effects on Home Ownership in Los Angeles, 1970 to 1980." *Urban Affairs Quarterly* 23: 601–15.

Orfield, Gary, and Carol Ashkinaze. 1991. *The Closing Door: Conservative Policy and Black Opportunity.* Chicago: University of Chicago Press.

Orfield, Myron. 2002. *American Metropolitics: The New Suburban Reality.* Washington: Brookings Institution Press.

Ornati, Oscar. 1966. *Poverty Amid Affluence.* New York: Twentieth Century Fund.

Orshansky, Mollie. 1977. *The Measure of Poverty.* Technical Paper I: Documentation of Background Information and Rationale for Current Poverty Matrix. Washington: U.S. Government Printing Office.

Ortiz, Vilma. 1994. "Women of Color: A Demographic Overview." In *Women of Color in U.S Society,* edited by Maxine Baca Zinn and Bonnie Thornton Dill. Philadelphia, Pa.: Temple University.

Ostergren, Robert C. 1991a. "European Settlement and Ethnicity Patterns on the Agricultural Frontier of South Dakota." In *Immigrants on the Land: Agriculture, Rural Life, and Small Towns,* edited by F. C. Luebke. London: Garland.

———. 1991b. "Land and Family in Rural Immigrant Communities." In *Immigrants on the Land: Agriculture, Rural Life, and Small Towns,* edited by G. E. Pozetta. New York: Garland.

Osterman, Paul. 1999. *Securing Prosperity: The American Labor Market: How It Has Changed and What to Do about It.* Princeton, N.J.: Princeton University Press.

Oxford English Dictionary Online. 1989. Oxford: Oxford University Press. Available at: http://dictionary.oed.com/cgi/entry/50007152?query_type=word& queryword=american&first=1&max_to_show=10&sort_type=alpha&result_ place=1&search_id=Tgwn-P9pnGs-800&hilite=50007152 (accessed October 24, 2005).

Ozawa, Martha N. 1995. "Anti-Poverty Effects of Public Income Transfers on Children." *Children and Youth Services Review* 17(1): 43–59.

Packaged Facts. 2002. "The Gay and Lesbian Market: New Trends, New Opportunities." New York: Packaged Facts. Available at: http://www. packagedfacts.com/product/display.asp?ProductID=761233 (accessed October 25, 2005).

Pacyga, Dominic A. 1991. *Polish Immigrants and Industrial Chicago: Workers on the South Side, 1880–1922.* Columbus: Ohio State University Press.

Pager, Devah. 2003. "The Mark of a Criminal Record." *American Journal of Sociology* 108(5): 937–75.

Palmer, Gladys L. 1939. "The Convertibility List of Occupations and the Problems of Developing It." *Journal of the American Statistical Association* 34(208): 693–708.

Parcel, Toby L. 1982. "Wealth Accumulation of Black and White Men: The Case of Housing Equity." *Social Problems* 30(2): 199–211.

Parenti, Christian. 1999. *Lockdown America: Police and Prisons in an Age of Crisis.* New York: Verso.

Pascarella, Ernest T. 1985. "Racial Differences in Factors Associated with Bachelor's Degree Completion: A Nine-Year Follow-Up." *Research in Higher Education* 23(4): 351–73.

Pascarella, Ernest T., G. C. Wolniak, and C. T. Pierson. 2003. "Influences on Community College Students' Educational Plans." *Research in Higher Education* 44(3): 301–14.

Passel, Jeffrey S. 2005. "Estimates of the Size and Characteristics of the Undocumented Population." Washington, D.C.: Pew Hispanic Center. http://pewhispanic.org/reports/print.php?ReportID=44.

Patterson, James T. 1981. *America's Struggle Against Poverty.* Cambridge, Mass.: Harvard University Press.

Pearce, Diane. 1978. "The Feminization of Poverty: Women, Work,and Welfare." *Urban and Social Change Review* 10: 28–36.

Pearce, Esther. 1957. "History of the Standard Industrial Classification." Executive Office of the President. Bureau of the Budget, Office of Statistical Standards. Washington: U.S. Government Printing Office.

Peck, Gunther. 2000. *Reinventing Free Labor: Padrones and Immigrant Workers in the North American West.* Cambridge: Cambridge University Press.

Pelavin, Sol H., and Michael Kane. 1990. *Changing the Odds: Factors Increasing Access to College.* New York: College Entrance Examination Board.

Pennsylvania Partnerships for Children. 2002. "The State of the Child in Pennsylvania: A 2002 Guide to Child Well-Being in Pennsylvania." Harrisburg: PPC.

Perlmann, Joel. 2001. *Toward a Population History of The Second Generation: Birth Cohorts of Southern-, Central- and Eastern-European Origins, 1871–1970.* Working Paper 333. Annandale-on-Hudson, N.Y.: The Jerome Levy Institute of Bard College.

———. 2001. "Young Mexican Americans, Blacks, and Whites in Recent Years: Schooling and Teen Motherhood as Indicators of Strengths and Risks." Working Paper 338. Annandale-on-Hudson, N.Y.: The Jerome Levy Institute of Bard College.

———. 2002a. "Census Bureau Long-Term Racial Projections: Interpreting Their Results And Seeking Their Rationale." In *The New Race Question: How The Census Counts Multiracial Individuals,* edited by Joel Perlmann and Mary C. Waters. New York: Russell Sage Foundation.

———. 2002b. "Poles and Italians Then, Mexicans Now? Immigrant-to-Native Wage Ratios, 1910 and 1940." Working Paper 343. Annandale-on-Hudson, N.Y.: The Jerome Levy Institute of Bard College.

———. 2002c. "Polish and Italian Schooling Then, Mexican Schooling Now? U.S. Ethnic School Attainments across the Generations of the 20th Century." Working Paper 350. Annandale-on-Hudson, N.Y.: The Jerome Levy Institute of Bard College.

Perlmann, Joel, and Roger Waldinger. 1999. "Immigrants, Past and Present: A Reconsideration." In *The Handbook of International Migration: The American Experience*, edited by C. Hirschman, P. Kasinitz and J. DeWind. New York: Russell Sage Foundation.

Perlmann, Joel, and Mary C. Waters. 2002. "Introduction." In *The New Race Question: How the Census Counts Multiracial Individuals*, edited by Joel Perlmann and Mary C. Waters. New York: Russell Sage Foundation.

Perloff, Harvey S., Edgar S. Dunn, Jr., Eric E. Lampard, and Richard F. Muth. 1960. *Regions, Resources, and Economic Growth*. Lincoln: University of Nebraska Press.

Perry, Marc J. 2003a. "Migration and Geographic Mobility in Metropolitan and Non-Metropolitan America." In *Census 2000 Special Reports*. Washington: U.S. Census Bureau.

———. 2003b. "State-to-State Migration Flows." In *Census 2000 Special Reports*. Washington: U.S. Census Bureau.

Persily, Nathaniel. 2002. "The Legal Implications of a Multiracial Census." In *The New Race Question: How The Census Counts Multiracial Individuals*, edited by Joel Perlmann and Mary C. Waters. New York: Russell Sage Foundation.

Peters, Enrique Dussel. 1998. "Recent Structural Changes in Mexico's Economy: A Preliminary Analysis of Some Sources of Mexican Migration to the United States." In *Crossings: Mexican Immigration in Interdisciplinary Perspectives*, edited by M. Suarez-Orozco. Cambridge, Mass.: Harvard University Press.

Peterson, George E., and Wayne Vroman, eds. 1992. *Urban Labor Markets and Job Opportunity*. Washington, D.C.: Urban Institute Press.

Peterson, Richard. 1996. "Statistical Errors, Faulty Conclusions, Misguided Policy: Reply to Weitzman." *American Sociological Review* 61(3): 539–40.

Peterson, Trond, and Laurie A. Morgan. 1995. "Separate and Unequal: Occupation Establishment Sex Segregation and the Gender Wage Gap." *American Journal of Sociology* 101(2): 329–65.

Phillips, Clifton J. 1968. *Indiana in Transition: The Emergence of an Industrial Commonwealth*, vol. IV, *The History of Indiana*. Indianapolis: Indiana Historical Bureau and Indiana Historical Society.

The Phyllis Schlafly Report. 1986. "A Short History of the E.R.A." September. Alton, Ill.: Eagle Forum. Available at: http://www.eagleforum.org/psr/1986/sept86/psrsep86.html (accessed October 25, 2005).

Piketty, Thomas, and Emmanuel Saez. 2001. "Income Inequality in the United States, 1913–1998." NBER Working Paper No. 8467. Cambridge, Mass.: National Bureau of Economic Research.

Piore, Michael. 1979. *Birds of Passage*. New York: Cambridge University Press.

Piven, Frances Fox, and Richard Cloward. 1977. *Poor People's Movements: Why They Succeed, How They Fail*. New York: Pantheon.

Plotnick, Robert D., Eugene Smolensky, Erik Evenhouse, and Siobhan Reilly. 2000. "The Twentieth-Century Record of Inequality and Poverty in the United States." In *The Cambridge Economic History of the United States. The Twentieth Century*, edited by S. L. Engerman and R. E. Gallman. Cambridge: Cambridge University Press.

"The 'Poorhouse State' Is the Right Name For It." 1949. *Saturday Evening Post*, November 19, 1949, pp. 10, 12.

Pope, Clayne. 2000. "Inequality in the Nineteenth Century." *In The Cambridge Economic History of the United States. The Nineteenth Century,* edited by S. L. Engerman and R. E. Gallman. Cambridge: Cambridge University Press.

Popenoe, David. 1988. *Disturbing the Nest: Family Change and Decline in Modern Societies.* New York: Aldine de Gruyter.

———. 1996. *Life Without Father: Compelling New Evidence that Fatherhood and Marriage are Indispensable for the Good of Children and Society.* New York: Free Press.

Population Reference Bureau. 2000. "Race and Ethnicity in the Census: 1860 to 2000." Washington, D.C.: Population Reference Bureau.

———. 2001. "Who Marked More Than One Race In The 2000 U.S. Census?" Washington, D.C.: Population Reference Bureau.

———. 2004. "Human Populations: Fundamentals of Growth Patterns of World Urbanization. Washington, D.C.: Population Reference Bureau.

Porter, Rebecca. 2000. "Supreme Court Delivers Narrow Ruling On Grandparents' Visitation Rights." *Trial* 36(8): 84.

Portes, Alejandro. 1999. "Immigration: Theory for New Century: Some Problems and Opportunities." In *The Handbook of International Migration: The American Experience,* edited by C. Hirschman, P. Kasinitz, and J. DeWind. New York: Russell Sage Foundation.

Portes, Alejandro, and Ruben G. Rumbaut. 2001. *Legacies: The Story of the Immigrant Second Generation.* Berkeley and New York: University of California Press and Russell Sage Foundation.

Portes, Alejandro, and Min Zhou. 1999. "Entrepreneurship and Economic Progress in the 1990s: A Comparative Analysis of Immigrants and African Americans." In *Immigration and Opportunity: Race, Ethnicity, and Employment in the United States,* edited by F. D. Bean and S. Bell-Rose. New York: Russell Sage Foundation.

Pozzetta, George E., ed. 1991. *Immigrants on the Land: Agriculture, Rural Life, and Small Towns.* New York: Garland.

Prather, Jane E. 1971. "When the Girls Move in: A Sociological Analysis of the Feminization of the Bank Teller's Job." *Journal of Marriage and the Family* 33(4): 777–82.

Preston, Samuel H. 1984. "Children and the Elderly in the U.S." *Scientific American* 251(6): 44–49.

Prewitt, Kenneth. 2002. "Race In The 2000 Census: A Turning Point." In *The New Race Question: How the Census Counts Multiracial Individuals,* edited by Joel Perlmann and Mary C.Waters. New York: Russell Sage Foundation.

Prison Index, The. 2003. Available at: http://www.westernprisonproject.org/model86.

Publisher's Weekly. 2000. "Sunnyvale: The Rise and Fall of a Silicon Valley Family (Book Review)." *Publisher's Weekly,* 247(23): 80.

Quadagno, Jill S. 1994. *The Color of Welfare: How Racism Undermined the War on Poverty.* New York: Oxford University Press.

"Questioning Age-Old Wisdom: The Legacy of Mandatory Retirement." 1992. *Harvard Law Review* 105: 889–907.

Raijman, Rebeca. 2001. "Determinants of Entrepreneurial Intentions: Mexican Immigrants in Chicago." *The Journal of Socio-Economics* 30(5): 393–401.

Raijman, Rebeca, and Marta Tienda. 1999. "Immigrants' Socioeconomic Progress

Post-1965: Forging Mobility or Survival?" In *The Handbook of International Migration: The American Experience,* edited by C. Hirschman, P. Kasinitz, and J. DeWind. New York: Russell Sage Foundation.

———. 2000. "Immigrants' Pathways to Business Ownership: A Comparative Ethnic Perspective." *International Migration Review* 34(3): 682.

———. 2000. "Training Functions of Ethnic Economies: Mexican Entrepreneurs in Chicago." *Sociological Perspectives* 43(3): 439.

Rainwater, Lee, and William Yancey. 1967. *The Moynihan Report and the Politics of Controversy.* Cambridge, Mass.: MIT Press.

Rank, Robert. 2004. *One Nation, Underprivileged: Why American Poverty Affects Us All.* New York: Oxford University Press.

Ransom, Richard, and Richard Sutch. 1986. "The Labor of Older Americans: Retirement of Men On and Off the Job, 1870–1937." *Journal of Economic History* 46(1): 1–20.

Ratner, Sidney. 1972. *The Tariff in American History.* New York: Van Nostrand.

Rauch, Jonathan. 2004. *Gay Marriage.* New York: Times Books, Henry Holt.

Rawlston, Valerie, and William E. Spriggs. 2002. "A Logit Decomposition Analysis of Occupational Segregation: An Update for the 1990s of Spriggs and Williams." *Journal of Black Political Economy* 29(4): 91–96.

Redd, Kenneth E. 2000. *HBCU Graduates: Employment Earnings and Success after College.* Indianapolis, Ind.: USA Group.

Reed, James. 1978. *From Private Vice to Public Virtue: The Birth Control Movement and American Society since 1830.* New York: Basic Books.

Rees, Albert, and Sharon P. Smith. 1991. "The End of Mandatory Retirement for Tenured Faculty." *Science* 253(5022): 838–39.

Reid, Lori L. 1998. "Devaluing Women and Minorities: The Effects of Race/Ethnic and Sex Composition of Occupations on Wage Levels." *Work and Occupations* 25(4): 511–36.

———. 2002. "Occupational Segregation, Human Capital, and Motherhood: Black Women's Higher Exit Rates from Full-Time Employment." *Gender & Society* 16(5): 728–47.

Reimers, Cordelia W. 2000. "The Effect of Tighter Labor Markets on Unemployment of Hispanics and African Americans: The 1990s Experience." In *Prosperity for All? The Economic Boom and African Americans,* edited by Robert Cherry and William M. Rogers III. New York: Russell Sage Foundation.

"Report Suggests National Assisted Living Center Is Needed To Manage Growth." 2003. *Contemporary Long Term Care* 26(7): 14.

Reskin, Barbara. 1998. *The Realities of Affirmative Action in Employment.* Washington, D.C.: American Sociological Association.

Reskin, Barbara F., and Catherine E. Roos. 1995. "Jobs, Authority, and Earnings Among Managers: the Continuing Significance of Sex." In *Gender Inequality at Work,* edited by J. A. Jacobs. Thousand Oaks, Calif.: Sage Publications.

Reskin, Barbara F., and Patricia A. Roos. 1990. *Job Queues, Gender Queues: Explaining Women's Inroads into Male Occupations.* Philadelphia, Pa.: Temple University Press.

Reyburn, John E. 1911. "Fourth Annual Message of John E. Reyburn, Mayor of the City of Philadelphia, with the Annual Reports of Henry Clay, Director of the Department of Safety and of the Chiefs of Bureaus, Constituting said De-

partment also Museum and Libraries for the Year ending December 31, 1910."
Philadelphia, Pa.: Dunlap Printing Company.

Reynolds, David R. 1999. *There Goes the Neighborhood: Rural School Consolidation at the Grassroots in Early Twentieth-Century Iowa*. Iowa City: University of Iowa Press.

Rifkin, Jeremy. 1995. *The End of Work: The Decline of the Global Labor Force and the Dawn of the Post-Market Era*. New York: G. P. Putnam's and Sons.

Riis, Jacob A. 1901. *The Making of an American*. New York: Grosset and Dunlap.

Riley, Matilda White. 1976. "Age Strata in Social Systems." In *Handbook of Aging and the Social Sciences*, edited by R. H. Binstock and E. Shanas. New York: Van Nostrand Reinhold.

Ritter, Gretchen. 1997. *Goldbugs and Greenbacks: The Antimonopoly Tradition and the Politics of Finance in America*. Cambridge: Cambridge University Press.

Rivkin, Steven G. 1995. "Black/White Differences in Schooling and Employment." The *Journal of Human Resources* 30(4): 826–52.

Roberts, Peter. 1920. *The Problem of Americanization*. New York: Macmillan.

Roberts, Steven V. 1986. "House Votes to End Mandatory Retirement." *New York Times*, October 18, 1986, p. 33.

Rockoff, Hugh. 2000. "Banking and Finance, 1989–1914." In *The Cambridge Economic History of the United States*, edited by S. L. Engerman and R. E. Gallman. Cambridge: Cambridge University Press.

Rodgers, Daniel T. 1998. *Atlantic Crossings: Social Politics in a Progressive Age*. Cambridge, Mass.: Harvard University Press.

Roediger, David R. 1991. *The Wages of Whiteness: Race and the Making of the American Working Class*. London: Verso.

Romero, Simon, and Janet Elder. 2003. "Hispanics in U.S. Report Opinion." *New York Times*, August 6.

Root, Maria P. P. 2003. "Five Mixed-Race Identities: From Relic to Revolution." In *New Faces in a Changing America: Multiracial Identity in the 21st Century*, edited by H. L. DeBose and L. I. Winters. Thousand Oaks, Calif.: Sage Publications.

Rose, James A. 1903. *Blue Book of the State of Illinois*. Springfield, Ill.: Phillips Bros, State Printers.

Rosenbaum, E. 1997. "Racial/Ethnic Differences in Home Ownership and Housing Quality, 1991." *Social Problems* 43: 403–26.

Rosenberg, Charles E. 1987. *The Care of Strangers: The Rise of America's Hospital System*. New York: Basic Books.

Rosenbloom, Joshua L. 1990. "One Market or Many? Labor Market Integration in the Late Nineteenth-Century United States." *Journal of Economic History* 50(1): 85–107.

———. 1998. "The Extent of the Labor Market in the United States, 1870–1914." *Social Science History* 22(3): 287–318.

———. 2002. *Looking for Work; Searching for Workers*. Cambridge: Cambridge University Press.

Rosenfeld, Michael J., and Marta Tienda. 1999. "Mexican Immigration, Occupational Niches, and Labor Market Competition: Evidence from Los Angeles, Chicago, and Atlanta, 1970 to 1990." In *Immigration and Opportunity: Race, Ethnicity, and Employment in the United States*, edited by F. D. Bean and S. Bell-Rose. New York: Russell Sage Foundation.

Rotella, Elyce J. 1981. *From Home to Office: U.S. Women at Work, 1870–1930.* Ann Arbor: UMI Research Press.

Rothman, Robert. 1991. "The Road Taken: Minorities and Proprietary Schools." In *The Education of African-Americans,* edited by C. V. Willie, Antoine M. Garibaldi, and Wornie L. Reed. New York: Auburn House.

Ruggles, Patricia. 1990. *Drawing the Line: Alternative Poverty Measures and their Implications for Public Policy.* Washington, D.C.: Urban Institute.

Ruggles, Patricia, and Robertson Williams. 1989. "Longitudinal Measures of Poverty: Accounting for Income and Assets Over Time." *Review of Income and Wealth* 35(3): 225–43.

Ruggles, Steven. 1994a. "The Origins of African-American Family Structure." *American Sociological Review* 59(1): 136–51.

———. 1994b. "The Transformation of American Family Structure." *American Historical Review* 99(1): 103–28.

———. 2000. *Living Arrangements and Well-Being of Older Persons in the Past.*

Ruggles, Steven, and Ron Goeken. 1992. "Race and Multigenerational Family Structure, 1900–1980." In *The Changing American Family Structure: Sociological and Demographic Perspectives,* edited by S. J. South and S. E. Tolnay. Boulder: Westview Press.

Ruggles, Steven, Matthew Sobek, Trent Alexander, Catherine A. Fitch, Ronald Goeken, Patricia Kelly Hall, Miriam King, and Chad Ronnander. 2004. Integrated Public Use Microdata Series: Version 3.0 [Machine Readable Database]. Minneapolis: Minnesota Population Center. Available at: http://www.ipums .org (accessed October 25, 2005).

Rumbaut, Ruben G. 1999. "Assimilation and Its Discontents: Ironies and Paradoxes." In *The Handbook of International Migration: The American Experience,* edited by C. Hirschman, P. Kasinitz and J. DeWind. New York: Russell Sage Foundation.

Rumbaut, Ruben G., and Alejandro Portes. 2001. "Introduction—Ethnogenesis: Coming of Age in Immigrant America." In *Ethnicities: Children of Immigrants in America,* edited by R. G. Rumbaut and A. Portes. Berkeley and New York: University of California Press and Russell Sage Foundation.

———, eds. 2001. *Ethnicities: Children of Immigrants in America.* Berkeley and New York: University of California Press and Russell Sage Foundation.

Rumberger, Russell W. 1983. "The Influence of Family Background on Education, Earnings, and Wealth." *Social Forces* 61(3): 755–73.

Rusk, David. 1996. "Cities Without Suburbs. Baltimore, Md.: Johns Hopkins University Press.

Sadayoshi, Ohtsu. 2004. "Changing Characteristics of International Labor Migration in Northeast Asia: With a Focus on the Russo-Chinese Border." *Slavic Eurasian Studies* 2.

Saenz, Roger. 2004. *Latinos and the Changing Face of America, The American People: Census 2000 Series.* New York and Washington, D.C.: Russell Sage Foundation and Population Reference Bureau.

Salary.com. 2000. "Right on Target—Reaching Minorities Through Ads." New York: Vault Inc. Available at: http://www.vault.com/nr/newsmain.jsp?nr _page=3&ch_id=265&article_id=18888&cat_id=1021 (accessed October 25, 2005).

Saloutos, Theodore. 1991. "The Immigrant in Pacific Coast Agriculture, 1880–1940." In *Immigrants on the Land: Agriculture, Rural Life, and Small Towns,* edited by G. E. Pozzetta. New York: Garland.

Salt, John. 1999. *Current Trends in International Migration in Europe: Social Cohesion and Quality of Life.* London: Council of Europe.

Sanchez, George J. 1993. *Becoming Mexican American: Ethnicity, Culture, and Identity in Chicano Los Angeles, 1900–1945.* New York: Oxford University Press.

Sassen, Saskia. 1991. *Global City: New York, London, and Tokyo.* Princeton, N.J.: Princeton University Press.

———. 1994. *Cities in a World Economy.* Thousand Oaks, Calif.: Pine Forge Press.

Savitch, H. V. 1988. *Post-Industrial Cities: Politics and Planning in New York, Paris, and London.* Princeton, N.J.: Princeton University Press.

Sawhill, Isabel V. 1988. "Poverty in the U.S.—Why Is It So Persistent?" *Journal of Economic Literature* 26(3): 1073–119.

Schachter, Jason R. 2003. *Migration by Race and Hispanic Origin: 1995 to 2000.* Census 2000 Special Reports. Washington: U.S. Census Bureau.

Schlesinger, Arthur M., Jr. 1998. *The Disuniting of America: Reflections on a Multicultural Society,* rev. ed. New York: W. W. Norton.

Schmitt, John. 2001. "Did Job Quality Deteriorate in the 1980s and 1990s?" In *Sourcebook of Labor Markets: Evolving Structures and Processes,* edited by Ivar Berg and Arne L. Kalleberg. New York: Plenum Publishers.

Schoeini, Robert, and Karen F. Ross. 2005. "Material Aid Received from Families during the Transition to Adulthood." In *On the Frontier of Adulthood: Theory, Research, and Public Policy,* edited by Frank E. Furstenberg, Jr., Ruben G. Rumbaut, and Richard A. Settensten, Jr. Chicago: University of Chicago Press.

Schulman, Bruce J. 1991. *From Cotton Belt to Sunbelt: Federal Policy, Economic Development, and the Transformation of the South, 1938–1980.* New York: Oxford University Press.

Schwartzberg, Beverly. 2004. "Lots Of Them Did That": Desertion, Bigamy, and Marital Fluidity in Late-Nineteenth Century America." *Journal of Social History* 37(3): 573–600.

Schwarz, John. 1983. *America's Hidden Success: A Reassessment of Twenty Years of Public Policy.* New York: W. W. Norton.

Scopp, Thomas, and John Priebe. 1993. "Census Occupational Classification System and the Standard Occupational Classification." Paper read at Proceedings of the International Occupational Classification Conference. Washington, D.C. (September).

Self, Robert. 1996. *American Babylon: Race and the Struggle for Postwar Oakland.* Princeton, N.J.: Princeton University Press.

Sentencing Project, The. 2003. *U.S. Prison Populations—Trends and Implications.* Briefing Sheet 1044. Washington, D.C.: The Sentencing Project. Available at: http://www.sentencingproject.org (accessed October 25, 2005).

Shalom, Stephen R. 1998. "Dubious Data: The Thernstroms on Affirmative Action in Higher Education." *Race and Society* 1(2): 125–57.

Shanahan, Michael J. 2000. "Pathways to Adulthood in Changing Societies: Variability and Mechanisms in Life Course Perspective." *American Sociological Review* 62: 667–92.

Sharpe, William, and Leonard Wallock. 1994. "Bold New City or Built-Up 'Burb? Redefining Contemporary Suburbia." *American Quarterly* 46(1): 1–30.

Shaw, Stephanie J. 1996. *What a Woman Ought to Be and Do: Black Professional Women Workers During the Jim Crow Era*, Women in Culture and Society. Chicago: University of Chicago Press.

Sheahan, Peggy Knee. 1994. "Estate Planning for the Post-Nuclear Family." *New Jersey Law Journal* 137(4): S6.

Sherraden, M. 1991. *Assets and the Poor: A New Direction for Social Policy*. Armonk, N.Y.: M. E. Sharpe.

Shklar, Judith. 1991. *American Citizenship: The Quest for Inclusion*. Cambridge, Mass.: Harvard University Press.

Shortman, Melanie. 2003. "Spencer Spreads Urban Sensibility Beyond the City." *PR Week*, August 25, 2003, p. 11.

Shulman, Steven. 1991. "Why is the Black Unemployment Rate Always Twice as High as the White Unemployment Rate?" In *New Approaches to Economic and Social Analyses of Discrimination*, edited by Richard R. Cornwall and Phanindra V. Wunnava. New York: Praeger.

Shulman, Steven, and William Darity, ed. 1989. *The Question of Discrimination: Racial Inequality in the U.S. Labor Market*. Middletown, Conn.: Wesleyan University Press.

Sitkoff, Harvard. 1981. *The Struggle for Black Equality, 1954–1980*. New York: Hill & Wang.

Skardal, Dorothy Burton. 1980. "Danes." In *Harvard Encyclopedia of American Ethnic Groups*, edited by Stephan Thernstrom. Cambridge, Mass.: Harvard University Press.

Skerry, Peter. 2002. "Multiracialism And The Administrative State." In *The New Race Question: How The Census Counts Multiracial Individuals*, edited by Joel Perlmann and Mary C. Waters. New York: Russell Sage Foundation.

Skocpol, Theda. 1992. *Protecting Soldiers and Mothers: The Political Origins of Social Policy*. Cambridge, Mass.: Harvard University Press.

Skolnick, Arlene. 1997. "Family Values: The Sequel." *The American Prospect* (May–June): 86–95.

Skrentny, John D. 1996. *Ironies of Affirmative Action: Politics, Culture and Justice in America, Morality and Society*. Chicago: University of Chicago Press.

Slavins, Joanna. 2001. "Credit Card Borrowing, Delinquency, and Personal Bankruptcy." *New England Economic Review*: 15–30.

Slevin, Kathleen F., and C. Ray Wingrove. 1998. *From Stumbling Blocks to Stepping Stones: The Life Experience of Fifty Professional African American Women*. New York: New York University Press.

Smeeding, Timothy, Lee Rainwater, and Gary Burtless. 2001. "United States Poverty in a Cross-National Context." *Focus* 21(1): 50–54.

Smelser, Neil J., and Jeffrey C. Alexander, eds. 1999. *Diversity and Its Discontents*. Princeton, N.J.: Princeton University Press.

Smith, D. Alton. 1980. "Government Employment and Black/White Relative Wages." The *Journal of Human Resources* 15(1): 77–86.

Smith, James P. 1987. "Recent Trends in the Distribution of Wealth: Data, Research, Problems, and Prospects." In *International Comparisons of the Distribu-*

tion of Household Wealth, edited by E.N. Wolff. New York: Oxford University Press.

———. 1993. "Broken Down by Age, Sex, and Race: Employment-Discrimination Litigation After 25 Years: Affirmative Action and the Racial Wage Gap." *The American Economic Review* 83(2): 79–84.

———. 1995. "Racial and Ethnic Differences in Wealth in the Health and Retirement Study." *Journal of Human Resources* 30: S158–S183.

Smith, James P., and Barry Edmonston. 1997. *The New Americans: Economic, Demographic, and Fiscal Effects of Immigration.* Washington, D.C.: National Academy Press.

Smith, James P., and Finis R. Welch. 1986. *Closing the Gap: Forty Years of Economic Progress for Blacks.* Santa Monica: The Rand Corporation.

———. 1989. "Black Economic Progress After Myrdal." *Journal of Economic Literature* 27(2): 519–64.

Smith, Jessie Carney, and Carrell Peterson Horton, ed. 1995. *Historical Statistics of Black America.* New York: Gale Research.

Smith, Neil, and Peter Williams, eds. 1986. *Gentrification and the City.* Boston, Mass.: Allen and Unwin.

Smith, Robert C. 2001. "Mexicans: Social, Educational, Economic, and Political Problems and Prospects in New York." In *New Immigrants In New York,* edited by N. Foner. New York: Columbia University Press.

———. 2002. "Gender, Ethnicity, and Race in School and Work Outcomes of Second-Generation Mexican Americans." In *Latinos In the Twenty-First Century,* edited by M. Suarez-Orozco and M. Paez. Berkeley and Los Angeles: University of California Press.

———. 2005. *Mexican New York: Transnational Lives of New Immigrants.* Berkeley: University of California Press.

———. 2005. "Racialization and Mexicans in New York City." In *New Destinations for Mexican Migration,* edited by R. Hernández-León and V. Zúñiga. New York: Russell Sage Foundation.

Smith, Sandra S. 2000. "Mobilizing Social Resources: Race, Ethnic, and Gender Differences in Social Capital and Persisting Wage Inequalities." *Sociological Quarterly* 41(4): 509–37.

Smith, Shelley A. 1991. "Sources of Earnings Inequality in the Black and White Female Labor Forces." *Sociological Quarterly* 32(1): 117–38.

Smith, Timothy L. 1972. *Native Blacks and Foreign Whites: Varying Responses to Educational Opportunity in America, 1880–1950,* vol. VI, *Perspectives in American History.* Cambridge, Mass.: Harvard University Press.

Smock, Pamela J., and Sanjiv Gupta. 2002. "Cohabitation in Contemporary North America." In *Just Living Together: Implications of Cohabitation on Families, Children, and Social Policy,* edited by A. Booth and A. C. Crouter. Mahwah, N.J.: Lawrence Erlbaum Associates.

Smull, William P. 1881. *Smull's Legislative Hand Book, Rules and Decisions of the General Assembly of Pennsylvania.* Harrisburg, Pa.: Lane S. Hart, State Printer.

Sobek, Matthew. 1996. "Work, Status, and Income: Men in the American Occupational Structure Since the Late Nineteenth Century." *Social Science History* 20(2): 169–207.

————. 1997. "A Century of Work: Gender, Labor Force Participation, and Occupational Attainment in the United States, 1880–1990." Ph.D. diss., History, University of Minnesota, Minneapolis.

Sokoloff, Natalie. 1992. *Black Women and White Women in the Professions*, Perspectives on Gender. New York: Routledge.

Sollors, Werner. 2002. "What Race Are You?" In *The New Race Question: How The Census Counts Multiracial Individuals*, edited by Joel Perlmann and Mary C. Waters. New York: Russell Sage Foundation.

Son, In Soo, Suzanne W. Model, and Gene A. Fisher. 1989. "Polarization and Progress in the Black Community: Earnings and Status Gains for Young Black Males in the Era of Affirmative Action." *Sociological Forum* 4(3): 309–27.

Sorenson, Andrew A. 1972. "Black Americans and the Medical Profession, 1930–1970." *The Journal of Negro Education* 41(4): 337–42.

Sorenson, Elaine. 1991. *Exploring the Reasons behind the Narrowing Gender Gap in Earnings*. Report 91-2. Washington, D.C.: Urban Institute Press.

Sorkin, Michael. 1992. "Introduction." In *Variations on a Theme Park: The New American City and the End of Public Space*, edited by M. Sorkin. New York: Hill & Wang.

Sowell, Thomas. 1975. *Race and Economics*. New York: David McKay.

Spain, Daphne, and Suzanne M. Bianchi. 1996. *Balancing Act: Motherhood, Marriage, and Employment Among American Women*. New York: Russell Sage Foundation.

Spencer, Ann Garlin. 1913. "The Age of Consent and its Significance." *Forum* 49: 406–13.

Spencer, Ethel. 1984. *The Spencers of Amberson Avenue: A Turn-of-the-Century Memoir*. Pittsburgh: University of Pittsburgh Press.

Spencer, Ranier. 2003. "Census 2000: Assessments in Significance." In *New Faces in a Changing America: Multiracial Identity in the 21st Century*, edited by H. L. DeBose and L. I. Winters. Thousand Oaks, Calif.: Sage Publications.

Spener, David, and Frank D. Bean. 1999. "Self-Employment Concentration and Earnings among Mexican Immigrants in the U.S." *Social Forces* 77(3): 1021–47.

Spriggs, William E., and Rhonda M. Williams. 2000. "What Do We Need to Explain About African American Unemployment?" In *Prosperity for All? The Economic Boom and African Americans*, edited by Robert Cherry and William M. Rogers III. New York: Russell Sage Foundation.

Stack, Carol. 1996. *Call to Home: African Americans Reclaim the Rural South*. New York: Basic Books.

Stanger-Ross, Jordan, Christina Collins, and Mark J. Stern. Forthcoming. "Falling Far From the Tree: Three Reinventions of the Transition to Adulthood in 20th Century America." *Social Science History.*

Steele, Shelby. 1990. *The Content of Our Character: A New Vision of Race in America*. New York: St. Martin's.

Steelman, Lala C., and Brian Powell. 1989. "Acquiring Capital for College: The Constraints of Family Configuration." *American Sociological Review* 54(5): 844–55.

Steinberg, Stephen. 1999. "Occupational Apartheid in America: Race, Labor Market Segmentation, and Affirmative Action." In *Without Justice For All: The New*

Liberalism And Our Retreat From Racial Equality, edited by A. Reed, Jr. Boulder, Colo.: Westview.

Stern, Mark J. 1987. *Society and Family Strategy: Erie County, New York, 1850–1920.* Albany: State University of New York Press.

———. 1991. "Poverty and the Life-Cycle, 1940–1960." *Journal of Social History* 24(3): 521–40.

———. 1993. "Poverty and Family Composition Since 1940." In *The "Underclass" Debate: Views from History,* edited by M. B. Katz. Princeton, N.J.: Princeton University Press.

———. 1999. "The Management of African-American Poverty." Unpublished manuscript. Available from author.

Sterner, Richard. 1973. *The Negro's Share: A Study of Income, Consumption, Housing, and Public Assistance.* New York: Harper and Brothers.

Stevens, Beth. 1988. "Blurring the Boundaries: How the Federal Government Has Influenced Welfare Benefits in the Private Sector." In *The Politics of Social Policy in the United States,* edited by M. Weir, A. S. Orloff, and T. Skocpol. Princeton, N.J.: Princeton University Press.

Stokley, William S. 1881. "Ninth Annual Message of William S. Stokley, Mayor of the City of Philadelphia with the Accompanying Documents, March 31, 1881." Philadelphia, Pa.: E. C. Markley and Son, Printers.

Stoll, Michael. 2004. *African Americans and the Color Line, The American People.* Census 2000 Series. New York and Washington, D.C.: Russell Sage Foundation and Population Reference Bureau.

Stoltzenberg, Ross M. 1975. "Education, Occupation, and Wage Differences Between White and Black Men." *American Journal of Sociology* 81(2): 299–323.

Stull, William J., and Janice Fanning Madden. 1990. *Post-Industrial Philadelphia: Structural Changes in the Metropolitan Economy.* Philadelphia: University of Pennsylvania Press.

Sugrue, Thomas J. 1996. *The Origins of the Urban Crisis: Race and Inequality in Postwar Detroit.* Princeton, N.J.: Princeton University Press.

———. 1998. "The Tangled Roots of Affirmative Action." *American Behavioral Scientist* 41(7): 886–97.

Sumner, William G. 1909. "The Family and Social Change." *American Journal of Sociology.* 14(5): 577–91.

Suro, Roberto, and Audrey Singer. 2003. "Changing Patterns of Latino Growth in Metropolitan America." In *Redefining Urban and Suburban America: Evidence From Census 2000,* edited by B. Katz and R. E. Lang. Washington, D.C.: Brookings Institution Press.

Szafran, Robert F. 2002. "Age-Adjusted Labor Force Participation Rates, 1960–2045." *Monthly Labor Review* 125(9): 25–38.

Taeuber, Irene B., and Conrad Taeuber. 1971. *People of the United States in the Twentieth Century.* Washington: U.S. Census Bureau.

Tafoya, Sonya, Hans Johnson, and Laura Hill. 2004. *Who Chooses to Choose Two?* edited by R. Farley and J. Haaga. New York and Washington, D.C.: Russell Sage Foundation and Population Reference Bureau.

Teaford, Jon C. 1984. *The Unheralded Triumph: City Government in America, 1870–1900.* Baltimore, Md.: Johns Hopkins University Press.

———. 2002. *The Rise of the States: Evolution of American State Government.* Baltimore, Md.: Johns Hopkins University Press.

Tempalski, Jerry. 1998. "Revenue Effects of Major Tax Bills." OTA Working Paper 81. Washington: U.S. Department of the Treasury. http://www.taxfoundation.org/Historical/RevenueEstHistory.pdf.

Tentler, Leslie Woodcock. 1979. *Wage-Earning Women: Industrial Work and Family Life in the United States, 1900–1930.* New York: Oxford University Press.

Testa, Mark, Marilyn Krogh, and Kathryn M. Neckerman. 1989. "Employment and Marriage Among Inner-city Fathers." *The Annals of the American Academy of Political and Social Science* 501: 79–92.

Texeira, Mary Thierry. 2003. "The New Multiracialism: An Affirmation of or an End To Race as We Know It? In *New Faces in a Changing America: Multiracial Identity in the 21st Century*, edited by H. L. DeBose and L. I. Winters. Thousand Oaks, Calif.: Sage Publications.

Thernstrom, Stephan. 1964. *Poverty and Progress: Social Mobility in a Nineteenth Century City.* Cambridge, Mass.: Harvard University Press.

———. 1973. *The Other Bostonians: Poverty and Progress in the American Metropolis, 1880–1970.* Cambridge, Mass.: Harvard University Press.

———, ed. 1980. *Harvard Encyclopedia of Ethnic Groups.* Cambridge, Mass.: Harvard University Press.

Thernstrom, Stephan, and Abigail Thernstrom. 1997. *America In Black and White: One Nation, Indivisible.* New York: Simon & Schuster.

Thomas, Melvin E. 1995. "Race, Class, and Occupation: An Analysis of Black and White Earning Differences for Professional and Non-Professional Males, 1940–1990." *Research in Race & Ethnic Relations* 8: 139–156.

Thomas, Ward. 2000. "Mitigating Barriers to Black Employment through Affirmative Action Regulations: A Case Study." *The Review of Black Political Economy* 27(3): 81–102.

Thomas, William Isaac, and Florian Znaniecki. 1920. *The Polish Peasant in Europe and America.* 5 vols. Boston, Mass.: Richard D. Badger.

Thorndike, Joseph J. 2002. "The Price of Civilization: Taxation in Depression and War, 1933–1945." Arlington, Va.: The Tax History Project. Available at: http://www.taxhistory.org/Articles/taxjustice.htm (accessed October 25, 2005).

Thwing, Charles Franklin. 1931. *American Society: Interpretations of Educational and Other Forces.* New York: Macmillan.

Tichenor, Daniel J. 2002. *Dividing Lines: The Politics of Immigration Control in America.* Princeton, N.J.: Princeton University Press.

Tienda, Marta, Katharine Donato, and Hector Cordero-Guzman. 1992. "Schooling, Color, and the Labor Force Activity of Women." *Social Forces* 71(2): 365–95.

Tienda, Marta, and Zai Liang. 1994. "Poverty and Immigration in Policy Perspective." In *Confronting Poverty: Prescriptions for Change*, edited by Sheldon Danziger and D. H. Weinberg. New York: Russell Sage Foundation.

Tienda, Marta, and Rebeca Raijman. 2000. "Immigrants' Income Packaging and Invisible Labor Force Activity." *Social Science Quarterly* 81(1, March): 291–310.

Tienda, Marta, and Shelley A. Smith. 1988. "The Doubly Disadvantaged: Women of Color in the U.S. Labor Force." In *Women Working: Theories and Facts in Perspective,* edited by A. H. Stromberg and S. Harkess. Mountain View, Calif.: Mayfield Publishing.

Tienda, Marta, and Haya Stier. 1996. "Generating Labor Market Inequality: Employment Opportunities and the Accumulation of Disadvantage." *Social Problems* 43(2): 147–65.

Tilly, Charles. 1998. *Durable Inequality.* Berkeley and Los Angeles: University of California Press.

Tilly, Louise A., and Joan W. Scott. 1978. *Women, Work, and Family.* New York: Holt, Rinehart and Winston.

Tolnay, Stewart E. 1999. *The Bottom Rung: African American Family Life on Southern Farms.* Urbana: University of Illinois Press.

———. 2001. "African Americans and Immigrants in Northern Cities: The Effects of Relative Group Size on Occupational Standing in 1920." *Social Forces* 80(2): 573–604.

Tomaskovic-Devey, Donald. 1993. *Gender and Racial Inequality at Work: The Source and Consequences of Job Segregation.* Ithaca, N.Y.: ILR Press.

———. 1995. "Sex Composition and Gendered Earnings Inequality." In *Gender Inequality at Work,* edited by J. A. Jacobs. Thousand Oaks, Calif.: Sage Publications.

Tompkins, Vincent. 1996. *American Decades 1900–1909.* Detroit, Mich.: Gales Research.

———. 1996. *American Decades 1910–1919.* Detroit, Mich.: Gale Research.

Toossi, Mitra. 2002. "A Century of Change: The U.S. Labor Force, 1950–2050." *Monthly Labor Review* 125(5): 15–28.

Treas, Judith. 1987. "The Effect of Women's Labor Force Participation on the Distribution of Income in the United States." *Annual Review of Sociology* 13: 259–88.

Treiman, Donald. 1977. *Occupational Prestige in Comparative Perspective.* New York: Academic Press.

Turner, Frederick Jackson. 1947. *The Frontier in American History.* New York: Henry Holt.

Tyre, Peg, Karen Springen, and Julie Scelfo. 2002. "Bringing Up Adultolescents." *Newsweek,* March 25, 2002, p. 34.

U.S. Bureau of the Census. 1904. *Abstract of the Twelfth Census of the United States 1900,* 3rd ed. Washington: U.S. Government Printing Office.

———. 1907. *Statistics of Cities Having a Population of Over 30,000: Special Reports 1905.* Washington: U.S. Government Printing Office.

———. 1913a. *Thirteenth Census of the United States Taken in the Year 1910. Abstract of the Census.* Washington: U.S. Government Printing Office.

———. 1913b. *Thirteenth Census of the United States Taken in the Year 1910,* vol. 5. *Agriculture.* Washington: U.S. Government Printing Office.

———. 1913c. *Thirteenth Census of the United States Taken in the Year 1910,* vol. 11. *Mines and Quarries 1909.* Washington: U.S. Government Printing Office.

———. 1913/1976. *Abstract of the Thirteenth Census,* repr. ed. New York: Arno Press.

———. 1914. *Thirteenth Census of the United States Taken in the Year 1910,* vol. IV, *Occupation Statistics.* Washington: U.S. Government Printing Office.

———. 1915. *Wealth, Debt, and Taxation, 1913.* Washington: U.S. Government Printing Office.

———. 1922. *Official Register of the United States 1921, Director.* Washington: U.S. Government Printing Office.

———. 1975. *Historical Statistics of the United States, Colonial Times to 1970.* Washington: U.S. Government Printing Office.

U.S. Bureau of Foreign and Domestic Commerce. 1921. *Statistical Abstract of the United States, 1920.* Washington: U.S. Government Printing Office.

U.S. Census Bureau. 1993. Economic Classification Policy Committee. "Issues Paper No. 1: Conceptual Issues." Washington: U.S. Government Printing Office. Available at: http://www.census.gov/epcd/naics/issues1 (accessed October 25, 2005).

———. 1997. "Businesses Classified as Providing Child Care Service, by Income Tax Status for State." Washington: U.S. Government Printing Office. Available at: http//www/census.gov/population/documentation/twps055/bus_1997.txt (accessed October 25, 2005).

———. 2000a. Poverty: 2000 Highlights, Table C. Washington: U.S. Government Printing Office. Available at: http://www.census.gov/hhes/poverty/poverty00/povoohi.

——— 2000b. "QT–P3. Race and Hispanic or Latino: 2000." American Fact Finder. Washington: U.S. Government Printing Office.

U.S. Census Bureau., U.S. Department of Commerce, and Economics and Statistics Administration. 2000. *Statistical Abstract of the United States, The National Data Book, 1920 Edition.* Washington: U.S. Government Printing Office.

U.S. Census Office. 1880. *Tenth Census of the United States.* Washington: U.S. Government Printing Office.

U.S. Census Office. 1895. In *Report on Wealth, Debt, and Taxation at the Eleventh Census: 1890.* Washington: U.S. Government Printing Office.

U.S. Census Office. 1902. *Twelfth Census of the United States Taken in the Year 1900.* Population, Part II. Washington: U.S. Government Printing Office.

U.S. Commission on Civil Rights. 1986. *Economic Progress of Black Men in America.* Washington: U.S. Government Printing Office.

———. 1990. *The Economic Status of Black Women: An Exploratory Investigation.* Washington: U.S. Government Printing Office.

———. 2002. *Beyond Percentage Plans: The Challenge of Equal Opportunity In Higher Education.* Washington: U.S. Commission on Civil Rights.

———. 2003. *The U.S. Department of Education's Race-Neutral Alternatives in Postsecondary Education: Innovative Approaches to Diversity—Are They Viable Substitutes for Affirmative Action?* Washington: U.S. Commission on Civil Rights.

U.S. Commission on Immigration Reform. 1997. *Becoming an American: Immigration and Immigration Policy; 1997 Report to Congress.* Washington: U.S. Government Printing Office.

U.S. Commission on Population Growth and the American Future. 1971. *Population Growth and the American Future.* Washington: U.S. Government Printing Office.

U.S. Congress. House. 1986. Subcommittee on Employment, Health, and Long-Term Care of the Select Committee on Aging. "The Removal of Age Ceiling

Cap Under the Age Discrimination in Employment Act." 99th Congr., 2d sess. (March 12, 1986). Washington.

U.S. Congress. Senate. 1909. Country Life Commission. *Report of the Country Life Commission and Special Message from the President of the United States.* 60th Congr., 2nd sess., S. Doc. 705. Washington.

———. 2001. *U.S.A. Patriot Act.* 107th Congr., 1st sess., S. Doc. 1510, Washington.

U.S. Department of Commerce. 1989. *200 Years of U.S. Census Taking: Population and Housing Questions, 1790–1990.* Washington: U.S. Government Printing Office.

U.S. Department of Commerce, Bureau of the Census. "Current Population Survey: Annual Demographic File, 2000 [Computer File]." 2000. Washington: U.S. Department of Commerce, Bureau of the Census [producer]. Ann Arbor, Mich.: Inter-University Consortium for Political and Social Research [distributor].

———. 2001a. "Current Population Survey: Annual Demographic File, 2000 [Computer File]." 2001. 2nd release. Washington: U.S. Department of Commerce, Bureau of the Census [producer]. Ann Arbor, Mich.: Inter-University Consortium for Political and Social Research [distributor].

———. 2001b. "Flow of Funds Account—Financial Assets and Liabilities of Foreign Sector: 1980–2000." *Statistical Abstract of the United States, 2001.* Washington: U.S. Government Printing Office. Available at: http://www.census.gov/prod/2002pubs/01statab/banking.pdf (accessed October 26, 2005).

———. 2001c. "U.S. Banking office of Foreign Banks—Summary: 1980 to 2000." In *Statistical Abstract of the United States, 2001.* Washington: U.S. Government Printing Office.

———. 2001d. "Businesses Classified as Providing Child Care Service, by Income Tax Status for State. 1987." Washington: U.S. Government Printing Office. Available at: http//www.census.gov/population/documentation/twps055/bus_1987.txt.

———. 2004a. "Current Population Survey Definitions. Head versus Householder." Washington: U.S. Government Printing Office. Available at: http://www.census.gov/population/www/cps/cpsdef.html (accessed October 26, 2005).

———. 2004b. "U.S. Trade in Goods—Balance of Payments(BOP) Basis vs. Census Basis Value in Millions of Dollars 1960 thru 2003." Foreign Trade Division. Washington: U.S. Government Printing Office. Available at: http://www.census.gov/foreign-trade/statistics/index.html (accessed October 26, 2005).

U.S. Department of Health and Human Services. 1997. "Trends in the Well-Being of America's Children and Youth: 1997." Office of the Assistant Secretary for Planning and Development. Washington: U.S. Government Printing Office.

U.S. Department of the Interior. Edward M. Dawson. 1901. *Official Register for the US Officers and Employees in the Civil Military and Naval Service,* vol. I, *Legislative, Executive, and Judicial.* Washington: U.S. Government Printing Office.

———. 1911. *Official Register of the US Officers and Employees in the Civil Miltary and Naval Service,* vol. I, *Legislative, Executive, and Judicial.* Washington: U.S. Government Printing Office.

U.S. Department of Labor. 1965. "The Older American Worker: Age Discrimination in Employment." Report of the Secretary of Labor to the Congress Under

Section 715 of the Civil Rights Act of 1964. June. Washington: U.S. Government Printing Office.

——. Bureau of Labor Statistics. 2004a. "International Comparisons of Hourly Compensation Costs for Production Workers in Manufacturing, revised data for 2002." Foreign Labor Statistics. Washington: U.S. Government Printing Office.

——. Bureau of Labor Statistics. 2004b. "Productivity and Costs, First Quarter 2004, Revised 2004." Washington: U.S. Government Printing Office. Available at: http://www.bls.gov/schedule/archives/prod_nr.htm (accessed October 26, 2005).

——. Office of Planning and Research. 1965. *The Negro Family: The Case for National Action.* Washington: U.S. Government Printing Office.

U.S. Department of State. Frequently Asked Historical Questions. Available at: http://www.state.gov/r/pa/ho/faq/ (accessed October 26, 2005).

U.S. General Accounting Office. 1994. "Federal Employment: How Government Jobs are Viewed on Some College Campuses: Report to Congressional Committees. Washington: U.S. Government Printing Office.

U.S. Immigration Commission. 1911. *Abstracts of the Reports of the Immigration Commission* [Dillingham Commission]. Washington: U.S. Government Printing Office.

U.S. Office of Management and Budget. 1977. "Directive No. 15: Race and Ethnic Standards for Federal Statistics and Administrative Reporting." Washington: U.S. Government Printing Office.

——. 1997a. "1997 North American Industry Classification System—1987 Standards Industrial Classification Replacement." Washington: U.S. Government Printing Office.

——. 1997b. "Recommendations from the Interagency Committee for the Review of the Racial and Ethnic Standards to the Office of Management and Budget Concerning Changes to the Standards for the Classification of Federal Data on Race and Ethnicity." In *Federal Register,* Part II. Washington: U.S. Government Printing Office.

——.1997c. "Report to the Office of Management and Budget on the Review of Statistical Policy Directive 15." Interagency Committee for the Review of Racial and Ethnic Standards. Washington: U.S. Government Printing Office.

University of Texas at Dallas Bruton Center. *Windows on Urban Poverty.* Available at: http://www.urbanpoverty.net (accessed October 26, 2005).

"The Urban Beat." 1999. *Maclean's,* July 19, p. 2.

Vallianatos, Corinna. 1997. "The Divorce Culture (Book Review)." *Washington Monthly* 29(3): 52–4.

Van Riper, Paul. 1957. History of the United States Civil Service. Evanston, Ill.: Row, Peterson.

Van Waters, Miriam. 1930. "Adolescence." In *Encyclopedia of the Social Sciences,* edited by Edwin R. A. Seligman. New York: Macmillan.

Vaughn, Gerald F. 1998. "Massachusetts Gave Leadership to America's Country Life Movement: The Collaboration of Kenyon L. Butterfield and Wilbert L. Anderson." *The Historical Journal of Massachusetts* 26(2): 124–44.

Vedder, Richard K., and Lowell E. Galloway. 1993. *Out of Work: Unemployment and Government in Twentieth Century America.* Independent Studies in Political Economy. New York: Holmes & Meier.

VermontCivilUnion.com. 2000. "Civil Union Resource Guide." Available at: http://www.vermontcivilunion.com/ (accessed October 26, 2005).

Vinovskis, Maris. 1988. *An "Epidemic" of Adolescent Pregnancy? Some Historical and Policy Considerations.* New York: Oxford University Press.

"Vital Signs." 1999. *Journal of Blacks in Higher Education* 23: 79–82.

Vitiello, Domenic. 2002. "Building the United States: Construction Labor and Laborers, 1880–1990." Unpublished paper. University of Pennsylvania History 580, Philadelphia.

———. 2004. "Urban America: What it Was and What it Is Becoming." Unpublished paper in authors' possession.

Vittoz, Stan. 1978. World War I and the Political Accommodation of Transitional Market Forces: The Case of Immigration Restriction." *Politics and Society* 8(1): 49–78.

Vobeda, Barbara. 1986. "Congress Voted To End Mandatory Retirement." *Washington Post,* October 18, 1986, p. A3.

Wadhwani, Rohit Daniel. 2004. "Citizen Savers: The Family Economy, Financial Institutions, and Social Policy in the Northeastern U.S. from the Market Revolution to the Great Depression." *Enterprise & Society* 5(4): 617–24.

Waldinger, Roger. 1993. "The Ethnic Enclave Debate Revisited." *Journal of Urban and Regional Research* 17: 444–52.

———. 1996. *Still the Promised City? African-Americans and New Immigrants in Post-Industrial New York.* Cambridge, Mass.: Harvard University Press.

———. 2001. "Conclusion: Immigration and the Remaking of Urban America." In *Strangers at the Gates: New Immigrants in Urban America,* edited by Roger Waldinger. Berkeley: University of California Press.

———. 2001. "Strangers at the Gates." In *Strangers at the Gates: New Immigrants in Urban America,* edited by Roger Waldinger. Berkeley: University of California Press.

———. 2001. "Up from Poverty? 'Race,' Immigration, and the Fate of Low-Skilled Workers." In *Strangers at the Gates: New Immigrants in Urban America,* edited by Roger Waldinger. Berkeley: University of California Press.

———, ed. 2001. *Strangers at the Gates: New Immigrants in Urban America.* Berkeley: University of California Press.

Waldinger, Roger, and Mehdi Bozorgmehr, eds. 1996. *Ethnic Los Angeles.* New York: Russell Sage Foundation.

Waldinger, Roger, and Claudia Der-Martirosian. 2001. "The Immigrant Niche: Pervasive, Persistent, Diverse." In *Strangers at the Gates: New Immigrants in Urban America,* edited by Roger Waldinger. Berkeley: University of California Press.

Waldinger, Roger, and Jennifer Lee. 2001. "New Immigrants in Urban America." In *Strangers at the Gates: New Immigrants in Urban America,* edited by Roger Waldinger. Berkeley: University of California Press.

Walker, Francis A. 1996. "Restriction of Immigration." *Atlantic Monthly* LXXVII(June): 828.

Walzer, Michael. 1992. *What It Means to Be An American: Essays on the American Experience.* New York: Marsilio Publishers.

Watkins, Susan Cott. 1994. "Introduction." In *After Ellis Island: Newcomers and Natives in the 1910 Census*, edited by S. C. Watkins. New York: Russell Sage Foundation.

Weeden, Kim A. 1998. "Revisiting Occupational Sex Segregation in the United States, 1910–1990: Results from a Log-Linear Approach." *Demography* 35: 475–87.

Weiner, Lynn Y. 1985. *From Working Girl to Working Mother: The Female Labor Force in the United States, 1820–1980*. Chapel Hill: University of North Carolina Press.

Weir, Margaret. 1992. *Politics and Jobs: The Boundaries of Employment Policy in the United States*. Princeton, N.J.: Princeton University Press.

Weisbrot, Robert. 1990. *Freedom Bound: A History of America's Civil Rights Movement*. New York: W. W. Norton.

Weitzman, Leonore J. 1985. *The Divorce Revolution: The Unexpected Social and Economic Consequences for Women and Children in America*. New York: Free Press.

Welch, Finis. 1990. "The Employment of Black Men." *Journal of Labor Economics* 8(1, part 2): S26–S74.

Wellington, Allison. 1993. "Changes in the Male/Female Wage Gap: 1976–1985." *Journal of Human Resources* 28(2): 383–411.

Wells, Thomas. 1999. "Changes in Occupational Sex Segregation during the 1980s and 1990s." *Social Science Quarterly* 80: 370–81.

Western, Bruce, Jeffrey R. Kling, and David F. Weiman. 2001. "The Labor Market Consequences of Incarceration." *Crime & Delinquency* 47(3): 410–27.

Western, Bruce, and Martina Morris. 1999. "Inequality in Earnings at the Close of the Twentieth Century." *Annual Review of Sociology* 25: 623–57.

Wetzel, James R. 1995. "Labor Force, Unemployment, and Earnings." In *State of the Union: America in the 1990s*, vol. 1: *Economic Trends*, edited by Reynolds Farley. New York: Russell Sage Foundation.

Whalen, Carmen Teresa. 2001. *From Puerto Rico to Philadelphia: Puerto Rican Workers and Postwar Economies*. Philadelphia, Pa.: Temple University Press.

Whelpton, P. K., and Edward Hollander. 1940. A Standard Occupational and Industrial Classification of Workers." *Social Forces* 18(4): 488–94.

White, Jack E. 1997. "I'm Just Who I Am." *Time*, May 5, 1997, p. 32.

Whitehead, Barbara Dafoe. 1993. "Dan Quayle Was Right." *The Atlantic* 271(4): 47–68.

———. 1997. *The Divorce Culture*. New York: Alfred A. Knopf.

Whitman, Walt. 1860. "Chants Democratic and Native American." In *Leaves of Grass*. Boston, Mass.: Thayer and Eldridge.

Wilcox, Delos F. 1911. *The American City: A Problem in Democracy*. New York: The Macmillan Company.

Williams, Kim M. 2003. "From Civil Rights to the Multiracial Movement." In *New Faces in a Changing America: Multiracial Identity in the 21st Century*, edited by H. L. DeBose and L. I. Winters. Thousand Oaks, Calif.: Sage Publications.

Williamson, Jeffrey G. 1995. "The Evolution of Global Labor Markets Since 1830: Background Evidence and Hypotheses." *Explorations in Economic History* 32(2): 141–96.

———. 1996. "Globalization and Inequality Then and Now: The Late 19th and

Late 20th Centuries Compared." NBER Working Paper 5491. Cambridge, Mass.: National Bureau of Economic Research.

———. 1998. "Globalization and the Labor Market: Using History to Inform Policy." In *Growth, Inequality, and Globalization: Theory, History, and Practice*, edited by P. Aghion and J. G. Williamson. Cambridge: Cambridge University Press.

Williamson, Jeffrey G., and Peter H. Lindert. 1980. *American Inequality: A Macroeconomic History*. New York: Academic Press.

Willrich, Michael. 2003. *City of Courts: Socializing Justice in Progressive Era Chicago*. New York and Cambridge: Cambridge University Press.

Willson, Andrea E. 2003. "Race and Women's Income Trajectories: Employment, Marriage, and Income Security over the Life Course." *Social Problems* 50(1): 87–110.

Wilson, Frank Harold. 1995. "Rising Tide or Ebb Tide? Recent Changes in the Black Middle Class in the U.S., 1980–1990." *Research in Race & Ethnic Relations* 8: 21–56.

Wilson, Joseph, ed. 1986. *Black Labor in America, 1865–1983: A Selected Annotated Bibliography*. New York: Greenwood Press.

Wilson, William Julius. 1978. *The Declining Significance of Race: Blacks and Changing American Institutions*. Chicago: University of Chicago Press.

———. 1987. *The Truly Disadvantaged: the Inner City, the Underclass, and Public Policy*. Chicago: University of Chicago Press.

———. 1996. *When Work Disappears: the World of the New Urban Poor*. New York: Alfred A. Knopf.

Winnick, Andrew. 1989. *Toward Two Societies: The Changing Distributions of Wealth in the United States Since 1960*. New York: Praeger.

Winters, Loretta I., and Herman L. DeBose, eds. 2003. *New Faces in a Changing America: Multiracial Identity in the 21st Century*. Thousand Oaks, Calif.: Sage Publications.

Woeste, Victoria Saker. 2001. "Land Monopoly, Agribusiness, and the State: Discovering the Family Farm in Twentieth-Century California." In *The Countryside in the Age of the Modern State: Political Histories of Rural America*, edited by C. M. Stock and R. D. Johnston. Ithaca, N.Y.: Cornell University Press.

Wolfbein, Seymour L. 1993. "Uses of an Occupational Classification System." Paper read at International Occupational Classification Conference. Washington, D.C. (September).

Wolfe, Alan. 1975. *The Limits of Legitimacy: Political Contradictions of Contemporary Capitalism*. New York: Free Press.

Wolff, Edward N. 1995. "The Rich Get Increasingly Richer: Latest Data on Household Wealth During the 1980s." In *Research in Politics and Society*, edited by R. E. Ratcliff, Melvin L. Oliver, and Thomas M. Shapiro. Greenwich, Conn.: JAI Press.

———. 2002. *Top Heavy*. New York: The New Press.

Wolff, Edward N., Ajit Zacharias, and Asena Caner. 2003. *Levy Institute Measure of Economic Well-Being: United States 1989 and 2000*. Annandale-on-Hudson, N.Y.: Levy Economics Institute.

"A Wonderful Year" and "The Outlook." 1900. *New York Times*, January 1, 1900, p. 1.

Woods, Harry. 1914. *Blue Book of the State of Illinois*. Danville: Illinois Printing Company.

Woodward, C. Van. 1951. *Origins of the New South, 1877–1913*. Baton Rouge: Louisiana State University Press.

Wright, Gavin. 1986. *Old South, New South: Revolutions in the Southern Economy Since the Civil War*. New York: Basic Books.

Wu, Lawrence L., and Jui-Chung Allen Li. 2005. "Marital and Childbearing Trajectories of American Women: 50 Years of Social Change." In *On the Frontier of Adulthood: Theory, Research, and Public Policy*, edited by Frank E. Furstenberg, Jr., Ruben G. Rumbaut, and Richard A. Settensten, Jr. Chicago: University of Chicago Press.

Wyman, Mark. 1993. *Round-trip to America: The Immigrants Return to Europe, 1880–1930*. Ithaca, N.Y.: Cornell University Press.

Yergin, Daniel, and Joseph Stanislaw. 1998. *The Commanding Heights: The Battle Between Government and the Marketplace that is Remaking the Modern World*. New York: Simon & Schuster.

Yu, Henry. 2003. "Tiger Woods Is Not the End of History: or, Why Sex across the Color Line Won't Save Us All." *American Historical Review* 108(5): 1406–14.

Zelizer, Viviana A. 1985. *Pricing the Priceless Child: The Changing Social Value of Children*. New York: Basic Books.

———. 1994. *The Social Meaning of Money: Pin Money, Paychecks, Poor Relief, and Other Currencies*. New York: Basic Books.

———. 1999. "Multiple Markets: Multiple Cultures." In *Diversity and its Discontents: Cultural Conflict and Common Ground in Contemporary American Society*, edited by N. J. Smelser and J. C. Alexander. Princeton, N.J.: Princeton University Press.

Zhou, Min. 1999. "Segmented Assimilation: Issues, Controversies, and Recent Research on the New Second Generation." In *The Handbook of International Migration: The American Experience*, edited by C. Hirschman, P. Kasinitz and J. DeWind. New York: Russell Sage Foundation.

———. 2001. "Progress, Decline, Stagnation? The New Second Generation Comes of Age." In *Strangers at the Gates: New Immigrants in Urban America*, edited by Roger Waldinger. Berkeley: University of California Press.

Zipp, John F. 1994. "Government Employment and Black-White Earnings Inequality, 1980–1990." *Social Problems* 41(3): 363–82.

Zúniga, Victor, and Rubén Hernández-León, eds. 2005. *New Destinations: Mexican Immigrants in the United States*. New York: Russell Sage Foundation.

Zwerling, Craig, and Hilary Silver. 1992. "Race and Job Dismissals in a Federal Bureaucracy." *American Sociological Review* 57(5): 651–60.

About the Authors

Michael B. Katz is Walter H. Annenberg Professor of History at the University of Pennsylvania.

Mark J. Stern is professor of social welfare and history and codirector of the Urban Studies Program at the University of Pennsylvania.

Index